The Essentials of Marketing Research

D0206425

Identifying and assessing the ways in which changes in the marketing mix affect consumer behavior is key to a successful marketing strategy.

The Essentials of Marketing Research guides the student in designing, conducting, and interpreting marketing research. This comprehensive textbook covers the full range of topics, including:

- secondary research and data mining
- Internet marketing research
- qualitative and exploratory research
- statistical analysis
- marketing research ethics.

With learning objectives at the beginning of each chapter, a host of cases, and a comprehensive companion website, this book offers a range of tools to help students develop and test their research and analytical skills.

Lawrence Silver is Associate Professor of Marketing and Management at the John Massey School of Business, Southeastern Oklahoma State University.

Robert Stevens is the John Massey Endowed Professor of Business at John Massey School of Business, Southeastern Oklahoma State University.

Bruce Wrenn is the Colson Endowed Chair Professor of Marketing at the School of Business Administration, Andrews University.

David Loudon is Professor of Marketing at the Brock School of Business, Samford University.

The Essentials of Marketing Research
Third Edition

**Lawrence Silver, Robert Stevens,
Bruce Wrenn, and David Loudon**

Routledge
Taylor & Francis Group

NEW YORK AND LONDON

Third edition published 2013
by Routledge
711 Third Avenue, New York, NY 10017

Simultaneously published in the UK
by Routledge
2 Park Square, Milton Park, Abingdon, Oxon OX14 4RN

Routledge is an imprint of the Taylor & Francis Group, an informa business

First edition published by Haworth 1999
Second edition published by Routledge 2006

Library of Congress Cataloging in Publication Data
The essentials of marketing research / Lawrence S. Silver ... [et al.]. – 3rd ed.
    p. cm.
  Rev. ed. of: Marketing research : text and cases / Bruce Wrenn, Robert E. Stevens, David L. Loudon. 2nd ed.
  Includes bibliographical references and index.
  1. Marketing research. 2. Marketing research – Case studies. I. Silver, Lawrence S., 1948– II. Wrenn, Bruce. Marketing research.
  HF5415.2.W74 2012
  658.8′3–dc23   2012016995

ISBN: 978-0-415-89929-1 (hbk)
ISBN: 978-0-415-89928-4 (pbk)
ISBN: 978-0-203-18259-8 (ebk)

Typeset in Garamond
by HWA Text and Data Management, London

Printed and bound in the United States of America
by Edwards Brothers, Inc.

Contents

About the Authors

Lawrence Silver, DBA, is an associate professor of marketing at Southeastern Oklahoma State University. He has taught at Louisiana Tech University, Troy University, and Mississippi College. He spent over 20 years as an independent insurance agent and holds the Chartered Property Casualty Underwriter (CPCU) and Chartered Life Underwriter (CLU) designations. Dr. Silver has taught marketing management, marketing research, consumer behavior, personal selling, and international marketing. He co-authored *The Concise Encyclopedia of Insurance Terms,* as well as over 40 articles and cases. He has published in a number of business journals and at numerous professional conferences. Dr. Silver serves on the editorial boards of *Health Marketing Quarterly* and *Services Marketing Quarterly* and is the director of the MBA program at the John Massey School of Business at Southeastern Oklahoma State University.

Robert Stevens, PhD, is John Massey Professor of Business, Management and Marketing Department in the John Massey School of Business at Southeastern Oklahoma State University, Durant, Oklahoma,. During his distinguished career, Dr. Stevens has taught at the University of Arkansas, the University of Southern Mississippi, Oral Roberts University, University of Louisiana Monroe and Hong Kong Shue Yan University. His repertoire of courses has included marketing management, business research, statistics, marketing research, and strategic management. He is the author or co-author of 30 books and well over 200 articles and cases. He has published his research findings in a number of business journals and numerous professional conference proceedings. He is co-editor of the *Health MarketingQuarterly* and *Services Marketing Quarterly,* and serves on the editorial boards of four other professional journals. Dr. Stevens has acted as a marketing consultant to local, regional, and national organizations and is the owner of two small businesses.

Bruce Wrenn, PhD, is the first recipient of the Colson Endowed Chair of Marketing at Andrews University. Prior to joining the Andrews faculty, he was Professor of Marketing at Indiana University South Bend where he taught for nineteen years. He received his PhD. in marketing from Northwestern University in 1989. Among the more than 100 scholarly and professional publications and presentations by Wrenn are a dozen books in marketing management, marketing research, marketing for religious organizations, and other marketing areas. He has received numerous awards for his teaching and research and is listed in *Who's Who in Finance and Business, Who's Who in American Education, Who's Who in Business Higher Education,* and *Who's Who in America.* He has been interviewed on National Public Radio, LifeTalk Radio, NBC, Hope Channel, and by numerous newspapers and magazines; and has served as an expert witness to the Federal Trade Commission. Wrenn serves on the editorial review board of several scholarly journals, and has consulted with organizations in pharmaceutical, food, high-tech, bio-medical, and hospital industries as well as numerous religious organizations on marketing matters. He currently serves as a Subject Matter Expert in marketing to the American Management Association and a Marketing Mentor in the Harvard Business School's ManageMentor program. His current research and service interests are in assisting churches adopting marketing practices to achieve their goals.

David Loudon, PhD, is a Professor of Marketing at Samford University. He holds the PhD (Marketing), MBA., and BS (Finance) degrees from LSU. He has also taught at the University of Louisiana, Monroe (where he served as a Department Head for many years), Shue Yan University (Hong Kong), University of Rhode Island, and Louisiana State University. Dr. Loudon's teaching interests focus on marketing management, consumer behavior, services marketing, and marketing communications. Dr. Loudon is the co-author of thirteen different books and has conducted research in the United States, Europe, Asia, and Latin America on such topics as consumer behavior, international marketing, services marketing, and marketing management. He has written over 100 papers, articles, and business cases, and his research findings have been published in a wide variety of journals and in the proceedings of numerous professional conferences. He co-founded and co-edited the Journal of Ministry Marketing & Management and was co-editor of Best Business Books, an imprint of Haworth Press, Inc. Dr. Loudon is a co-editor of Services Marketing Quarterly and Health Marketing Quarterly published by Taylor & Francis. He also serves on the editorial boards of several other professional journals. Dr. Loudon has been listed in eight Who's Who directories.

Acknowledgments

Many individuals contributed to the development of this book. We owe special thanks to Stephanie Metts, Special Assistant to the Dean of Instruction at Southeastern Oklahoma State University who helped with the development of the test bank, instructor's manual, and formatting of the material in the book.

Special thanks to the following contributors of cases and case teaching notes: Dr. Henry S. Cole, Dr. Bruce C. Walker, Dr. Stanley G. Williamson, Dr. Marlene M. Reed, Michael R. Luthy, Dr. Phylis Mansfield, Dr. C. William McConkey, Robert Howard, and Dr. Edward L. Felton.

Part I
The Marketing Research Process and Decision Making

1 Introduction to Marketing Research

Learning Objectives

Upon completing this chapter, you should understand:

1. what is involved in the decision making process;
2. how research contributes to the decision making process;
3. the differences between the following: management problems and opportunities, decisional alternatives, and decisional criteria;
4. the nature of the marketing research process;
5. how the research questions lead to formulating research hypotheses.

The Marketing-Decision Environment

Marketing decisions in contemporary organizations are some of the most important decisions made by managers. The decisions of what consumer segments to serve with what products/services, at what prices, through which channels, and with what type and amounts of promotion not only determine the marketing posture of a firm, but also affect decisions in other areas as well. The decision to emphasize quality products, for example, affects decisions on procurement, production personnel, quality control, etc.

Many companies are discovering that the decisions involved in creating and distributing goods and services for selected consumer segments have such long-run implications for the organization that they are now being viewed as strategic decisions necessitating input by top management. Some marketing decisions, such as those relating to strategy, may involve commitments and directions that continue to guide efforts as long as they prove successful. A belief that future success requires the organization to become "market oriented"[1] or "market sensitive" has increased the importance of the intelligence function within organizations as they seek to make the right responses to a marketplace. Right responses become increasingly important as competition heats up in markets. Firms are discovering that they must be market driven in order to make decisions that meet with market approval.

Developing an understanding of consumer needs, wants, perceptions, etc., is a prerequisite to effective decision making. Consider the different results of marketing Pepsi AM in the United States and Chee-tos in China. Pepsi AM was introduced without research, which would have revealed that the name suggested it to be drunk only in the morning, thereby restricting market size to specific-occasion usage. Frito-Lay did extensive research on the market for snack foods in China before introducing Chee-tos there. They learned that cheese was not a common item in the diet of Chinese, that traditional Chee-tos flavors did not appeal to consumers there, but that some flavors were appealing (savory American cream and zesty Japanese steak). They also researched Chinese reaction to Chester Cheetah, the cartoon character on the bag, and the Chinese translation of "Chee-tos" (luckily corresponding to Chinese characters *qu duo* or "new surprise"). Pepsi AM was a flop; Chee-tos were such a success that Frito-Lay could not keep store shelves stocked.[2]

Marketing research is the specific marketing function relied upon to provide information for marketing decisions. However, it should be stressed at the outset that merely doing marketing research does not guarantee that better decisions will be made. The quality of each stage of a marketing research project will either contribute to better decision making or will make it an ever elusive goal. If research results are correctly analyzed and imaginatively applied, studies have shown that increased profitability is often the outcome.[3]

Marketing Research

The American Marketing Association defines marketing research as follows:

> Marketing research is the function which links the consumer, customer, and public to the marketer through information—information used to identify and define marketing opportunities and problems; generate, refine, and evaluate marketing actions; monitor marketing performance; and improve understanding of marketing as a process.
>
> Marketing research specifies the information required to address these issues; designs the method for collecting information; manages and implements the data collection process; analyzes the results; and communicates the findings and their implications.[4]

This rather lengthy definition suggests the connection between research and decision making in business organizations.

Research, in a business context, is defined as an organized, formal inquiry into an area to obtain information for use in decision making. When the adjective marketing is added to research, the context of the area of inquiry is defined. Marketing research, then, refers to procedures and techniques involved in the design, data collection, analysis, and presentation of information used in making marketing decisions. More succinctly, *marketing research produces the information managers need to make marketing decisions.*[5]

Although many of the procedures used to conduct marketing research can also be used to conduct other types of research, marketing decisions require approaches that fit the decision-making environment to which they are being applied. Marketing research can make its greatest contribution to management when the researcher understands the environment, industry, company, management goals and styles, and decision processes that give rise to the need for information.

Marketing Research and Decision Making

Although conducting the activities of marketing research requires using a variety of research techniques, the focus of the research *should not* be on the techniques. Marketing research should focus on decisions to be made rather than the collection techniques used to gather information to facilitate decision making. This focus is central to understanding the marketing research function in terms of what it should be and to the effective and efficient use of research as an aid to decision making. Any user or provider of marketing research who loses sight of this central focus is likely to end up in one of two awkward and costly positions: (1) failing to collect the information actually needed to make a decision or (2) collecting information that is not needed in a given decision-making context.[6] The result of the first is ineffectiveness—not reaching a desired objective, and the result of the second is inefficiency—failing to reach an objective in

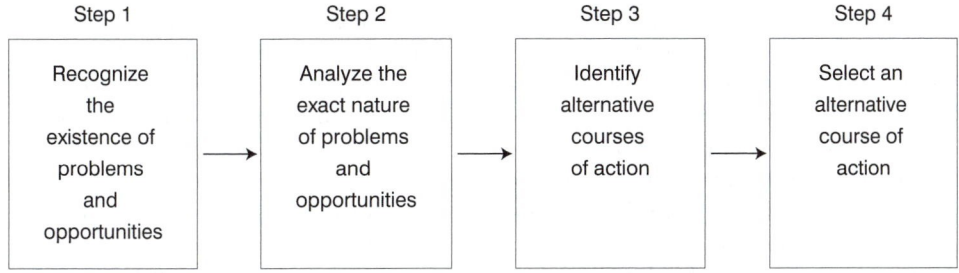

Step 1	Step 2	Step 3	Step 4
Recognize the existence of problems and opportunities	Analyze the exact nature of problems and opportunities	Identify alternative courses of action	Select an alternative course of action

Figure 1.1   Steps in Decision Making

the least costly manner. The chances of either of these occurring are greatly reduced when the decision to be made is the focus of the research effort.

To maintain this focal point, an understanding of the purpose and role of marketing research in decision making is necessary. The basic purpose of marketing research is to reduce uncertainty or error in decision making. It is the uncertainty of the outcome surrounding a decision that makes decision making difficult. If the outcome of choosing one alternative over another is known, then choosing the right alternative would be simple, given the decision-making criteria. If it were certain that alternative A would result in $100,000 in profit and that alternative B would result in $50,000 in profit, and the decision criterion was to maximize profits, then the choice of alternative A would be obvious. However, business decisions must be made under conditions of uncertainty—it is unknown if alternative A will produce $50,000 more than B. In fact, either or both alternatives may result in losses. It is the ability to reduce uncertainty that gives information its value.

Analyzing what is involved in making a decision will help in understanding how information aids decision making. Decision making is defined as a choice among alternative courses of action. For purposes of analysis, a decision can be broken down into four distinct steps (see Figure 1.1): (1) identify a problem or opportunity, (2) analyze the problem or opportunity, (3) identify alternative courses of action, and (4) select a specific course of action.

Identify a Problem or Opportunity

A problem or opportunity is the focus of management efforts to maintain or restore performance. A problem is anything that stands in the way of achieving an objective, whereas an opportunity is a chance to improve overall performance.

Managers need information to aid in recognizing problems and opportunities because before a problem can be defined and alternatives developed, it must be recognized. An example of this type of information is attitudinal data that compares attitudes toward competing brands. Since attitudes usually are predictive of sales behavior, if attitudes toward a company's product were less favorable than before, the attitudinal information would make the managers aware of the existence of a problem or potential problem. Opportunities may depend upon the existence of pertinent information, such as knowing that distributors are displeased with a competitor's new policy of quantity discounts and as a result may be willing to place increased orders for your product.

Analyze the Problem or Opportunity

Once a problem or opportunity has been recognized, it must be analyzed. Until the nature and sources of the problem have been analyzed, no alternative courses of action can be considered. Sometimes the symptoms of the problem are recognized first and there may be several problems that produce the same set of symptoms. An analogy using the human body may help in understanding this point. A person experiencing a headache (symptom) may be suffering from a sinus infection, stress, the flu, or a host of other illnesses (potential problems). Treating the headache may provide temporary relief, but not dealing with the root problem will ensure its return, perhaps worsening physical conditions.

The same type of phenomenon occurs in marketing. A firm, experiencing a decline in sales (symptom), may find it to be the result of a decline in total industry sales, lower prices by competitors, low product quality, or a myriad of other potential problems. No alternative courses of action should be considered until the actual problem has been analyzed. Thus, information aids the manager at this stage in the decision-making process by analyzing the problem.

In some cases an entire research project must be devoted to defining the problem or identifying an opportunity because of a lack of prior knowledge of a particular area. This type of study is usually called an exploratory study and will be discussed more fully in Chapter 4.

Identify Alternatives

The third stage in the decision-making process involves identifying viable alternatives. For some problems, developing alternatives is a natural outcome of analyzing the problem, especially if that particular problem or opportunity has occurred before. A manager's past knowledge and experiences are used to develop the alternatives in these situations. However, in other situations a real contribution of research is to inform the decision maker of the options available to him or her. A company considering introduction of a new product may use consumer information to determine the position of current offerings to evaluate different ways its new product could be positioned in the market. Information on the significant product attributes and how consumers position existing products on these attributes would be an evaluation of possible "openings" (options) available at a given time.

Select an Alternative

The final stage in the decision-making process is the choice among the alternative courses of action available to the decision maker. Information provided by research can aid a manager at this stage by estimating the effects of the various alternatives on the decision criteria. For example, a firm considering introduction of a new product may test market two versions of that product. The two versions of the product are two alternatives to be considered and the sales and profits resulting from test marketing these two versions become the information needed to choose one alternative over another. Another example is the pre-test of television commercials using different themes, characters, scripts, etc., to provide information on consumer reactions to alternative commercials. This information also aids the decision maker in selecting the best advertising approaches to use.

Information collected through research must be directly related to the decision to be made in order to accomplish its purpose of risk reduction. Thus, the focus of research should be the decision-making processes in general and, specifically, the decision to be made in a given situation, rather than the data or the techniques used to collect the data. There is always the danger of a person involved in marketing research viewing himself or herself as a research technician rather than as someone who provides information to help managers make decisions to solve problems and take advantage of opportunities. In fact, it is safe to say that the best researchers think like decision makers in search of information to make decisions rather than as researchers in search of answers to research questions.

Strategic Versus Tactical Information Needs

Managers are called upon to make two broad categories of decisions—strategic and tactical. The strategic decisions are those that have long-run implications and effects. These decisions are critical to a firm's success and may not be altered if successful. Tactical decisions are short-run in scope and effect and are usually altered on a regular basis. An example of these two types of decisions will help clarify the distinction and also clarify what many researchers and managers have failed to understand.

A company analyzing a market for possible entry would be considering a strategic move— entering a new market. This requires information on such things as competitor strengths and weaknesses, market shares held by competitors, market growth potential, production, financial and marketing requirements for success in the industry, strategic tendencies of competitors, etc. This is strategic information. Once the decision to enter the market has been made, information on current prices charged by specific competitors, current package designs and sizes, etc., is needed to make the tactical decisions for the short run—a year or less. This is tactical information.

Thus, strategic decisions require strategic information, and tactical decisions require tactical information. Failure to recognize the distinction between decision types and information types will result in information that deals with the right areas—prices for example—but with the wrong time frame. For tactical decisions, a manager needs to know competitive prices and their emphasis by both competitors and consumers. For strategic decisions, the manager is more interested in competitors' abilities and tendencies to use pricing as a retaliatory weapon.

The researcher and the manager must be certain the time frame for the decision is specified in advance to ensure that the right type of information is collected. This should be a joint effort by both information user and provider.

The Nature of Marketing Research

It is obvious at this point that the key to understanding when marketing research can be of greatest value to organizations is to understand the decisions facing marketing managers. These areas and the related forms of marketing research include:

- *Concept/product testing.* A concept or product test consists of evaluating consumer response to a new product or concept. This is often a part of the test market in the development of a new product. It is also used to determine how a product or service can best be positioned in a particular sector of the marketplace. For example, product testing would answer what the consumer's perception of new products or services to be offered might be. It can also examine how users perceive a product's value as well as its attributes and benefits or how perceived values and attributes relate to actual need and demand.
- *Tracking study.* A tracking study is an ongoing periodic survey of pre-recruited consumers who record their use of various products or services. Specific preferences are measured and compared to evaluate changes in perceptions, preferences, and actual usage over time.
- *Product/brand service usage.* Product or brand usage studies serve to determine current demand for the various brands of a product or service. This type of approach may also determine which brand name has primary awareness in the consumers' minds or which they prefer as well as how often and why it is used.
- *Advertising penetration.* Advertising penetration analyses evaluate the message that is actually being communicated to the target audience. This type of study serves to determine if the intended message is understood, how persuasive it is, or how well it motivates. These studies may also evaluate the effectiveness of individual media for a particular target market.

- *Image evaluation.* Image studies provide feedback relative to the image a company, product, or service has in the eyes of the consumers. Image studies may reveal attribute perceptions of a particular brand or determine its strengths and weaknesses.
- *Public opinion surveys.* Public opinion surveys determine the key issues in the minds of the public or specific customers (or investors), relative to specific issues, individuals, or business sectors. They reveal whether opinion is positive or negative, determine the degree of importance of specific issues, or evaluate awareness levels of key issues.
- *Copy testing.* Copy testing allows for an evaluation of consumer response to ad copy being considered. It determines how well the intended message is actually being communicated. Copy tests ensure the wording used is consistent with the language of the target audience. Copy testing is used most effectively in the conceptual stages of copy development to allow for consumer feedback on concepts portrayed by various preliminary ad copy.
- *Test marketing/product placements.* Product placements are a bit more extensive than product tests. Product tests take place in a controlled setting, such as a shopping mall where consumers are recruited to test a product. In a product placement study, the product to be test marketed is placed in the home of the consumer for a specific period of time. After this period a personal or telephone interview is used to record the specific responses of the user concerning the product. This type of study will determine how consumers respond to a product that often has no name or packaging appeals associated with it.
- *Taste tests.* Taste tests are conducted in a controlled environment where consumers are recruited to taste a product and give their evaluations. Taste tests serve to determine the acceptance of a product, without brand or packaging appeals, relative to attributes of flavor, texture, aroma, and visual appeal. Taste tests may be conducted with variations of a single product or with samples of competitors' products tasted for comparison testing.
- *Market segmentation.* Market segmentation studies determine how a market is segmented by product usage, demand, or customer profiles. These studies usually develop demographic, psychographic, product preference, and lifestyle profiles of key market segments.
- *Media measurement.* These studies determine what share of the market the medium being tested actually has and how a target market is identified demographically and psychographically. Media studies also evaluate preferences in programming as well as promotional appeals that are most effective in reaching and expanding a particular target audience.
- *Market feasibility.* A market feasibility study analyzes the market demand for a new product, brand, or service. This type of study usually evaluates potential market size, determines what kind of demand might be expected, what market dynamics are interacting, and what market segments might be most receptive to the introduction of a new product or brand. Feasibility studies may also determine market feedback relative to similar product or services, attributes sought, as well as pricing and packaging perspectives.
- *Location studies.* For local customer-intensive businesses, the location must be determined. Location studies serve to evaluate the size of the potential market surrounding a proposed location and whether local demand will support the facility.
- *Market share/market size studies.* Market share/market size studies determine what products are being purchased at what volume and the actual size of sales being realized by each competitor. These studies can also identify and determine the strength of new firms that have recently entered the market in a strong growth mode.
- *Competitive analysis.* A competitive analysis is often part of a market share/market size study. It consists of an evaluation of the strengths and weaknesses of competitors. It may also include pertinent data relative to locations, sales approaches, and the extent of their product lines and manufacturing capabilities.
- *Positioning studies.* Positioning studies evaluate how leading companies or brands are viewed in the minds of consumers concerning key product or image attributes. This type of study

will evaluate perceived strengths and weaknesses of each, as well as determine key attributes consumers associate with their idea of an "ideal" supplier of a particular product or service.

- *Customer satisfaction studies.* Customer satisfaction studies evaluate the level of satisfaction existing customers have with the products or services of a company or organization. The basic philosophy is that it is cheaper to keep an existing customer than to try to attract a new one. Therefore, continuous analysis of existing customers provides input on how to change what is being done to increase satisfaction or lessen dissatisfaction.

Marketing Research for Small Organizations

While it is true that larger corporations would account for the largest share of expenditures for the aforementioned applications of research, small businesses and entrepreneurial ventures are certainly interested in obtaining research results that can help them make better decisions in these areas. Such firms would typically seek answers to the following types of questions as well.

Customer Research

- Which customer groups represent the best target markets for my product or service?
- How large is the existing and potential market? What is its rate of growth?
- What unfulfilled needs exist for my product? How are customers currently fulfilling those needs?
- Under what circumstances would customers use the product? What benefits are customers seeking to gain in these circumstances?
- Where would customers expect to buy the product? What decision process do they go through when buying the product?
- Who makes the purchase decision for this type of product? How are they influenced by others in the household (or company) when making this decision?
- What is the value customers place on having their needs fulfilled by this type of product?

Competitor Analysis

- Who are my competitors (i.e., alternatives to addressing the needs of potential customers)?
- How brand-loyal are customers to my competitors?
- How do potential buyers perceive competitors' offerings?
- What are my competitors' competitive advantages and how are they exploiting them through their marketing programs?

Operational Environment

- By what means (channels, methods) is this type of production made available to customers? Is there an opportunity to innovate here?
- How are customers made aware of this type of product? What opportunities exist to increase efficiency and effectiveness in promotion?
- What technological developments are likely to occur in this market and how will they affect our competitive position?
- What cultural/social environmental trends could impact our business? How?
- What will be the impact of the regulatory environment on our business now and in the foreseeable future?
- What economic and demographic trends are occurring which could affect the nature of the market opportunity? How?

These examples of issues of interest to small businesses are typical of the kinds of questions that marketing research can seek to answer. How research arrives at the answers to these questions can vary from project to project.

The Nature of Conventional and Unconventional Research

It is important to reiterate that a study of marketing research should begin with this understanding—marketing research is not focused on the use of surveys or experiments or observations (i.e., techniques). Marketing research is about finding solutions to management problems and aiding in better decision making. Therefore, the goal of using marketing research is not to propagate convention in the use of research methods, but rather to find solutions. When it is obvious that the best method of finding a solution to a problem is to conduct a survey (or conduct an experiment, or use observational methods, etc.), then it is important to use such techniques scientifically, so that we have faith that the findings contain as much "truth" as we can afford. Sometimes the method we use to search for the truth in order to reduce uncertainty and make better decisions follows convention. Sometimes it is unique and unconventional. We do not "score points" for conventionality; we succeed by finding efficient and effective means of gathering information which aids decision making. The following example will help to illustrate this point:

> A producer of frozen dinner entrees set an objective that the company's food products should not just be good heat-and-serve meals, but should aim higher and be considered excellent cuisine in general. At an advanced stage of product development they wanted to see how close they were getting to their objective, and decided upon a somewhat unconventional method of testing product quality. They rented the ballroom of a local hotel noted for its excellent catering service and under the guise of a professional organization invited local business professionals to attend a meeting where a well-known speaker would make a presentation on a topic of interest to the business community. Unbeknownst to the attendees, the company had the hotel kitchen heat and serve the food company's frozen entrees instead of the hotel's usual catered meal. At each table of eight in the audience the company had a member of its staff playing the role of just another invited guest. During the meal the employee would engage others at the table in a discussion of the quality of the food (e.g., "I see you got the lasagna while I got chicken Kiev. How is the lasagna here?"). After the meal and speech the other guests at each table were debriefed about the ruse.

By taking this approach the firm was able to obtain insights into how close they were to having a product that could compare favorably to cuisine prepared by chefs and with high expectations by diners. Although not the only research conducted by the firm for this line of products, this rather unconventional method gave them good insights at this stage of the process that might have exceeded what traditional taste tests could have achieved. Once again, our overriding objective is to improve decision making, not pursue convention.

We would be remiss, however, if we did not follow-up that admonition with this caveat—we are not suggesting an "anything goes" approach to research. We must always ensure that we pursue research that is both related to the management problem and its related decisional issues, *and* must make certain our methods are scientific and represent the most efficient means of seeking answers to our questions. Figure 1.2 helps to show the possible combinations of these variables.

Better decision making by using research results only comes from research which falls in cell #1. However, you can imaginatively apply scientific methodology that goes against "convention," and still end up in cell #1. The point here being that when we set out to do our research we do not set out to write a questionnaire, or conduct in-depth interviews, or run an experiment,

		Is research relevant to a real management problem?	
		YES	NO
Does the research follow scientific methods?	YES	1. Results are relevant and believable.	2. Results are believable, but not relevant.
	NO	3. Results are relevant, but not believable.	4. Results are neither relevant nor believable.

Figure 1.2. Outcomes of Research

1. Define the management problem
2. State research objectives
3. Determine the research methodology
4. Collect data
5. Analyze and intrepret the findings
6. Present the results

Figure 1.3 Basic Steps in a Marketing Research Project

etc.; we set out to solve a problem, to evaluate an opportunity, to test hypotheses, etc., so that we can reduce uncertainty and improve our decision making. So, we need to understand that it is possible to be both scientific *and* unconventional, and we must be open to using whatever method represents the most efficient and effective means of generating relevant and believable results, and not be bound by our past proclivities to use certain "comfortable" methods.

Steps in a Marketing Research Project

Ensuring that data collected in a research project not only is related to management's information needs but also fits management's time frame, requires an approach to research that is centered on the management problem—the decision to be made. Such an approach is shown in Figure 1.3.

A venerable work adage states, "Plan your work; work your plan," and this is the approach that should be used in carrying out a research project. A research project does not begin with a questionnaire or a focus group interview or any other research technique, but with a carefully thought-out plan for the research that includes: (1) a statement of the management problem or opportunity, (2) a set of research objectives, and (3) a statement of the research methodology to be used in the project.

Define the Management Problem

The starting point in a research project should be an attempt by both the user and the provider of information to clearly define the problem. Mutual understanding and agreement are vitally necessary at this point in the research process. Failure by either party to understand or clearly define the major issue requiring information will surely lead to disappointment and wasted effort. Studies have shown that the proper utilization of the findings from marketing research by managers is directly affected by the quality of interactions that take place between managers and researchers, plus the level of researcher involvement in the research decision-making process.[7] Many information users, especially the uninitiated, have been "burned," never to be "burned" again, by someone who has collected some data, then collected the money and left them with a lot of "useful" information.[8]

A health care administrator recently related such a story. He had heard a great deal about marketing and the need for having information on consumers, although he was unclear about both. He was approached by a marketing research firm that offered to supply a lot of "useful marketing information" for a reasonable fee. Several months after he had received the final report and the marketing research firm had received his check, he realized that he had no idea of how to use the information or if it was what he really needed.

This type of problem can be avoided, or at least minimized, through user–provider interaction, analysis, and discussion of the key management issues involved in a given situation. The information provider's task is to convert the manager's statement of symptoms to likely problems and decision issues and then finally to information needs. Two key questions that must always be dealt with at this stage are: (1) what information does the decision maker believe is needed to make a specific decision and (2) how will the information be used to make the decision? Asking these questions will cause the information user to begin thinking in terms of the information needed to make the decision rather than the decision itself. Also, the user can move to a level of thinking specifically about how the information will be used.

An example of this interaction process will help clarify this point. An executive vice president for a franchise of a national motel-restaurant chain was evaluating his information needs with one of the authors about a major remodeling of one of the chain's restaurants. The author posed the question about how the information was going to be used in the decision-making process. The chain's vice president then realized that corporate policy would not permit deviating from the established interior designs currently used even if information were available that an alternate design would be more acceptable to consumers. He then concluded that he did not need the information! The information could have been easily obtained through a survey, but the bottom line would have been management's inability to act on it. The manager realized that he needed to work on a policy change at the corporate level and if information was needed, it would be to evaluate that particular policy.

Research Project Tip

A problem exists when there is a difference between the ideal state and the actual state. An opportunity exists when the market favorably values something the organization can do. Ask the client to describe "the bottom line" of what he or she sees as the problem or opportunity that requires research in order to make decisions. This is a starting point, but more work is needed to determine the focus of the research.

One type of question that can aid in the process of identifying the real problem in its proper scope is the "why" question. The researcher uses the why question to help separate what is known (i.e., facts) from what is merely assumed (i.e., hypotheses). The following example of a manufacturer of capital equipment will help illustrate the use of the why question.

The Compton Company was a capital equipment manufacturer with a market share larger than its next two competitors combined. All companies in this business sold through independent distributors who typically carried the lines of several manufacturers. Compton had for several years been suffering a loss of market share. In an effort to regain share they fired their ad agency. The new agency conducted a study of end-use customers and discovered that the fired ad agency had done an outstanding job of creating awareness and interest in the Compton line. The study also revealed that these end-users were buying competitor's equipment from the distributors. The switch from interest in Compton to the competition was not a failure of the advertising, but rather the result of distributors' motivation to sell the products of manufacturers' running sales contests, offering cash bonuses, and supplying technical sales assistance.[9]

If a marketing researcher had been called in to help address Compton's problem the resulting conversation might have been as follows:

Manager:	We need you to help us find a new advertising agency.
Researcher:	*Why* do you believe you need a new ad agency?
Manager:	Because our market share is slipping.
Researcher:	*Why* do you believe that is the fault of your ad agency?
Manager:	Because we think they have not created a high enough level of awareness and interest in our product among target market members.
Researcher:	OK, but *why* do you believe that? What evidence do you have that ties your declining market share to a problem with advertising?

At this point it will become obvious that the company does not have any evidence that supports the contention that poor advertising is the source of the decline in market share. This realization should open the door for the researcher to suggest that the issue be defined as a decline in market share, and that some research could be done to identify the source of the problem. Asking "why" questions allows all parties involved to separate facts from hypotheses and give direction to research that can help solve real problems in their proper scope. Once the problem has been determined, the researcher can enter into discussions with the decision maker regarding the appropriate purpose for the research.

Research Project Tip

You will need to ask "why" questions similar to the Compton Company example to distinguish between facts and hypotheses. Sometimes the client believes a hypothesis so strongly that it has become a "fact" in the client's mind. Asking "why" questions helps focus researchers and decision makers on the "real" problem (i.e., the problem in its proper scope).

Specify Research Proposal[10]

It is important to establish an understanding between the decision maker and the researcher as to the role the research will play in providing information for use in making decisions. This suggests that one of the first things researchers should do is identify the decision alternatives facing the decision maker.

Identify Decision Alternatives

As has been repeatedly stressed in this chapter, effective research is research that results in better decision making. Hence, as a first step in determining the role of research in solving the management problem, the researcher should ask "what if" questions to help identify the decisions under consideration. For example, continuing the Compton Company dialog between researcher and decision maker:

Researcher: *What if* the research revealed that potential customers believed our products failed to offer features comparable to our competitors, and so bought competitor's products?

Manager: Well, I do not think that is happening, but if it were then we would change our product to offer those features.

A review of such "what if" questions will identify those areas in which decisions might be made to solve the management problem. If the answer to the question is that knowing such information would not make a difference in the decisions made, then the researcher knows not to include that issue in the research since it would not positively influence decision making. It is obvious that it is necessary for the researcher to "think like a decision maker" in order to know what questions to ask. Putting yourself in the position of a decision maker, thinking what decisions you might be faced with, and then asking "what if" questions to determine if the actual decision maker sees things as you do is an effective means of beginning the process of determining the research purpose.

Research Project Tip

You may have to ask a series of probing questions intended to get the client to reveal what information in what form he or she will need in order to make the decisions faced. Sometimes these criteria have not been explicitly identified before such questioning. By "thinking like a marketing decision maker" you can determine if the client might be interested in the same information you might use if you were in the client's position.

Determine Decisional Criteria

Once the decision alternatives facing the decision maker seeking to solve the management problem have been specified, the researcher must determine what criteria the manager will use to choose among the alternatives. Different managers facing a choice among alternatives might desire different information, or information in different forms to feel comfortable in distinguishing which alternative is best. The decisional criteria are those pieces of information that can be used to identify which alternatives are truly capable of solving the problem. For example, in the Compton Company case the dialog to help identify one of the decisional criteria might have looked like the following:

Researcher: So, one area we might want to consider making a decision in would be redesigning the product with the latest features. What information would you need to have in order to make those types of decisions?

Manager: I would want to know the features desired by our target market customers, and how those features are expected to deliver specific benefits to those customers. I would also like to see how our customers compare our products to our competitors' products.

A similar dialog would help to identify other decisional criteria. Through this process of specifying decisional alternatives and the criteria used to choose among the alternatives, the researcher is also helping the decision maker to clarify in his or her own mind how to arrive at a decision to solve the real management problem.

Indicate Timing and Significance of Decisions

Other areas of concern to the researcher trying to arrive at a statement of research purpose are the amount of time available to the decision maker within which to make the decision, and how important the decision is to the firm. The same management problem could result in very different research purposes if decision makers see the timing and significance of the research differently. Researchers are responsible for ensuring that the research purpose not only fits the decisional criteria needs, but is also consistent with the timing and significance accorded the research and the associated decision-making process.

STATEMENT OF RESEARCH PURPOSE.

Once the decision alternatives, criteria, and timing and significance of the decisions have been considered it is useful for the researcher to construct a one (or two) sentence declaration of the research purpose. For the Compton Company case such a sentence might be as follows:

> Research Purpose: To determine the cause(s) of the decline in our market share and identify possible actions that could be taken to recover the lost share.

The researcher would need to obtain agreement with the decision maker as to the appropriateness of such a statement, as well as agreement with the research questions.

State Research Objectives

Research objectives consist of questions and hypotheses. The research questions represent a decomposition of the problem into a series of statements that constitute the end results sought by the research project. The questions should be stated in such a way that their accomplishment will provide the information necessary to solve the problem as stated. The objectives serve to guide the research results by providing direction, scope of a given project, and serve as the basis for developing the methodology to be used in the project.

In the area of research questions, both the user and provider should interact to maximize the research results that the user and provider are anticipating. The provider of the information usually assumes the role of interpreting needs and developing a list of questions that serve as a basis of negotiation for final research objectives. It is helpful to use the form of questions so that the researcher can think in terms of finding ways to provide answers to those questions. The following illustration will help make this clear.

In the Compton Company case the research questions might be framed as follows:

- Where has market share declined (e.g., products, geographic areas, channel type, etc.)?
- What is the level of awareness and interest in our products among target market members?
- What competitive actions have attracted our customers?
- What are the perceptions of our dealers and distributors for our policies and practices (i.e., what is the status of our relationships with dealers)?
- How do customers rate the quality, features, price, etc., of our products versus competitors?

Other questions could be stated. Note that in each case research must be done (sometimes internal to the company, sometimes external) to discover information that can answer the research questions

Research Project Tip

Be sure your research questions are in the form of questions, and require research of some type (internal or external to the organization) to get answers to the questions. Plan on spending a fair amount of time developing these questions (and hypotheses) since all the remaining steps of the research process will be seeking to get answers to these questions (and testing your hypotheses)

Hypotheses are speculations regarding specific findings of the research. They are helpful to researchers when their presence results in actions taken by the researcher that might not have occurred in the absence of the hypothesis. If the presence of an hypothesis in no way affects the research or the analysis of the data, the hypothesis is superfluous and does not need to be stated. If, on the other hand, the hypothesis influences the research in any one of the following ways, it should be included:

Research Project Tip

Hypotheses can be very helpful in identifying issues for the research to investigate, but are superfluous if they do not "work for you" as the two examples illustrate. Include them when their presence results in the research being somehow different than it would be if they were not there.

Research Project Tip

Since the research process from this point on will focus on achieving the research objectives (i.e., answering the research questions and testing the hypotheses), the researcher needs to "step back" and objectively look at these objectives and ask the question: Do I really believe that getting answers to these questions (and testing these hypotheses) will provide the information needed to make the necessary decisions to solve management's problem? Sometimes all the research questions look good individually, but collectively they just do not provide the information necessary to make the decisions. In this case more research questions are needed.

1. CHOICE OF RESPONDENTS

If the researcher believes that an important part of the research is to determine if a speculated difference in attitudes, behaviors, preferences, etc., exists between two groups of respondents, the hypothesis is useful to the research. For example:

Hypothesis: Customers on the west coast favor this product feature more than customers on the east coast.

Such a hypothesis affects the research by causing the researcher to include customers from both coasts in the sample. Without the need to test such a hypothesis, the sample may not include enough customers on the east and west coasts to allow for comparisons. Of course, as with all research questions and hypotheses, there should be some decision-making relevance in pursuit of an answer to the question or testing the hypothesis.

2. QUESTIONS ASKED

A second area where hypotheses "work for" researchers is in influencing the questions asked of respondents. For example:

> *Hypothesis:* Customer interest in our product declines when they see what it costs.

To test this hypothesis the researcher must find some way to ask questions that determine the role of price in affecting customer interest in the product. So, hypotheses that aid the researcher by suggesting variables to be included in the data collection instrument are "keepers."

3. ANALYSIS OF DATA

Another use of hypotheses that argues for their inclusion is when the hypothesis identifies analytical tasks that must be performed to test the hypothesis, as shown below:

> *Hypothesis:* Sales declines for this product are not uniform across the country.

Here, a test of the hypothesis requires the researcher to examine the sales data on a regional, district, state, or some other appropriate geographical breakout. Absent such a hypothesis, the data might not be examined in this manner.

Research Project Assignment

Prepare a short (no more than three single-spaced pages) Statement of Management Problem, Research Purpose (include decision alternatives, criteria, timing, and importance), Research Objectives, and Hypotheses based on your dialogs with the client. Get the client's reactions, revise as necessary, and submit to your instructor.

Develop Research Design

Once we have established the research questions and hypotheses we must plan a research design by which we will get answers to our research questions and test our hypotheses. While it is important that the researcher be precise and comprehensive in the development of research questions and hypotheses in order that the research design directly address those research needs, the researcher must also be flexible in order to make changes to both the research questions/hypotheses and the design in the course of conducting the research. This flexibility is important because unanticipated discoveries during the research may require reformulation of questions/hypotheses and the research design followed to address them.

The research design will involve the use of one or more of three broad categories of research approaches: exploratory, descriptive, and causal. Exploratory research is usually called for if the management problem is vague or can be only broadly defined. Research at this stage may involve

Definition of Terms: Management Problems/Opportunity, Research Purposes, Research Questions, Hypotheses

Management Problem/Opportunity

Idle curiosity is an insufficient reason to undertake research. To justify research, management must need research information in order to reduce the risk of making decisions intended to either solve a problem or investigate an opportunity. A problem exists whenever the ideal state differs from the actual state (e.g., sales are down and management doesn't know why). An opportunity is a chance to improve performance if the correct decisions can be made (e.g., what do we need to know about the market that can help us determine whether we should introduce this new product line or not?).

Research Purpose

Decision Alternative

What actions might we take to solve the problem or exploit the opportunity if the research reveals those actions are warranted (e.g., change our target market, promote "convenience" as our competitive advantage)?

Decisional Criteria

The information we need to know from the marketplace that helps us choose among the decision alternatives (e.g., if we discovered the opportunities to grow our current target market we'll better know if we should change our target market; if we know the prospective customers' attraction to "convenience" as a selling point we'll know if that should be our Unique Selling Proposition).

Research Purpose

A declarative statement that indicates how the research will contribute to solving the problem or evaluating the opportunity (e.g., "To determine the cause(s) of our sales decline and the possible actions to reverse the decline.").

Research Questions

The specific questions that must be answered by the research in order to provide all the decisional criteria information needed. In other words, what exactly does the research need to discover that will help us know what we should do to ultimately solve our problem or exploit our opportunity. For example, our decision alternatives include changing our target market, our criteria is the extent of the opportunity to grow our current target market, and our questions might include:

- What are our current target market's needs? Have they changed? Why?
- Does our current target market believe our product fully satisfies their needs? Why or why not?
- How well do our competitors satisfy the needs of the target market?
- What is the expected growth rate of the current target market (i.e., people who share this need)? Other market segments?

We'll need numerous questions answered before we are fully ready to choose among our decision alternatives.

Research Hypothesis

Possible findings from the research that could make a difference in what we decide to do (e.g., Hypothesis: Our product appeals more to the older market segment than the younger.).

This possible finding (we don't know whether it is true or not until we do the research) could affect our target market selection. To determine whether it is true or not requires that we ask both young and old consumers in our research about the attractiveness of our product.

a variety of techniques (literature review, focus groups, in-depth interviews, psychoanalytic studies, and case studies) and is characterized by the flexibility allowed to researchers in the exploration of relevant issues. Descriptive research is conducted when there is a need to measure the frequency with which a sampled population behaves, thinks, or is likely to act or to determine the extent to which two variables covary. Research must be highly structured in descriptive research so that any variation in the variables under investigation can be attributed to differences in the respondents rather than to variations in the questioning. Causal research is also highly structured, and includes exercise of control over variables in order to test cause-and-effect relationships between variables. While exploratory research is used to generate hypotheses, both descriptive and causal research are used to test hypotheses.

Select Data-Collection Methodology

A research design provides the overall plan indicating how the researcher will obtain answers to the research questions and test hypotheses. The researcher must also identify the specific methodology that will be used to collect the data. These decisions include determining the extent to which the questions can be answered using secondary data—data that have already been collected for other purposes than the research under investigation—or must be answered by the use of primary data— which are collected explicitly for the research study at hand. If primary data must be collected, decisions must be made with regard to the use of communication and/or observation approaches to generating the data, the degree of structure and disguise of the research, and how to administer the research—observation by either electronic, mechanical, or human methods; communication in person, through the mail, over the phone; or via computer or Internet link.

Determine Measurement and Data-Analysis Methods

The next research decision area concerns the methods used to measure and analyze the data. The major criterion used in making this decision is the nature of the data to be analyzed. The purpose of the analysis is to obtain meaning from the raw data that have been collected.

For many researchers the area of data analysis can be the most troublesome. While some data-analysis techniques do require an understanding of statistics, it is not true that all research results must be managed by statistical experts to be interpretable or useful. However, use of the *proper* data-analysis approach will mean the difference between capitalizing on all the careful work done to generate the data versus not being able to discover the answers to research objectives, or worse, drawing erroneous conclusions.

It is important to identify how the information will be measured before a data-collection instrument is developed because it is necessary to know how one plans to use the data in getting answers to research objectives before the question that generates the data can be asked. For example, if one needs to examine the differences in attitudes of people aged 13 to 16, 17 to 20, 21 to 24, and 25 to 28, one cannot ask about the respondent's age by using categories less than 18 years, 18 to 25, or 25 and older.

The researcher is therefore trying to determine the answer to this difficult question: "How will we measure what we need to measure?" For example, if attitudes are to be measured, which technique will be used? The method of equal-appearing intervals? The semantic differential? The Likert technique? In many cases no validated measuring techniques are available, so the researcher must rely on what has been used in past studies and on his or her own judgment to decide upon the appropriate technique.

It is extremely important that the researcher develop operational definitions of the concepts to be measured and that these be stated explicitly. Even seemingly simple concepts, such as awareness, can be defined in several ways, each having different meaning and relative importance. To know that 60 percent of the respondents said they had heard of Kleenex is not the same as 60 percent saying that Kleenex is what comes to mind when they think of facial tissues. Yet both of these approaches could be considered as measuring awareness.

Design Data-Collection Forms

The specific instruments (forms) that will be used to measure the variables of interest must now be designed. This would involve the design of the observation form or questionnaire. In either case, these forms should coincide with the decisions made with respect to what should be measured and how.

Constructing a data-collection form is part art and part science. We are attempting to construct an instrument that is capable of generating the measures and allowing for the data analysis procedures determined in the previous step. However, we are also focusing on the decision that we are faced with making that were both the beginning point and the end point of our research. Thus the data collection instrument must accomplish more than merely generating measures, it must provide the insights needed that lead to better decision making. As we'll see in Chapter 6, there is a great deal more to achieving such a goal than merely converting our needed measures (data) into questions capable of producing those measures. For example, in addition to expressing the study objectives in question form (i.e., obtaining measures), a questionnaire must contextualize the information collected, create harmony and rapport with the respondent, and generate data that might not have been specified in the study objectives, but that is needed to direct decision making. These goals require a blend of both art and science to be successfully achieved. We won't ultimately be successful, however, if we ask the wrong people the right questions. Hence the importance of our next step in the process.

Define Sampling Methods

The next step in the research is to define the population or universe of the study. The research universe includes all of the people, stores, or places that possess some characteristic management is interested in measuring. The universe must be defined for each research project and this defined universe becomes the group from which a sample is drawn. The list of all universe elements is sometimes referred to as the sampling frame.

It is extremely important that the sampling frame include all members of the population. Failure to meet this requirement can result in bias. If, for example, the researcher is trying to estimate the average income in a given area and intends to use the telephone book as the population listing or sampling frame, at least three problems would be encountered. First, not everyone has a telephone and those who do not tend to have low incomes. Second, there are usually 15 to 20 percent in an area with unlisted numbers. Third, new residents would not be listed. Thus, the difference between the sampling frame (telephone book) and area residents could be substantial and would bias the results.

It is imperative that the population be carefully identified and a sampling technique used that minimizes the chance of bias introduced through the sampling frame not containing all elements of the population. Sampling methods also include determination of techniques and sample size. Two separate decisions are called for in this step. The first is how specific sample elements will be drawn from the population. There are two broad categories of sampling techniques: probability and nonprobability. The approach selected depends on the nature of the problem and the nature of the population under study. For probability designs the objective is to draw a sample that is both representative and useful. For nonprobability designs the objective is to select a useful sample even though it may not be representative of the population it comes from. These distinctions will be clarified later, but it is important to note that the sample design influences the applicability of various types of statistical analysis—some analysis types are directly dependent upon an assumption about how sample elements are drawn.

Sampling issues are pertinent even when we are dealing with decision makers who say "I cannot afford the time or money to do a big survey. I just want to get a feel for the market opportunity and then I will take my chances." For example, if in the Compton Company case the decision makers held such an opinion about what competitor policies were with dealers, the researcher is still faced with the need to define the population of interest (all dealers, dealers of a certain volume of business or location, etc.), develop a sampling frame (list) of the dealers, and determine how many and who to talk with in order to get answers to the research questions.

Sample size represents the other side of the decision to be made. Determining how many sample elements are needed to accomplish the research objectives requires both analysis and judgment. The techniques for determining sample size are discussed in Chapter 9, including a whole series of other nonstatistical questions, such as costs, response rate, homogeneity of sample elements, etc., which must be considered to determine sample size. In some studies the cost may dictate a lower sample size than would be required given requirements about sampling reliability.

Collect, Analyze and Interpret the Data, and Present the Results

Once the previous steps have been completed and the planning stage of the research project has been carried out, the plan is now ready for execution. The execution stages involve collecting the data from the population sampled in the ways specified, and analyzing the data using the analysis techniques already identified in the research plan. If the research plan or proposal has been well thought out and "debugged" early through revisions of objectives and research designs, then the implementation steps will flow much better.

Once the data are collected and analyzed the researcher must interpret the results of the findings in terms of the management problem for which the data were collected. This means determining what the results imply about the solution to the management problem and recommending a course of action to management. If the purpose of the research project was to determine the feasibility of introducing a new product and the results of the research project show that the product will produce an acceptable level of profits, then the research should recommend introduction of the product unless there are known internal or external barriers to entry that cannot be overcome. This means the researcher must move beyond the role of the scientist in objectively collecting and analyzing data. Now a researcher must assume the role of a management consultant in a science that states: Given these facts and this interpretation, I recommend this action. This does not, of course, mean that the action recommended will be followed by management. Since the researcher is usually in a staff capacity, only recommendations for action can be offered. Management can accept or reject the recommendations; this is management's prerogative. However, to be effective in getting results implemented, the researcher must assume this role of recommending action. The researcher should be involved in the problem definitions and objectives to be able to recommend courses of action based on interpretation of results.

To some this approach may seem to be overstepping the researcher's responsibilities to make recommendations. Yet most managers appreciate this approach since it at least represents a starting point in deciding what action should be taken given certain research results. Remember, information has not really served its basic purpose until it is used in decision making.

Marketing Information Systems

Some organizations have moved beyond the stage of thinking of information needs in terms of projects and have focused attention on creating information systems that provide a continuous flow of information to users. While such a focus may shift priorities in terms of the amount spent on information for a database and that spent for specific projects, it should be pointed out that even if information is collected on a regular basis as a part of the information system, the principles of good marketing research set forth in this book are still applicable to these information systems. The fact that information is collected on a regular basis does not negate the need for relating it to the decisions to be made, for using correct sampling techniques, etc. The basic principles outlined are applicable to all information flows; some directly and others indirectly, but nonetheless applicable. Therefore, an understanding of these principles will help ensure better quality of information regardless of the nature of the system or procedures used to provide the information.

Summary

This chapter focused on the purpose, use, and overall approaches to gathering information for making marketing decisions. An understanding of the decision-making process and how information can aid management is the basis for planning and implementing research projects. Research projects, in turn, should be carried out in such a way that this focus of providing problem-solving information is central to the research process.

Discussion Questions

1   "The best marketing researchers think like marketing decision makers." Discuss the validity of this statement, using examples from the text, class discussion, and other readings to make your point.

2   The Compton Co. made a serious error in problem formulation. Describe what happened and what lessons we can learn from their experience.

3   Describe what should have been the statement of management problem, research purpose, and research questions for Compton had they done research instead of making a decision without collecting information.

4   Which is more important to "get right" if research that contributes to better decision making will occur: the management problem, the research purpose, or the research objectives? Defend your answer.

5   Why is it necessary for marketing research to be both managerially relevant and scientifically "believable" to result in better management decision making. Use examples from the text and class to help illustrate your answer.

6 Define the following terms and describe the process used by the researcher in determining what they would be for a research project: management problem or opportunity, decisional alternatives, decisional criteria, research questions, research hypotheses. Use specific examples to illustrate your points.

2 Ethics in Marketing Research

Learning Objectives

Upon completing this chapter, you should understand:

1 differences in approaches to ethics;
2 what it means to do research in an ethical manner;
3 what is meant by the term "informed consent" and why it is critical to ethical research;
4 how codes of ethics aid in making ethical decisions in research.

The word "ethics" comes from the Greek *ethos* which is translated as character in English. Yet, *ethos* means more than character. It also refers to the fundamental set of values one uses to make decisions. Thus, we can define ethics, for our purposes, as the set of values and standards we use to make decisions about right and wrong. In terms of marketing research, these values should include that no harm comes from our research to subjects, clients, society, or the environment.

People use several approaches in governing their ethical decision making. These include: moral philosophy, the rights principle, utilitarianism, relativism, and justice. It is important to note, that these approaches are not mutually exclusive. That is, most people use some combination of these to make their decisions.

Moral Philosophy

Also known as virtue ethics, this school of thought posits that ethical decisions are based on one's moral virtue. As described by Aristotle, a decision in a certain situation is the one a mature person with good character would make. The virtues that constitute good moral character are timeless and can be taught. Moreover, these virtues transcend and are a higher order than community standards or consensus.

Aristotle believed that a person learned character from the people he or she associated with. If one associates with others of good moral character, then that person will develop the proper virtues. Many adherents of virtue ethics today believe that such institutions as places of worship and schools should be used to foster the proper virtues.

The Rights Principle

Underlying the rights principle are the rights of individuals and the intentions of behavior with respect to those rights. Originally expressed by Emanuel Kant (1724–1804) this principal holds that a decision is ethical when it is the same decision most people would make based on universal morals (i.e., morals held by all people such as respect for life). This leads to the concept that an ethical decision is correct if it can be applied to all similar situations. For example, if it is wrong to lie, it is wrong to lie at all times including "white" lies one may tell to spare someone's feelings. This is known as Kant's "moral imperative." The concept goes beyond legal requirements and insists that people volunteer the truth in situations where they are not obligated to reveal information. As an example, when buying a used car, the salesperson is not obligated to reveal information not requested by the buyer. Under the moral imperative, the salesperson is obligated to reveal the information whether asked or not. The rights principle is often compared to the Golden Rule. Therefore, decision makers need to ask, is this decision the same decision that I would expect most moral people to agree with?

Utilitarianism

Another approach to ethics is called utilitarianism (also known as *teleology*), which means the greatest good for the greatest number of people. Teleology comes from the Greek word *telos* which means "end." Thus, individuals who espouse utilitarianism seek a decision that benefits everyone in the best way. This is commonly referred to as the "greatest good for the greatest number." Often this process includes a cost/benefit analysis. That doesn't mean this approach will yield the best ethical result. For example, an automobile defect may injure only a few people. Instead of recalling the defective model, however, the automobile company pays the damages to the few injured. The injured get compensation while the automobile manufacturer saves money. It may appear that everyone in this situation wins, but there is still a risk that other consumers will be harmed by the defects, even if these consumers are notified of the defects. This is an example of how utilitarianism suggests that resources be implemented in the most efficient form. Even though there is still a risk of harm to consumers, individuals who use this approach feel they have made the best ethical decision.

The Justice Principle

The justice principle refers to the fairness of processes and rewards when dealing with others. There are three categories, 1) distributive justice, 2) procedural, and 3) interactive. Distributive justice deals with the equitable determination of rewards. For example, if it is announced that promotion to sales manager will go to the year's top salesperson, then the top salesperson should get the position. To give the sales manager job to someone who came in second or third violates the equitable determination of rewards.

Procedural justice involves the "rules of the game" and if they are followed. In the above example, if the one salesperson falsely manipulates sales figures and comes out as number one for the year, the rules have been violated. Once procedural justice has been breached, distributive justice is also brought into doubt.

Interactive justice involves the communication used in the relationship. Again, using the example above, if the announced rules for the promotion are that the position goes to the top salesperson but management fails to make it clear that it is the most profit on sales and not the most revenue, the lack of communication will violate the concept of interactive justice. Such a violation will undermine employees' beliefs in distributive and procedural justice as well.

Relativism

Relativists make ethical decisions based on the people around them or the specific context in which they find themselves. Often, they simply follow a group's consensus rather than applying any ethical standards of their own. As consensus or context changes, the relativist changes his or her ethical decisions. Everyone has heard the old saying, "When in Rome, do as the Romans do." This sums up the relativist position – ethics change as context changes.

There is a strong tendency for market researchers and other business practitioners to become relativists in international situations. Despite the temptation, core standards still need to be followed in foreign cultures. It is also important to understand the law both in the host country and in the United States. Researchers and other business professionals may be prosecuted for violation of U.S. law (e.g., bribery) while in a foreign country.

Ethics in Marketing Research

It is critically important that market research be conducted in an ethical manner because consumers often rely on such research to make purchase decisions. Data and information improperly collected and/or interpreted has the potential to mislead consumers in their purchase decision process. Thus, ethical market research requires market researchers to use honesty in all research techniques. To know more about the market, researchers need respondents or study subjects. In order to ensure their rights and encourage their participation, respondents need to be treated with respect. Subjects also need to know that they are free to make a choice about whether or not to participate in a research project. Respondents have the right to be informed about the research being conducted, how their information is going to be used and a right to privacy. The safety of respondents is extremely important because of legal requirements, and because respondents quit participating if their safety is at risk. In conducting the study, the researcher needs to practice the concepts of justice discussed above.

A helpful tool to guide market research is to have a code of standards. Companies that develop such standards have employees who are better equipped to distinguish between ethical and unethical scenarios. A code of standards may aide researchers from the beginning of the research process including development of the research question. For example, a proposal to study smokers' reaction to tobacco advertising raises ethical questions even if the research is never conducted. The idea of research on tobacco advertising presupposes that increased tobacco consumption or persuading consumers to change cigarette brands is preferable to encouraging people to quit using tobacco.

Code of Standards

Organizations that conduct market research often develop a code of standards to guide investigators, employees, and any subcontractors involved in the research process. Several research and marketing trade groups have written codes of ethics to guide their members. A list of the groups and their web addresses are displayed in Table 2.1.

These organizations offer templates for a research firm or other organization to develop its own code of standards tailored to the firm's particular situation. There are several steps involved in the process of developing a code that applies not only to research but to the entire organization. These steps are outlined in Table 2.2.

Table 2.1 Websites of Research Groups

American Marketing Association	http://www.marketingpower.com
Council of American Survey Research Organizations	http://www.casro.org
Marketing Research Organization	http://www.marketingresearch.org
Association of Internet Researchers	http://www.aoir.org

Table 2.2 Steps in the development of a code of standards

Get everyone involved	Employees will feel more ownership if they help craft the document. Other shareholders such as customers and vendors can also add valuable insight
Decide whether to do the job in-house or outsource to a consultant	If the firm lacks the knowledge and expertise necessary to write a code of standards, a consultant may be helpful. The consultant's role, however, is just that – to consult. The firm still needs to take ownership of the document.
Make sure the standards apply to everyone in the organization	A code of standards is ineffective if anyone in the organization is held to a different criterion. This is especially true if senior executives are allowed to engage in behavior for which other employees would be sanctioned.
Avoid legalese	Keep the firm's code of standards in simple language, easily understood by those who will implement it.
Publicize	Publicize the code of standards on the firm's Web page, in brochures and in sales presentations. Publication aides in implementation, provides good publicity, and builds pride among employees.
Provide training	Employees, subcontractors, and others should not be held to standards of behavior of which they are not aware. Hold regular training on the code of standards and make sure all new hires understand the conduct expected.
Implement and follow-up	Make sure all supervisory personnel are implementing the new plan. At the same time, gather feedback from employees and other stakeholders and make necessary adjustments. It is a good idea to have a regular timeframe (e.g., annually) to revise the standards to keep up with changing conditions and technology.
Enforcement	Have procedures in place to sanction those who violate the standards. Apply the concepts of procedural and distributive justice to the enforcement process.
Ombudsman	Provide employees, clients, and other stakeholders with a senior executive to whom violations can be reported outside of the chain of command. Employees need to be assured that they can report a supervisor's unethical behavior without fear of retaliation.

The term *code of standards* is used in lieu of "code of ethics" to illustrate that the firm should go beyond traditional ethical issues. A "code of standards" is more inclusive. As well as ethics, a code of standards addresses:

- client confidentiality
- duty of care to the environment and community
- conflicts of interest
- fair pricing policies
- equitable treatment of employees
- quality management/assurance
- non-discriminatory policies
- corporate citizenship.

Other Organizational Factors in Marketing Research

Institutional context is also an important ethical concern. This is especially true when there is a perceived power difference between the institution conducting the research and the research subjects. Academic research provides an illustration of this power difference. A professor may require students to participate as research subjects in a study regarding sex and advertising. Some students may view such a study as creating a hostile environment of sexual harassment. Yet, the power and authority of the professor may cause reluctant students to keep silent.

Organizations that either commission or conduct market research have a responsibility to conduct and report such research in an unbiased manner. An organization that conducts research on its own products may influence the design, execution, and reported results of a study. For example, Merck and Company, Inc. had to withdraw its pain reliever Vioxx because of potentially dangerous side effects. The U.S. Food and Drug Administration accused the company of presenting false results and that Merck employees knew all along of the potential serious problems.[1]

Other problems may arise when advertising agencies have subsidiary market research firms. Pressure to bias the research process or results may be put on researchers if the client has a large account with the agency. Additionally, because the firm is a subsidiary, executives at the agency may assign it research for which it is not qualified and which should be outsourced.

One particularly troubling aspect of market research is known as *advocacy research* where a firm conducts a study in order to defend a legal action. Advocacy research design is determined by the court and may not adhere to common market research guidelines. Further, researchers may find themselves in an ethical dilemma when they are commissioned to conduct a study aimed not at finding the truth but at supporting the sponsoring organization's specific claim.

In order to avoid many of the ethical problems associated with sponsored research, firms may take the following steps:

1   price the research adequately so that pressure for bias is reduced;
2   state to clients that bias in interpretation of data will not be condoned;
3   treat respondents with dignity and respect;
4   when selling research services, avoid unnecessary promotion or pressure on salespeople;
5   conduct research in accordance with accepted codes of ethics such as the American Marketing Association, the Marketing Research Association, or the Council of American Survey Research.[2]

International Organization for Standardization

The International Organization for Standardization (ISO) has developed ISO 2052 which applies ISO quality management standards to market, opinion, and social research. The standards were developed to standardize market research worldwide, including ethical standards such as consistency and transparency, so that consumers and research clients can be confident of study results. The standards apply to the manner in which market research studies are planned, conducted, supervised, and reported. According to the Council of American Survey Research, the key elements of the standards are:[3]

- documented quality management system that can be audited;
- staff training and development;
- control of subcontractors;
- transparency to clients including client review of key steps and reporting;
- proposal/quotation content;
- validation and verification of major process steps.

ISO also developed standards, definitions, and guidelines for researchers using panels in market, opinion, and social research (ISO 26362). Each of these standards should benefit both research clients and study participants. Clients are assured that the research process has been conducted in ways recognized by the research industry and that research firms are accountable for the quality of their results. Study participants know that ethical standards relating to research have been consistently applied.

Institutional Review Board (IRB)

Governments at all levels have developed rules and regulations for research involving human subjects. These laws have led to the creation of the Institutional Review Board (IRB) that is required for any institution that conducts research for the federal government and specifically the Department of Health and Human Services. Beyond the federal government, states have also insisted on IRBs at state-funded universities and state agencies that conduct research. Most private universities have also put boards in place.

The purpose of the IRB is to approve, monitor, and review any research that involves humans. At universities this normally applies to education and the social sciences. Increasingly, however, it also applies to marketing and management studies.

The process requires researchers who wish to study human behavior to submit an outline of the study to the review board, including the name of the investigator, title of the project, time period of the study, any outside funding, how the study will be conducted, how privacy and confidentiality will be assured and a copy of the informed consent form the researcher will use.

An advantage of the human subjects form is that it requires the researcher to develop a sound and valid research methodology. A well-designed study is less likely to encounter unexpected ethical problems than one that is not well thought out. Planned research studies also require proper interpretation and application of research findings. This is important because often the results of a study will find its way to the popular press. Most of the people who read about the study will not be trained in interpretation of the information. Additionally, the limitations of the results and conclusions of the study will not likely be revealed because of the space required and the lack of reader interest. Therefore, it is imperative upon the researcher to design the study well, interpret the data accurately, and disclose any limitations or lack or generalizability about the results. Figure 2.1 is a sample of an IRB request form.

Common Ethical Research Issues

There are various issues that are common to almost every study. It is imperative that the researcher understand and address each of these issues before, during, and after the study as appropriate. An understanding of these common concerns avoids ethical problems, misunderstandings of participants, and aides in completing Institutional Review Board requests.

Beneficence

One purpose of Institutional Review Boards is to ensure that the principle of beneficence is followed. In research terms, beneficence refers to the benefits of a study as opposed to its risks. In short, the IRB asks the researcher to answer the question, "Does this study benefit more people than are the risks associated with it?" Additionally, investigators need to show that while their research may be of benefit to one group it does not harm or disadvantage another group. For example, in the case of the Tuskegee Syphilis Study, hundreds of African American men who had syphilis were studied to determine the outcomes of the disease. The study lasted 40 years, but there was an effective treatment within the first 10 years of the study. Even though the researchers learned a great deal about the effects of syphilis, it was unethical for the study to continue after a treatment became available. The broader population had the advantage of

Request For Approval of Human Subjects Research

This application should be submitted to the Chair of the Human Subjects Research Review Committee.

1. Principal Investigator's Name: _____
   Department & Campus Address: _____
   Campus Phone No.: _____
   Home No.:_____
2. If you are a student, provide the following:
   Home Address of Student: _____
   Name of Faculty Sponsor:_
   Phone Ext:_____
   Is this your thesis research? Yes___ No___
3. Title of Project: _____
4. Total Project Period: From:_____To:_____
5. Is a proposal for external support being submitted? Yes__ No__
   If "Yes," you must submit one complete copy of that proposal as soon as it is available and complete the following:
   a) Is notification of Hum. Subj. Approval Required? Yes__ No__
   b) Is this a renewal application? Yes___ No___
   c) Funding agency's name: _____
6. Has this proposal already been approved and you are seeking annual renewal? Yes_No
7. In making this application, I certify that I have read and understand the guidelines and procedures developed by the University for the protection of human subjects, and I fully intend to comply with the letter and spirit of the University's policy. I further acknowledge my responsibility to report any significant changes in the protocol, and to obtain written approval for these changes, in accordance with the procedures, prior to making these changes. I understand that I cannot initiate any contact with human subjects before I have received approval and/or complied with all contingencies made in connection with that approval.
   Signature of Principal Investigator Date

   _____ _____
8. Approval by Faculty Sponsor (required for all students): I affirm the accuracy of this application, and I accept the responsibility for the conduct of this research and supervision of human subjects as required by law.
   Signature of Faculty Sponsor Date

   _____ _____
9. I have included copies of all pertinent attachments including, but not limited to: questionnaire/survey instrument, informed consent, letters of approval from cooperating institutions, copy of external support proposal if applicable, etc.
   Yes____ No____ (If no, explain on an attached sheet)
   For the following items, attach your answers, appropriately numbered on a separate sheet of paper.
10. Identify the sources of the potential subjects, derived materials or data. Describe the characteristics of the subject population, such as their anticipated number, age, sex, ethnic background, and state of health. Identify the criteria for inclusion or exclusion. Explain the rationale for the use of special classes of subject, such as fetuses, pregnant women, children, institutionalized mentally disabled, prisoners, or others, especially those whose ability to give voluntary informed consent may be in question.
11. Provide a description of the procedures to be used in the study including major hypotheses and description of the research design.
12. Describe the recruitment and consent procedures to be followed, including the circumstances under which consent will be solicited and obtained, who will seek it, the nature of information to be provided to prospective subjects, and the methods of documenting consent. (Include applicable consent form(s) for review purposes). If written consent is not to be obtained, specifically point this out and explain why not. (Note: Informed consent must normally be obtained in a written form which requires the subject's signature or that of the subject's legally authorized representative. A waiver of this requirement may be granted by the HSRRC if adequate justification for the requirement is provided by the investigator in # 12. However, if the procedures pose no more than minimal risk to the subjects, informed consent may be documented via a written cover letter which does not require the subject's signature. In all cases, **a copy of the written informed consent must be given to the subject**. Consult the document "Research Involving Human Subjects at _____ University" for more information on informed consent requirements and specific examples of possible informed consent documents.)
13. Include a discussion of confidentiality safeguards, where relevant.
14. Describe the anticipated benefits to subjects, and the importance of the knowledge that may reasonably be expected to result.
15. Describe the risks involved with these procedures (physical, psychological, and/or social) and the precautions you have taken to minimize these risks. Do the benefits described above outweigh the described risks?

NOTE: While every effort is made to ensure the accuracy of these pages, errors may occur on occasion

Figure 2.1 Institutional Research Board Request For Approval Of Human Subjects Research

understanding the disease, but the study participants were a disadvantaged group because of the research.

Informed Consent

Autonomy refers to people's freedom to make their own decisions and to choose the activities they wish to engage in and which activities to avoid. Therefore, potential participants need to understand that they have complete freedom to participate or refuse to participate in a research study. In order to ensure autonomy, participants must give their informed consent to participate in a study.

Informed consent is at the heart of market research ethics and involves communication between the research participants and the researcher. The ethical researcher fully discloses the purposes and procedures involved in each study. Subsequent to this disclosure, the researcher may ask the potential subject to consent to participation in the project. If the research involves children (e.g., effects of TV advertising on children), a parent or legal guardian needs to agree to the child's participation.

In order for a person to make an informed consent concerning participation in a study, the researcher should identify the sponsor, estimate the time needed to complete the interview or survey, and remind the subject that participation is completely voluntary. Mail surveys, on the other hand, do not normally require signed or verbal consent. If the participant completes and returns the survey, consent is implied. A sample informed consent form is at the end of this chapter. Figure 2.2 is a sample informed consent form.

Privacy and Confidentiality Rights

Privacy follows the concept of informed consent and requires market researchers to protect the privacy of respondents and the confidentiality of their information. Privacy, in terms of research, is concerned with participation in the research process. Even if a subject signs an informed consent form, he or she has the right to not answer specific questions, not to admit a researcher into his or her home, and to refuse to answer the telephone. In addition to informed consent, problems in these areas can be addressed by scheduling times for interviews, respecting the subject's time, and reminding them of their right to refuse to answer questions.

Privacy requires that the person conducting the research identify him- or herself when conducting the study, avoiding any unwanted intrusion, and setting interview times that are mutually convenient. Additionally, researchers must comply with all applicable privacy laws whether at the state or federal level. If the research is being conducted in an international context, the privacy laws of the country where the research takes place should be obeyed. Research organizations with subsidiaries or subcontractors are responsible for such entities following privacy laws. After the conclusion of a study, firms may want to destroy any unneeded information such as survey responses, audio or videotapes.

Privacy on the Web

A recent development in market research ethics involves privacy concerns when conducting online market research. Hiding one's status as a researcher is of particular concern, especially for netnographers and other qualitative researchers. As Robert Kozinets explains, netnographers are "professional lurkers."[4] Specifically, is online information public or private? Moreover, how does one obtain proper informed consent for online research? Finally, is it ethical to deliberately hide the researcher's identity online?

For example, in terms of online information, is there a difference in information posted on Facebook and information discussed in a limited chat room? An additional concern involves

(Name of the Study)

Introduction

The following information is provided for you to decide whether you wish to participate in the present study. You may refuse to sign this form and not participate in this study. You should be aware that even if you agree to participate, you are free to withdraw at any time. If you do withdraw from this study, it will not affect your relationship with the researcher or the research sponsor in any way.

Purpose of the study

(Insert description of the purpose of the study).

Procedures

(Insert description of the procedures that will be followed in the study. Address the participants, i.e. "you will be asked to…" Include the time commitment involved. If you plan to use video or audiotapes, state that here. Also state what will be done with the tapes, i.e. used by the researchers only and stored in a locked cabinet).

Risks

(Insert a description of all burdens, inconveniences, pain, discomforts and risks associated with participation in the study. If no risks are anticipated, this should be stated explicitly).

Benefits

(Insert a description of the potential benefits, if any, to the research subject. Clarify if these are direct benefits – e.g., to the subject – or indirect benefits – e.g., to society. If there are no anticipated benefits, this should be stated explicitly).

Payment to participants

(Insert a statement regarding whether or not participants will be paid and if so, how much and on what schedule. Include the following statement if participants are being paid:

Investigators may ask for your social security number in order to comply with federal and state tax and accounting regulations).

Participant confidentiality

(Include a general statement about confidentiality and the length of time the researcher intends to keep the information).

If researchers are sharing respondents' information in any way, respondents should be informed and given a choice on whether they agree to the use of their private information. Researchers must not share respondents' information in other research studies, or with other researchers. The research should clearly explain how the information is going to be used and researchers must follow those guidelines to keep the respondents information private.

Refusal to sign consent and authorization

You are not required to sign this Consent and Authorization form and you may refuse to do so without affecting your rights in any way.

Cancelling this consent and authorization

You have the right to cancel your permission to use and disclose further information collected about you, in writing, at any time, by sending your written request to: (Name and address of researcher or research firm).

If you cancel permission to use your information, the researchers will stop collecting additional information about you. However, the research team may use and disclose information that was gathered before they received your cancellation, as described above.

Participant certification:

I have read this Consent and Authorization form. I have had the opportunity to ask, and I have received answers to, any questions I had regarding the study. I understand that if I have any additional questions about my rights as a research participant, I may call (name and address or researcher or research firm).

I agree to take part in this study as a research participant. By my signature I affirm that I am at least 18 years old and that I have received a copy of this Consent and Authorization form. (Form is modified if a parent or legal guardian needs to consent for the research subject).

_____   _____
Type/Print Participant's Name   Date

_____
Participant's Signature
(Researcher contact information goes here)

Figure 2.2 Example Of Adult Informed Consent Statement

the age of the online subject. Facebook requires a person to be thirteen to have a Facebook page, yet this is below the normal age of eighteen required for informed consent. Researchers also need to consider if the participants in the online community consider themselves study subjects or simply people who are voluntarily sharing information with the public. One question a researcher can ask to determine the answer to these questions is, "If the content of a subject's communication were to become known beyond the confines of the venue being studied – would harm likely result?"

Whether a netnographer should act as a member of, or remain outside, the community under study is another ethical issue. Participation in the online community as a member will impact the results of the research. For marketing research, influencing the study results is counterproductive. Thus, market researchers should honestly disclose that their interest in the online group is that of researcher despite that such disclosure may make it more difficult to gain trust and participant influence.

Honest disclosure leads to the key ethical concept of informed consent. Netnographers and other online researchers may find obtaining informed consent difficult. Some online conversations involve thousands of people, many of whom are transient through the community. Nonetheless, the market researcher should disclose his or her actions and let subjects know they can opt out by not participating.

Additionally, people who participate in chat rooms and other online forums often use pseudonyms. The researcher needs to ask if he or she is under the same obligation to protect the privacy of a pseudonym as would be the case for a real person. There are no easy answers to these questions and the researcher's judgment is critical for addressing these matters.

Survey research on the Internet also presents privacy concerns. When conducting survey research via email, study participants should have a reasonable expectation that they may be contacted for survey purposes. This happens when there is a pre-existing relationship between the potential subjects and the firm supplying the email addresses or the research firm itself. This also presupposes that the participants have not opted out of email communication. Finally, the firm conducting the research is required to disclose the same information as a survey that is conducted face-to-face.

Active agent technology is software designed to track people's behavior on the Internet including sites visited, online transactions, and advertising click-through and purchase information. The software is also capable of obtaining information from emails and other documents. Active agents are not cookies. Cookies gather much less data and are less intrusive. Moreover, computer users can easily disable cookies.

Downloading of active agent software to someone's computer without permission is clearly unethical. The concept and procedures associated with informed consent must be followed. In addition to consent, research firms need to disclose the types and amount of data sought. As the study continues, participants should be reminded periodically of the presence of the active agent software. Further, active agent software should not disable anti-spam, anti-virus programs or otherwise disable or disrupt participants' computers.

In summary, the issues for online research are varied and complex. Various organizations, including The Association of Internet Research (http://aoir.org/documents/ethics-guide) and the Council of American Survey Research (http:www.casro.org) have published ethics codes for online research.

Confidentiality

Confidentiality concerns what is done with the data collected. Since study subjects often provide researchers with personal information, it is imperative that this information not be shared in such a way that it can be identified with any particular individual. Any disclosure of personal information requires informed consent by the study subject. Moreover, market research studies should clearly explain how information obtained will be used and privacy protected. As noted in the informed consent form discussed above, the length of time research data will be held by the research, the disposition of that data (locked in a safe, password protected, etc.), and with whom the data will be shared all need to be disclosed to the participant. It should be noted, the smaller the research group, the more easily it can be identified with a particular subject. This could be especially true in certain qualitative studies where only a few subjects participate in depth interviews. In these cases, it is imperative that extra caution be taken to avoid disclosure of the identity of participants.

Participant data is protected when research firms properly train and supervise employees who interact with the subjects or have access to the subjects' data. A further step is to have front-line researchers remove as much of the participants' information as possible (e.g., telephone numbers, addresses, etc.).

There are instances where a subject's data may be disclosed. For example, a research firm may disclose specific participant information so that its client may compare the data with that of its customers. In such cases, the research firm should obtain, in writing, a commitment from the client firm to use the information only for comparison or model building purposes. In no case should such information be used to embarrass or harass the participant or to use the information as a lead generation for salespeople.

The concept of confidentiality of participant information applies to legal proceedings as well. Information subject to subpoena should be opposed by the research firm until the release of such information is ordered by the court.

Avoiding Deception

Deception occurs when study subjects are lead to believe something the researcher knows is not true. Examples of deception involve misleading promises of privacy/confidentiality, improper/false disclosure of sponsors, and a lack of informed consent. Researchers, for example, may guarantee privacy and at the same time track survey responses with numbered questionnaires or invisible ink. In another situation, researchers may not inform study subjects that they are being observed with two-way mirrors or hidden cameras. These instances of deception violate the important tenet of informed consent.

The disclosure of a researcher sponsor is an area of ethical concern for marketing researchers. Often a firm may conduct market research to determine the viability of a new product or to gather information on entering a new market. In these instances, the company may want to remain anonymous so as not to inform the competition of its activities. In this instance, the researcher will want to safeguard the identity of the sponsor while at the same time informing the subject of the general nature of the study. The confidentiality of the sponsor is perfectly acceptable as long as it does not in any way harm participants or interfere with their informed consent.

Institutional review boards in academic settings and ethics committees in industry may approve deception in the research process if the goals of the research cannot otherwise be achieved or the expected benefits of the research are sufficient to justify the deception. If deception is used, it should be disclosed to the participants during the debrief.

Paying people to participate in research is a common practice. Many mail survey researchers will include a token payment of a one dollar bill, for example while some medical studies pay considerably more. Research participation has been declining for the past few years for mail, telephone, and interview research.[5] Therefore, paying research subjects may increase mail survey response and aid in recruitment for sensitive research studies, yet this practice may create more problems than it solves.

One problem is that paying participants may violate the tenet of informed consent. Depending on the situation, compensation may cause participants to feel coerced to participate in a study. The researchers who choose to pay participants must decide on an amount that provides incentive but does not coerce participants – particularly subjects who are members of disadvantaged populations.

Another problem associated with paying participants is that it may cause study subjects to tell the researcher what the subject thinks the researcher wants to hear. For example, a month's supply of free laundry detergent in order to study consumer attitudes toward the product may cause the participants to feel obligated to give the detergent a favorable review.

A clearly deceptive method of increasing response rates is to mislead participants about the length of the questionnaire. For example, a market research firm may call homes in a particular neighborhood to determine attitudes toward a new product. In order to gain participants, the phone solicitor tells the subject that the survey will take less than five minutes. At the end of the survey, the researcher tells the participant that a supervisor just handed him or her a few more questions and would the participant mind just a few more minutes. The researcher is relying on the subject's initial commitment to the process and goodwill to continue although the researcher knew all along that the survey would take more than five minutes.

Researchers may also tell potential research subjects that many others, including the subject's friends and family, have completed the survey indicating that refusal to participate will result in becoming a social outcast. Even if the statement of others' participation is true, the method contains an element of deception.

Debrief

Participants should be debriefed after the study is completed. The debrief includes information about the results and conclusions of the research. Any questions participants may have are answered. Researchers may also take this opportunity to express gratitude to study participants. The debrief also allows the researcher to lay the groundwork for any future study participation.

If deception has been used (e.g., intentionally misleading the participants as to who the sponsoring organization is), this is the time to explain what deception was used and why. As previously noted, there are times deception may be justified. However, after the study is completed, there should not be any mistaken ideas about the research.

Natural Environments

In addition to not harming study subjects in any way, researchers should take care not to harm the environment as well. Research must avoid harming the planet's resources. The community the research is conducted in needs to be out of harm's way as well. This may require consent on the part of the community as well as individual participants.

Market researchers need to protect the world we live in, by making business decisions in the world's best interest. Consumers are judging businesses based on the ways they are preserving or damaging the planet. For consumers to accept market research data, the research needs to be conducted in a way that isn't harmful to the environment. Businesses can make these decisions based on the 3Rs which are, reuse, recycle, and reduce.[6]

Dangers of unethical market research

To better understand the dangers of unethical market research, it helps to understand troubles that market researchers are faced with. These problems that market researchers are faced with may cause distortions of data that leads to loss of credibility. Communication problems with

Table 2.3 Factors to consider when assessing an ethical decision

Follow the rules that are mutually understood and agreed upon. Everyone needs to operate under the same rules of the game.
Be able to discuss and defend your choices. An ethical decision maker needs to be open about how a decision was reached. Openness indicates a confidence in one's attempt to make the right decision.
Employ the Golden Rule. That is, would you want to be on the receiving end of your actions? Additionally, consider what society would look like if everyone acted as you did.
Consider the decision alternatives. This is best done by seeking input from those with different points of view who are inside and outside of the firm.

Adapted from L.G Bolman and T.E. Deal, (2008). *Reframing Organizations: Artistry, Choice, and Leadership*, 4th edn. Jossey-Bass: San Francisco, CA.

employers may lead to data distortion. Unethical research by another employee may risk the credibility of other employees. Pressures from clients lead to time constraints, incomplete research, unobtainable data, and information being held from respondents, which all can lead to distortion of data. When distorted data is given to research users, poor decisions are made. All these problems hurt the credibility of the research firm and researcher.

Communication Problems with Clients

Market researchers can have communication problems with their clients. The client may take the information that the researcher has provided and translate it in a different manner. The market researcher may have conducted the research ethically, but the client is translating the information unethically. It is extremely important that the market researcher explain the data and present it without any distortions. The research user should clearly understand that it is unethical to distort the data that has been given to them. When clients distort the data that has been presented to them the research firm may lose credibility.

Another Employee Makes an Unethical Decision

It is important for all market researchers to work together ethically and hold each other accountable for unethical actions. It becomes difficult when a supervisor or other senior employee is making unethical decisions. For example, a marketing vice president deliberately distorted research findings. The marketing research director decided to ignore it because the marketing vice president is above his position, and therefore knows what he or she is doing. Market researchers need to be careful with situations such as these because they can be held responsible for the unethical action. The firm's code of standards and the position of ombudsman may help alleviate this situation.

Time Constraints

Due to time constraints, a researcher may not finish conducting a survey or interview. A market researcher may be tempted to invent an outcome or data that never was discovered. The market researchers may not falsify the outcome, but do the research in a way they know will show the desired results. Researchers may be running out of time and omit information that doesn't support what the client wants. This is no different than changing the information and makes a market researcher's work dishonest.

Incomplete Research

Another pressure clients may force on market researchers, involves stopping the research when a trend is noticed. A market researcher plans to conduct a set number of interviews, but discovers a trend in the findings. The employer wants the interviewing to stop because of time constraints and the trend has been the same in the respondents that have already been interviewed. The researcher has saved time, but this can greatly affect the findings; and once again the credibility of the researcher and research firm. There may be a current trend, but maybe another trend might have been discovered. It can't be concluded that there even is a trend at all until the research is completed.

Client Wants Unobtainable Data

Market researchers need to have good business judgment. A client may want to conduct research that a market researcher knows won't yield the results that the client expects. Should the market researcher take the job? The most ethical action is to inform the client, in a professional manner, that the research will not yield the desired results. While the researcher may cite previous studies in support of his or her contention, one should keep in mind that proof from a previous client's research can't be shared without that client's permission.

There are those who would argue that the client wants the information and therefore the researcher should do it. The suggestion is that another firm will do the research for the client anyway. However, to take the job and not inform the client of your professional opinion, the researcher is putting the firm at risk of losing credibility. The researcher has wasted time and resources and the results will not satisfy the client. The result will be negative publicity and a reputation for poor research.

Making Poor Business Decisions from Faulty Data

When faulty data is used, clients may introduce a new product or service that should've been avoided. When clients make poor decisions from faulty data they imperil the financial health of their firms. Clients may also miss out on an opportunity when faulty data is presented and used to make decisions. The client isn't the only one that loses from a poor decision. Consumers and society at large are also harmed. For the research firm, negative word of mouth will destroy the organization's credibility.

Ethical Decision Making

An old Chinese proverb is, "To starve to death is a small thing, but to lose one's integrity is a great one." To keep our integrity, we need to make good ethical decisions. Unfortunately, most ethical situations do present themselves as simple right or wrong problems, but instead, are most often complex and ambiguous. Ethical situations may also be ill-defined and difficult to recognize. As business becomes more globalized, technology advances, and workers gain more knowledge, ethical problems take on increasing complexity. These factors put ethical decision makers at "ethical risk."[7] That is, managers and others who make the wrong ethical decisions put their organizations, employees, and the public at risk of physical, social, or environmental harm.

Ethical decision making will remain difficult, but there are guidelines researchers can employ to aide in making the right choices. Table 2.3 illustrates these guidelines.

In addition to these factors, ethical decision makers should reflect on their own moral philosophy. A person's values guide actions and the better one understands his or her values, the easier ethical decisions will be.

Summary

Ethics involves the study of how individuals govern their decisions of right or wrong behavior. In market research, right behavior is to protect study subjects, research clients, the community at large, and the environment. Ethical problems, however, are often not clear and easy to understand. Thus, it is incumbent upon market researchers to understand the different schools of ethical thought and to employ a set of ethical standards to their studies. While there are standards common to all ethical market research, individual firms need to develop a more detailed code of standards that applies additional contextual criteria.

Additionally, as ethical decision makers, market researchers need to understand their own values. This requires a certain amount of reflection *before* one is presented with an ethical dilemma. There are factors to consider when making an ethical decision and a number of resources to aide in making the best choice.

Discussion Questions

1   Characterize the differences between *utilitarianism* and *the rights principle*. Discuss if it is ever morally acceptable to lie. Explain your answer.
2   Do you agree with Aristotle that virtue can be taught? Explain your answer.
3   What is the purpose of an Institutional Review Board? How do such boards help market researchers?
4   Why is informed consent so central to research ethics?
5   What organizational pressures might market researchers face? What are some ways for investigators to deal with these situations?
6   What is the value of a Code of Standards? What are the steps in developing one?
7   What are some guidelines in making good ethical decisions?

Appendix

Resources for Ethics

American Counseling Association: http://www.counseling.org
American Marketing Association: http://www.marketingpower.com
American Psychological Association: http://www.apa.org
Aspen Institute: http://www.aspeninstitute.org
Association of Internet Researchers:http://www.aoir.org
Council of American Survey Research Organizations: http://www.casro.org
Ethics Resource Cente:http://www.ethics.org
Global Ethics: http://www.globethics.net
Josephson Institute: http://www.josephsoninstitute.org
Marketing Research Association: http://www.marketingresearch.org
Online Ethics Center: http://www.onlineethics.org
Public Relations Society of America: http://www.prsa.org
Resources for Research Ethics Education: http://www.research-ethics.net

Part II
Secondary Data and Research Designs

3   Secondary Data

Learning Objectives

Upon completing this chapter, you should understand:

1   the difference in secondary and primary data;
2   the advantages and disadvantages of secondary data;
3   what is meant by a "search strategy";
4   how secondary data can help in the collection of primary data;
5   the different sources of secondary data.

Research design, as discussed in Chapter 4, is the "road map" for the researcher, indicating the route the researcher will take in collecting the information to ultimately solve the management problem or evaluate the market opportunity in question. The types of data collected in executing this research design will be either (1) *primary data* or (2) *secondary data*. Primary data are those data that are collected for the first time by the researcher for the specific research project at hand. Secondary data are data previously gathered for some other purpose. There is some confusion about the terms "primary" and "secondary." These terms have nothing to do with the relative importance of the information. Whether the data are primary or secondary is determined by whether they originated with the specific study in consideration or not.

The first tenet of data gathering among researchers is to exhaust all sources of secondary data before engaging in a search for primary data. Many research questions can be answered more quickly and with less expense through the proper use of secondary information. However, caution must be used to ensure that primary sources of secondary data are used since they are generally more accurate and complete than secondary sources of secondary data.

Uses of Secondary Data

There are several important uses of secondary data even though the research design might require the use of primary data. The most common uses are:

1   In some cases the information and insights gained from secondary data are sufficient to answer the research question.
2   Secondary data can provide the background necessary to understand the problem situation and provide an overview of the market dynamics.
3   Secondary data often can provide exploratory information that can aid in the planning and design of the instruments used to gather primary data.
4   Secondary data can serve as a check and standard for evaluating primary data.

5   Secondary data can give insight into sample selection.
6   Secondary data can suggest research hypotheses or ideas that can be studied in the primary data phase of the research process. The extensive use of secondary data reduces the possibility of "reinventing the wheel" by gathering primary data that someone else has already collected.

Advantages of Secondary Data

Secondary data are data gathered for some purpose other than the research project at hand. Consequently, researchers must understand and appreciate the relative advantages and disadvantages of this secondary information. To properly use and evaluate secondary information, its value must be assessed.

Secondary data possess the following advantages:

1   *Low cost.* The relatively low cost of secondary data is one of its most attractive characteristics. The cost of this data is relatively low when it is obtained from published sources. There is no design cost and only the cost of the time required to obtain the data is incurred. Even when the secondary information is provided by a commercial firm, it is normally less expensive than primary data because it is available on a multi-client basis to a large number of users rather than being custom designed on a proprietary basis for a single client.
2   *Speed.* A secondary data search can be accomplished in a much shorter time frame than can primary data collection that requires design and execution of a primary data-collection instrument.
3   *Availability.* Some information is available only in the form of secondary data. For example, census information is available only in secondary form. Some types of personal and financial data can not be obtained on a primary basis.
4   *Flexibility.* Secondary data is flexible and provides great variety.

Disadvantages of Secondary Data

Since secondary data, both internal and external, were generated for some purpose other than to answer the research question at hand, care must be taken in their application. The limitations of secondary data must be considered. Secondary data have the following potential limitations or disadvantages:

1   *A poor "fit."* The secondary data collected for some other research objective or purpose may not be relevant to the research question at hand. In most cases, the secondary data will not adequately fit the problem. In other cases, secondary data collected from various sources will not be in the right intervals, units of measurement or categories for proper cross-comparison. The secondary data may not be collected from the correct or most representative sample frame.
2   *Accuracy.* The question of accuracy takes several things into consideration. First of all, there is the question of whether the secondary data came from a primary or secondary source. Secondary sources of secondary data should be avoided. The next consideration is the organization or agency that originally collected the data. What is the quality of their methodology and data-gathering design? What is their reputation for credibility?
3   *Age.* A major problem with published and secondary data is the timeliness of the information. Old information is not necessarily bad information; however, in many dynamic markets, up-to-date information is an absolute necessity.
4   *Quality.* Information quality is sometimes unknown. The reputation and capability of the collecting agency is important to assess the quality of the information provided. To verify

the overall quality of secondary information, it may be necessary to know how the data were collected, what the sampling plan was, what data collection method was used, what field procedures were utilized, what training was provided, what degree of nonresponse was experienced, and what other sources of error are possible.

Secondary Data Sources

The first problem that confronts a researcher in initiating a secondary data search is the massive amount, wide variety, and many locations of secondary data. Some method of logically summarizing the sources of secondary data is helpful. Most textbooks on the subject divide secondary data sources into two groups: (1) internal data sources and (2) external data sources.

Internal secondary data sources are closest at hand since they are found within the organization initiating the research process. These internal data have been collected for other purposes but are available to be consolidated, compared, and analyzed to answer the new research question being posed. This is particularly true of organizations that have sophisticated management information systems that routinely gather and consolidate useful marketing, accounting, and production information.

Specific internal records or sources of internal secondary data are:

- invoice records
- income statements (various cost information)
- sales results
- advertising expenditures
- accounts receivable logs
- inventory records
- production reports and schedules
- complaint letters and other customer correspondence
- salesperson's reports (observations)
- management reports
- service records
- accounts payable logs
- budgets
- distributor reports and feedback
- cash register receipts
- warranty cards

Even though most research projects require more than just internal data, this is a very cost-efficient place to begin the data search. Quite often a review of all internal secondary data sources will inexpensively give direction for the next phase of data collection. The internal search will give clues to what external data sources are required to gather the information needed to answer the research question.

External secondary data originate outside the confines of the organization. There is an overwhelming number of external sources of data available to the researcher. Good external secondary data may be found through libraries, Web searches, associations, and general guides to secondary data. Most trade associations accumulate and distribute information pertinent to their industry. Quite often this includes sales and other information gathered from their members. The *Directory of Directories* and the *Encyclopedia of Associations* are excellent sources for finding associations and organizations that may provide secondary information for a particular industry.

Data mining is a term commonly used to describe the process by which companies extract consumer behavioral patterns from analysis of huge databases containing internally and externally generated data. These databases contain information gleaned from customer Web site visits, warranty cards, calls to toll free numbers, retail purchases, credit card usage, car registration information, home mortgage information, and thousands of other databases, including the U.S. Census. The use of neural network and parallel processing technology allows marketers to search through these databases to find behavioral patterns that can help identify the best prospects for:

- upgrading customers to more profitable products;
- cross-selling different products or services offered by the company;
- special offers or offers combining several companies (e.g., travel packages);
- continued long-term relationship building;
- "weblining"—similar to the practice of "redlining" where vigorous customer service is reserved for only a firm's best customers and withheld from the marginal customers, all based on the customer records in the database.[1]

The use of the Internet as a key channel of distribution has allowed many companies to develop even more sophisticated databases for marketing purposes.[2] For example, customers clicking on NextCard, Inc.'s ad for a credit card on the Quicken.com financial website can have their credit history checked and a card issued (or application rejected) in 35 seconds.

Secondary Data Sources on the Worldwide Web

The Web has become the first, and too often the only, source to be used by the marketing researcher in search of pertinent secondary data. It is reasonable to assume the reader of this text has had experience "surfing the Web," and therefore is familiar with Web browsers (Microsoft Internet Explorer, Firefox, Safari), search engines or portals (e.g., AltaVista, Infoseek, HotBot, Google, Excite, Yahoo!, etc.), indexes of business and other periodical literature (e.g., EBSCOhost), Web search strategies (e.g., use of parentheses, and, or, not, +, –, quotation marks, asterisk, etc.), and use of newsgroups (i.e., Internet sites where people can post queries or respond to other people's queries or post comments; hundreds of thousands of newsgroups exist, each devoted to a specific topic). The savvy researcher can harness these and other resources and methods of using the Internet to discover relevant secondary data available over the Worldwide Web. Our objective in this section is not to inundate the reader with a long list of websites, but rather to focus on those "megasites"—sites with the most comprehensive information databases including links to other sites—that can be "bookmarked" and regularly used in secondary research. Perhaps the best way to conceptualize the types of secondary information on the Web is the pyramid in Figure 3.1

At the top of the pyramid are the search engines that provide access to all that is on the Web. Underneath that are two types of searches: those that seek information about markets (either business to business markets (B2B), or business to consumer markets (B2C)) or marketing (either companies that offer marketing services, or the process of marketing itself). We will provide some suggestions for websites of primary interest for each of these categories.

General Search Engines

- Google (www.google.com) or Yahoo! (www.yahoo.com): while virtually everyone reading this book will have had experience using Google or Yahoo! as their portal to the web, it bears mentioning that a well-designed search (using appropriate Boolean logic, field searches, proximity operators, truncation, nesting, and limiting) will generate thousands, perhaps millions, of "hits" where the object of the search appears on the web. Readers unfamiliar

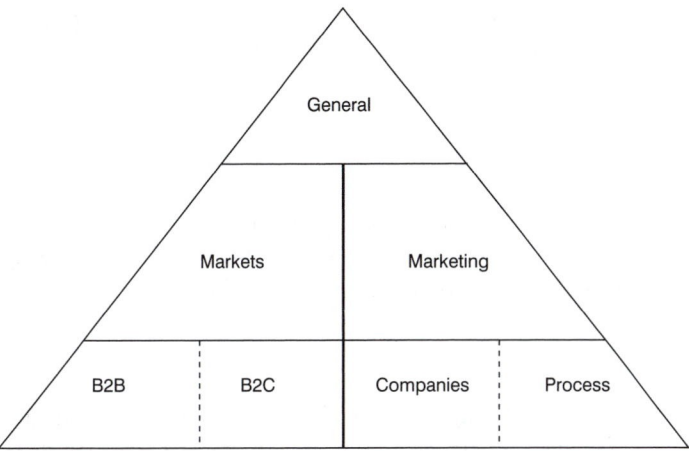

Figure 3.1 Categories of Secondary Information on the Internet

with the use of sophisticated search strategies can save considerable time and frustration by learning how to do targeted searches before using these engines.

- Teoma (www.Teoma.com): bought by Ask Jeeves in 2001, this search engine quickly finds "communities" (groups of websites related to the search topic) without generating unproductive links, as is sometimes the case with Google.
- Multi-search engines which search multiple search engines for information. The most popular are Dogpile.com, Metrocrawler.com, and Search.com.

Markets

BUSINESS TO BUSINESS MARKETS

Government Sources: FedWold (www.fedworld.gov) links to 100 federal agencies issuing statistical data. B2B researchers will probably be most interested in information contained in the Economic Census (see www.bea.gov). Of particular interest will be data contained in the North American Industry Classification System (NAICS) at www.census.gov/eos/www/naics.

Commercial Sources: www.marketingpower.com The website of the American Marketing Association has hyperlinks to other websites that identify over 40,000 research reports, including many on B2B markets.

BUSINESS TO CONSUMER MARKETS

Government Sources: See www.fedworld.gov for government information about the consumer market of interest.

Commercial Sources: In addition to search www.marketingpower.com for reports on the consumer market of interest, commonly used websites for determining the size of a market would include the Survey of Buying Power at www.salesandmarketing.com and a similar database called DemographicsUSA at www.tradedimensions.com which offers calculation of a Buying Power Index (BPI) like the Survey of Buying Power, but at a more specific level (e.g., a BPI for high tech products). Also of use to the marketer of consumer goods is the geodemographic information available at www.claritas.com, whose PRIZM system is perhaps the best known of the geodemographic consumer market segmentation sources.

Marketing

COMPANIES

To see a directory of marketing service firms that can be used for a wide variety of marketing services (e.g., advertising, new product or brand development, research, etc.) go to www.marketingpower.com and see their marketing services directory.

PROCESS

By "process" we mean the marketing process itself. That is, when you are seeking information about some aspect of marketing (e.g., sales promotion customer satisfaction research, etc.) that has been published in a business periodical or is otherwise available to the public. Primary sources of information for business related material are OCLC, Proquent, dialog, Lexis Nexis, and Ebsco which cover hundreds of sources.

Your Local Library

One source of secondary data that should never be underestimated is a local public or college library, particularly if it is a federal depository. A well-equipped library will not only contain many of the sources mentioned below but will also have a variety of helpful indexes, directories, abstracts, and personnel who can assist in locating specific information. Any thorough search for secondary data should include a comprehensive library search. Not only is the public library an important source of information, but various institutions maintain excellent libraries in their various areas of specialization. Research foundations, financial institutions, energy companies, engineering firms, utilities, universities, and manufacturing establishments often maintain good libraries. The reference librarian can help you find your way through the maze of data sources.

Syndicated Data Sources

Specific syndicated sources are available to provide marketing information. Several specific syndicated services are mentioned below:

- *Nielsen Retail Index*—This service measures consumer activity at the point of sale. It is based on national samples of supermarkets, drug stores, mass merchandisers, and beverage outlets. The store audits track volume at the retail level such as sales to consumers, retail inventories, out-of-stock conditions, prices, dealer support, and number of days' supply. http://nz.acnielsen.com/products/crs_retailindex.shtml
- *Roper Reports and the Harris Survey*—These surveys deal with public opinion on social, political, and economic subjects. Both involve large national samples and are conducted approximately every month. http://www.ropercenter.uconn.edu/data_access/tag/presidential_approval.html and http://nod.org/research_publications/nod_harris_survey/
- *National Purchase Diary Panel (NPD)*—This diary panel of over 13,000 families provides monthly purchase information about approximately fifty product categories. https://www.npd.com/wps/portal/npd/us/home
- *Nielsen Television Index*—Perhaps the most well-known service, the Nielsen Television Index measures television show ratings and shares among a panel of 1,200 television viewers

who are matched according to U.S. national statistics. http://www.nielsen.com/us/en/measurement/television-measurement.html

- *Arbitron Radio Market Reports*—These reports, based on a representative sample in each market, provide information concerning radio listening habits. http://www.arbitron.com/home/content.stm
- *Simmons MRB Media/Marketing Service*—Based on extensive data collection from a national sample of about 20,000 individuals, this service reports information concerning media exposure as well as purchase behavior about several hundred product categories. Simmons offers a software package (Choices) which allows the user to create almost unlimited comparisons and cross-tabulations of the extensive database. http://www.simmonssurvey.com/
- *Starch Readership Reports*—These reports provide measures of exposure to print ads in a wide variety of magazines and newspapers using a large number of personal interviews. http://www.starchresearch.com/services.html
- *BehaviorScan*—This service, provided by Information Resources, Inc. (IRI), uses supermarket scanners to measure the consumption behavior of a panel of consumers. http://www.symphonyiri.com/SolutionsandServices/Detail.aspx?ProductID=187

Consumer Data Sources

- *Total Economy Database.* Published annually by Conference Board, this source provides data on the behavior of consumers, under the headings of: population, employment, income, expenditures, production and distribution, and prices. http://www.conference-board.org/data/economydatabase/
- *Historical Statistics of the United States from Colonial Times to 1970.* This volume was prepared as a supplement to the *Statistical Abstract.* This source provides data on social, economic, and political aspects of life in the United States. It contains consistent definitions and thus eliminates incompatibilities of data in the Statistical Abstracts caused by dynamic changes over time. http://www.census.gov/prod/www/abs/statab.html
- *County and City Data Book.* Bureau of the Census (Government Printing Office). Published every 5 years, this publication gives statistics on population, income, education, employment, housing, retail, and wholesale sales for various cities, SMSAs, and counties. http://www.census.gov/statab/www/ccdb.html
- *Census of the Population* (Government Printing Office). Taken every ten years, this source reports the population by geographic region, with detailed breakdowns according to demographic characteristics, such as sex, marital status, age, education, race, income, etc. http://www.census.gov/prod/www/abs/decennial/
- *Editor and Publisher Market Guide.* Published annually by Editor and Publisher Co., it contains information on 265 metro areas including population, number of households, industries, retail sales, and climate. http://www.editorandpublisher.com/Subscribe/MarketGuide/

Company Data Sources

- *Fortune Directory.* Published annually by *Fortune* magazine, this source presents information on sales, assets, profits, invested capital, and employees for the 500 largest U.S. industrial corporations. http://money.cnn.com/magazines/fortune/fortune500/2012/faq/index.html
- *Middle Market Directory.* Published annually by Dun & Bradstreet, this source lists companies with assets in the range of $500,000 to $999,999. The directory offers information on some 30,000 companies' officers, products, sales, and number of employees. http://www.dnbmdd.com/mddi/

- *Million Dollar Directory.* Published annually by Dun & Bradstreet, this source offers the same information as the Middle Market Directory, only for companies with sales over $9 million or 180 employees. http://www.dnbmdd.com/mddi/
- *Thomas Register of American Manufacturers.* Published annually by the Thomas Publishing Company, this source gives specific manufacturers of individual products, as well as the company's address, branch offices, and subsidiaries. http://www.thomasnet.com/
- *Moody's Manuals.* This source list includes manuals entitled *Banks and Finance, Municipals and Governments, Public Utilities, Transportation.* These manuals contain balance sheet and income statements for various companies and government units. http://www.moodys.com/
- *Standard and Poor's Register of Corporations, Directors, and Executives.* Published annually by Standard and Poor, this source provides officers, sales, products, and number of employees for some 75,000 U.S. and Canadian corporations. http://www.netadvantage. standardandpoors.com/login/NASApp/NetAdvantage/NET/login/login.jsp
- *Wall Street Journal Index.* Published monthly, this source lists corporate news, alphabetically, by firm name, as it has occurred in *The Wall Street Journal.* http://online.wsj.com/mdc/ public/page/marketsdata.html#mod=djmr_mdcpodcast
- *Moody's Manual of Investments.* This source documents historical and operational data on selected firms and five years of their balance sheets, income accounts, and dividend records. http://www.moodys.com/
- *State Manufacturing Directories.* Published for each state, these sources give company addresses, products, officers, etc., by geographic location. http://www.mnistore.com/
- *Fortune Double 500 Directory.* Published annually in the May-August issues of *Fortune* magazine, this source offers information on assets, sales, and profits of 1,000 of the largest U.S. firms, 50 largest banks, life insurance companies, and retailing, transportation, utility, and financial companies. In addition, this source ranks foreign firms and banks. http:// money.cnn.com/magazines/fortune/fortune500/2012/faq/index.html
- *Directory of Corporate Affiliations.* Published annually by LexisNexis this source lists approximately 3,000 parent companies and their 16,000 divisions, subsidiaries, and affiliates. http://www.lexisnexis.com/dca/
- *Moody's Industrial Manual.* Published annually, this source provides information on selected companies' products and description, history, mergers and acquisition record, principal plants and properties, principal offices, as well as seven years of financial statements and statistical records. http://www.moodys.com/
- *Reference Book of Corporate Management.* Published annually by Dun & Bradstreet, this source gives a list of 2,400 companies and their 30,000 officers and directors. http://www. dnbmdd.com/mddi/
- *Hoover's Handbook of American Business.* Published by Hoover's Business Press, this two-volume work provides profiles of 750 large companies in the U.S. http://www.hoovers. com/products/100000859-1.html#
- *Mergent's Manuals.* Published annually, this source provides income statements and balance sheets for companies and government units. http://www.mergent.com/downloads-newsReports.html

Market Data Sources

- *Bureau of the Census Catalog* (Government Printing Office). Published quarterly, this source is a comprehensive guide to Census Bureau publications. Publications include agriculture, foreign trade, governments, population, and the economic census. http://www.census.gov/ prod/www/abs/catalogs.html

- *Economic Indicators.* Council of Economic Advisors, Department of Commerce (Government Printing Office). Published monthly, this source gives current, key indicators of general business conditions, such as GNP, personal consumption expenditures, etc. http://bookstore.gpo.gov/actions/GetPublication.do?stocknumber=752-004-00000-5
- *Federal Reserve Bulletin* (Washington, DC: Federal Reserve System Board of Governors). Published monthly, this publication offers financial data on interest rates, credit, savings, banking activity; an index of industrial production; and finance and international trade statistics. http://www.federalreserve.gov/pubs/bulletin/
- *Monthly Labor Review.* Bureau of Labor Statistics (Government Printing Office). Published monthly, this source presents information on employment, earnings, and wholesale and retail prices. http://www.bls.gov/opub/mlr/
- *Survey of Current Business.* Bureau of Economic Analysis, Department of Commerce (Government Printing Office). Published monthly, this source presents indicators of general business, personal consumption expenditures, industry statistics, domestic trade, earnings and employment by industry, real estate activity, etc. http://www.bea.gov/scb/index.htm
- *Census of Business* (Government Printing Office). Published every five years, this source supplies statistics on the retail, wholesale, and service trades. The census of service trade compiles information on receipts, legal form of organization, employment, and number of units by geographic area. http://www.census.gov/econ/susb/
- *Census of Manufacturer* (Government Printing Office). Published every five years, this source presents manufacturers by type of industry. It contains detailed industry and geographic statistics, such as the number of establishments, quantity of output, value added in manufacture, employment, wages, inventories, sales by customer class, and fuel, water, and energy consumption. http://www.census.gov/econ/overview/ma0100.html
- *County Business Patterns.* Departments of Commerce and Health, Education and Welfare. Published annually, this source gives statistics on the number of businesses by type and their employment and payroll broken down by county. http://www.census.gov/econ/cbp/
- *Commodity Yearbook.* Published annually by the Commodity Research Bureau, this source supplies data on prices, production, exports, stocks, etc., for 100 commodities. http://www.crbyearbook.com/
- *Business Statistics.* Department of Commerce. Published biennially, this source is a supplement to "The Survey of Current Business." It provides information from some 2,500 statistical series, starting in 1939. http://www.esa.doc.gov/about-economic-indicators
- *Standard and Poor's Trade and Securities Statistics.* Published monthly by Standard and Poor Corporation, this source contains statistics on banking, production, labor, commodity prices, income, trade, securities, etc. http://www.netadvantage.standardandpoors.com/login/NASApp/NetAdvantage/NET/login/login.jsp
- *Market Analysis.* A Handbook of Current Data Sources. Written by Nathalie Frank and published by Scarecrow Press of Metuchen, NJ, this book offers sources of secondary information broken down on the basis of indexes, abstracts, directories, etc. http://www.abebooks.com/servlet/BookDetailsPL?bi=5540772959&searchurl=kn%3DMarket%2BAnalysis.%2BA%2BHandbook%2Bof%2BCurrent%2BData%2BSources%26sts%3Dt%26x%3D43%26y%3D9
- *Statistics of Income.* Internal Revenue Service, published annually, this source gives balance sheet and income statement statistics, prepared from federal income tax returns of corporations, and broken down by major industry, asset size, etc. http://www.irs.gov/taxstats/article/0,,id=120303,00.html
- *Public Affairs Information Services Bulletin (PAIS).* Similar to, but different from, the Business Periodicals Index, this source includes more foreign publications, and it includes

many books, government publications, and many nonperiodical publications. http://www.csa.com/factsheets/pais-set-c.php

- *Census of Retail Trade* (Government Printing Office). Taken every five years in the years ending in 2 and 7, this source provides information on 100 retail classifications. Statistics are compiled on number of establishments, total sales, sales by product line, size of firms, employment and payroll for states, SMSAs, counties and cities of 2,500 or more. http://www.census.gov/econ/census07/
- *Census of Selected Service Industries* (Government Printing Office). Taken every five years, in years ending in 2 and 7, this source compiles statistics on 150 or more service classifications. Information on the number of establishments, receipts, payrolls, etc., is provided for various service organizations. http://www.census.gov/econ/census07/
- *Census of Wholesale Trade* (Government Printing Office). Taken every five years, in years ending in 2 and 7, this source provides statistics of 150 wholesale classifications. Information includes numbers of establishments, sales, personnel, payroll, etc. http://www.census.gov/econ/census07/
- *Census of Transportation* (Government Printing Office). Taken every five years, in years ending in 2 and 7, this source presents three specific surveys: Truck Inventory and Use Survey, National Travel Survey, and Commodity Transportation Survey. http://www.census.gov/econ/census07/
- *U.S. Industrial Outlook* (Government Printing Office). Published annually, this source provides a detailed analysis of approximately 200 manufacturing and nonmanufacturing industries. It contains information on recent developments, current trends, and a ten-year outlook for the industries. This source is useful in forecasting the specific marketing factors of a market analysis. http://www.allcountries.org/uscensus/industrial_outlook.html
- *Standard and Poor's Industry Survey.* Published annually, this source offers current surveys of industries and a monthly Trends and Projections section, useful in forecasting market factors. http://www.netadvantage.standardandpoors.com/login/NASApp/NetAdvantage/NET/login/login.jsp
- *Monthly Labor Review.* Published monthly by the U.S. Bureau of Labor Statistics, this source compiles trends and information on employment, wages, weekly working hours, collective agreements, industrial accidents, etc. http://www.bls.gov/mlr/

Cost Data Sources

- *Moody's Investors Services, Inc.* Published by Standard and Poor Corporation (NY), this is a financial reporting source that includes many large firms. http://www.moodys.com/Pages/atc002.aspx
- *Standard Corporation Records.* Published by Standard and Poor Corporation (NY), this is a publication of financial reporting data of the larger firms. http://www.netadvantage.standardandpoors.com/login/NASApp/NetAdvantage/NET/login/login.jsp
- *Business Publication Rates and Data.* Published by Standard Rate & Data Service, Inc. This index lists various trade publication sources. http://next.srds.com/media-data/business
- *Economic Census* (Government Printing Office). A comprehensive and periodic canvass of U.S. industrial and business activities, taken by the Census Bureau every five years. In addition to providing the framework for forecasting and planning, these censuses provide weights and benchmarks for indexes of industrial production, productivity, and price. Management use these in economic or sales forecasting, and analyzing sales performance, allocating advertising budgets, locating plants, warehouses and stores, and so on. http://www.census.gov/econ/census07/

- *Gale Directory of Databases*. Published by Gale Research Co. twice a year, this directory lists more than 12,000 databases, 3,000 database producers and 2,000 online services and vendors. http://www.gale.cengage.com/servlet/SearchResultServlet

General Advice

There is no question that the number and complexity of information sources may discourage the novice secondary source researcher from pursuing this line of research. Our advice to the uninitiated researcher is to take the problem to the business reference librarian at the nearest university library. He/she can save considerable wasted time and effort by directing the researcher to those sources most likely to provide the solution to information problems. We also recommend the following short list of sources for those researchers who want to pursue their searches alone, but who need a few broad-based sources to get started.

- *Directories in Print—Gale Research Co.* Indexes over 10,000 published directories. http://www.gale.cengage.com/servlet/SearchResultServlet
- *Encyclopedia of Business Information Sources—*Also by Gale Research, this encyclopedia is updated frequently. http://www.gale.cengage.com/servlet/SearchResultServlet
- *Business Information, How to Find It, How to Use It—*Michael R. Lavin, author. The second edition was published in 1992 by Oryx Press. http://www.amazon.com/Business-Information-How-Find-Use/dp/0897745566
- *Directory of On-Line Databases—*Cuadra Associates, Santa Monica, CA. Updated periodically. http://www.cuadra.com/about/about.html
- *Encyclopedia of Associations—*Gale Research lists over 20,000 trade associations by subject area, including addresses and phone numbers. Many trade associations are very helpful in meeting information needs. http://www.gale.cengage.com/servlet/SearchResultServlet

Summary

Whenever research requirements are defined, secondary data should be exploited first to give background, direction, and control over the total research process. Beginning with a secondary data search will ensure that the maximum benefit is derived from the collection of primary data. All pertinent secondary data should be gathered before moving to the primary gathering stage because it is generally quicker and cheaper to collect secondary data. Good secondary data can be found both internally and externally. Library facilities, as well as the Web, should be used as a starting point in gathering secondary data, while the federal government is the largest single source of secondary information.

Although secondary information may answer the research question, generally it provides only the springboard for a collection of specific custom-designed information.

Research Project Tip

Virtually all research projects will benefit from conducting a literature review of secondary data sources. While this will undoubtedly include the use of the Web, you should also visit a university and/or public library. It is not enough to merely print out those articles available as a "full-text" print option on EBSCOhost, for example. Other very important articles and secondary data sources are available only by visiting your library. Conducting a literature review only from in front of your computer screen is not sufficient. This is not a time to take shortcuts. Key information may be available only with the expenditure of time and hard work.

Discussion Questions

1   Why is a search of secondary data almost always a good way to begin a research project? Provide an example from your research project to illustrate your points.
2   What precautions need to be observed when using secondary data to get answers to research questions? Provide an example from your research project to illustrate your points.
3   Describe in depth a search strategy you would use to get an answer to this question: How have conceptions of what constitutes "good customer service" changed over time for American consumers, and what has been the trend in customer complaints about airline travel in the past decade?

4 Research Designs
Exploratory and Qualitative Research

Learning Objectives

Upon completing this chapter, you should understand:

1 differences in exploratory, descriptive, and causal research;
2 how exploratory/qualitative research differs from quantitative research;
3 when exploratory/qualitative research should be used;
4 how exploratory/qualitative research can improve the development of the quantitative research process;
5 different types of exploratory/qualitative methodologies.

As described in our outline of the research process, the next step after stating the management problem, research purpose, and research hypotheses and questions, is to formulate a research design. The starting point for the research design is, in fact, the research questions and hypotheses we have so carefully developed. In essence, the research design answers the question: How are we going to get answers to these research questions and test these hypotheses? The research design is a plan of action indicating the specific steps that are necessary to provide answers to those questions, test the hypotheses, and thereby achieve the research purpose that helps choose among the decision alternatives to solve the management problem or capitalize on the market opportunity (see Figure 4.1).

Types of Research Designs

A research design is like a roadmap—you can see where you currently are, where you want to be at the completion of your journey, and can determine the best (most efficient and effective) route to take to get to your destination. We may have to take unforeseen detours along the way, but by keeping our ultimate objective constantly in mind and using our map we can arrive at our destination. Our research purpose and objectives suggest which route (design) might be best to get us where we want to go, but there is more than one way to "get there from here." Choice of research design is not like solving a problem in algebra where there is only one correct answer and an infinite number of wrong ones. Choice of research design is more like selecting a cheesecake recipe—some are better than others but there is no one which is universally accepted as "best." Successfully completing a research project consists of making those choices that will fulfill the research purpose and obtain answers to the research questions in an efficient and effective manner.

Choice of design type is not determined by the nature of the strategic decision faced by the manager such that we would use research design "A" whenever we need to evaluate the extent of

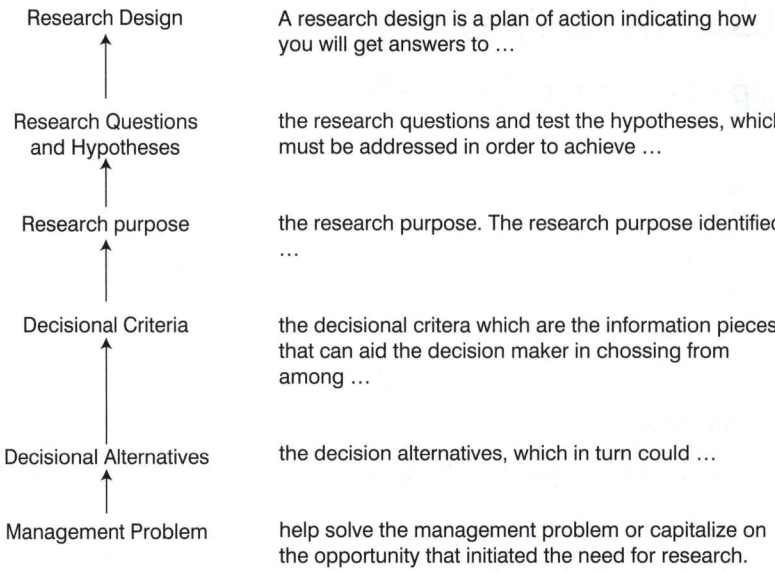

Figure 4.1 The relationship between research design and the solution to management's problem

a new product opportunity, or design "B" when deciding on which of two advertising programs to run. Rather, choice of research design is influenced by a number of variables such as the decision maker's attitude toward risk, the types of decisions being faced, the size of the research budget, the decision-making time frame, the nature of the research objectives, and other subtle and not-so-subtle factors. Much of the choice, however, will depend upon the fundamental objective implied by the research question:

- To conduct a general *exploration* of the issue, gain some broad insights into the phenomenon, and achieve a better "feel" for the subject under investigation (e.g., What do customers mean by "good value"?).
- To describe a population, event, or phenomenon in a precise manner where we can attach numbers to represent the extent to which something occurs or determine the degree two or more variables vary (e.g., determine the relationship between age and consumption rate).
- To attribute *cause* and effect relationships among two or more variables so that we can better understand and predict the outcome of one variable (e.g., sales) when varying another (e.g., advertising).

These three broadly different objectives give us the names of our three categories of research designs: exploratory, descriptive, and causal. Before we discuss each of these design types a cautionary note is in order. Some might think that the research design decision suggests a choice among the design types. Although there are research situations in which all the research questions might be answered by doing only one of these types (e.g., a causal research experiment to determine which of three prices results in the greatest profits), it is more often the case that the research design might involve more than one of these types performed in some sequence. For example, in the case of the Compton Company described in Chapter 1, if research had been conducted, the research objectives might first have required exploratory research to more precisely define the problem, followed by descriptive research which could have determined the frequency that distributors recommended a competing brand, or the extent to which purchase intent covered by previous experience with the Compton brand. Some research questions might have been completely answered using just one of the research design types, while others required a sequence of two or all three types. The overall research design is intended to indicate exactly how the different design types will be utilized to get answers to the research questions or test the hypothesis.

A further cautionary note is needed to warn the reader that while it may appear that if sequencing is done the sequence would be exploratory, then descriptive, then causal, that is not always the case. For example, some companies may do an annual survey of consumers to determine the frequency with which certain behaviors are performed (e.g., washing dishes by hand) followed by exploratory research that probes to gain an in-depth understanding of the circumstances surrounding that behavior (i.e., descriptive then exploratory rather than exploratory then descriptive). It is not hard to imagine a research design that might sequence as exploratory, then descriptive, then exploratory again; or causal, then descriptive. It is important to remember that because a research design is a plan of action to obtain answers to the research questions, it is those questions that suggest which design types are necessary and the sequence of conducting those design types, if a sequence is needed. An example later in this chapter will be used to illustrate this point. With these cautions in mind we will discuss exploratory research in this chapter and address descriptive and casual methods in Chapter 5.

Exploratory Research

Exploratory research is in some ways akin to detective work—there is a search for "clues" to reveal what happened or is currently taking place, a variety of sources might be used to provide insights and information, and the researcher/detective "follows where his or her nose leads" in the search for ideas, insights, and clarification. Researchers doing exploratory research must adopt a very flexible attitude toward collecting information in this type of research and be constantly asking themselves what lies beneath the surface of what they are learning and/or seeing. An insatiable curiosity is a valuable trait for exploratory researchers.

Such curiosity will serve the exploratory researcher well when, for example, he or she sees the need to ask a follow-up question of a respondent who has mentioned some unanticipated answer to a researcher's query. The follow-up question is not listed on the researcher's interview guide, but the curious interviewer instinctively knows that the conversation should begin to deviate from the guide because the unexpected response may be revealing much more important issues surrounding the topic for investigation than were originally anticipated by the researcher. A willingness to follow one's instincts and detour into new territory is not only acceptable in exploratory research, it is commendable! Inspired insight, new ideas, clarifications, and revelatory observations are all the desired outcomes from exploratory research and decision makers should not judge the quality of the idea or insight based on its source.

Although we do not want to give the impression that any approach is acceptable for doing exploratory research, or that all methods are of equal value in providing desired information, it is true that exploratory research is characterized by a *flexibility* of method that is minimal with descriptive and causal designs.

Exploratory research is needed whenever the decision maker has an objective of:

1 more precisely defining an ambiguous problem or opportunity (e.g., "Why have sales started to decline?");
2 increasing the decision maker's understanding of an issue (e.g., "What do consumers mean by saying they want a 'dry beer'?");

3   developing hypotheses that could explain the occurrence of certain phenomena (e.g., "Different ethnic groups seek different levels of spice in our canned beans.");

4   generating ideas (e.g., "What can be done to improve our relationships with independent distributors?");

5   providing insights (e.g., "What government regulations are likely to be passed during the next year that will affect us?");

6   establishing priorities for future research or determining the practicality of conducting some research (e.g., "Should we try to survey all our salespeople on this issue or just talk with the leading salesperson in each region?");

7   identifying the variables and levels of variables for descriptive or causal research (e.g., "We will focus our attention on determining the level of consumer interest in these three product concepts because exploratory research shows no interest in the other two.").

Tools Used to Conduct Exploratory Research

As previously noted, our research design is a plan of action indicating the specific steps that are necessary to provide answers to the questions we have developed and, in some cases to test hypotheses. It is possible, however, that we do not know enough about a question to formulate a hypothesis, or we are more interested in describing a particular event or discovering the meaning of an event for the research subjects than we are in frequency of event occurrence or differences between groups. The research method we use in these situations is known as *qualitative* research and is outlined below.

Explanation of the Qualitative Research Process

Qualitative research is beneficial for studying ill-structured problems, which are defined as "non-routine problems that have no clear solution."[1]

Research Project Tip

Your choice of a research design goes beyond simply saying which type(s) of approaches you will use (exploratory, descriptive, or causal). You must indicate the specific way you will get answers to each research question.

Traditional survey research methods are inadequate for this type problem because, by definition, the problem cannot be verbalized. Effective qualitative methods may help by eliciting images, nonverbal cues, and unconscious thoughts that lead to a statement of the problem.

Qualitative research refers to a variety of methods and, as such, a variety of definitions. There are differences between qualitative and quantitative research, that address not only research questions to be investigated but the role of the researcher and assumptions about the world in which we live. Additionally, qualitative research is often a multi-method process with the particular method employed depending, at least to some extent, on the results of the ongoing study.

Qualitative research is often conducted in a natural setting. An underlying assumption is that humans create their own reality and that observation and description of this reality is the only way to understand human behavior. Often a qualitative researcher will immerse herself in the situation. For example, in order to understand the consumption behavior of homeless people, the researcher may join a homeless community and live as they do for the duration of the study.

Thus, qualitative research is phenomenological in that it is concerned with the meanings people attach to events, the dominant culture, advertising, and marketing.

Qualitative methods include ethnography, extended case studies, immersion techniques, in-depth interviews, focus groups, projective techniques, and grounded theory. Data is collected in a variety of ways including field notes, videos, voice recordings, historical artifacts, company reports and advertisements, and storytelling. Thus, qualitative research may be defined as a set of methods that are investigative in methodology, naturalistic in approach, and are dependent on description, observation, and categorization.[2]

As previously noted, market researchers employ qualitative methods when not enough is known about a problem to develop a workable hypothesis or the researcher is interested in discovering the root cause or deeper meaning of an event, such as a purchase decision. Thus, researchers may use qualitative research to explore questions people are unwilling or unable to answer. For example, a study subject may be unwilling to admit his decision to buy a gift for his girlfriend was to reflect on his financial success rather than attempting to please her. A more acceptable answer would be that the gift was practical or the right color. Various qualitative methods (such as projective techniques discussed below) can develop the true reason for the purchase.

People often make decisions for reasons they do not understand or cannot articulate. Depth interviews, projective techniques, ethnography, and other qualitative research methods can help the researcher tap the subject's subconscious and help him or her articulate the decision process. These methods are also valuable in discovering which sensory feelings are important in areas such as purchase decisions.

Qualitative methods differ from quantitative research methods and there is tension between those who favor one method over the other. We will examine these differences and the controversy surrounding them next.

Qualitative versus Quantitative

Many academic and practitioner market researchers are skeptical of the value of qualitative research. Increased sophistication of statistical software results in less measurement error than was true in the past. Additionally, marketers and market researchers find value in the ability of quantitative studies to generalize from a sample to the population. Qualitative research, however, is catching the attention of both industry and researchers. There are three primary issues that arise in the qualitative versus quantitative argument.

First, there is a difference between a numbers and word approach to research. Words, actions, and records are emphasized in qualitative research while numerical assignments to words, actions, and records signify qualitative methods.

Next, the qualitative researcher attempts to understand study subjects in the context of their environment In fact, many qualitative researchers do not consider themselves objective observers as do quantitative investigators but as actors who are part of the research process. That is, they are observers and participants.

Finally, qualitative research is designed to discover patterns and trends that take place in a particular context. This differs from quantitative research that takes a relatively small sample and attempts to generalize findings across contexts.[3]

Table 4.1 outlines the differences in qualitative and quantitative research in terms of various research processes.

Qualitative research has been criticized as "soft science" or just plain journalism. Qualitative researchers who immerse themselves in the study context are accused of bias, value-laden results, or even a political agenda. At best, critics of qualitative research believe that it is valuable only as an exploratory method and is unsuited for descriptive or causal research designs. Yet, each

Table 4.1 Qualitative vs. Quantitative Methods

	Qualitative	*Quantitative*
Objective/purpose	Gain understanding of underlying motives; explore ill-structured problems.	Test hypotheses; generalize from sample results to the population of interest.
Sample/data collection	Small sample; unstructured, flexible, data collection involving observation, interviews, and field notes.	Large sample; numerical values assigned to subjects' responses; primary survey data or secondary data.
Data analysis	Continuous as data is collected; analysis affects next step in the research; non-statistical analysis.	Analysis takes place after all data collected; statistical methods used.
Planned outcome	Develop an initial understanding and/or description; begin theory development.	Provide a specific recommendation.

approach has limitations. Quantitative methods tend to force people into groups that are artificial while qualitative research often fails to provide results that can be generalized beyond the current study. Despite these criticisms, consumer-oriented businesses have embraced qualitative research as part of an overall, effective market research program.

Another criticism of qualitative research is that, because of the methods used, there is no way to statistically determine the validity of a study. To answer this criticism, there are several steps the qualitative researcher can take. First, and most importantly, researchers should be very careful and precise in designing the study from deciding on the management question to the interpretation and reporting of results.

Another method of increasing the validity of a qualitative study is to view the management question from different perspectives. This method is known as triangulation. In this approach, the same questions are addressed from a different perspective. For example, an ethnographic study may observe children's television viewing habits. To look at the question from a different perspective, depth interviews may be conducted with the children's parents.

A third approach is to combine qualitative and quantitative methods into one study. This often happens when one method alone is not sufficient to measure all aspects of a phenomenon. Refer to the example of children's TV viewing habits; a survey may be given to the parents while the children are observed in their homes.

Designing the Qualitative Study

Qualitative methods require the researcher to be able to tolerate ambiguity and vagueness. Both require flexibility and patience on the part of the researcher. Ambiguity refers to a situation that can be understood in more than one way while vagueness means the situation lacks precision. Qualitative researchers need to approach a project with a willingness to change qualitative methods as the situation begins to take a specific direction or the meaning becomes clearer. With qualitative methods, data unfolds as the study progresses. In this sense, qualitative research is in some ways akin to detective work—there is a search for "clues" to reveal what happened or is currently taking place and the detective follows where his or her nose leads in the search for ideas, insights, and clarifications. The keys to success in qualitative research are flexibility and an insatiable curiosity.

In contrast to quantitative methods that use random sampling to recruit study participants, qualitative researchers rely on purposive sampling where the research participants and/or the setting (school, business, consumption experience) are carefully selected depending on the study question. A qualitative sample needs to be "information rich." For example, if we are conducting a study to determine the consumption pattern of problem gamblers, we would look for participants who display this characteristic, rather than recreational gamblers who stay within their budgets. In other cases we may want to select participants who are experts on the subject under study or we may want the most heterogeneous sample we can assemble. The qualitative researcher needs to be aware, however, that as the study progresses, newer participants may be very different from those originally chosen. Again, as previously noted, the qualitative researcher needs to be flexible and go where the study leads. Below is a list of factors to consider when designing a qualitative study.

1   The management question should not be narrowly drawn, but should be exploratory and descriptive. Qualitative studies evolve as data is collected and analyzed. The analysis of collected data often determines the next set of questions or subjects to be interviewed.

2   Spend time determining the initial sample of participants. Study subjects live, work and play in the context of the phenomena being investigated. For example, if we are studying the breakfast eating habits of elementary school children, we would want to select families where both parents worked outside the home and families where one parent stayed home. This gives us variability in our sample. In contrast, quantitative methods use random sampling, which is designed to achieve the same variability with a large sample size.

3   An important characteristic of qualitative research is that personal meaning is tied to the context within which a behavior takes place. Therefore, it is best to collect data from participants where they live, work, or play.

4   The data we collect in qualitative research is often people's language and behavior. In order to be accurate, researchers may use field notes, audio, or videotapes, and collection of relevant documents. It is important that the data collection process be organized and complete as the decision about which data is relevant may change as the study progresses.

5   Data is constantly analyzed and interpreted during a qualitative study. This allows for important aspects of the study to emerge as it processes. Again, this process differs from quantitative research in several ways. First, data is analyzed at the end of a quantitative study. Second, quantitative research is designed "upfront" and the design does not change as the study progresses. Finally, but not critically, the quantitative researcher decides what is important in a study while the qualitative researcher takes a participant perspective. That is, the data collected and analyzed is based on what is important to the study participants.

6   Qualitative findings are best reported in a narrative such as a case study. The length of the report may range from a few pages to an entire book. The longer the report, the more excerpts from interviews and observations can be included. While quantitative reports suggest to readers that generalizing the results depends on the sample, qualitative reports provide enough information for readers to make this determination on their own.

Qualitative Research Methods

Literature Review

More often than not the proper place to begin a research study is to investigate previous work related to the research issues under study. Exploratory research seeks to generate ideas, insights, and hypotheses, and reading what others have done and discovered about the topic in which you are interested can save valuable time and resources in the search for those ideas. For example, if your research objective consists of developing an instrument to measure customer's satisfaction with your product or service, a search of previously published studies measuring customer satisfaction could generate many ideas and insights useful in developing your own instrument. This may be done by using one or more of numerous books on the subject currently available, or by doing a search of a library database where key words such as "customer satisfaction" or "customer service" are used to reveal articles published on the subject during a specific time period (e.g., the previous three years) or searching the Web for information. Chapter 3 discussed sources and uses of secondary data in more depth.

In-Depth Interviews

One of the best ways to obtain desired insights, hypotheses, clarifications, etc., is to talk with someone whose experience, expertise, or position gives them unique perspective on the subject of interest. While in some cases such key informants are obvious, such as talking with secretaries about changes in your word-processing software, sometimes valuable insights come from not-so-obvious sources, such as talking with shoeshine people about executive footwear or golf caddies about golf equipment. The key to achieving your research objective of gaining insight, ideas, etc., through exploratory personal interviews is to be flexible and think about what you are hearing. Your objective in conducting the interview is not to get your predetermined questions asked and answered in the course of the conversation. The questions are the means to the objective of gaining insights; they are not the objective itself. Your objective is to gain *insight* and you may be able to achieve that objective far better by asking questions related to what you are hearing than doggedly pursuing your original questions.

Researchers should never confuse the exploratory in-depth interview with one conducted in descriptive research. Descriptive-research interviewing requires a consistency in the questions asked and the way the questions are asked which is not conducive to achieving exploratory objectives. With descriptive research, we need to eliminate the variance of results due to differences in interviewing circumstances so that we can attribute the results to variances in respondent attitudes and behaviors, hence the need for consistent interviewing behavior. With exploratory research, we are not trying to precisely measure some variable, we are trying to gain penetrating insights into some important issue. Hence, each of our exploratory interviews may take a different tack as we seek to probe and query each key informant to gain full benefit of their unique experiences.

For example, if we are researching the use of digital music storage/player devices by college students, the exploratory in-depth interviews may probe issues about what features are desired, when and how they are used, which devices are currently popular and why, etc. The order these topics are addressed in the interviews and how the question is asked to elicit discussion of these topics is immaterial and can vary from interview to interview. We are looking for insights, not numbers here, and we must let the interview flow naturally to cover these topics and perhaps digress into areas we hadn't anticipated if those areas promise even greater insights. We might find that after 20 or so of these interviews we start hearing the same responses, so we stop conducting interviews. Or, we are continuing to generate more and more ideas from these interviews that we explore in subsequent interviews, and end up conducting 40 interviews instead of the 25 we had originally planned. Again, flexibility in both conducting the interviews and knowing when to stop is the key to getting the most from our exploratory research.

Researching this same topic in descriptive research interviews would not afford such flexibility. Here we want to know how many students prefer one product feature over another, would pay $50 more for twice as much storage capacity, intend to buy in the next 6 months, etc. Every interviewer in the descriptive research must ask each question in the same way and in the same order for each interview in this research design. This is necessary so that the data generated reflects the market characteristics instead of the peculiarities of the interviewer–interviewee interaction.

In other words, in descriptive research interviews we want the results of the interview to be the same no matter who did the interviewing. In exploratory research interviewing, each interview can be a unique experience that results in original insights, ideas, etc.

In the same sense, descriptive research interviewing may require a probability sample of respondents so that we can compute sampling errors and be able to make statements such as "We are 95 percent confident that somewhere between 77 percent to 81 percent of dealers prefer brand A over brand B." Never, however, should exploratory research use a probability sample since our entire objective in talking with people is to select those who are in a position to shed an unusual amount of light on the topic of interest. Another way of thinking about this is to answer the question "How many people do you need to talk with to get a good idea?" The answer, of course, is one person—the *right* person. In exploratory research we are not measuring behavior, we are seeking inspiration, clarification, perspective, etc., so we must seek out those people who can do that for us. Chapter 8 discusses in more detail interviewing approaches that would be used in descriptive research.

Focus Groups

One of the most popular techniques for conducting exploratory research is the focus group, a small number of people (usually eight to twelve), convened to address topics introduced by a group moderator. The moderator works from a topic outline developed with input from moderator, researcher, and decision maker. Focus groups have proven to be of particular value in:

- allowing marketing managers to see how their consumers act, think, and respond to the company's efforts;
- generating hypotheses that can be tested by descriptive or causal research;
- giving respondent impressions of new products;
- suggesting the current temperament of a market;
- making abstract data "real"—such as seeing how a "strongly agree" response on a survey appears in the faces and demeanor of "real" people.

Focus groups are popular because they not only are an efficient, effective means of achieving these goals but also because decision makers can attend them, observing the responses of the participants "live." This observation can be a double-edged sword, for while it does make the abstract "real," it can deceive the novice into believing that the entire market is represented by the consumers in the focus group. Conducting more focus groups to see a larger number of respondents does not convert the exploratory findings into descriptive data. Focus groups are one of several means of achieving the objectives of exploratory research and should not be overused or believed to be generating results that were never the intent of this technique.

Why Conduct Focus Groups?

The standard reasons for conducting focus groups include:

- *Idea Generation.* Consumers or knowledgeable experts may provide a good source of new products or other ideas in the fertile environment of a group setting.
- *Reveal Consumers' Needs, Perceptions, Attitudes.* Probing consumers on why they think or act the way they do may reveal less obvious, but no less important, reasons for their behavior.
- *Help in Structuring Questionnaires.* Hearing the way consumers think and talk about a product, activity, or consumption experience not only generates hypotheses that might be

tested in a descriptive research design, but also informs the researcher about how to word questions in ways directly relevant to the consumer's experience.

Some less frequently mentioned reasons for conducting focus groups include:

- *Post Quantitative Research.* Focus groups are most often mentioned as research done prior to a survey, but they might be of equal value in helping researchers to "put flesh on the bones" of quantitative research. Discovering that a certain percentage of consumers behave in a particular fashion may make it desirable to probe a group of those consumers in some depth to discover why and how they came to act in that manner.
- *Making the Abstract Real.* One of the most memorable qualities of focus groups is their ability to make "real" what was heretofore only considered in a very abstract manner. For example, it is one thing for a product manager of a brand of dog food to know that many dog owners really love their dogs. It is quite another for that product manager to see dog owners in a focus group take obvious delight in recounting their Ginger's latest adventure with a raccoon, or grow misty-eyed in remembering Jason, now dead ten years, or hear the soft lilt in their voice as they describe the relationship they have with Kate and Bailey, their golden retrievers. Attendance at a focus group can infuse lifeless market data with new meaning and make its implications more memorable and meaningful. One checklist for management using focus groups to obtain a more "three-dimensional" understanding of their actual customers includes the following advice:
  1. Do not expect the people in the focus group to look like "idealized customers." Fitness seekers may not look like aerobic instructors— they are just *trying* to.
  2. It can be shocking to find that your customers may not like you very much. Listening to what they have to say about your company's products and personnel and your ideas can be ego-bruising. You cannot argue with them—be prepared to listen to the good and bad news.
  3. Your customers are unlikely to think or care as much about your product as you do. It may be what you worry about for ten hours a day, but not them.
  4. Do not expect focus group participants to be just like you are—or to be totally different either.
  5. People are not always consistent in what they say. That does not mean they are liars or hypocrites—just human.
  6. Your moderator is a good resource to put the study in a context with other research he or she has done. Are the responses more or less positive than he or she has seen in other focus groups?
  7. If your screening process was effective, you are looking at real customers—whether you like what you see or not.
  8. Be honest about what you expected to see. We all have preconceptions, just ask whether yours are based on research or prejudice.
- *Reinforcing Beliefs.* Judith Langer recounted an experience by The Gillette Company, which illustrated the ability of focus groups to convey a message much more powerfully to employees than repeat admonitions by management:

  > A focus group with women showed that consumers are more demanding and "educated" about quality than in the past. This comment was typical:
  >
  > "I think as consumers we're becoming more aware of what goes into a product. For myself, I have become more aware of the ingredients—food or clothing or whatever. I feel that I'm not the same shopper I was perhaps six years ago. That was just fad buying. Now I look at something."

Marketing, market research, and research and development people observe the group; the videotape of the session has since been shown to others in the company. Hans Locater, Gillette's research director, says that the focus group made what top management has been saying more tangible and believable

- *Early Barometer.* Focus groups may provide an early warning system of shifts in the market. Probing consumers on lifestyle changes, consumption patterns, opinions of new competitive entries, etc., may reveal threats and opportunities entering the market long before they might be revealed in a large-scale survey. Keeping an open mind and maintaining an active curiosity allow for researchers to see the far-reaching significance of seemingly innocuous observations made by focus group participants.

Focus Group Composition

Conventional industry wisdom suggests that focus groups should consist of eight to twelve people selected to be homogeneous along some characteristic important to the researcher (e.g., do a lot of baking, own foreign luxury cars, manage their own retirement account with more than $100,000 invested, etc.). Usually recruitment of focus group participants strives to find people who fit the desired profile but who do not know each other—thus reducing the inhibitions of group members to describe their actual feelings or behaviors. Typically, group sessions last from one and a half to two hours. Going against such conventional wisdom may be necessary in some cases. For example, one of the authors conducted research for a food company that wanted a few direct questions asked prior to presenting participants with prepared versions of their food products, as well as their competitor's. While not a taste test *per se*, the client wanted to hear the subjects' reactions to the products and a discussion of the circumstances under which the products would be used in their homes. For this study a series of one-hour group sessions were run with five people per group. The more structured discussion and the desire to query each participant made the shorter time and smaller group more conducive to achieving the study's objectives.

Selection and Recruitment of Group Participants

The research objectives and research design will indicate the types of people to be recruited for a focus group. If a facility especially designed for focus group use is contracted with, the management of the facility typically will conduct recruitment of focus group members. If a marketing research firm is being hired to conduct the groups, they usually hire the facility; identify, recruit, and select the participants; moderate the groups; and make an oral and written report of the findings. Sometimes the client organization will provide a list of possible participants taken from a master list of customers, members, users, etc. It is usually necessary to provide *at least* four names for every respondent needed (i.e., approximately fifty names per focus group).

Prospective participants are screened when contacted to ensure their eligibility for the group, but without revealing the factors used to assess their eligibility. For example, if the researcher is interested in talking with people who have traveled to Europe in the past year, he or she would also ask about other trips or activities to camouflage the central issue under investigation. This deception is helpful in discouraging respondents from answering in ways strictly intended to increase or diminish chances for an invitation, and to discourage selected participants from preparing "right" answers for their participation in the group sessions. It is advisable to provide a general idea of the topic for discussion (e.g., personal travel) to encourage participation. Actual participants are usually rewarded with an honorarium (say $25 to $50 per person) for their time.

The size of the honorarium depends upon the type of participant (e.g., physicians expect more than homemakers). The focus group facility's management usually covers the cost of recruiting, hosting, and compensating the groups in their fee. The following are six rules for recruiting focus group members:

1   Specifically define the characteristics of people who will be included in the groups.
2   If an industrial focus group is being conducted, develop screening questions that probe into all aspects of the respondents' job functions. Do not depend on titles or other ambiguous definitions of responsibilities.
3   If an industrial focus group is being conducted, provide the research company with the names of specific companies and employees, when possible. If specific categories of companies are needed, a list of qualified companies is critical.
4   Ask multiple questions about a single variable to validate the accuracy of answers. Therefore, if personal computer users are to be recruited, do not simply ask for the brand and model of personal computer they use. In addition, ask them to describe the machine and its function; this will ensure that they are referring to the appropriate equipment.
5   Do not accept respondents who have participated in a focus group during the previous year.
6   Have each participant arrive fifteen minutes early to complete a prediscussion questionnaire. This will provide additional background information on each respondent, reconfirm their suitability for the discussion, and help the company collect useful factual information.

Moderator Role and Responsibilities

The moderator plays a key role in obtaining maximum value from conducting focus groups. The moderator helps design the study guide, assists the manager/researcher who is seeking the information, and leads the discussion in a skillful way to address the study's objectives while stimulating and probing group participants to contribute to the discussion. The following are ten characteristics of a good focus group moderator.[4]

1   Be experienced in focus group research.
2   Provide sufficient help in conceptualizing the focus group research design, rather than simply executing the groups exactly as specified.
3   Prepare a detailed moderator guide well in advance of the focus group.
4   Engage in advance preparation to improve overall knowledge of the area being discussed.
5   Provide some "added value" to the project beyond simply doing an effective job of conducting the session.
6   Maintain control of the group without leading or influencing the participants.
7   Be open to modern techniques such as visual stimulation, conceptual mapping, attitude scaling, or role-playing, which can be used to delve deeper into the minds of participants.
8   Take personal responsibility for the amount of time allowed for the recruitment, screening, and selection of participants.
9   Share in the feeling of urgency to complete the focus group while desiring to achieve an excellent total research project.
10 Demonstrate the enthusiasm and exhibit the energy necessary to keep the group interested even when the hour is running late.

Trends in Focus Groups

Several new variations in the traditional focus group approach are being successfully used by some companies. One is two-way focus groups, which involves conducting a focus group, then having a second, specific group of respondents interested in the comments of the first focus group view the video of the focus group during their own focus group session. This approach could be expanded to a three-way focus group setting. One of the authors of this text worked with a company that supplied food products to fine restaurants that used a three-way focus group approach. In this instance the first group consisted of patrons of expensive restaurants talking about their experiences at such restaurants. The video of these consumers was then viewed in a focus group of chefs and restaurant managers who commented on what they were seeing and were asked what they might do to address the needs of these consumers. The video of the chef's focus group was then observed by the food brokers used by the food service company who talked about what they could do differently to better serve the needs of the chefs. Managers from the sponsoring food service company attended all three focus groups (multiple groups of each "level" of focus groups were conducted).

Quads is another variation of focus groups that has been used. In these groups usually four respondents (hence the name quads) discuss a limited set of topics, perhaps engage in a taste test, and might complete a short evaluation of products. These take less time to complete than the usual focus group (less than one hour as opposed to one and one half to two hours), allowing for more of these to be conducted in an evening than traditional focus groups. The attraction of these quads is the ability to get 100 percent participation of respondents (in a ten-person focus group participation by each person is more limited) on a short, specific set of issues, allowing observers to more easily focus on the differences in responses and generate hypotheses regarding those observations. Conducting more groups allows for more "fine tuning" of discussion questions and methodology and changes to be made from one group session to the next. Both two-way and quad variations of focus group approaches (and many more variations practiced by research firms) illustrate the flexibility inherent in conducting good exploratory communication research.

Internet focus groups are rapidly gaining in popularity. Internet focus groups are, like all focus groups, an exploratory research technique that capitalizes on the efficiency afforded by the Internet to engage people in diverse geographic locations together in a discussion of a topic of interest to the researcher and participants. Such groups can be conducted within a company with employees or externally with customers or members of a target market. If confidentiality is a concern with employees, they can use a hyper-link embedded in e-mail to go to a secure Web site where they can participate anonymously.

Internet focus groups with consumers have an obvious advantage in cost savings over traditional focus groups (approximately one-fifth to one-half the cost) as well as allowing for greater diversity among participants. Participants may in some situations be able to enter their input and reactions to other participants anytime during the extended focus group time frame— twenty-four hours a day. Use of IRC (Internet Relay Chat) and/or Web chat sites make it easy for participants to contribute to a discussion set up at that specific site for a specific purpose. It is then possible to immediately generate transcripts of twenty to thirty pages of verbatim responses for analysis. Advantages include speed of recruitment, savings in travel costs and time away from the office, respondents are able to participate from the comfort of their own home, and anonymity of responses. Disadvantages include a loss of observable information (e.g., facial expressions, body language, sense of excitement, confusion, etc.), which veteran focus group moderators use in analyzing traditional group sessions. Also, it is not possible to ensure that the person engaging in the focus group session is really the person you wanted. It is not possible to effectively screen people for certain desirable and easily verifiable characteristics (e.g., age, gender, racial background, etc.), and be certain the person on the Internet actually fits the desired profile. Also, unless the topic is about the use of the Internet itself, the people who are available for Internet focus groups may or may not be representative of the complete target market.

Some research companies operate Internet focus groups by recruiting and building a database of respondents from screening people visiting their Web site or through other recruitment methods. These people are then profiled through a series of questions, which allows the research firm to select respondents with the characteristics desired by the client organization. Potential respondents are emailed, asking them to go to a particular Web site at a particular time (using a hyperlink embedded in the e-mail). The "moderator" types in questions and responds, probes, and clarifies during the session by typing in queries. Several companies do these types of focus groups.

Immersion Groups

Some marketers are turning away from the traditional format of focus groups with a moderator and 8–10 people, and have instead begun interacting directly with fewer consumers in what has begun being called "Immersion Groups."[5] At Yahoo, for example, marketers meet directly with four or five consumers in work sessions to design new services. A new online community for auto buffs who desire more opportunities to chat with other members was designed using immersion research. The advocates of these immersion groups believe that some consumers are not honest about their feelings and behaviors in front of other consumers around the focus group table. "Hands on" work sessions with consumers break down such inhibitions.

Ethnography

Companies are increasingly adapting the ethnographic research methodologies of cultural anthropologists to study consumers. Typically, marketing ethnography involves a marketer experiencing life events along with their consumers—asking questions, observing, and recording their own feelings as they share the experience. Volkswagen engineers couldn't understand why Americans treat their cars as homes on wheels until they spent three and a half grueling hours on a Greyhound bus traveling between Seattle and Portland. That experience and spending 18 months traveling across the U.S. by car, talking with fellow travelers at rest stops and fast food outlets, going to malls, visiting the Rock and Roll Hall of Fame, tailgating at a NASCAR race, attending drag races, and observing other travelers on similar long car trips helped drive home the differences in the American and European car cultures. "If you lose your car here you're done", was the revelation of one of the researchers.[6] Additionally, they took subways, drove rental cars, and took red-eye flights. They shadowed mothers who spent the day taking kids to soccer practice, picking up the dry cleaning, and shopping for groceries. Their conclusion: "In Germany it's all about driving, but here it's about everything but driving." Designs for all VW products sold in the U.S. market are expected to be impacted from the ethnographic research results.

Procter & Gamble likewise conducts ongoing ethnographic studies to keep abreast of consumption practices. The company routinely sends scores of researchers armed with video cameras into consumer households around the world to tape daily routines and procedures of consumers in all their boring glory. Typically the ethnographer-filmmakers arrive at the home of the participant when the alarm clock goes off, and stay until bedtime, usually for a four-day stretch. Sometimes the camera is left on without an attendant in a room while family members go about their daily tasks. Taping a mother feeding a child in the consumer's own home can reveal many actions that would go unreported in a focus group session on that subject. Observing multitasking behaviors occurring during such sessions could inspire packaging and product designs that could provide a competitive advantage when they reach the market.[7] Each year more companies pursue such ethnographic studies to supplement other exploratory research methods.

Netnography

In recent years, e-commerce has become an important component of retail sales. Moreover, consumers join discussion boards, chat rooms, and other online forums to trade information about products, services, and businesses. Thus, methods to conduct research on the World Wide Web have been developed. One such method is *netnography*, which is ethnography that studies the consumer behavior of online communities. The research methodology is the same as traditional ethnography in that the researcher should begin with specific marketing questions and learn as much as possible about the online groups to be studied. Data collection can consist of copies of computer-mediated communications of the online community and/or transcriptions of what the researcher observes in monitoring online forums.

For example, while many may believe that the coffee market has been adequately addressed by Starbucks, a study of coffee drinkers using netnography indicates that there is an online community of coffee drinkers with an almost religious fervor about coffee that has yet to be exploited by marketers. These consumers possess discriminating tastes and snob appeal. They also are not interested in the in-person social aspects of coffee consumption at a place like Starbucks but are more interested in products they can use at home.[8]

Grounded Theory

Grounded theory is based on the concept that people act in response to environmental clues, objects and other people based on the meanings people assign to them. That is, grounded theory researchers believe that personal conduct is programmed by social norms. In order to understand behavior in a particular situation, then, the researcher enters into the subject's context.

A variety of research methods may be used in grounded research including depth interviews, ethnography, and immersion groups. A researcher may choose to use only one method or they may use more than one method in the same study. The method to use after the initial method is chosen is driven by the research.

The key concept of grounded theory is that the theory evolves during the research process. That is, unlike quantitative methods where the researcher tests an existing theory, grounded theory research is designed to *develop* a theory. Another important element of grounded theory is that there is a constant interplay between the data collected and its analysis. Thus, as data is collected the theory evolves along with the method. Additionally, there is no pre-determined sample with grounded theory. Researchers continue to collect data until they learn nothing new from additional data. This is known as theoretical sampling.

Grounded theory is used when researchers want to study an area of interest without preconceptions. Thus, the method is more difficult for study subjects with long, empirically based literature. Grounded theory researchers attempt to avoid even any unconscious predispositions concerning the area of study.

Analysis of Selected Cases

Another means of achieving the objectives of exploratory research is to conduct in-depth analysis of selected cases of the subject under investigation. This approach is of particular value when a complex set of variables may be at work in generating observed results and intensive study is needed to unravel the complexities. For example, an in-depth study of a firm's top salespeople and a comparison with the worst salespeople, might reveal characteristics common to stellar performers. Here again, the exploratory investigator is best served by an active curiosity and willingness to deviate from the initial plan when findings suggest new courses of inquiry might prove more productive. It is easy to see how the exploratory research objectives of generating insights and hypotheses would be well served by use of this technique.

Projective Techniques

Researchers might be exploring a topic where respondents are either unwilling or unable to directly answer questions about why they think or act as they do. Highly sensitive topics involving their private lives are obviously in this category, but more mundane behaviors may also hide deep psychological motivations. For example, in a case investigating why some women persisted in preferring a messy, expensive spray to kill roaches instead of using a more efficient trap that the women acknowledged to have more benefits than their sprays, researchers discovered that the women transferred hostilities for the men who had left them to the roaches and wanted to see the roaches squirm and die. The method used to uncover these hidden motives is one of the so-called projective techniques, named because respondents project their deep psychological motivations through a variety of communication and observable methods. These methods typically include:

1   *Word association.* Respondents are given a series of words and respond by saying the first word that comes to mind. The response, the frequency of the response, and time it takes to make the response are keys to understanding the underlying motives toward the subject. If no response is given, it is interpreted to mean that emotional involvement is so high as to block the response.

2   *Sentence completion.* Similar to word association, sentence completion requires the respondent to enter words or phrases to complete a given sentence such as: People who use the Discover credit card are _____. Responses are then analyzed for content.

3   *Storytelling.* Here respondents are given a cartoon, photograph, drawing, or are asked to draw a scene related to the subject under investigation and tell what is happening in the scene. In theory, the respondent will reveal inner thoughts by using the visual aid as a stimulus to elicit these deep motivations. Therefore, if the picture is of two people sitting and looking at a computer screen in an office, the story that is told about the people will reveal how the respondent feels about using computers in a work environment.

4   *Third-person technique/role-playing.* This technique is a reflection of what Oscar Wilde meant when he said "A man is least himself when he talks in his own person; when he is given a mask he will tell the truth." Respondents are told to explain why a third person (a co-worker, neighbor, etc.) might act in a certain way. For example, a stimulus might appear as: We are trying to better understand what features people might consider when buying a garden tractor. Please think about people you know and tell us what features would be important to them for such a product. Role-playing requires the respondent to play the role of another party in a staged scenario, such as asking a retailer to play the role of a customer coming into a retail establishment.

5   *Collages.* This technique involves asking the respondent to cut pictures out of magazines and arrange them on poster board to depict some issue of interest to the researcher. For example, respondents might be asked to choose pictures that tell a story of how they decided to start exercising daily, or to find pictures that convey their image of the Compaq computer brand.

6   *Music association.* Here the researcher plays a variety of music selections and asks the respondent to associate the music with one of the brands being evaluated. The objective is to determine a brand's emotional content for the respondent (e.g., associating one brand of vodka with hard rock music and another brand with cool jazz).

7   *Anthropomorphicizing.* In this approach the respondent is asked to describe what the product or service being researched would look like if it were a person—age, gender, attractiveness,

how would he or she be dressed, what would his or her occupation be, what kind of car would he or she drive, or health status, etc. A variation of this is asking what famous person the product or service would be.

As can be seen from the description of these techniques, one must be skilled not only in structuring these approaches, but also must be an experienced professional in interpreting the results. Also, their use is often bimodal—either an organization (such as an advertising agency or marketing consulting firm) uses them extensively or not at all. They have been shown to provide intriguing new insights into behavior, but are best left to experts to operate and interpret.

The Value of Exploratory Research

All of these exploratory techniques, when properly applied, can be successfully used to achieve the research objectives of generating ideas, hypotheses, clarifying concepts, etc. Quite often in a multistage research project, one might start with exploratory research, then use the results to help structure a descriptive research questionnaire or a causal research experiment. While that is frequently the case, exploratory results do not have value only as preliminary work before the "real" research takes place. Depending on the research purpose or attitude of the decision maker toward risk, exploratory research may be the only research that is done. For example, if in-depth interviews with 20 selected purchasing agents generate only ridicule of a new product idea, it is not necessary to conduct a structured survey of 500 to kill the idea. However, if you want to ultimately produce an ad that says your paintbrush is preferred two to one over a major competitor's by professional painters, exploratory research will not be sufficient to support your claims. If a decision maker is a high risk taker, exploratory research may be all that is desired before a decision can be reached. If the stakes increase, however, that same decision maker may want to follow up the exploratory research with more structured and quantifiable descriptive or causal research.

The point we are trying to make here is that well-conducted exploratory research can be extremely valuable in achieving the objectives endemic to that type of research, apart from its contributing to later phases of the research study. The fact that it does not generate precise quantifiable data is not a "weakness" of the approach. When properly conducted and interpreted it can serve as a powerful aid to decision making, depending upon the decisions being faced and the decision-making style of the manager.

To know whether exploratory research is alone sufficient or should be followed by descriptive or causal research, the researcher should examine the research questions, the decisional criteria, the time available to do the research, and the research budget. An example might help to illustrate the interplay of these factors in determining whether exploratory research should be followed by quantitative research.

In the case of the Compton Company described in Chapter 1, the managers decided, incorrectly as it turned out, to get a new advertising agency instead of doing research to discover the cause of their declining market share. If they learned a lesson from this experience and next time decide to do research before making a decision, their preferred decision-making style might be to rely on exploratory approaches rather than a full-scale quantitative study.

So, a research question such as: "Are our dealer policies competitive?" might with some decision makers involve doing exploratory research to first clarify concepts, formulate the issue more precisely, gain valuable insights into dealer relations, etc., then descriptive research to discover the frequency with which dealers rate your company's policies as fair, motivating, understandable, etc., compared to your competitors. The Compton Company managers, however, may merely want you to have in-depth conversations with a few key dealers (i.e., the decision criteria of Compton's decision makers), report the results of your conversations, and then they are ready to make their decision. Whether the research would be staged as exploratory followed by descriptive, or exploratory only would therefore depend upon how the decision makers (with the help of the researchers, see Chapter 1) defined the decision alternatives and criteria that would be used to choose among the alternatives, the time available for the research, and the research budget.

In some cases the research question itself suggests descriptive research will be needed to follow up exploratory findings. If, in collaboration with the decision maker, the researcher writes the research question as: "What percentage of dealers rate our company as having the best customer service?", then it will be necessary to follow the exploratory research with descriptive research. Here the exploratory clarifies terms such as "best" and "customer service" and identifies what areas of customer service are most important to dealers, and the descriptive determines the percentage of dealers rating the company's and its competitors' customer service along those important dimensions. It is descriptive, not exploratory, that provides quantification of responses.

Summary

Research designs are like roadmaps that help us determine the most efficient and effective methods to conduct our marketing studies. The three basic research designs are exploratory, descriptive, and causal.

In this chapter, we focused on exploratory research design with an emphasis on qualitative methods. It was noted that exploratory research helps us gain broad insights to an issue or an ambiguous problem. Exploratory research may also help us develop hypotheses we will use in descriptive and causal research designs.

Qualitative research methods are one set of tools we can use to conduct exploratory research. Qualitative research is often a multi-method process that is flexible in design and depends on the researcher's observation and interpretation of behavior and or non-numerical data. Methods include case analysis, ethnography, netnography, immersion groups, depth interviews, grounded theory, and projective techniques.

Qualitative methods are still rejected by many who consider them to be "soft science" that fails to reflect objective reality. Despite these reservations, many companies are incorporating qualitative methods into their market research activities.

Discussion Questions

1   What are the objectives of exploratory research?
2   How does exploratory research differ from descriptive and causal research?
3   Define qualitative research.
4   What are the main issues in the debate between qualitative and quantitative researchers?
5   If you were asked to study the breakfast cereal consumption habits of children 8–10, which qualitative method would you use? Why?

5 Research Design
Descriptive and Causal Research

Learning Objectives

Upon completing this chapter, you should understand:

1 how exploratory/qualitative, descriptive, and causal research methodologies differ;
2 the factors influencing the choice of research design;
3 how descriptive designs differ from experimental designs;
4 the differences between a quasi-experimental, pre-experimental, and true experimental designs;
5 what is meant by the terms: treatments, experimental units, and experimental designs;
6 different applications of experiments to test marketing.

As the name implies, descriptive research seeks to *describe* something. More specifically, descriptive research is conducted when seeking to accomplish the following objectives:

1 Describe the characteristics of relevant groups such as the 20 percent of our customers who generate 80 percent of our business. Having a description of our "heavy users" can define a target for our future marketing efforts intended to find more prospects similar to our best customers.
2 Determine the extent to which two or more variables co-vary. For example, does consumption rate vary by age of consumer?
3 Estimate the proportion of a population who act or think a certain way. For example, how often do childless couples eat at restaurants in a typical month?
4 Make specific predictions. For example, we might want to forecast the number of wholesalers who will be converting to a new inventory tracking software system in the next year.

Descriptive research is highly structured and rigid in its approach to data collection compared to exploratory research's unstructured and flexible approach. As such, descriptive research presupposes much prior knowledge on the part of the researcher regarding *who* will be targeted as a respondent, *what* issues are of highest priority to be addressed in the study, *how* the questions are to be phrased to reflect the vocabulary and experience of the respondents, *when* to ask the questions, *where* to find the respondents, and *why* these particular questions need to be answered in order to make decisions. Thus, exploratory research may often be needed to allow descriptive research requirements to be met.

While exploratory research may generate a hypothesis (e.g., Hispanics offer a more attractive market for our product than do Asians), it is descriptive research (or causal) that provides for a test of the hypothesis. Exploratory research may be needed to answer the who, what, when, where, why, and how of doing descriptive research (e.g., who should be the respondents of the survey), while descriptive research answers these same questions about the market (e.g., who are the high consumers of our product). Whereas exploratory research *suggests,* descriptive *quantifies.*

Finding answers to these who, what, when, where, why, and how questions in descriptive research demands disciplined thinking on the part of the researcher. This is illustrated by the following example:[1]

> Suppose a chain of food convenience stores was planning to open a new outlet and wanted to determine how people begin patronizing such a store. Imagine some of the questions that would need to be answered before data collection for this descriptive study could begin.
>
> - Who is to be considered a "patron"? Anyone who enters the store? Even those who participate in only the grand-opening prize giveaway? Someone who purchases anything from the store?
> - Should patrons be defined on the basis of the family unit or as individuals?
> - What characteristics should be measured: age, gender, where they live, or how they learned about the store? Should we measure them before, during, or after shopping? Should they be studied during the first weeks of operation, or after sales have stabilized? Should they be measured outside or inside the store, or at home? Should we measure them by using a questionnaire or by obsving their behavior? If using a questionnaire, will it be administered by telephone, mail, or personal interview?[2]

Research Project Tip

While a detailed description of what you plan to do in conducting the descriptive phase of the research might need to wait until you have done the exploratory research (i.e., get specifics of the who, what, etc. for the descriptive research), you should be able to describe in general terms the rationale for doing descriptive research. Provide a preliminary description in your research design of which research question and hypotheses will require descriptive research, a rationale for why descriptive is needed, and your initial ideas for answers to the who, what, etc. questions, understanding that these may change after reviewing the exploratory findings.

These questions reveal the need for the researcher to arrive at answers by "thinking like a decision maker." That is, the researcher must think how the research findings will be used to make the decisions facing the decision maker. If you are trying to attract more single, elderly patrons to food convenience stores, for example, you know the "who" question would need to include a representative sample of that group. Your exploratory research might have been needed to identify the importance of that type of patron (helping supply the answer to the "who" question), but the descriptive research can not be conducted until that and other questions such as those listed above have been answered. All answers should be supported by an underlying rationale related to the decisions being faced.

Descriptive research is more than an efficient means of collecting quantifiable facts. Facts can be a plentiful and useless commodity unless coupled with the "glue of explanation and understanding, the framework of theory, the tie-rod of conjecture."[3] We should determine how the information collected in a descriptive research study will be analyzed and used to test hypotheses, indicate the characteristics of a population, etc., before we ever design the data-collection instrument. For example, exploratory research conducted by a hospital may have generated the hypothesis that women of child-bearing age with higher incomes and education demand a variety of birthing options, education classes, and father participation and presence in the delivery room, including during a cesarean section. Secondary data may reveal that the hospital is located in an area of high concentration of women of above average income and education, and that pregnancy rates are average for the area. Descriptive research may seek to test the hypotheses that these women:

- do demand and expect their hospital to provide an obstetrics program with those characteristics;
- are not presently satisfied with the options available from other hospitals;
- are looking for and would be attracted to a hospital that did offer an obstetrics program that satisfied their wants and needs.

Here, the exploratory research generated, but could not test, the hypotheses, and the descriptive research generated facts in a form that provided the means of testing the hypotheses. It is important to note that researchers would have determined how the hypotheses would be tested *before* they designed questions in the questionnaire to generate the desired facts. That is, they would have set up dummy tables or chosen the multivariate statistical techniques to be used to test the hypotheses, then determined how data would be collected to allow for the use of these procedures for hypotheses testing. For example, sample dummy tables can be seen in Table 5.1.

Table 5.1. Sample table for hypothesis testing

Sibling Education Classes

	Household Income Per Year			
	≤$25,000	$25,001–$40,000	$40,001–$55,000	>$55,000
High				
Medium				
Low				

Father in Delivery Room

	Household Income Per Year			
	≤$25,000	$25,001–$40,000	$40,001–$55,000	>$55,000
High				
Medium				
Low				

Nurse Midwife

	Household Income Per Year			
	≤$25,000	$25,001–$40,000	$40,001–$55,000	>$55,000
High				
Medium				
Low				

Physician Referral Service

	Household Income Per Year			
	≤$25,000	$25,001–$40,000	$40,001–$55,000	>$55,000
High				
Medium				
Low				

Importance of Service or Program Feature in Determining Hospital Choice

By setting up this table before we even design the questionnaire or determine the number and type of respondents to survey, we have in effect helped specify the parameters for those parts of the research design. One hypothesis is that we should see the percentages on the top row of these tables get larger as we move to higher incomes (e.g., higher-income expectant mothers put more emphasis on such services in choosing a hospital than do lower-income expectant mothers). Other dummy tables would be developed to show how other hypotheses would be tested. This table was developed because researchers were intent on testing the hypotheses arising out of the exploratory research, and will be used once completed to influence decisions about service design, promotion, and other aspects of the marketing program. Design of such a table also permits researchers to develop a data-collection instrument such as a questionnaire that can provide the data in a form that permit the hypotheses to be tested. While sounding somewhat convoluted, it is true that we determine how the data will be analyzed before we develop the questions that provided the data. Remember, "No problem is definitely formulated until the researcher can specify how [he or she] will make [his or her] analysis and how the results will contribute to a practical solution."[4] The basic types of descriptive research studies used to provide such data are cross-sectional and longitudinal studies.

Cross-Sectional Designs

The best known and most frequently used descriptive design, cross-sectional analysis, involves a sampling of a population of interest at one point in time. This technique is sometimes referred to as a *sample survey*, because it often involves a probability sampling plan intended to choose respondents who will be representative of a certain population. As with all descriptive research, sample surveys are characterized by a high degree of structure—in both the data-collection instrument and in the data-collection process itself. The only way we can be sure we are measuring frequency or variation in the phenomenon under investigation is to build a high degree of structure into the instrument and process. That structure was not only *not* needed in exploratory research, it would have been a deterrent to achieving our objectives of insight, ideas, hypotheses, clarification, etc. Chapter 7 will discuss how to conduct sample surveys via questionnaires or observation in order to achieve the goals of a descriptive research study.

Cross-sectional surveys do not always have to involve selection of a one-time sample of respondents from the population. Several firms such as The Home Testing Institute, Market Facts, and National Family Opinion (NFO) operate omnibus panels that consist of hundreds of thousands of U.S. households that have been selected to proportionately represent the U.S. population along key dimensions such as age, income, sex, ethnic composition, and geographic dispersion. Members of such households are recruited to serve on the panel and agree to participate in answering questionnaires or trying products when requested to do so by the company maintaining the panel. Using such a panel allows an organization to select certain demographic characteristics for respondents (e.g., single males under thirty-five years of age) and send a questionnaire to them, knowing that the cost of finding and getting a response from a targeted number of this group (e.g., 1,000 completed questionnaires) is much less than trying to complete such a project in the general population where response rates may be as low as one or two percent.

These panels are particularly cost-effective when research is being conducted on a topic where the incidence rate in the population is very low (e.g., vegetarians, people with three-car garages, people with weight training machines in their homes, etc.). In such cases it is possible to buy a few screening questions on the monthly questionnaire sent to, say, 50,000 panel members to identify those members who fit the desired profile, then send only those qualified panellists a longer questionnaire to obtain the detailed information being sought. Firms maintaining such omnibus panels turn over membership frequently to avoid participating households becoming "professional respondents," which would reduce the respondents' representativeness for the general population.

Some organizations recruit and maintain their own panels. For example, Parker Pen maintains a panel of people who use writing pens frequently. Such corporate panels are useful when the company wants to assess targeted consumers' attitudes on a scheduled basis, try out potential new products in an in-home setting before making a go/no-go decision, or seek information on awareness and knowledge of competitive promotions. These panels are used more than once over time, similar to the longitudinal panels discussed below, but since the subject of the research changes constantly it is best to think of these panels as company-run omnibus cross-sectional survey research panels.

Longitudinal Studies

Whereas cross-sectional studies are like taking snapshots of a target population at a point in time, longitudinal studies are similar to filming videotapes of the respondents. The primary objective of longitudinal research is to monitor behavior over time and thereby identify behavioral (or attitudinal) changes. Sometimes referred to as *true panels,* these longitudinal panels report the same information (e.g., grocery store purchases, or purchases and use of a particular product or service) at specific points in time. This information can be combined with other pertinent information to determine, for example, if brand switching occurred after exposure to a trial sample, coupon, or advertisement.

One of the best-known panels for consumer goods is Information Resource's BehaviorScan, which continuously tracks tens of thousands of households in a number of different markets by having panel members use a specially coded card that tracks optically scanned purchases by household members at selected grocery stores. BehaviorScan can be used for test-marketing purposes by splitting the panel into two or more matched groups based on household demographics, and then sending different promotional appeals to the groups via direct mail, newspaper ads, or even TV. Changes in purchasing patterns can be measured after the promotional appeal is made. A.C. Nielsen Company offers a similar service, where households use hand-held scanners in their homes to track purchases.

The ability to use longitudinal panels for tracking changes in purchase behavior and brand loyalty has advantages over the use of cross-sectional surveys. For example, consider Table 5.2 and information taken from two cross-sectional sample surveys.

Table 5.2 Two Cross-Sectional Sample Surveys

	Number of consumers buying	
	Period 1	*Period 2*
Brand A	100	100
Brand B	150	150
Brand C	250	250
Total	500	500

Table 5.3 Longitudinal Panel

Brand purchasedin Period 1	Brand purchased in Period 2			
	Brand A	*Brand B*	*Brand C*	*Total*
Brand A	50	20	30	100
Brand B	20	80	50	150
Brand C	30	50	170	250
Total	100	150	250	

It appears that no brand switching occurred between the two surveys taken in time periods 1 and 2. A longitudinal analysis, however, might reveal a very different story, as shown in Table 5.3.

Table 5.3 shows that in fact there was considerable brand-switching behavior, and that Brand C enjoyed the greatest brand loyalty, Brand A the least. Longitudinal panels also have an advantage over sample surveys in that panel members record purchases immediately and therefore generate accurate purchase data, whereas cross-sectional surveyors often must rely on respondents' memories for reporting purchases. However, cross-sectional studies may often be more representative of the target population, due to the difficulties of recruiting and maintaining a representative sample in a panel design.

Causal Research

While descriptive research is effective in identifying co-variation between variables (e.g., blue packages outsell red ones, consumption rate varies by education level) it cannot truly indicate causality (e.g., color causes sales, education causes consumption). When we are in need of determining if two or more variables are causally related we must turn to causal-research procedures. While there might be a tendency to see many research objectives from a causal perspective ("We really want to know what causes consumers to act that way"), there is a difference between causality in the vernacular and how it is defined by scientists. Quite often decision makers do not need to test for a causal relationship in order to make good decisions. I might need to know only that blue packages outsell red ones or that consumption of my product increases with educational level in order to make appropriate marketing decisions. Testing for causality is a risky, expensive, time-consuming proposition and may not in the end permit better decisions than those made by simply acknowledging the co-variation that descriptive research identified.

However, in some cases a test of our hypothesis requires causal research (e.g., greater sales will result from having four shelf offerings of our product in stores under 60,000 square feet than having two facings in stores over 80,000 square feet). Remember that we stated that descriptive research is characterized by its more structured approach as compared to exploratory? Causal research is also highly structured, but is characterized also by the use of *control* procedures used during the experimental designs associated with tests of causal relationships.

Our interest in causal research is to determine the degree to which one variable is causally related to another (e.g., Does ad A cause people to remember its message better than ad B? Does a 10 percent decrease in price cause an increase in profit compared to no price change?). Obviously, in all such cases we are concerned with truly determining the impact of our independent variable (ads A and B, or price in the examples above) on our dependent variable (ad recall or profit in the examples), and not some extraneous variable that "leaks" into our test (e.g., a competitor's actions, an environmental event). Therefore, when we conduct a causal experiment we do three things:

1   *Manipulation:* We manipulate the causal or independent variable such as ad message or price.
2   *Measure:* We measure the effect or dependent variable such as ad recall or profit.
3   *Control:* We control other variables which could have an impact on our dependent variable, such as making sure that our product with price P1 in store S1 is found on the same shelf level as that product with price P2 in store S2.

In addition to manipulation, measurement, and control, we should also think of causal research as requiring three types of evidence: concomitant variation, time order of occurrence, and elimination of other possible causal factors.

- *Concomitant Variation.* Cause and effect must vary together in some predictable manner. They may vary in a positive (i.e., the cause and effect both increase or decrease together) or inverse relationship (i.e., one increases while the other decreases). Statistical tests indicate the degree of the concomitant variation, such as chi-squared tests, correlation, regression, or analysis of variance. Concomitant variation, when we are dealing with the actions of people as with marketing research, is a matter of degree and is not absolute or perfect in the correlation of movement between cause and effect. Scientists infer cause and effect relationships if the presence of the cause makes the occurrence of the effect more likely from a statistically significant standpoint. However, no matter how strong that relationship, mere concomitant variation alone is insufficient to infer a causal relationship. We must see the next two pieces of evidence present.
- *Time Order of Occurrence.* To demonstrate that X causes Y, we must be able to consistently see that X occurs first before we see Y, and not vice versa.
- *Elimination of Other Possible Causal Factors.* Conducting experiments under actual market conditions ("in the field") makes it difficult to control for other possible factors that could influence the effect variable. For example, if we are trying to determine how the amount of shelf space influences the sales for a particular brand of cereal, we realize that other variables such as price, advertising, sales promotion and environmental events (e.g., good or bad publicity about the product), not to mention the activities of our competition could also influence sales. So when we say we must design an experiment that involves manipulation, measurement, and control, what we are saying is that we must find ways of holding all other possible causal factors "constant" while manipulating the causal factor(s) under investigation. Otherwise, when we measure our effect variable we will not know if the observed change was due to our manipulated variable, shelf space, or some other variable, such as competitor pricing.

When we cannot exercise physical control (i.e., physically putting the products on the same level of store shelf), we can in effect still have control over the experiment by measuring the nonphysically controlled variable. For example, we cannot control our competitor's pricing in our test markets, but if we can measure the competitor's price, we can use our statistical analysis procedure to control for differences in competitive pricing by "making all else equal" and just measuring the effect of our price change on our sales. How this is done is beyond the scope of this discussion, but researchers should be aware that control can be exerted through both "physical" means as well as via measurement. The key in both cases is to anticipate what variables, other than the ones being manipulated, could have an effect on the dependent variable and then exercise control in some form over those variables. Manipulation, like control, may also occur in two ways: "physical" manipulation (e.g., altering the price) or "naturally occurring" manipulation. For example, if you are seeking to determine if store size has an effect on sales of a particular product, store size is the causal variable, and would be manipulated. Obviously you can't "physically" manipulate store size but you can find stores of different sizes naturally occurring in the market and randomly assign product placement in 10,000 or 20,000, etc. square-foot-sized stores. Why can't you merely check existing sales data to determine store size effect on sales? Because you haven't also met the conditions we've discussed here, and therefore can't know for sure if a cause-effect relationship exists.

As previously mentioned, causal research is often conducted through the use of controlled experiments to allow for testing of cause and effect. We will now discuss experimentation in marketing research.

Experimentation

What Is Experimentation?

Experimental designs differ from other research designs in the degree of control exerted by the researcher over the conditions under which data are collected. When observational or survey descriptive designs are employed, the researcher measures the variables of interest but does not attempt to manipulate or control the variables. However, in experimental (causal) designs, researchers are exercising control over the variables of interest.

For example, a retailer trying to isolate the influence of price changes on the sales volume of a product, must identify the nonprice variables such as location of the product in the store, time period of the day/week, promotion, etc., and control these variables because they also influence sales volume. Simply altering price and measuring sales is not an adequate design because of the impact of nonprice variables on sales.

Essentially, the key differences in experimentation and other designs are:

1   In an experiment, one or more of the independent variables are deliberately manipulated while others are controlled.
2   Combinations of conditions (particular values of the independent variables, e.g., different prices) are assigned to sample elements (e.g., different stores) on a random basis. This reduces the likelihood of preexisting conditions affecting the results.

The Terminology of Experimentation

There are several terms that are used to describe the concepts involved in an experiment. Knowledge of these terms is essential to understanding experimental designs.

Experimental Treatments

The term "treatment" is used to describe a specific manner of manipulating an independent variable. For example, if an experiment was designed to measure the influence of three different levels of advertising on sales, then each level of advertising would be a different treatment. If the effects of the three levels of advertising were combined with two levels of price, then there would be six experimental treatments as shown in the following:

Price level one with
  Advertising level one
  Advertising level two
  Advertising level three

Price level two with
  Advertising level one
  Advertising level two
  Advertising level three

Since price level one with advertising level one represents a specified combination of independent variables, it is referred to as an experimental treatment. Each combination of price and advertising levels creates another experimental treatment. Therefore, this example consists of six different treatments.

Experimental Units

Experimental units are the geographic areas, stores, or people whose responses are measured in determining the effect of the different treatments. If the price and advertising levels described earlier are used in different geographical areas, then the areas represent experimental units. Each group of experimental units is a sample of all possible units and is used for comparing the impact of the treatments. Continuing the example, each of the six treatments may be assigned to 40 different geographic locations for a total of 240 units. If we took a measure of sales before and after each treatment in each location, we would have a total of 480 (i.e., 240 × 2) "observations."

Experimental Designs

The experimental design is the specific process used to arrange independent variables into treatments and then assign treatments to units. There are many possible designs and great care should be exercised in choosing and/or modifying the design. Choosing the best design is the most important aspect of experimentation. Several designs will be discussed in a later section, but it should be noted that researchers unfamiliar with experimentation should seek advice in setting up an experiment.

Control Group

In many experiments the use of a control group is a necessary element of the design. A control group is randomly selected just like other groups of units in the experiment. However, the control group does not receive a treatment and thus serves as a benchmark for comparing the effects of treatments. If an experiment was used to determine the impact of two new levels of price on sales, prices held at the previous level in some areas would enable these areas to serve as controls in analyzing the results.

Validity and Experimentation

While there are a number of different types of validity, the two major varieties are considered here: internal validity and external validity. Internal validity has to do with whether the independent variables that were manipulated caused the changes in the dependent variable or whether other factors involved also influenced the dependent variable. There are many threats to internal validity. Some of the major ones are:

1   *History.* During the time that an experiment is taking place, some events may occur that affect the relationship being studied. For example, economic conditions may change, new products may be introduced, or other factors may change that alter the results.
2   *Maturation.* Changes may also take place within the subject that are a function of the passage of time and are not specific to any particular event. These are of special concern when the study covers a long period of time, but may also be a factor in tests that are as short as an hour or two. For example, a subject can become hungry, bored, or tired in a short time and this can affect response results.
3   *Testing.* When pre-treatment and post-treatment measures are used, the process of taking a test can affect the scores of a second measurement. The experience of participation in the first measurement can have a learning effect that influences the results on the second measurement.
4   *Instrumentation.* This threat to internal validity comes from changes in measuring instruments or observers. Using different questions or different observers or interviewers is a validity threat.

5 *Selection.* One of the more important threats to internal validity is the differential selection of subjects to be included in experimental and control groups. The concern is over initial differences that exist between subjects. If subjects are randomly assigned to experimental and control groups, this problem can be overcome.

6 *Statistical regression.* This potential loss of validity is of special concern when subjects have been selected on the basis of their extreme scores. For example, if the most productive and least productive salespeople are included in an experiment, there is a tendency for the average of the high scores to decline and the low scores to increase.

7 *Mortality.* Mortality occurs when the composition of the study groups changes during the experiment. Subjects dropping out of an experiment, for example, cause the makeup of the group to change.

While internal validity concerns whether experimental or nonexperimental factors caused the observed differences, external validity is concerned with whether the results are generalizable to other subjects, stores, or areas. The major threats to external validity are:

1 *Subject selection.* The process by which test subjects are selected for an experiment may be a threat to external validity. The population from which subjects are selected may not be the same as the target market. For example, if college students were used as subjects, generalizing to other types of consumers may not be appropriate.

2 *Other factors.* The experimental settings themselves may have an effect on a subject's response. Artificial settings, for example, can give results that are not representative of actual market situations. If the subjects know they are participating in a price experiment, they may be more sensitive to price than normal.

Field versus Laboratory Experiments

There are two types of settings in which experiments are conducted—field and laboratory. Field experiments result in an experimental setting which is more realistic in terms of modeling actual conditions and is therefore higher on external validity. Field experiments are carried out in a natural setting with a minimum of artificial elements in the experiment. The downside of field experiments is that they usually cost more, have lower internal validity due to lack of control over variables that influence the dependent variable, and also may alert competition to changes a company is contemplating in marketing their products.

Laboratory experiments are experiments conducted under artificial conditions, such as testing television ads in a movie theater rather than in buyers' homes. Such experiments usually are lower in costs, have higher internal validity due to more control of the experimental environment, and provide greater secrecy of potential marketing actions. It is also possible to use more elaborate measurement techniques in a laboratory setting than in field experiments.

Disadvantages of laboratory experiments include loss of realism and lower external validity. These are due to the artificial conditions used in the experiment. For example, an experiment where people are given play money and asked to shop in a laboratory setting may reveal a great deal about some aspects of consumer behavior but there would be great difficulty in trying to generalize the findings to the purchase environment encountered in the marketplace.

The type of information to be generated from the experiment and its intended use dictate which type of experimental setting is more appropriate in a given situation. It is even possible to use both—a laboratory experiment followed by a field experiment—to validate the findings of the laboratory study under actual market conditions.

Experimental Design Symbols

Certain symbols have been developed to help describe experimental designs. These symbols have been used because they help in understanding the designs. These symbols include:

- X = exposure of a group of subjects to an experimental treatment or a level of an independent variable (e.g., to a particular ad or product price, etc.). If different levels are used, then such as $X_1, X_2, X_3, \ldots, X_n$ are used.
- O = observation or measurement of the dependent variable in which the researcher is interested.
- R = random assignment of people to groups or groups to treatments.

Other notions are also helpful. The left-to-right notation indicates the time sequence of occurrence of events. Thus the notation

$$RO_1XO_2$$

would mean that subjects were randomly assigned to this group (R); a before measure (O_1) was taken; the subjects were then exposed to the treatment (X); and then an after measure (O_2) was taken.

All the notations on a single line refer to a single group of respondents, and notations that appear together vertically identify events that occurred at the same point in time. Thus,

$$O_1X_1O_2$$
$$X_1O_3$$

refers to two groups of subjects, one of which received a pre-test measure and a post-test measure (O_1 and O_2), whereas the other received only a post-test measure (O_3). Both groups were exposed to the same treatment (X_1) and that the treatment and post-test measures occurred at the same time for both groups.

Ethics and Experimentation

Over the past few years, there has been increasing concern for protecting the rights of subjects used in research projects. This is a potential problem in all studies involving human subjects. The researcher should give careful consideration to the potential negative effects on those participating in an experiment to avoid violating the subjects' rights and deflect potential lawsuits. Luckily, most marketing research experiments are not likely to involve negative effects, but the possibility of such effects should be carefully evaluated.[5]

Experimental Research Designs

There are many possible experimental designs to choose from and they vary widely in terms of both complexity and effectiveness. The most widely accepted classifications of designs are: (1) pre-experiments, (2) true experiments, and (3) quasi-experiments. While complete coverage of experimental designs is beyond the scope of this book, a brief explanation and examples of these follows:

Pre-experimental Designs

Pre-experimental designs are designs that are weak in terms of their ability to control the various threats to internal validity. This is especially true with the one-shot case study.

One-Shot Case Study. This design may be noted as:

$$X_1 O_1$$

An example of such a study would be to conduct a sales training program without a measure of the salespeople's knowledge before participation in the training program. Results would reveal only how much they know after the program but not how effective the program was in increasing knowledge.

One-Group Pre-test-Post-test. This design can be represented as:

$$O_1 X_1 O_2$$

It is an improvement on the one-shot case study because of the addition of the pre-test measurement, but it is still a weak design in that it fails to control for history, maturation, and other internal validity problems.

Static-Group Comparison. This design provides for two study groups, one of which receives the experimental treatment while the other serves as a control. The design is:

$$X_1 O_1$$
$$O_2$$

The addition of a control group makes this design better than the previous two designs. However, there is no way to ensure that the two groups were not different before the introduction of the treatment.

True Experimental Designs

The major deficiency of the previous designs is that they fail to provide groups that are comparable. The way to achieve comparability is through the random assignment of subjects to groups and treatments to groups. This deficit is overcome in the following true experimental designs.

Pre-test-Post-test Control Group. This design is represented as:

$$RO_1 X_1 O_2$$
$$RO_3 \quad O_4$$

In this design, most internal validity problems are minimized. However, there are still some difficulties. For example, history may occur in one group and not the other. Also, if communication exists between the groups, the effect of the treatment can be altered.

Post-test-Only Control Group. Pre-test measurements are not used in this design. Pre-test measurements are well-established in experimental research design but are not really necessary when random assignment to groups is possible. The design is represented as:

$$RX_1 O_1$$
$$R \quad O_2$$

The simplicity of this design makes it more attractive than the pre-test-post-test control group design. Internal validity threats from history, maturation, selection, and statistical regression are adequately controlled by random assignment. This design also eliminates some external validity problems as well. How does this design accomplish such notable achievements? We can think of the O_1 observation as a combination of the treatment effect (e.g., a change in price, or the advertising campaign we ran, or a change in package design, etc.), plus the effect of all the extraneous variables (i.e., history, maturation, testing effect, instrumentation, selection, statistical regression, and mortality). However, since O_2 will theoretically be subject to all the same extraneous variables, the only difference between what we observe between O_1 and O_2 (e.g., a measure of sales at two stores) will be the fact that O_1 (e.g., sales at store #1) was measured after the treatment X_1 (e.g., where prices were lowered), and O_2 (e.g., sales at store #2) did not receive the treatment. Therefore, all the other extraneous variable effects "wash" or cancel out between the two observations, so any difference in the observations must be due to the treatment. These results are dependent, however, on the random assignment of multiple units (stores in this example) to either the test or control conditions. Sample sizes for each of the test and control conditions must be large enough to approach a "normal distribution" of stores so that we can assume that the only difference that we see between O_1 and O_2 is the result of the treatment, and not due to some extraneous variable differences between the test and control stores.

Quasi-Experiments

Under actual field conditions, one often cannot control enough of the variables to use a true experiment design. Under such conditions, quasi-experiments can be used. In a quasi-experiment, comparable experimental and control groups cannot be established through random assignment. Often the researcher cannot even determine when or to whom to expose the experimental variable. Usually, however, it is possible to determine when and whom to measure. The loss of control over treatment manipulation (the "when" of the experimental variable exposure) and the test unit assignment (the "who" of the experimental variable exposure) greatly increases the chance of obtaining confounded results. Therefore, we have to build into our design the ability to account for the possible effects of variables outside our control in the field, so that we can more safely conclude whether the treatment was, in fact, the thing that caused the results we observed.

A quasi-experiment is not as effective as a true experiment design, but is usually superior to available nonexperimental approaches. Only two quasi-experimental designs will be discussed here.

Nonequivalent Control Group. This is one of the most widely used quasiexperimental designs. It differs from true experimental design because the groups are not randomly assigned. This design can be represented as follows:

$$O_1 X_1 O_2$$
$$O_3 \quad O_4$$

Pre-test results are one indicator of the degree of comparability between test and control groups. If the pre-test results are significantly different, there is reason to doubt the groups' comparability. Obviously, the more alike the O_1 and O_3 measures are, the more useful the control group is in indicating the difference the treatment has made (i.e., comparing the difference in the O_2 to O_1 with the difference between O_4 to O_3). Close similarity allows for control over the extraneous variables of history, maturation, testing, instrumentation, selection, and mortality. However, statistical regression can be a problem if either the test or control group has been selected on the basis of extreme scores. In such a case, the O_2 or O_4 measures could be more the result of simply regressing back from the extreme to the average score, rather than the result of anything that intervened between the first and second observation of either group.

Separate Sample Pre-test-Post-test. This design is most applicable in those situations where we cannot control when and to whom to introduce the treatment but can control when and whom to measure. The design is:

$$R \quad O_1$$
$$R \, X_1 O_2$$

This design is more appropriate when the population is large and there is no way to restrict who receives the treatment. For example, suppose a company launches an internal marketing campaign to change its employees' attitudes toward customers. Two random samples of employees may be selected, one of which is interviewed regarding attitudes prior to the campaign. After the campaign the other group is interviewed.

Limitations of Causal Research

It is natural for managers to be attracted to the results that can be gained from doing experimentation. After all, are we not often looking to know what really causes the effects we see such as satisfied customers, rising (or falling) sales, motivated salespersons, etc.? However attractive causal research may be, managers should recognize the following limitations:[6]

1   Field experiments can involve many variables outside the control of the experimenters, resulting in unanticipated differences in conditions surrounding treatment groups.
2   It may be difficult or expensive to gain the cooperation of retailers and wholesalers when setting up the experiment.
3   Marketing personnel may lack knowledge of experimental procedures, reducing the chance of results which demonstrate causality.
4   Experiments are notoriously expensive and time consuming.
5   The experimenter must be careful not to introduce bias into the experiment by saying or doing something that may consciously or unconsciously affect the behavior of the test participants.

Ex Post Facto Research

Ex post facto (after the fact) studies are those that try to discover a causal relationship without manipulation of the independent variable or control over respondent exposure to treatment conditions. These studies are characterized by an observance of an outcome followed by attempts to find the causal factor that caused the observed outcome. Consider this example:

> A research manager for a regional bank was concerned with assessing customer images of their various branch locations. A mail survey asked whether they were satisfied with the services provided by the branch location that they used. Each respondent rated his or her branch location on a number of attributes: for example, friendliness of bank personnel, convenience of location, parking facilities, and so forth. After receiving the questionnaires, the manager divided the sample into two groups: those who expressed satisfaction with the branch location and those who expressed dissatisfaction. An analysis of these two groups revealed that compared with customers who expressed satisfaction, dissatisfied customers rated their branch location as unsatisfactory with respect to friendliness of service. The researcher concluded that friendliness of services is the primary factor leading to customer satisfaction, and, consequently, it plays an important part in the decision about which bank to use.[7]

In this example, there is an attempt to identify a cause-effect relationship ex post facto, without manipulation of variables, assignment of respondents to treatments, or control of extraneous variables. The observed association between friendliness of service, customer satisfaction, and choice of bank may in fact be spurious and the correlation was in fact due to another variable not included in the analysis.

For example, the people who rated their branch lower on the friendliness and satisfaction scales may be from an area populated by high-income households and who may have higher expectations of all aspects of service and who are more difficult to please in general. In such a case, the same level of service and friendliness of personnel among the branches is perceived differently by respondents, as is their level of overall satisfaction. It is obvious that any causal inference drawn from ex post facto research, while indicating a *possible* causal relationship, must be supplemented with true experimental or quasi-experimental studies before we can draw cause-effect conclusions. However, in some cases, merely demonstrating co-variation between variables of interest is sufficient for marketing planning purposes. We merely must be careful not to assume we know more than we can legitimately claim we do.

Test Marketing

Test marketing is the name given to a set of experimental or quasi-experimental (field) studies that are intended to determine the rate of market acceptance for (usually) a new product. A company typically would use test marketing to determine such information as:

- the sales volume and market share expectations of the new product;
- some estimate of the repurchase cycle and likelihood of repurchase;
- a profile of trier-adopters;
- an understanding of competitor reactions to the new product;
- some feel for the effect of the new product sales on existing product sales;
- performance of new product package design in generating trial and satisfaction.

With the cost and likelihood of new product failure, it is easy to see the incentive of marketers conducting test markets to avoid large-scale introduction of products destined to fail. On the other hand, test marketing itself may cost millions of dollars, delay the cash flow of a successful new product, and alert competitors to your plans, so the costs may be high in either case. However, when the stakes are high and the costs of failure are very significant, test marketing may be the best of the unattractive options available.

There are several points to ponder when making the decision whether or not to test market a product.[8]

1   It is necessary to weigh the cost and risk of product failure against the profit and profitability of success. The higher the probability of success and lower the costs of failure, the less attractive is test marketing.
2   The difference in the scale of investment involved in the test versus national launch route has an important bearing on deciding whether to test. The greater the investment called for in manufacturing, the more valuable a test market becomes in indicating the payout of such an investment before it is made.
3   Another factor to be considered is the likelihood and speed with which the competition will be able to copy the new product and preempt part of your national market or overseas markets, should the test market prove successful.
4   Investments in plant and machinery are only part of the costs involved in a new product launch. The investment in marketing expenses and effort may be extensive, as well as the

fact that sometimes the new product will only be given space at the retail level previously occupied by your existing products. Stock returns and buy-backs for unsuccessful products likewise increase the costs of failure, not to mention the psychological impact of failing on a national scale. The higher these associated costs, the greater the potential value of test marketing in helping decision makers arrive at the best decision regarding large-scale product launch.

A.C. Nielsen data indicate that 75 percent of products that undergo test marketing succeed, while 80 percent of products not test marketed fail.[9] Careful readers, however, may identify this implied causal relationship between test marketing and success as ex post facto research—we observe the relationship and identify the implied causal factor instead of conducting a controlled test to determine causality. In this case, it could be that the type of firms doing test marketing (large, big-budget firms with considerable marketing expertise), or not doing test marketing (small, low-budget firms without high-priced marketing talent), may explain more of the success rate than does test marketing itself.

Three Types of Test Markets

STANDARD TEST MARKETS

In standard test markets the firm uses its own regular distribution channels and sales force to stock the product in selected test areas. Test site selection is an important consideration. Some criteria for selecting test sites are:[10]

1   There should be a balance in the size of a test area between being large enough to generate meaningful results but not so large as to be prohibitively expensive (a good rule of thumb is that test areas should comprise at least two percent of the potential market).
2   They should provide representative media that would be used in a national launch, but be self-contained so that media in test areas will not "bleed over" into other test areas or control sites.
3   They should be similar along demographic dimensions with the full-scale market area (i.e., region or entire United States).
4   The trading area should be self-contained to avoid transhipments between test and control areas or two test areas.
5   Competition should be representative in test areas.
6   Test areas should provide for testing under different conditions that will be encountered on a national scale (e.g., both hard and soft water sites for water soluble products).

Additional considerations include what measures will be used to indicate performance (e.g., trial rates, repeat purchase rates, percentage of households using, sales, etc.) and length of the test (e.g., depends upon the repurchase cycle, competitive response, and consumer response, but a minimum of ten months for new consumer brands). Standard test markets are subject to the problems associated with after-only experimental designs and are time consuming and expensive.

CONTROLLED STORE TEST MARKETS

Controlled store test markets are run by a research firm such as Audits & Surveys Worldwide, or A.C. Nielsen, who, for a fee, handle warehousing, distribution, product pricing, shelving, and stocking. Typically, these organizations pay a fee to distributors to guarantee shelf space. Sales and other performance measures are also gathered by the research firm.

Advantages of controlled test markets are that competitors can not "read" test results because they are available only to the research firm conducting the test and are not available through syndicated sales tracking services, which would track standard test market data, they are faster to run since it is not necessary to move the product through a distribution channel, and they are less costly to operate than standard test markets. Disadvantages include use of channels that might not be representative of the firm's channel system; the number of test sites is usually fixed and limited, making projections difficult; firms will not get a read on the willingness of the trade to support the product under normal conditions; it can be difficult to mimic nationally planned promotional programs; and the care of the research firms to avoid stock-outs, optional shelf positioning, correct use of point-of-purchase materials, and so on may not duplicate conditions existing with the normal launch of a product. Nevertheless, controlled store test markets are often used as a check before going to standard test markets. If the results are promising, a standard test market follows. If not, the product is killed or revised.

SIMULATED TEST MARKETS

A simulated test market is not conducted in the field, but rather in a laboratory setting. Firms providing such services (e.g., Burke; M/A/R/C; NPO Research; Yankelovich Clancy Shulman; Custom Research, Inc.) follow a procedure that usually includes the following:

1   Respondents are recruited and screened to fit the desired demographic and usage patterns of the target market.
2   Respondents are shown ads for the tested products as well as competitive products, or are shown product concepts or prototypes.
3   Respondents are asked to record their attitudes toward the product on structured questionnaires and are either asked to indicate their purchase interest or are given a chance to buy the product or competitive products in a simulated shopping environment. For example, an aisle might be set up similar to an aisle in a drugstore with your tested cough syrup along with competitive cough syrups. Respondents can purchase any of the brands they desire.
4   Those who choose the tested products take it home and use it as they would under normal conditions, and are contacted after an appropriate time period and asked a series of attitudinal, repurchase intent, and usage-related questions.
5   Data from these steps are processed by a computer programmed to calculate estimated sales volume, market share, and other performance data based on assumptions of a marketing mix incorporated into the program.

Simulated test markets do *not* assume that the attitudes and behaviors evidenced in the simulation will be exactly duplicated in the market, but rather depend upon observed relationships that have been discovered historically between laboratory and eventual market findings. While costing in the low six-figures, simulated test markets are cheap compared to a full-blown standard test market, they are confidential, and permit easy modifications in a marketing mix to calibrate the most successful plan for introduction. The disadvantage is that they operate under a series of assumptions about what will really happen, while standard test markets *are* the real thing. Reported accuracy of simulated test markets are within 29 percent of forecast 90 percent of the time.[11]

Exploratory, Descriptive, Or Causal Observation

The previous discussion of research designs followed the generally accepted practice of discussing the techniques for carrying out the research without distinguishing between the data-collection methods of communication or observation. We will discuss those two methods at greater length in Chapter 7, but the reader should be alerted to the fact, at this point, that observation can be legitimately conducted as a part of exploratory, descriptive, or causal research. The use of observation for collecting causal data is perhaps most obvious (e.g., sales data collected in a test market represents observation). Less obvious is the use of observation in exploratory or descriptive research. This situation is at least partly explained by the lack of categories used to classify observation techniques such as exist for communication methods (e.g., focus groups, cross-sectional sample surveys, etc.).

The difficulty in classifying observational techniques does not diminish the value of these techniques, however; it just makes their discussion a little more difficult. It is perhaps best to think of observational research, whatever the technique, as being appropriately used when it is consistent with the overall objectives of the research design under which it is being applied. Therefore, observational research in exploratory designs is being used to gain insights, ideas, clarification, etc., while descriptive observational research is determining frequency of occurrence, the extent to which two observational behaviors co-vary, etc., and causal observation is conducted in a controlled setting to determine if a causal relationship exists between carefully defined variables. Such desirable consistency is the rule whether observation is the sole data-collection method, or combined with communication. For example, in a focus group intended to gain insight into consumer attitudes about a brand, the body language of consumers observed by the researchers provides additional insights into their feelings. Likewise, in descriptive research, coupling survey information with diary of purchases (i.e., observed data) can provide opportunity to see if attitudes and behavior co-vary. However observation is done, it is the objective of research that will determine how it is applied—flexibility inherent in exploratory observation, structure inherent in descriptive observation, and control inherent in causal observation.

In another example, observation data collected by optical scanners in supermarkets could be used to generate ideas or hypotheses in the exploratory phase of a research project (e.g., maybe large packages are outselling smaller packages because they seem to offer better value), test hypotheses via co-variation in the descriptive phase (e.g., package size purchases co-vary with number of people in the household), or test hypotheses via experimental design in the causal phase (e.g., varying coupon amounts has a greater effect on sales of the 16 oz. package size of Brand A than the 8 oz. size). In this example it is important to note that the only reason the data could be used in the descriptive and causal research designs is that it was originally collected by using a methodology that generated "quantifiably precise" data. In other words, you cannot use information that was originally generated using exploratory research methodology in making descriptive or causal research calculations (e.g., focus groups cannot generate descriptive data if you do a hundred of them instead of three because the methodology is not intended to generate quantifiable information—it was intended to provide insights, ideas, etc.).

Dangers of Defining Design By Technique

Just as it is not appropriate to define a research design by data-collection method (e.g., exploratory research is not always done via communication; causal, not always by observation), it is also inappropriate to think research "tools" are the province of only one design. While some techniques are associated with only one design, such as experiments with causal and projective techniques for exploratory, other techniques may be used successfully under all three designs. Therefore, it is dangerous to define a design by a technique. Rather, designs are defined by the objectives and resulting methodology pursued which is consistent with the methodology. An example will help make this point. Table 5.4 shows the difference in using a survey when doing exploratory, descriptive, or causal research.

Table 5.4 Differences in using a survey by research design type

	Exploratory Research	*Descriptive Research*	*Causal Research*
Objectives	Gain insights, ideas	Quantify	Test variables for causal relationships
Hypotheses	Generated	Tested via co-variation	Tested via experimentation
Sampling method	Nonprobability	Probability	Random assignment to treatments
Survey questions	Can change over course of research	Fixed	Fixed
Structure of data collection	Loosely structured	Highly structured	Controlled
Example of survey question	"Why did you first start using Tide?"	"Which of the following reasons best explains why you first started using Tide?"	"Do you recall seeing any TV commercials in the past 24 hours for a laundry detergent?" (Unaided recall measures after testing a new TV commercial.)

While acknowledging that surveys can and are used for exploratory research, we should emphasize that the preferred methods for achieving the objectives of exploratory research remain the five techniques (literature review, in-depth interviews, etc.) discussed earlier in this chapter. They are more capable of generating the depth of insight desired as an outcome from exploratory research.

Research Project Assignment

Describe the design to be used in conducting the research for your project. Be as specific as possible in detailing exactly how you will get answers to your research questions and test your hypotheses. For example, don't just say you will do exploratory research; rather say you will do a literature search of census data for research question #4, which will provide information needed to do descriptive research in the form of a mailed sample survey to get answers to research questions #6 and #7, etc.

Summary

Good strategy and good marketing decisions do not just "happen." They are grounded in accurate, timely, and useful market intelligence. Such information is obtained only through the careful translation of management problems into a research purpose, a research purpose into a set of research objectives, and those research objectives into a research design. Such a design is a road map that helps us arrive at our planned destination of having the information we need for decision making. The research design may involve one or more of the three categories of research: exploratory, descriptive, or causal. Our research objectives suggest that one or combinations of these types will be needed to obtain the desired information.

Whenever researchers must find answers to research questions dealing with cause and effect inferences they must consider the need for experimentation. Experimental designs differ from exploratory or descriptive designs in the degree of control exerted by the researcher over relevant variables. Experiments involve manipulation, control, and measurement of variables in order to allow for causal inference. In some cases such experiments must be conducted in the field, rather than in a controlled laboratory setting and are referred to as quasi-experiments. Several experimental designs were discussed, along with test marketing, one of the most commonly conducted causal experimental approaches used by marketers.

Discussion Questions

1   Explain why the three keywords ("flexible" for exploratory, "rigid" for descriptive, "control" for causal) were chosen to indicate the approaches used for each of the three types of research designs. Use examples to illustrate your points.

2   How do you know which one, or combination, of the three research designs to use to achieve your research purpose in any given situation? How do you know which technique (focus groups, sample survey, etc.) to use for the research design? Use examples to help illustrate your points.

3   What do we mean by stating that descriptive research requires a clear specification of the who, what, where, why, and how of the research before you can design the descriptive study? Why is this required?

4   If you had been asked by the Compton Co. to design research to help them solve their problem, what research would you have suggested? Describe and defend your choice.

5   There have been a number of complaints in your city that minorities have received discriminatory treatment from local retailers of major appliances with respect to trade-ins, prices, sales assistance, and credit terms. How would you investigate this issue (i.e., describe and defend a research design and data collection method).

6   You are the marketing research manager at Proctor & Gamble. A brand manager comes to you and says she wants you to design a causal research study that will allow her to determine the motivations people have for buying Tide detergent. How would you respond? Be comprehensive in your response.

Part III

Measurement, Data Collection, and Sampling

6 Measurement

Learning Objectives

Upon completing this chapter, you should understand:

1 what is meant by the measurement process;
2 the differences in nominal, ordinal, interval, and ratio levels of measurements;
3 the concepts of validity and reliability of measurements;
4 what is meant by a measurement scale;
5 how scales are used in marketing research.

Introduction

In Chapter 1 we described marketing research as producing the information managers need to make marketing decisions. In that chapter we also listed numerous examples of how the results of marketing research can inform marketing decisions such as in concept/product testing, market segmentation, competitive analysis, customer satisfaction studies, etc. These, and many other examples of marketing research studies, illustrate the need for *measurement*—"rules for assigning numbers to objects in such a way as to represent quantities of attributes."[1] Several things we should note about this definition:

1 Not all of what researchers do involves measurement. Researchers are interested in generating *information,* which leads to *knowledge,* which leads to better *decisions.* Sometimes that information is in the form of insights from exploratory research studies such as focus groups, in-depth interviews, projective research, and similar methods. For these techniques we are generating information, but we are not "assigning numbers to objects," so we are not "measuring." As we have said before, information does not have to have numbers attached to it to have value, and we are dangerously oversimplifying our analysis when we favor information with numbers over that without, simply because it has the appearance of being "hard evidence."

2 The "rules for assigning numbers" will be discussed in greater depth in this chapter, but we should note here that those rules exist so that we can be more scientific in our measures, and can place more confidence in the numbers that those rules help generate (see Figure 1.2). We want to make decisions that are grounded in information that we believe correctly represent reality. This means the assignment of numbers should map the empirical nature isomorphically (i.e., on a "one-to-one" basis).

   For example, if we assign the number "5 lbs" to represent the weight of an object, we want to make sure that the weight is 5 lbs and not 8 lbs or 3 lbs. Using a carefully calibrated scale is how we ensure in this example that we have correctly measured the item's weight—assigned numbers to the object to accurately represent the quantity of its attribute of weight. The mundane quality of this example disappears when we find ourselves confronted with the need to measure variables of interest to marketers such as intentions, attitudes, perceptions, etc. How can we be sure that the number "4" correctly captures the intensity with which a respondent holds an intention, for example? We will devote further discussion to the ways of ensuring good measures in our research in this chapter.

3   The definition states that we attach numbers to the attributes of an object and not to the object itself. For example, we cannot measure the quantity of what you are now holding in your hand. There is no scale for measuring the amount of "bookness" in a book. We can, however, measure the attributes of a book—its weight, dimensions in inches, number of pages, and so forth. We can even measure qualities less obvious such as its stature as great literature or its educational value; but, as described in point number 2, the rules for assigning numbers to those attributes will involve different measuring devices than those used to measure its physical properties. This caveat also holds true for the measurement of variables of interest to marketers.

We measure a consumer's attitudes, income, brand loyalty, etc., instead of measuring the consumer. In some cases, such as attitudes, we go a step further and measure the subcomponents of the variable. Attitudes, for example, are said to consist of cognitive, affective, and conative components that we would want to measure to ensure we have captured the essence of how strong one's attitude was toward an object. For example, if we are to claim we have measured a parent's attitude toward a new product concept for a child's fruit drink, we need to measure beliefs and knowledge (the cognitive component of attitudes), how positive or negative he or she feels about the concept (the affective component), and the parent's predisposition to behave toward the product (the conative component).

4   Scientists in the physical sciences such as physics, chemistry, and biology have something of an advantage over behavioral scientists because the things they are interested in measuring have a physical reality, and the devices used to measure these things can be physically calibrated. "Good measures" are generated by carefully calibrating the measuring devices (e.g., micrometers, weight scales, etc.). Behavioral scientists, such as marketing researchers, cannot see or feel those things of interest to them (e.g., perceptions, intentions, brand loyalty, attitudes, etc.), and so must find ways of determining if the process they use to attach numbers is trustworthy in order to know if the numbers resulting from that process are trustworthy. In other words, while a chemist can trust that the weight of a chemical is what a carefully calibrated scale says it is, the marketing researcher can trust that he or she has obtained a good measure of intent to purchase only by having faith in the measurement process used to attach numbers to that intention. There is no way of comparing the numbers on the intention scale to a standardized measure for intentions the way a chemist can check the measures of weight against a standardized scale for weight. We trust the numbers because we trust the process used to attach those numbers.

The Process of Measurement

Information gained from conducting marketing research contributes to better decision making by reducing risk, which can happen only if researchers are able to collect information that accurately represents the phenomenon under study. When it is appropriate to measure that phenomenon, that is, attach numbers to reflect the amount of an attribute inherent in that object of interest, then we must try to ensure that the process we use to take those measures is a "good" process. We have nothing to compare those numbers with to determine if they are "good" numbers, so we make sure the process is trustworthy so that we can believe the numbers

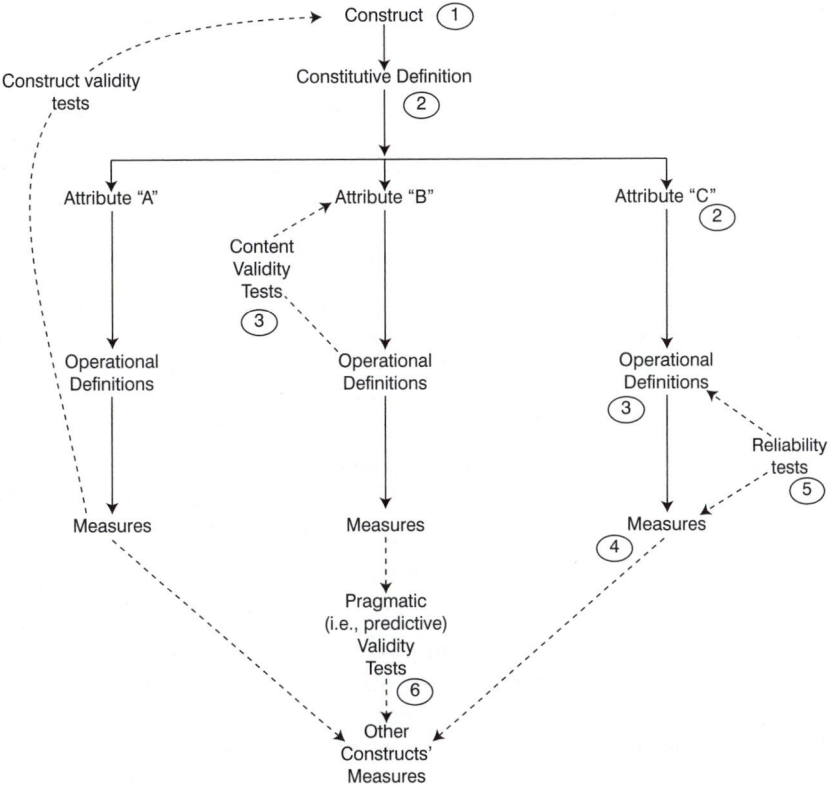

Figure 6.1 Measurement Hierarchy

resulting from the process are trustworthy and can indeed reduce the risk of decision making. The following process can help generate good measures (see Figures 6.1 and 6.2).

Step 1: Determine the Construct(s) of Interest

Constructs are abstract "constructions" (hence, the name) that are of interest to researchers. Some examples of constructs of interest to marketing researchers are customer satisfaction, heavy users, channel conflict, brand loyalty, marketing orientation, etc. These constructs are typical of the type of constructions of interest to marketers—they have no tangible reality apart from our defining them (unlike, for example, a botanist's plant), and we define them and study them because we need to understand them in order to make decisions based on that understanding (e.g., changing our policies on return of purchases in order to increase customer satisfaction). Because they have no tangible reality they are generally not directly observable. We cannot see customer satisfaction, but we can indirectly observe it by asking customers a series of questions that we believe reveal how satisfied customers are with our firm in specific areas. As an example of measuring a construct we will use "marketing orientation"—a core construct of the marketing discipline.

Step 2: Specify the Construct's Domain

We must take care that we are accurately capturing what should be included in the definition of that construct. We previously mentioned that the tricomponent model indicates that an attitude contains in its domain cognitive, affective, and conative components. Social scientists have studied the construct "attitude" over many years and have generally agreed that its domain

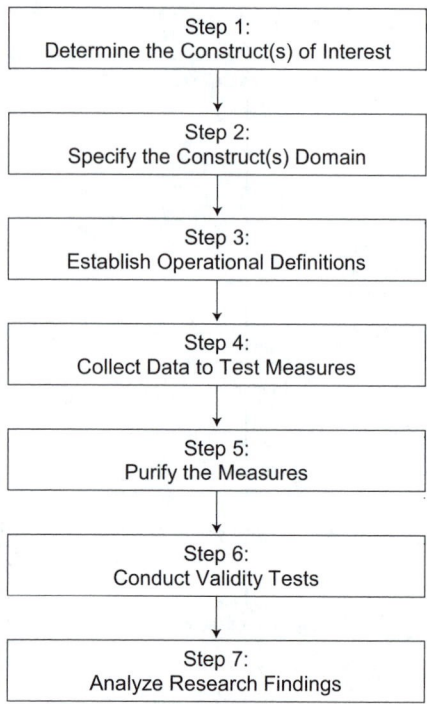

Figure 6.2 Developing Good Measures: The Measurement Process

includes these three components. We specify a construct's domain by providing a constitutive definition for the construct. A constitutive definition defines a construct by using other constructs to identify conceptual boundaries, showing how it is discernable from other similar but different constructs. A construct's constitutive definition is what has been generally accepted in the marketing literature as a definition. Consider the constitutive definitions for the following related, but different, constructs:

Marketing orientation is the attention to identifying and satisfying customer needs, integration of effort by all areas of the organization to satisfying those needs, and focusing on the means by which an organization can achieve its goals most efficiently while satisfying those needs. *Market orientation* is the systematic gathering of information on customers and competitors, both present and potential, the systematic analysis of the information for the purpose of developing marketing knowledge, and the systematic use of such knowledge to guide strategy recognition, understanding, creation, selection, implementation, and modification.[2]

The definition of *market* orientation is distinguished from *marketing* orientation by what it adds (a focus on potential customers as well as present customers and on competitors as well as customers), and subtracts (an interfunctional coordination).

Step 3: Establish Operational Definitions

The constitutive definition makes it possible to better define the construct's domain by use of an operational definition. An operational definition indicates what observable attributes of the construct will be measured and the process that will be used to attach numbers to those attributes so as to represent the quantity of the attributes. Often, a construct's attributes are identified in the constitutive definition.

Figure 6.3 Strength of Marketing Orientation

We need to establish operational definitions of our constructs to move them from the world of abstract concepts into the empirical world where we can measure them. Marketing orientation remains an abstract concept until we say exactly what its attributes are and how, specifically, we intend to measure those attributes.

One example of operationalizing the marketing orientation construct[3] in a hospital setting involved identifying five attributes of the construct (customer philosophy, marketing information systems, integrated marketing effort, strategic orientation, and operational efficiency), and then generating a set of nine statements for each attribute which fell along a strength of marketing orientation continuum anchored by the end points of "primitive" to "world class." These statements were assigned a score on the nine-point scale by a panel of expert judges. The following are two examples of statements whose average score by the judges fell at different points on the scale (Figure 6.3). Respondents (hospital administrators) would choose which statements most accurately reflected the marketing practices at their hospital.

"The feeling in my organization is that marketing activity is often contrary to the values of this hospital." (1.25)

"Marketing here is more than a staff function—it is heavily involved in line decision making." (8.35)

These example statements were two of forty-five item statements (nine statements for each of five attributes), which represent the operationalization of the marketing orientation construct.

Another operationalization[4] of marketing orientation involved identifying four attributes of the construct (intelligence generation, intelligence dissemination, response design, and response implementation), and then generating thirty-two item statements, each of which would be scored on a five-point scale ranging from "strongly disagree" to "strongly agree." Some examples of these operationalizations of the intelligence dissemination attribute (respondents were executives at manufacturing firms) are:

We have interdepartmental meetings at least once a quarter to discuss market trends or strategies.

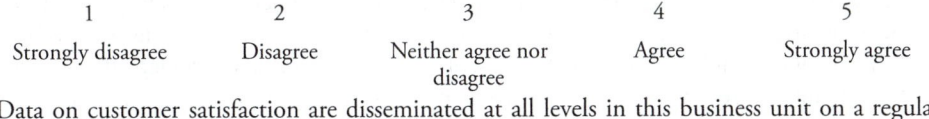

Data on customer satisfaction are disseminated at all levels in this business unit on a regular basis.

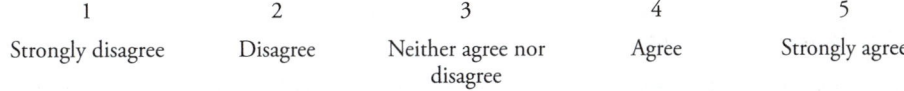

Note that these two operational approaches differ in the identification of the construct attributes, the item statements used to operationalize the attributes, and the method used to attach numbers to the item statements (also part of the operationalization process). Both examples, however, share in common the operationalization process of describing a specific set of operations that must be carried out in order to empirically measure the construct's attributes (i.e., move it from mere abstract conceptualization to the "real world" where it can be measured by establishing a process for attaching numbers to represent the quantity of the attribute—in these cases the degree to which a firm exhibits marketing oriented behavior). Researchers may not choose the same means of operationalizing the constructs of interest. How can we tell if our chosen approach represents "good measurement" methods if it is different from the methods used by other researchers, perhaps who can demonstrate that their methods have resulted, in fact, in good measures? The answer to this question lies in the next steps of the measurement process.

Step 4: Collect Data to Test Measures

In this step we use our operationalized measures to collect data from our target population (i.e., the "measures" in Figure 6.1). We need this data to help us determine if we are on the right track with our operationalized measures. That is, have we done a good job in developing the operational definitions and measuring processes so that they accurately represent our constructs of interest? As was mentioned before, since we have no standardized measures that can be calibrated to give us accurate data, such as a chemist using a carefully calibrated weight scale, we must use data to help us determine if the methods used to collect that data were "good." If the process of measurement is good the results of the process will also be assumed to be good. "Collecting data" in the previous two examples would consist of using the questionnaires to collect responses from the target populations (hospital administrators in the first example, executives at manufacturing firms in the second).

Step 5: Purify the Measures

In Step 5 we use the data collected in Step 4 to determine which items in our original list of operationalized items have "made the cut." Some items we thought would be good ways to operationalize our abstract constructs may not be as good as we thought. We can determine which item statements are keepers and which are to be rejected for our final item list by conducting reliability tests. We will discuss reliability in greater detail later in this chapter, but suffice it to say for now that we are using some statistical procedures to help identify which item statements "hang together" as a set, capturing the various aspects of the construct's attributes we were seeking to measure in our operationalizations.

For example, the two statements that were used to illustrate the attributes for marketing orientation in the two studies described in Step 2 were keepers— they passed the statistical tests intended to use the collected data to determine which item statements were appropriate pieces of the whole attribute we sought to measure. Other item statements might have failed those tests (i.e., the statements did not contribute to describing the attribute as we thought they would), and are eliminated from the final version of our measuring device (questionnaires in these two cases).

Step 6: Conduct Validity Tests

Once we have purified the scale by eliminating item statements that fail to pass our reliability test we are ready to conduct another test to determine how much faith we will place in the results of our research. Here we are testing for validity—did we actually measure what we were trying to measure? Validity will also be discussed in greater depth later in this chapter. Here, we should merely make note of the need to determine how successful we were in establishing measures that did correctly reflect the quantities of those attributes of our constructs of interest (e.g., Did we, in fact, accurately measure the degree to which an organization was marketing oriented?).

Step 7: Analyze Research Findings

If we have successfully developed measures that are reliable (Step 5) and valid (Step 6) we are now ready to analyze our data to achieve the objectives of our research study: answer research questions, test hypotheses, check for cause and effect relationships, describe the extent to which a population behaves in a specific manner, etc. A report can then be written that states the results of the research.

Commentary on the Measurement Process

Note that in this seven-step process data are actually analyzed two different ways. In Steps 5 and 6 data are being analyzed not to determine what are the findings of the research itself (i.e., not to obtain answers to the research questions), but rather to determine if the process used to collect the data generated results which can be trusted—that is, did the process generate reliable, valid information. Both of these measures of "data trustworthiness" are matters of degree instead of binary yes or no conclusions. We determine the degree of reliability and validity rather than determining whether the data is or is not reliable or valid. Once we have established degree of reliability and validity we are in a better position to know how secure we can be in our research conclusions when we analyze the same data in Step 7 to achieve the purpose of doing the research study itself.

We should also point out that some measurement processes[5] suggest collecting data twice—once to determine which item statements are reliable (i.e., after Step 4), then again after unreliable item statements have been eliminated (i.e., between Steps 4 and 5), performing reliability and validity tests on the second set of data, followed by analysis of the data for research findings (Step 7).

Now a reality check: Do all or most marketing research studies actually follow a measurement process similar to the seven-step process outlined here? Well, yes and no. Marketing scholars doing research on topics of interest to the discipline of marketing (such as "Does being marketing oriented increase a firm's profit?"), would have to do something like this process or they might not get their research results published! However, applied marketing-research studies, such as described in this text, are less vigilant in conducting such measurement processes. It should be obvious that all researchers are concerned whether or not they have measures that can be trusted before drawing conclusions and making decisions based on research findings. Therefore, attention to issues of construct domain, proper operational definitions, appropriate data-collection methods, and reliability and validity checks are efforts intended to generate data that accurately represents the object of the research and can lead to better decisions.

What Is To Be Measured?

There are many different types of measures used in marketing research. However, most measures fall into one of the following three categories:[6]

1 states of being—age, sex, income, education, etc.
2 behavior—purchase patterns, brand loyalty, etc.
3 states of mind—attitudes, preferences, personality, etc.

Table 6.1 shows examples of the types of measures frequently used in consumer and industrial marketing research. The criterion for selecting what to measure is based on our knowledge or expectation that what we want to measure will provide insight into or help solve the marketing decision problem for which data are being collected. Thus, the relevant measures for any study are based on the research objectives, which indicate the types of information needed.

Table 6.1. Types of Measures

Measurement type	Type of buyer	
	Ultimate consumers	*Industrial customers*
States of being	Age	Size or volume
	Sex	Number of employees
	Income	Number of plants
	Education	Type of organization
	Marital status	
Behavioral	Brands purchased	Decision makers
	Coupon redemption	Growth markets
	Stores shopped	Public vs. private
	Loyalty	Distribution pattern
	Activities	
States of mind	Attitudes	Management attitudes
	Opinions	Management style
	Personality traits	Organizational culture
	Preferences	

The research objectives indicate the concepts (constructs) that must be measured. For example, customer satisfaction, store loyalty, and sales performance are all concepts that relate to marketing problems. However, most concepts can be measured in more than one way. Store loyalty, for example, could be measured by: (1) the number of times a store is visited, (2) the proportion of purchases made at a store, or (3) shopping at a particular store first. These alternate measurement approaches are our operational definitions. We develop operational definitions for two types of variables: discrete and continuous.

Discrete variables are those that can be identified, separated into entities, and counted. The number of children in a family is an example of a discrete variable. Although the average may be 3.5, a given family would have 1, 2, 3, or, 4 or more children, but not 3.5.

Continuous variables may take on any value. As a simple rule, if a third value can fall between the two other values, the variable is continuous. It can take on an infinite number of values within some specified range. Temperature, distance, and time are continuous variables, and each can be measured to finer and finer degrees of accuracy. Frequently, continuous variables are rounded and converted to discrete variables expressed in convenient units such as degrees, miles, or minutes.

Who Is To Be Measured?

The question of the object of the measurement process may appear to have obvious answers: people, stores, or geographic areas. However, more thoughtful answers would reveal a multiplicity of possible objects to be measured.

For example, the level of influence on decision making of a husband and wife depends in part upon the product or service being purchased. The resulting decision might be wife-dominated, husband-dominated, joint, or autonomic (either solitary or unilateral). Moreover, such decision-making influence can change over time, as evidenced in recent trends toward female heads of households making financial decisions.[7] Husband–wife decision making also varies from culture to culture.[8] In a study of children's influence on decision making in the family, it was discovered that about 17 percent of the 9- to 12-year-old children survey considered themselves the main decision maker with regard to a decision to go to a restaurant, and 40 percent thought themselves the primary decision maker in choice of restaurant.[9] Thus, collecting data from the "decision maker" does not always represent an obvious choice of respondent.

The buying-center concept used in understanding organizational buying patterns provides a useful framework for other consumer and industrial purchasers.[10] A buying center consists of everyone involved in a buying action.

Buying-center participants play different roles. These roles must be identified and understood to select the type of respondents to be measured in a research project. These roles are:

- users—those who actually use the product;
- gatekeepers—those who control the flow of information or access to decision makers;
- influencers—those who influence the choice of product or supplier by providing information;
- deciders—those who actually make the choice of product and/or supplier;
- buyers—those who actually complete the exchange process for a family or organization.

The major point of this discussion is to emphasize the need to judiciously select the respondents, stores, areas—i.e., the "who" to be measured. If we ask questions of the wrong people, we will still get answers; they just will not be meaningful and could even be misleading.

How To Measure What Needs To Be Measured

Measurement involves a system of logical decision rules incorporated into a scale. Four scales widely used in marketing research are nominal, ordinal, interval, and ratio scales. These are listed in order of the least sophisticated to the most sophisticated in terms of the amount of information each provides. The scale classification of a measure determines the appropriate statistical procedure to use in analyzing the data generated through the measurement process.

The Nominal Scale

The nominal scale is the lowest level of measurement. It measures difference in kind (e.g., male, female, member, nonmember, etc.). Many people consider a nominal scale a qualitative classification rather than a measurement. It produces categorical data rather than the metric data derived from more advanced scales. While numbers may be used as labels (e.g., 0 for males, 1 for females), they can be replaced by words, figures, letters, or other symbols to identify and distinguish each category. Nominal scales are said to recognize differences in kind, but not differences in degree. As a result, nominal scales tend to oversimplify reality. All items assigned to the same class are assumed to be identical.

Summaries of data from a nominal scale measurement are usually reported as a count of observations in each class or a relative frequency distribution. A mode, or most frequently observed case, is the only central tendency measure permitted. Since the nominal scale does not acknowledge differences in degree, there are no useful measures of dispersion (such as range, standard deviation, variance, etc.). This scale calls for nonparametric statistical techniques such as chi-squared analysis.

The Ordinal Scale

The ordinal scale goes a step further than the nominal scale to introduce a direction of difference. If measurement can be ordered so that one item has more than or less than some property when compared with another item, measurement is said to be on an ordinal scale. Ordinal scales are frequently used in ranking items such as best, second best, etc. Such a ranking reveals position, but not degree. For example, if favorite vacation destinations are rank ordered, it may be determined that Florida ranks first, the Rocky Mountains second, and New England third, but it is not clear if all three are relatively close in desirability, or if Florida is much more desirable and the Rockies and New England are a distant second and third choice.

The most appropriate statistic describing the central tendency on an ordinal scale is the median. Dispersion can be quantified using the range, interquartile range, and percentiles.

The Interval Scale

Measurement is achieved on an interval scale with two features: (1) a unit of measurement, and (2) an arbitrary origin. Temperature, for example, is measured by interval scales. Each scale has a unit of measurement, a degree of temperature. An interval scale indicates a difference, a direction of difference, and a magnitude of difference, with the amount expressed in constant scale units. The difference between 20 and 30 degrees represents the same difference and direction as the difference between 100 and 110 degrees.

The arbitrary origin of the interval scale means there is no natural origin or zero point from which the scale derives. For example, though both Fahrenheit and Celsius scales are used to measure temperature, each has its own zero point.

The arithmetic mean is the most common measure of central tendency or average. Dispersion about the mean is measured by the standard deviation. Many researchers will assume their measures are interval level measures to permit the use of more powerful statistical procedures. Great care must be used here to avoid the use of inappropriate statistical procedures.

The Ratio Scale

The most advanced level of measurement is made with a ratio scale. This scale has a natural origin. Zero means a complete absence of the property being measured. Properties measured on a ratio scale include weight, height, distance, speed, and sales. Measurement on a ratio scale is less frequent in marketing research than in the physical sciences. All the common descriptive and analytical statistical techniques used with interval scales can be used with ratio scales. In addition, computation of absolute magnitudes are possible with a ratio scale, but not with an interval scale. Therefore, while it cannot be said that 100°F is twice as hot as 50°F (it is not when converted to Celsius), it can be said that $2 million in sales is twice as much as $1 million in sales.

Table 6.2 is a summary of these measurement levels along with sample types of variables and questions used in their measurement.

Assessing Reliability And Validity Of Our Measures

In a perfect world our measures would exactly represent the construct under study, with no bias or error introduced into the measurement process. Since we live in an imperfect world we must expect that the numbers we collect in our research to represent our constructs will contain a certain amount of error. In other words, if M represents our measures (i.e., numbers) and T represents the true, accurate quantity of our construct we are trying to measure, we could represent the relationship as

$$M = T + E$$

where E represents errors introduced into the measure. Here we see that any numbers that are collected in the measurement process to represent the attributes of the construct of interest contain the true quantity of the attribute plus a certain amount of error. How does this error enter into our measures? There are several explanations why we might see a difference between the measured value and the true value:[11]

Table 6.2 Scales of Measurement

Measure	Results	Sample questions	Measure of central tendency
Nominal	Classification of variables	Which brand do you own? A ___ B ___ C ___	Mode
Ordinal	Order of variables	Rank your preference for stores. First ___ Second ___ Third ___	Median
Interval	Differences in variables	The salespeople were friendly. Strongly agree ___ Agree ___ Neutral ___ Disagree ___ Strongly disagree	Mean
Ratio	Absolute magnitude of differences in variables	What was your sales volume by store last year? Store A $___ Store B $ ___ Store C $ ___	Mean, geometric mean

Source: Adapted from Robert F. Hartley, George E. Prough, and Alan B. Flaschner, *Essentials of Marketing Research*, 1983, p. 145. Tulsa, OK: PennWell Books, Inc

1   short-term characteristics of the respondent such as mood, health, fatigue, stress, etc.;
2   situational factors such as distractions or other variations in the environment where the measures are taken;
3   data-collection factors introducing variations in how questions are administered (e.g., different tone of voice for different interviewers, etc.) and variations introduced by the interviewing method itself (i.e., Internet, phone, mail, personal contact);
4   measuring instrument factors such as the degree of ambiguity and difficulty of the questions and the ability of the respondent to provide answers;
5   data-analysis factors introduced during the coding and tabulation process.

Reliability

A reliable measure is one that consistently generates the same result over repeated measures. For example, if a scale shows that a standardized 1 lb weight actually weighs 1 lb when placed on the scale today, tomorrow, and next Tuesday, then it appears to be a reliable scale. If it reads a different weight, then it is unreliable, the degree of unreliability indicated by how frequently and by how much it reads an inaccurate weight. A reliable scale will also indicate that a different weight placed on the scale consistently shows a different measure than the 1 lb weight (i.e., a scale is not reliable if it says a 1 lb weight weighs 1 lb consistently, but says every other weight is also 1 lb because it is stuck on that measure). We can determine whether our measures of psychological constructs are reliable using one of several types of tests.

• *Test-Retest Reliability.* The objective with test-retest reliability assessment is to measure the same subjects at two different points in time under approximately the same conditions as possible and compare results. If there was actually no change in the object of measurement (e.g., someone's preferences, attitudes, etc.), a reliable measuring device (e.g., questionnaire) would generate the same results. Obvious problems are that it may not be possible to get the same respondents to respond to the test, the measurement process itself may alter the second responses, and conditions may be difficult to duplicate.

- *Alternative Form.* The deficiencies of test-retest reliability measures can be overcome to some degree by using an alternative form of the measuring device. If you have at least two equivalent measuring forms (e.g., questionnaires), researchers can administer one form and then two weeks later administer the alternate form. Correlating the results provides a measure of the reliability of the forms.
- *Internal Consistency.* Measuring reliability using an internal consistency approach usually involves the use of different samples of respondents to determine reliability of measures. A typical way to assess internal consistency would be to use a split-half technique, which involves giving the measuring instrument (e.g., questionnaire) to all the respondents, then randomly dividing them into halves and comparing the two halves. High correlation represents good reliability. Another type of split-half comparison involves randomly splitting the item statements intended to measure the same construct into halves and comparing the results of the two halves of the statements for the entire sample. Again, high correlation of results (e.g., the way the respondents answered the item statements) suggests good reliability. Another way of testing for internal consistency is to use a statistical test such as Cronbach's alpha for intervally scaled data or KR-20 for nominally scaled data. These measures will indicate how well each individual item statement correlates with other items in the instrument. A low correlation means the item statement should be removed from the instrument. Cronbach's alpha is a common test done in Step 5: Purify the Measures of Our Measurement Process (see Figure 6.2). Also note that in Figure 6.1, reliability tests are using "measures" (e.g., data such as answers to questionnaires) to test whether our "operational definitions" (e.g., questionnaire questions) are reliable (e.g., internally consistent).

Validity

Validity is the extent to which differences found among respondents using a measuring tool reflect *true* differences among respondents. The difficulty in assessing validity is that the true value is usually unknown. If the true value were known, absolute validity could be measured. In the absence of knowledge of the true value, the concern must be with relative validity, i.e., how well the variable is measured using one measuring technique versus competing techniques. Validity is assessed by examining three different types of validity: content, predictive, and construct.

The *content* validity of a measuring instrument is the extent to which it provides adequate coverage of the topic under study. To evaluate the content validity of an instrument, it must first be decided what elements constitute adequate coverage of the problem in terms of variables to be measured. Then the measuring instrument must be analyzed to assure all variables are being measured adequately. Thus, if peoples' attitudes toward purchasing different automobiles are being measured, questions should be included regarding attitudes toward the car's reliability, safety, performance, warranty coverage, cost of ownership, etc., since those attributes constitute attitudes toward automobile purchase.

Content validity rests on the ability to adequately cover the most important attributes of the concept being measured. It is testing to determine how well we have specified the domain of our construct (see Figure 6.1). It is one of the most common forms of validity addressed in "practical" marketing research. A common method of testing for content validity is to ask "experts" to judge whether the item statements are what they purport to be. For example, if you are trying to develop item statements intended to measure customer satisfaction with the content of a website you could get several experts on customer satisfaction for websites to judge the adequacy of your item statements, or use item statements previously found to have passed content validity tests.

Predictive or *pragmatic* validity reflects the success of measures used for estimating purposes. The researcher may want to predict some outcome or estimate the existence of some current behavior or condition. The measure has predictive validity if it works (see Figure 6.1). For example, the ACT test required of most college students has proved useful in predicting success in college courses. Thus, it is said to have predictive validity. Correlation of the independent (ACT test score) and dependent (college GPA) variables is often used to test for predictive validity.

Construct validity involves the desire to measure or infer the presence of abstract characteristics for which no empirical validation seems possible. Attitude scales, aptitude tests, and personality tests generally concern concepts that fall in this category. In this situation, construct validity is assessed on how well the measurement tool measures constructs that have theoretically defined models as an underpinning. For example, a new personality test must measure personality traits as defined in personality theory in order to have construct validity. Construct validity is usually determined by testing to see if measures converge (i.e., convergent validity) when they are supposed to measure the same thing, but by different means or by different respondents, and discriminate (i.e., discriminant validity) when you are measuring different things. Construct validity is obviously important—if we are not really measuring what we thought we were measuring (e.g., we thought we were measuring brand loyalty but we were actually measuring store loyalty), we cannot have confidence that our decisions based on the research will achieve their goals. When two independent methods of measuring the same construct converge as expected (e.g., two different measures of the degree of a consumer's brand loyalty), then we have some degree of convergent validity (see Figure 6.1). When two measures diverge as expected (e.g., brand loyalty and eagerness to try a new brand), then we have some degree of discriminant validity. How each of these tests of construct validity are determined varies for different research studies.

Commentary on Reliability and Validity

As stated previously, researchers conducting research in order to make marketing decisions rarely conduct the kinds of formal tests of reliability and validity described here. However, it should be obvious to the reader that good research is "good," at least to some degree, because it generates data you have faith in as a picture of reality—i.e., it used a data collection instrument which could consistently generate similar results when used repeatedly (it is reliable), and it measured what it was intended to measure (it is valid). An illustration will help make the point about the wisdom of being concerned about these issues when doing research, even nonacademic practical research. Let's say our construct of interest is an "accurate rifle." If we were living on the frontier, an accurate rifle would not only be an abstract concept of intellectual interest, it could be a life or death matter! That is practical in the extreme! We want to do reliability and validity tests on the rifle before we "make decisions" based on its use, so we clamp it in a vise to make it steady (and remove the variability of the skill of the rifleman) and sight it at the center of a target a reasonable distance away. We do this at an indoor shooting range where conditions are held constant (so we can avoid the problems previously mentioned about environmental variables that can affect our measures). The rifle is then fired numerous times using a mechanical triggering device. Figure 6.3 displays several different possible results of our test.

As shown in (a), the rifle is very inconsistent (i.e., unreliable) in its shot pattern, and does not hit the center of the target very often (i.e., it is not valid as an "accurate rifle"). In (b), there is much better consistency (i.e., it is reliable), but it still fails to be what it is supposed to be—an accurate rifle. That is, the construct "accurate rifle" means it hits what it is aimed at, and the rifle in both (a) and (b) does not do that. Reliability is obviously less important than validity here. You would take little comfort in knowing your rifle could consistently hit six inches above and a foot to the left of a charging mountain lion. In (c) we see that the rifle can consistently (reliably)

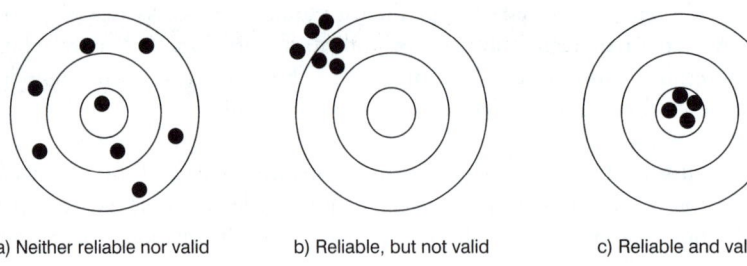

a) Neither reliable nor valid   b) Reliable, but not valid   c) Reliable and valid

Figure 6.4 Possible Results of Firing a Rifle to Test for Reliability and Validity of an "Accurate Rifle"

hit what it is aimed at (it is a valid "accurate rifle"), which increases our faith in it as a tool of practical value.

In the same way, we will have more faith in our ability to make good decisions if we believe the data we analyze to make those decisions were generated using valid and reliable data collection instruments. As mentioned at the beginning of the chapter, since we do not have a standard, calibrated set of results to compare our results to in order to know if the results are "good," we must determine if the results were collected using good measuring devices. If the devices (e.g., questionnaires, observation methods, etc.) are good, then we believe the results from use of those devices are good—that is, reliable and valid representations of the reality we sought to measure. For example, we want to be sure that our efforts to measure consumer preference and intention to purchase product designs A or B have accurately represented consumer actual desires and likely behavior, so that we can have faith in our decision to introduce design A instead of B because the research supports that decision.

If we do not know whether we can trust the results of the research, why do research at all? The alternative to good research is to make your decision and hope for the best. By doing marketing research we are saying that we want to reduce the uncertainty of the decision making process. But we can only reduce the uncertainty by a reliable and valid representation of the "real" state of our constructs of interest. So, even if formal methods of testing for validity and reliability are not used, it is the wise researcher who devotes thought to the construction of research instruments and using research methods that have proven over time to generate valid and reliable results. Interested readers should refer to some of the major works on the subject.[12]

Research Project Tip

Indicate how you will check to ensure that the results of your research are reliable and valid. This may not necessarily involve statistical tests, but should involve actions that check to ensure that you are in fact measuring what you say you are measuring and that the results are replicable. At a minimum you should indicate how you will test for content validity. Also, take special care in establishing your operational definitions. A careful and thorough literature search of research previously conducted on your topic is one of the best ways to improve the reliability and validity of your data collection instrument. You are able to better define the domain of your construct and perhaps even find questionnaires that have been tested for validity and reliability in the literature.

Measuring Psychological Variables

Measurement of most variables depends upon self-report, that is, by the respondents volunteering the information when asked, instead of through observation. While a state of mind is obviously not directly observable (e.g., you cannot see a "motive" for purchasing an item), many behaviors are also not observable. Consequently, marketing researchers must ask people to respond to questions intended to measure (attach numbers to) an attribute of a construct in ways that reveal the quantity of the attribute. Researchers have developed scales that are believed to capture the quantity or intensity of the construct's attribute.

Many of the states of mind mentioned are typically measured using scales developed for that purpose. We will describe several scales used for measuring various states of mind after discussing attitude measurement, a common object of measurement for marketing researchers.

Attitude Measurement

Attitudes are one of the most frequently measured constructs by marketing researchers. Why are attitudes of such universal interest? Because marketing-decision makers are interested in them. Why are marketing-decision makers interested in attitudes? Because they believe there is a close connection between the way a person thinks (i.e., their attitude) and what they are likely to do (i.e., their behavior). Why then, don't we just study behavior, since marketers are actually ultimately interested in understanding and influencing a person's behavior, not just their attitudes? There are several good reasons why marketers do focus on attitudes instead of exclusively on behavior:

1 Marketers may not have access to observation of or reporting of a person's behavior. The behavior may occur over a long period of time or in private settings only, and therefore observation is either not possible or prohibitively expensive. Also, sometimes the behavior itself is of a nature that people will not voluntarily report it, but will answer attitude questions related to the behavior.
2 Sometimes the behavior cannot be reported because it has not yet occurred. Marketers seeking to determine the best combination of attributes for a new product must ask attitudinal questions about the desirability of those features since the product itself has yet to be produced and, hence, there is no behavior that can be recorded concerning the product.
3 Attitudes, under certain circumstances, are reasonably good predictors of behavior. Consequently, by measuring someone's attitudes we can obtain a good indication of their likely behavior in the future. The connection between attitudes and behavior has, however, been the subject of extended debate among marketing researchers.[13] Attitudes can help us understand *why* certain behaviors occur.

If attitudes are such good surrogates for behavior, why do we hear of the marketing blunders like "New Coke," (see Exhibit 6.1) where making decisions on the basis of attitudes got marketers in some very hot water? The answer is that the research focused on only a limited set of attitudes toward the new formula versus the old (taste), and failed to measure other attitudes (how people felt about the idea of altering a formula for a product they had used for many years). Consider also the problems of using attitudes to predict behavior (see Exhibits 6.2 and 6.3).

In Exhibit 6.2 we see that peoples' attitudes toward their diet resulted in their being classified in specific groups. Separate measures of their behavior indicate not all of what they eat would be predicted from their attitudes. Why this inconsistency? Just as in the "New" Coke example,

Exhibit 6.1. Coca-Cola's "New" Coke Fiasco

When the Coca-Cola Company unveiled its formula for "New" Coke, executives were certain that it was the right move to make. They described as "overwhelming" the results of taste tests with 190,000 consumers, most of whom preferred the new recipe over old Coke.

The record is now clear that the introduction of "New" Coke ranks right up there with the debut of the Edsel as one of the greatest marketing debacles of all time. What went wrong? After all, if a marketer cannot rely on the findings from 190,000 consumer taste tests, then what good is research in aiding marketing decisions?

Analysts now agree that the problem was Coke failed to measure the psychological impact of tampering with a venerable 99-year-old soft drink brand. "When you have a product with a strong heritage that people could always count on being there, the mind becomes more important than physiological responses," said the research director for a rival cola.

Source: Adapted from Ronald Alsop, "Coke'sFlip-Flop Underscores Risks of Consumer Taste Tests," *The Wall Street Journal,* July 18, 1985, p. 27.

Exhibit 6.2 Do Attitudes Predict Behavior? Part I

Food companies have usually conducted their market research by asking people about their eating habits and preferences. Then they develop new products based on the results. The problem is that people do not always tell the truth. To counter this problem, NPD distributed the usual questionnaires to members of 1,000 households asking them questions about their attitudes on nutrition and food. In addition, the company asked each household to record in a diary every snack or meal consumed during a two-week period in each of the two years the survey spans.

NPD found that its subjects divide roughly into five groups: meat and potato eaters; families with kids, whose cupboards are stocked with soda pop and sweetened cereal; dieters; natural-food eaters; and sophisticates, those moneyed urban types. The study focused mainly on the last three groups because food companies are mostly interested in them. It was found that, as expected, each group frequently consumed the following:

*   Naturalists—Fresh fruit, rice, natural cereal, bran bread, wheat germ, yogurt, granola bars
*   Sophisticates—Wine, mixed drinks, beer, butter, rye/pumpernickel bread, bagels
*   Dieters—Skim milk, diet margarine, salads, fresh fruit, sugar substitutes

More surprisingly, however, each group was also found to frequently consume:

*   Naturalists—French toast with syrup, chocolate chips, homemade cake, pretzels, peanut butter and jelly sandwiches
*   Sophisticates—Prepackaged cake, cream cheese, olives (probably in drinks), doughnuts, frozen dinners
*   Dieters—Coffee, zucchini, squash

Source: Adapted from Betsy Morris, "Study to Detect True Eating Habits Finds Junk-Food Fans in the Health-Food Ranks," *The Wall Street Journal,* February 3, 1984, p. 19.

Exhibit 6.3. Do Attitudes Predict Behavior? Part II

Early lifestyle travel studies conducted by a Chicago ad agency showed a positive trend in the attitude that "meal preparation should take as little time as possible." It would be safe to predict, therefore, that during the same period consumer use of frozen vegetables would also increase.

Wrong, according to the agency's senior vice president and director of research services. "There was actually a precipitous decline in the use of frozen vegetables," he said, "when an extraneous factor entered the picture. During the years of the study, the real price of frozen vegetables increased sharply, especially when compared with the cost of other ways to simplify meal preparation. Remember that frozen vegetables represent only one of a number of acceptable ways to shorten meal preparation time. The link between the desire to make meal preparation easier and the use of frozen vegetables is neither necessary nor direct."

The ease of meal preparation/frozen vegetable case illustrates the point that broad attitude trends do not always predict specific trends in consumer behavior.

Source: Adapted from "Broad Attitude Trends Don't Always Predict Specific Consumer Behavior," *Marketing News,* May 16, 1980, p. 8.

---

we see that people hold a multiplicity of attitudes toward an object, and not all attitudes will be consistent with a specific behavior (solid lines indicate consistency, dotted lines inconsistency).

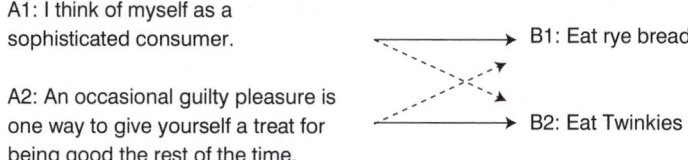

Here, we see that attitude A_1 is consistent with behavior B_1, but not with behavior B_2, while attitude A_2 is consistent with behavior B_2, but not B_1. In other words, because people have a *multiplicity of attitudes,* focusing on any one attitude (i.e., A_1) may not permit successful prediction of a single behavior (i.e., B_2).

In Exhibit 6.3, we see that people were increasingly in agreement with the attitude that meal preparation should take as little time as possible. This fact failed to lead to an increase in sales of frozen vegetables. Why this inconsistency? In this case a *multiplicity of behaviors* are possible, only some of which are consistent with the attitude concerning meal preparation time.

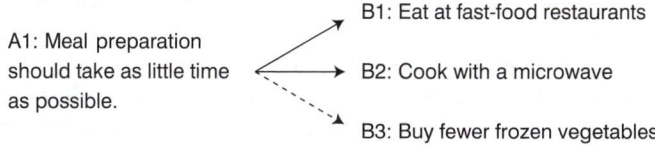

Lesson

Attitudes and behavior are complex phenomena. When we try to simplify what is inherently complex for our own convenience we often draw erroneous conclusions. We are seekers after truth, not simplicity. If truth is complex, let's try to understand its complexity. If it is simple, let's just be thankful for its simplicity. What these examples do tell us is that we must strive very hard to make sure we have correctly sampled the domain of the attitudes we are seeking to measure (i.e., have good content validity). For example, if we are trying to measure peoples' attitudes toward eating healthfully, we would want to have a number of item statements that would be divided among the three components of attitudes. Example attitude questions about eating healthfully might be:

		Strongly agree				Strongly disagree
Affective	I like the taste of healthy foods.	____	____	____	____	____
Cognitive	I believe eating healthfully will increase my life span.	____	____	____	____	____
Conative	I try to buy healthy foods whenever possible.	____	____	____	____	____

We would also want to correctly sample from the domain of the behavior of interest to us. We will now discuss the use of scales to measure attitudes and other psychological variables of interest to marketers.

Itemized Rating Scales

Itemized rating scales are just that—the points on the scale are "itemized," with a description of the scale point provided. Several choices confront the researcher using an itemized rating scale:

1   The number of item statements and scale points. Research has indicated that scale reliability improves, up to a point, with increases in the number of item statements and scale points.[14] So, for example, a questionnaire that asks for attitudes toward healthy eating is more reliable if it uses twelve attitude item statements (e.g., an example of an item statement is a declarative statement with itemized responses such as "I like the taste of most healthy foods" with responses like strongly agree, agree, neither agree nor disagree, disagree, strongly disagree), rather than three item statements, but thirty item statements is probably less reliable than twelve. Why? Because of the fatigue factor—respondents get fatigued in answering too many questions and their responses are made more to "get it over with" rather than as a true representation of their state of mind. The same is true for response points on the scale—five is better than three, but more than ten points does not improve reliability. Typically, the number of scale points vary between five to seven (see Figure 6.4).

2   Odd or even number of points. Is a scale with an even number of points preferable to an odd number, or is the odd number preferable? There is no hard evidence that supports either choice. The odd number provides a midpoint on the scale, while the even number forces respondents to "choose sides" (lean toward one end of the scale or the other). This remains a matter of researcher preference.

ATTITUDES

Strongly Agree	Agree	Neither Agree Nor Disagree	Strongly Disagree	Disagree
5	4	3	2	1

PERFORMANCE OR QUALITY

Excellent	Very Good	Good	Fair	Poor
5	4	3	2	1

SATISFACTION

Completely Satisfied		Very Satisfied		Fairly Well Satisfied		Somewhat Dissatisfied		Very Dissatisfied	
10	9	8	7	6	5	4	3	2	1

IMPORTANCE

Of Critical Importance	Very Important	Somewhat Important	Of Little Importance	Not At All Important
5	4	3	2	1

EXPERIENCE

Far Exceeded my Expectations	Exceeded My Expectations	Met My Expectations	Did Not Meet My Expectations	Far Below My Expectations
5	4	3	2	1

INTENTION

Extremely Unlikely	Very Likely	Somewhat Likely	About 50-50 Chance	Somewhat Unlikely	Very Unlikely	Extremely Unlikely
7	6	5	4	3	2	1

BEHAVIOR

Always	Frequently	Occasionally	Infrequently	Not At All
5	4	3	2	1

More Than Once a Week	About Once a Week	Two or Three Times a Month	About Once a Month	Less Than Once a Month	Almost Never	Never
7	6	5	4	3	2	1

Figure 6.5 Examples of Itemized Rating Scales

3   Use of "don't know" and "no opinion." The general tendency for interviewers is to discourage respondents from choosing a "don't know" or "no opinion" option when responding to a scaled item statement. Many respondents then select the midpoint of an odd-number scale as the default option. Obviously, researchers analyzing the data are then unable to determine how many people marked "3" on the five-point scale because that expressed the intensity with which they held an attitude, and how many marked "3" because they did not know how they felt, and chose the midpoint because it was the safest option available. These kinds of compromises to the validity of the instrument argue persuasively for a scale that provides for both a "don't know" and a "no opinion" option for respondents, and for instructions to interviewers to accept these responses from respondents.

It is generally conceded that itemized rating scales generate intervally scaled data, although there is an ongoing debate in the social sciences as to whether that position is defensible or not (some researchers believe itemized rating scales generate only ordinal data).

Likert Scales

Strictly speaking, a Likert scale is a five-point itemized rating scale with specific descriptors for the scale points. We list it separately here because it is one of the most frequently used scales for measuring attitudes. Developed by Rensis Likert,[15] it has undergone many variations over the years. It consists of five points of agreement for measuring intensity of an attitude.

Strongly agree	Agree	Neither agree nor disagree	Disagree	Strongly disagree

Variations have been made to turn it into a seven-point scale.

Strongly agree	Agree	Somewhat agree	Neither agree nor disagree	Somewhat disagree	Disagree	Strongly disagree

Or a bipolar scale, which is not technically an itemized rating scale since the points of the scale are not "itemized" with a description.

Strongly agree	____	____	____	____	____	____	____	Strongly disagree

The Likert scale is sometimes referred to as a summated ratings scale, because you can determine the strength of someone's attitude, positive or negative, toward an object by summing their scores for each of the item statements. Consider, for example, how persons A and B answered the following questions:

	Strongly agree 5	Agree 4	Neither agree nor disagree 3	Disagree 2	Strongly disagree 1
The hotel has helpful employees.	A		B		
The hotel is conveniently located.		A	B		
The hotel has reasonable rates.	A			B	

The summated rating score for person A is 5+ 4+ 5=14, and for person B it is 3+ 3+ 2= 8. Person A then has an overall more positive attitude toward the hotel than person B. Note that we would not then state that person A's attitude is 75 percent more positive (14 / 8 = 1.75) than person B's. Such a statement requires ratio-scaled data, and attitudes can never be measured on a ratio scale (there is no absolute zero point for attitudes). At best, a Likert scale generates interval data.

Rank-Order Scales

In a rank-order scale the respondent puts objects in an order of some variable under study (e.g., order of liking, preference, intention to buy, quality, etc.), generating ordinal data. An example of such a scale is shown below:

> Rank-order the following sporting events in terms of most desirable to least desirable for you to attend (1 = most desirable, 2 = second most desirable, etc.)
> —— Super Bowl
> —— World Series
> —— NBA Championship Game
> —— NHL All-Star Game
> —— NCAA Basketball Championship
> —— Masters Golf Tournament

The advantages of a rank-order scale are that it is easy for the respondent to understand and respond to, and it is a realistic representation of choice behavior (i.e., some objects would be purchased before others according to the rank order). The disadvantages are that the rank order appears without the researcher knowing his or her location on a like–dislike continuum. That is, all the items may be toward the highly liked end of the scale, or spread out along the scale so that number one is liked while the bottom numbered item is disliked, or all located at the disliked end of the scale (e.g., even the item ranked number one is only the least disliked of the entire group of disliked items rank-ordered). Another disadvantage is that data analysis is limited to those procedures permissible for ordinal-ranked data. Also, the respondents actual first choice may not have been included on the list, but researchers would not know this. Finally, we do not know how far apart the items are on the list in terms of desirability (e.g., 1 and 2 may be highly desirable and close together, 3, 4, and 5 are much less desirable and far down the list), and we do not know why the items were ranked in that order.

Comparative Rating Scales

The comparative rating scale (also called a constant-sum scale) requires respondents to divide a fixed number of points, usually 100, among items according to their importance to the respondent. The result provides researchers with some understanding of the magnitude of the difference between the items importance to the respondent. An example is:

> Please allocate 100 points among the items below such that the allocation represents the importance of each item to your choice of a hotel. The higher the number of points, the greater its importance. If an item has no importance you would assign no points to it. Please check when finished to ensure that your point total is 100.
>
> | | |
> |---|---|
> | Hotel belongs to a national chain | —— |
> | I receive frequent guest "points" for my stay | —— |
> | Location is convenient | —— |
> | Is good value for the money | —— |
> | Listed as a top quality hotel in guide book | —— |
> | Total | 100 points |

The task of allocating points becomes more difficult with a large number of items. Ten items are generally considered the maximum limit for the comparative rating scale.

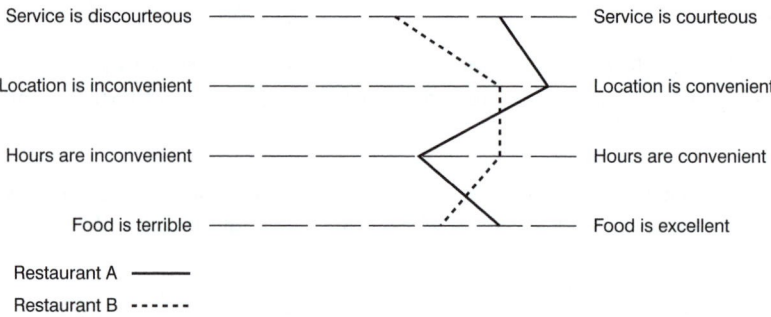

Figure 6.6 Profiles of Two Restaurants Using a Semantic Differential Scale

Semantic Differential Scales

The semantic differential scale is a seven-point scale using pairs of adjectives or phrases that are opposite in meaning. Each pair of adjectives measures a different dimension of the concept. The respondent chooses one of the seven scale positions that most closely reflects his or her feelings. A large number of dimensions would be needed to completely measure a concept.

Two forms of a semantic differential scaled statement are:

Clean	1	2	3	4	5	6	7	Dirty
The store was clean.	1	2	3	4	5	6	7	The store was dirty.

Again, the numbers assigned to the positions on the scale indicate order, so at least an ordinal level of measurement has been achieved, although many researchers assume interval level data are obtained through this method. Semantic differential scales can also be graphed to show comparisons by group or objects by plotting medians or means (Figure 6.6).

Stapel Scales

The Stapel scale is used as a substitute for the semantic differential when it is difficult to construct pairs of bipolar adjectives. The following example illustrates a Stapel scale for measuring airline performance on seating comfort.

	Delta	United	American	Northwest
Comfortable Seating	+3	+3	+3	+3
	+2	+2	+2	+2
	+1	+1	+1	+1
	−1	−1	−1	−1
	−2	−2	−2	−2
	−3	−3	−3	−3

Respondents would be instructed to circle positive numbers for when the adjective increasingly accurately describes the airline seating in economy class, and negative numbers when the adjective is increasingly less accurate in describing the airline. Stapel scales generate results similar to the semantic differential, but are easier to construct and administer, particularly over the phone.

Commentary on Scales

Some types of scales are designed to collect measures of a specific type of construct, while others can be used for more than one type of construct. For example, Likert, semantic differential, and Stapel scales were all originally designed as attitude-rating scales. They are also generally thought of as interval scales (i.e., generating intervally scaled data).

A comparative rating scale, in contrast, is an interval scale (or quasi-interval—scientists are not in agreement about this) that could be used to measure several constructs. See the following examples.

Motives. Allocate 100 points among this list of items with respect to their importance in selecting a university for an undergraduate degree:

Parents attended the university	_____
National reputation for quality	_____
Student-teacher ratio	_____
Cost of tuition	_____
Close to home	_____
Total	100 points

Preferences. Allocate 100 points among this list of items with respect to your preference for places to vacation:

Disneyworld	_____
Mountains	_____
Beach	_____
Golf Resort	_____
Total	100 points

A rank-order scale is similar in versatility to the comparative rating scale (e.g., could measure motives, preferences), but is an ordinal scale.

Example: Rank-order your preferences for places to vacation (first choice = 1, second choice = 2, etc.):

Disneyworld	_____
Mountains	_____
Beach Golf	_____
Resort	_____

See Table 6.3 for further clarification.

Table 6.3. Types of Scales and Their Properties

	Types of Data	*Used to Measure*	*Typical Number of Scale Points*
Itemized Ratings	Interval	Many different constructs (see examples in this chapter)	Varies
Likert	Interval	Attitudes	Five
Rank-orders	Ordinal	Several constructs	Varies
Comparative Rating (Constant-Sum)	Interval or quasi-interval	Several constructs	Varies
Semantic Differential	Interval	Attitudes	Seven
Stapel	Interval	Attitudes	Six

Summary

The researcher must be sure that the measurement process is carefully analyzed to ensure good measurement tools are used in research. All the questions of what, who, and how to measure must be dealt with to yield valid and reliable measures of marketing concepts. Failure to exercise care throughout measurement procedures can result in misleading information and ineffective decisions. The process of developing measures to be used in research projects should constitute a substantial part of the researcher's time and effort in the planning stages of each project. Using the proper scale for responding to questions measuring psychological variables is an important step in obtaining good measures. Care should be taken that attitude measures do not lead to improper and erroneous predictions of behavior.

Discussion Questions

1 Do you test for construct and pragmatic (predictive) validity before or after you use the questionnaire to collect data from respondents? Explain.
2 Discuss how a thorough literature search can help improve the validity of the measures you will obtain in the descriptive research phase of a research project.
3 Describe how you could use Figures 6.1 and 6.2 to develop a questionnaire that could be used to measure attitudes and behavior toward a healthy diet. Provide examples of questions that could be generated from this process. Discuss how you would test the questionnaire for reliability and validity.

7 Primary Data Collection

Learning Objectives

Upon completing this chapter, you should understand:

1 what is meant by the term primary data;
2 the different types of primary data that can be collected in a research project;
3 basic methods of collecting primary data;
4 the advantages and disadvantages of the different methods of data collection.

The search for answers to our research questions, or the tests of our hypotheses to determine whether or not they are supported by the information we collect, may require us to go beyond the examination of existing data. When we find ourselves in such a situation we are in need of *primary* data— data not available in a secondary form that must be collected to address the specific needs of our research. Research studies can be at any point on a continuum, which at one end answers all research questions with secondary data and at the other end where no existing secondary data can be used to answer the research questions (Figure 7.1). Chapter 3 provided guidance on how and where to look for secondary sources of information. In this chapter we examine the search for primary data.

It is important not to lose sight of how we arrived at the point of acknowledging our need for primary data. We are seeking to make decisions to solve a management problem (or assess a market opportunity, etc.), and we want those decisions to be *informed* decisions, rather than be based on hunches or guesswork. Consequently, we have identified a purpose for the research and a specific set of research questions to keep ourselves on track as we seek information to inform our decision making. Thus, the primary data we seek is in a form needed to answer a question, test a hypothesis, or in some way contribute to better decision making. We would know, for example, that we needed to measure consumer preferences because they were one of the criteria decision makers want to consider when choosing among decision alternatives (e.g., do consumers prefer product design A or design B). In other words, we do not "automatically" include any particular type of primary data in our research—there must be a reason for its inclusion, which ultimately can be traced to its contribution to making better decisions.

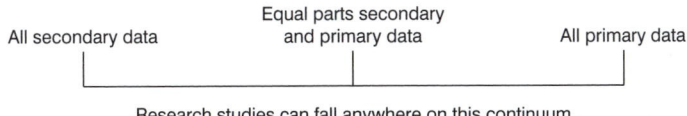

Figure 7.1. Continuum of Answers to Research Questions

Sources of Primary Data

Primary data originate from various sources. Some of the major sources are:

1 *The organization itself.* We generally think of the organization as a source of internal secondary information; however, the organization can also be a valuable beginning source of primary data for answering research questions (e.g., a survey of the sales force).

2 *The environment.* The market environment includes customers and potential customers, as well as competitors. Customers are very important sources of information related to their demands and intentions. An emerging factor relative to the market environment is competition. Competition is increasing in importance and the next decade will be one of severe marketing warfare among competitors. Customers, and even potential customers, can be surveyed and information can be gathered from them much easier than from competitors. It is difficult to obtain information directly from competitors, however. Competitive intelligence and analysis is an important type of primary data.

3 *The distribution channel.* Wholesalers, retailers, manufacturers, and various suppliers and users can be vital sources of information for an organization. In fact, the role of wholesalers and retailers has increased greatly in importance in recent years in many product categories.

Types Of Primary Data

Primary data come in a variety of forms. Some of the more common types of primary data are:

Demographic/Socioeconomic Data

Information such as age, education, occupation, marital status, sex, income, ethnic identification, social status, etc., are of interest to marketers because when combined with other types of primary data (e.g., consumption rates, attitudes, etc.), these descriptions help marketers profile target market members or other groups of interest. Consequently, through media plans, channels of distribution, and other ways, marketing plans can reflect the type of people who are our targets. In other words, this information is quite often of interest to us because the means by which we get our message and product to our target market is most often described in terms of demographic/socioeconomic data (e.g., magazine subscription lists, typical retail customers, TV viewers, etc.). The equivalent of demographics for industrial marketers (e.g., sales volume, number of employees, location, North American Industrial Classification System [NAICS] code, etc.) is likewise used in combination with other information for targeting purposes.

Another reason for collecting this information is to test hypotheses that are related to groupings of people by demographic/socioeconomic category (e.g., young people will prefer concept A and middle-aged people will prefer concept B; consumption rate is directly correlated with income; people with college degrees do this behavior more frequently than those with no college education, etc.).

Please check the highest educational level you have achieved:	
Less than high school	☐
High school graduate	☐
Some college	☐
College graduate	☐
Some graduate school	☐
Post-graduate degree	☐

Attitudes

Attitudes refer to a person's feelings, convictions, or beliefs for an object, idea, or individual. Attitudes are a common object of measurement for marketing researchers because it is believed that they are precursors of behavior. While marketers are ultimately responsible for influencing behavior, not just attitudes, we are not always able to observe and measure behaviors. For example, for a potential new product we may have to measure attitudes toward the product concept instead of behavior toward a product that does not yet exist. Also, attitudes help us to understand why people behave as they do, and marketers always want to know *why* behavior occurs, in addition to the frequency with which it occurs. Chapter 5 discusses some of the more common means of measuring attitudes.

I like the taste of healthy foods.	
Strongly agree	☐
Agree	☐
Neither Agree or Disagree	☐
Disagree	☐
Strongly Disagree	☐

Psychographics/Lifestyle Data

This type of data is concerned with people's personality traits, what interests them, how they live, and their values. It is sometimes referred to as a person's AIOs—activities, interests, and opinions. While empirical evidence linking someone's personality with their purchase and consumption behavior is weak, marketers find that combining psychographics and lifestyle information with demographics provides a "three-dimensional" perspective of a target market, permitting a much better focus to a marketing program.

If I have an hour of free time I would rather (check one):	
Read a book	☐
Watch TV	☐
Pursue my hobby	☐
Take a walk	☐

Intentions

Intentions refer to the anticipated future behaviors of an individual. This is a subject of interest to marketers who factor the planned behavior of their consumers heavily into marketing plans. Intentions may be specific to the research project under investigation, or may be the kinds of purchase intentions routinely measured by such organizations as the Survey Research Center at the University of Michigan. While there will always be some disparity between what consumers say they will do, and what they actually do, marketers feel that obtaining some measure of planned future behavior is useful in distinguishing the potential of several alternative offerings.

Read the product concept below and indicate the likelihood you will buy such a product:						
Definitely Will Purchase						Definitely Will Not Purchase
7	6	5	4	3	2	1

Awareness/Knowledge

Referring to what subjects do or do not know about an object of investigation, awareness, and knowledge is of interest to marketers who wish to distinguish the image, experience, feelings, etc., of consumers who are familiar with a product from those who are not. If I am interested in determining my brand's image, for example, I want to first determine which consumers are aware of and knowledgeable about my brand. Other areas for determining awareness (unaided or aided) and extent of knowledge are advertisement recall, retail store familiarity, manufacturers, country of product origin, and so on.

Which brands of riding lawn mowers have you ever heard of?
[Interviewer: Do not read list. Check all brands mentioned.]
☐ John Deere   ☐ White
☐ Simplicity   ☐ Case
☐ Craftsman   ☐ Lawn Boy
☐ Other: _____

Motivations

Motives consist of inner states that direct our behavior toward a goal. Other terms used to describe motives are urges, drives, or impulses. Our concern with motives centers around an interest in why people act as they do. When we ask respondents to indicate how important each of several product attributes is in influencing their choice we are attempting to identify what motives are influencing their behavior. Other ways of assessing motives include projective techniques (see Chapter 2), open-ended questions asking why people acted as they did, and a variety of other exploratory, descriptive, or even causal techniques intended to probe the needs that channel a person's actions.

How important are each of the following in influencing your choice of a laundry detergent for the first time?

	Very Important	Somewhat Important	Important	Not Very Important	Not at All Important
Advertisement	☐	☐	☐	☐	☐
Consumer Magazine Test	☐	☐	☐	☐	☐
Coupon	☐	☐	☐	☐	☐
Friend or Relative	☐	☐	☐	☐	☐
Sale	☐	☐	☐	☐	☐
Sample	☐	☐	☐	☐	☐

Behaviors

Behaviors are the actual actions taken by respondents. Marketers may have an interest in any number of specific behaviors enacted by selected groups of respondents, but typically purchase and consumption behaviors are of significant interest. Obtaining information about a person's behaviors might be accomplished through either self-report (e.g., asking someone to indicate how often they consume a particular product), or through observation, either disguised or undisguised, of a subject's behavior as it occurs.

How often do you go out to see a movie?
☐ Less than once a month
☐ Once a month
☐ Two or three times a month
☐ Once a week or more

Methods of Collecting Primary Data

The design of any research project is developed to obtain answers to the questions and objectives of the study. This will call for specific types of information and also indicate specific methods of gathering the data. The primary methods of collecting primary data are (1) *communication* and (2) *observation.* Communication includes various direct approaches of asking questions of respondents either by personal interview, telephone survey, electronic survey, or mail questionnaire. Observation, on the other hand, involves the process of viewing market situations either in the field or in laboratory settings. In this method of data collection, an observer records activities of the entity being observed, either in a structured (descriptive or causal research) or unstructured (exploratory) fashion. Sometimes the actions of interest are recorded by mechanical devices instead of using an observer.

Choosing Between Observation and Communication Methods

How does a researcher know when to use communication or observation to collect primary data? Each approach has inherent advantages and disadvantages that can affect the decision of when to appropriately use it for collecting information.

Advantages and Disadvantages of the Communication Method

Communication methods have the advantages of versatility, speed, and cost. *Versatility* is the ability to cover a wide spectrum of types of primary data. Examining our list of primary data types reveals that communication is the preferred (and sometimes only) method of collecting information on attitudes, intentions, awareness/knowledge, motives, demographics/socioeconomic, and behaviors (e.g., self-report of past behaviors). Obtaining accurate and truthful answers to questions on these topics is always a concern, but certainly communication methods are a versatile means of addressing the need for information in such areas.

Communication also provides the benefits of speed and cost. These two benefits are interrelated and refer to the degree of control the researcher has over data collection. It is much faster and less expensive to develop questions that ask people to recount their experiences (behaviors) than it is to set up an observational research process and wait for the behavior to occur in order to record it. A telephone interviewer, for example, may conduct four extensive interviews in the same hour the observational researcher is still waiting to observe the first relevant behavior.

Disadvantages of the communication method involve the lack of cooperation on the part of the research subject. Some subjects may either be unable or unwilling to answer questions. Perhaps worse than being unable to answer questions is when they do not recall the facts in questions yet invent an answer so as to not disappoint the interviewer! Another disadvantage, then, is the bias in responses that may be introduced in the process of asking questions. We will discuss this at greater length in Chapter 8.

Advantages and Disadvantages of the Observation Method

Observation has several advantages over the communication method. The disadvantages of the communication method—inability or unwillingness for subject to communicate, interviewer bias—are not present with observation. Also, some types of behavior, such as observing small children at play or solving problems, lend themselves much more readily to observational study than communication. Observational information is thought to have an advantage over communication in objectivity and accuracy. Subjects wishing to portray themselves in the most positive light will respond to questions accordingly, but when unknowingly observed, a record of their behavior may reflect more objectivity and accuracy. Also, descriptive observational research, such as scanner data from a supermarket, generates more accurately and objectively determined data than achieved by communication (e.g., trying to recall purchases and list them on a questionnaire).

Two disadvantages characterize the observation method. First, some information internal to subjects such as attitudes, intentions, motives, etc., cannot be observed. It is important to remember this when tempted to attribute such things to people based on an observation of their behavior. For example, you might observe someone examining the back of a food carton and believe they are studying the product's nutritional content when they were looking for the name of the producer. Second, the observed behavior must be of short duration and occur frequently enough to permit a cost-effective plan for its measurement.

Often communication may be productively combined with observation to gain the benefits of both, with none of the disadvantages, since the disadvantages of one method are the advantages of the other. The usual sequence would be to observe behavior and then ask questions about why the person behaved as he or she did. For example, if a company were trying to build a better infant highchair they might observe mothers feeding their infants using currently available brands, then ask what they liked or disliked about them, why they performed particular acts in using the highchairs, etc.

Research Project Tip

When writing up the preliminary results of your research you should describe the methodology you used in detail. It is not enough, for example, to say you conducted a search of the literature and then completed four in-depth interviews with consumers. You should describe the databases you used in your search, the key words used in searching the computer databases (e.g., LexisNexis), include a photocopy of the printout of the results of the search (e.g., articles list, abstracts, or first page of published article or report). In-depth interviews should indicate the criteria you used in selecting people to interview, a description of the people interviewed, a copy of interview guides, etc.

Communication Methods

At the risk of repeating ourselves, we will note that the communication method (and observation too) can be used for information collection using exploratory, descriptive, or causal research designs. As we have already indicated, the most commonly used communication method, the survey, can be used in all three research designs, although it is most commonly thought of as a primary tool of descriptive research. We will discuss a common exploratory research communication method—focus groups—then discuss the descriptive communication survey research method.

Exploratory Communication—Focus Group Interviewing

As discussed in Chapter 4, one of the most popular exploratory research techniques, focus group interviewing, consists of a small group of people (usually eight to twelve) assembled for the purpose of discussing in an unstructured, spontaneous manner topics introduced by a group moderator. The objective of conducting focus groups is *not* to accomplish the goals of a survey at a lower cost. In fact, focus groups, as an exploratory research technique, cannot be substituted for a descriptive research's survey design.

Focus Group Composition

Conventional industry wisdom suggests that focus groups should consist of eight to twelve people selected to be homogeneous along some characteristic important to the researcher (e.g., do a lot of baking, own foreign luxury cars, manage their own retirement account with more than $100,000 invested, etc.). Usually recruitment of focus group participants strives to find people who fit the desired profile but who do not know each other—thus reducing the inhibitions of group members to describe their actual feelings or behaviors. Typically, group sessions last from one and a half to two hours. Going against such conventional wisdom may be necessary in some cases. For example, one of the authors conducted research for a food company that wanted a few direct questions asked prior to presenting participants with prepared versions of their food products, as well as their competitor's. While not a taste test per se, the client wanted to hear the subjects' reactions to the products and a discussion of the circumstances under which the products would be used in their homes. For this study a series of one-hour group sessions were run with five people per group. The more structured discussion and the desire to query each participant made the shorter time and smaller group more conducive to achieving the study's objectives.

Selection and Recruitment of Group Participants

The research objectives and research design will indicate the types of people to be recruited for a focus group. If a facility especially designed for focus group use is contracted with, the management of the facility typically will conduct recruitment of focus group members. If a marketing research firm is being hired to conduct the groups, they usually hire the facility; identify, recruit, and select the participants; moderate the groups; and make an oral and written report of the findings. Sometimes the client organization will provide a list of possible participants taken from a master list of customers, members, users, etc. It is usually necessary to provide *at least* four names for every respondent needed (i.e., approximately fifty names per focus group).

Prospective participants are screened when contacted to ensure their eligibility for the group, but without revealing the factors used to assess their eligibility. For example, if the researcher is interested in talking with people who have traveled to Europe in the past year, he or she would also ask about other trips or activities to camouflage the central issue under investigation. This deception is helpful in discouraging respondents from answering in ways strictly intended to increase or diminish chances for an invitation, and to discourage selected participants from preparing "right" answers for their participation in the group sessions. It is advisable to provide a general idea of the topic for discussion (e.g., personal travel) to encourage participation. Actual participants are usually rewarded with an honorarium (say $25 to $50 per person) for their time. The size of the honorarium depends upon the type of participant (e.g., physicians expect more than homemakers). The focus group facility's management usually covers the cost of recruiting, hosting, and compensating the groups in their fee. The following are six rules for recruiting focus group members:[1]

1   Specifically define the characteristics of people who will be included in the groups.

2   If an industrial focus group is being conducted, develop screening questions that probe into all aspects of the respondents' job functions. Do not depend on titles or other ambiguous definitions of responsibilities.

3   If an industrial focus group is being conducted, provide the research company with the names of specific companies and employees, when possible. If specific categories of companies are needed, a list of qualified companies is critical.

4   Ask multiple questions about a single variable to validate the accuracy of answers. Therefore, if personal computer users are to be recruited, do not simply ask for the brand and model of personal computer they use. In addition, ask them to describe the machine and its function; this will ensure that they are referring to the appropriate equipment.

5   Do not accept respondents who have participated in a focus group during the previous year.

6   Have each participant arrive fifteen minutes early to complete a pre-discussion questionnaire. This will provide additional background information on each respondent, reconfirm their suitability for the discussion, and help the company collect useful factual information.

Moderator Role and Responsibilities

The moderator plays a key role in obtaining maximum value from conducting focus groups. The moderator helps design the study guide, assists the manager/researcher who is seeking the information, and leads the discussion in a skillful way to address the study's objectives while stimulating and probing group participants to contribute to the discussion. The following are ten traits of a good focus group moderator.[2]

1   Be experienced in focus group research.

2   Provide sufficient help in conceptualizing the focus group research design, rather than simply executing the groups exactly as specified.

3   Prepare a detailed moderator guide well in advance of the focus group.

4   Engage in advance preparation to improve overall knowledge of the area being discussed.

5   Provide some "added value" to the project beyond simply doing an effective job of conducting the session.

6   Maintain control of the group without leading or influencing the participants.

7   Be open to modern techniques such as visual stimulation, conceptual mapping, attitude scaling, or role-playing, which can be used to delve deeper into the minds of participants.

8   Take personal responsibility for the amount of time allowed for the recruitment, screening, and selection of participants.

9   Share in the feeling of urgency to complete the focus group while desiring to achieve an excellent total research project.

10   Demonstrate the enthusiasm and exhibit the energy necessary to keep the group interested even when the hour is running late.

Reporting the Results of Focus Groups

In writing the findings of focus groups, care must be taken not to imply that results typify the target population. The groups were not formed in an effort to generate inferential statistics, but rather to clarify concepts, generate ideas and insights, make the abstract real, etc. Therefore, it is the qualitative rather then quantitative conclusions that should be the focus of the written report. Goldman and McDonald make the following suggestions about writing the report on focus group findings:[3]

1   The report should not be a sequential summary or transcript of the sessions, but rather a "logically organized and coherent interpretation of the meaning of these events."

2   The report should begin with an introductory section that reviews the research purpose, research objectives, and a short description of the research methodology. This is followed by a report of findings, the marketing implications, recommendations, and suggestions for future research phases.

3   An "Executive Summary" at the beginning of the report should cover the major discoveries as well as the relevant marketing implications that can be justifiably concluded based on the qualitative research results.

4   The results section is not necessarily best done by following the sequence of topics covered in the discussions. It may rather be approached as focusing on marketing problems or market segments, and discuss the findings from the groups that might have been addressed in diverse order during the group sessions.

5   The written analysis should progress from the general to the more specific. For example, a report on a new snack product concept might start with a discussion of general observations about snack eating, then go to a discussion of brand image and loyalty, then address the response to the new snack concepts.

6   The marketing implications section should provide guidance for the development of marketing response to the findings without overstating the conclusiveness of the qualitative findings. Everyone, report writers and readers, should remain aware of the limited objectives for conducting the groups, as well as the limitations of this type of research method in general.

Trends in Focus Groups

Several new variations in the traditional focus group approach are being successfully used by some companies. One is two-way focus groups, which involves conducting a focus group, then having a specific group of respondents interested in the comments of the first focus group view the video of the focus group during their own focus group session. This approach could be expanded to a three-way focus group setting. One of the authors of this text worked with a company that supplied food products to fine restaurants that used a three-way focus group approach. In this instance the first group consisted of patrons of expensive restaurants talking about their experiences at such restaurants. The video of these consumers was then viewed in a focus group of chefs and restaurant managers who commented on what they were seeing and were asked what they might do to address the needs of these consumers. The video of the chef's focus group was then observed by the food brokers used by the food service company who talked about what they could do differently to better serve the needs of the chefs. Managers from the sponsoring food service company attended all three focus groups (multiple groups of each "level" of focus groups were conducted).

Quads is another variation of focus groups that has been used. In these groups usually four respondents (hence the name quads) discuss a limited set of topics, perhaps engage in a taste test, and might complete a short evaluation of products. These take less time to complete than the usual focus group (less than one hour as opposed to one and one half to two hours), allowing for more of these to be conducted in an evening than traditional focus groups. The attraction of these quads is the ability to get 100 percent participation of respondents (in a ten person focus group participation by each person is more limited) on a short, specific set of issues, allowing observers to more easily focus on the differences in responses and generate hypotheses regarding those observations. Conducting more groups allows for more "fine tuning" of discussion questions and methodology and changes to be made from one group session to the next. Both two-way and quad variations of focus group approaches (and many more variations practiced by research firms) illustrate the flexibility inherent in conducting good exploratory communication research.

Internet focus groups are rapidly gaining in popularity. Internet focus groups are, like all focus groups, an exploratory research technique that capitalizes on the efficiency afforded by the Internet to engage people in diverse geographic locations together in a discussion of a topic of interest to the researcher and participants. Such groups can be conducted within a company with employees or externally with customers or members of a target market. If confidentiality is a concern with employees, they can use a hyper-link embedded in e-mail to go to a secure Web site where they can participate anonymously.

Internet focus groups with consumers have an obvious advantage in cost savings over traditional focus groups (approximately one-fifth to one-half the cost) as well as allowing for greater diversity among participants. Participants may in some situations be able to enter their input and reactions to other participants anytime during the extended focus group time frame—twenty-four hours a day. Use of IRC (Internet Relay Chat) and/or Web chat sites make it easy for participants to contribute to a discussion set up at that specific site for a specific purpose. It is then possible to immediately generate transcripts of twenty to thirty pages of verbatim responses for analysis. Advantages include speed of recruitment, savings in travel costs and time away from the office, respondents are able to participate from the comfort of their own home, and anonymity of responses. Disadvantages include a loss of observable information (e.g., facial expressions, body language, sense of excitement, confusion, etc.), which veteran focus group moderators use in analyzing traditional group sessions. Also, it is not possible to ensure that the person engaging in the focus group session is really the person you wanted. It is not possible to effectively screen people for certain desirable and easily verifiable characteristics (e.g., age, gender, racial background, etc.), and be certain the person on the Internet actually fits the desired profile. Also, unless the topic is about the use of the Internet itself, the people who are available for Internet focus groups may or may not be representative of the complete target market.

Some research companies operate Internet focus groups by recruiting and building a database of respondents from screening people visiting their Web site or through other recruitment methods. These people are then profiled through a series of questions, which allows the research firm to select respondents with the characteristics desired by the client organization. Potential respondents are e-mailed, asking them to go to a particular Web site at a particular time (using a hyperlink embedded in the e-mail). The "moderator" types in questions and responds, probes, and clarifies during the session by typing in queries

Sequencing of Focus Groups and Surveys

While the usual sequence of focus groups and surveys is to do focus groups first to generate hypotheses and then a descriptive survey to test the hypotheses, there are some advantages to doing focus groups after descriptive research as well as before. Advantages of conducting focus groups after doing descriptive research are:

1   Managers are not as likely to be unduly influenced by anomalous responses. When you have already determined the frequency with which certain behaviors are performed, you have a perceptual framework to use when listening to people describe their behavior and the motives behind it. When you hear something that deviates significantly from the norm you do not have to wonder if the person represents a significant number of people in the market, you already know the frequencies with which such behavior is performed. You can concentrate on probing to understand the relevant behavior.

2   The descriptive data allows you to better screen focus group respondents to ensure they represent the people you are most interested in understanding in greater depth.

3   You are better able to delve into the nuance of consumer phenomenon understood in statistical terms from the descriptive research. For example, identifying the statistical profile of your heavy users is undoubtedly useful information, but understanding what makes them "tick" and how vulnerable they are to competitor appeals may be best determined through qualitative (focus group) work.

4   Descriptive data will usually reveal information that cannot easily be explained with existing knowledge of consumers. Sometimes the statistics are merely puzzling, sometimes they are counterintuitive. The possible competing explanations of the data need to be tested through probing qualitative research to determine *why* the results look as they do. Without such probing, the explanation settled upon may or may not be appropriate, but if repeated often enough it will take on an undeserved verity which could be dangerous. Making the effort to check out the various explanations before making a decision could in some instances be the best money spent in the research project.

Other forms of exploratory communication techniques were discussed in Chapter 2. We will now discuss what is perhaps the most frequently used of all communication research techniques: the descriptive research sample survey.

Descriptive Communication—Survey Research

In the discussion of descriptive research in Chapter 2, we noted that the primary methods of collecting descriptive data were through cross-sectional sample surveys and panels. Panel data may be collected via surveys or through observation (scanner-based data or the like), but our concern in this section is to describe the use of the cross-sectional sample survey method of collecting descriptive data.

Surveys are frequently used to collect all the types of primary data described earlier in this chapter. Surveys generate data that make it possible to test various types of hypotheses that suggest relationships between those variables and between respondent groups. For example, we might use a survey to segment a consumer population and then test hypotheses that some segments are more price sensitive than other segments, or that some segments acquire more information by using the Internet than other segments. A test of a hypothetical relationship between variables might involve determining the degree of influence a set of demographic, attitudinal, or behavioral variables had in explaining a consumer decision (e.g., membership in a health club). As we will see in our chapters on data analysis, statistical analytical techniques to test such hypotheses require that the data being analyzed be collected through descriptive or causal data collection methods, and most frequently the method for descriptive research is a survey.

Survey Methods

Descriptive research surveys can be conducted in a variety of ways using many combinations of people and electronics and conducted in a variety of locations. Table 7.1 displays a few of the types of survey delivery methods possible from such combinations. We will first discuss the more "traditional" methods of conducting surveys by telephone, mail, or in person, then discuss some of the newer ways these methods and the computer and fax technologies are being used in survey research.

Telephone Interviewing

Telephone interviewing is usually employed when the study design requires speedy collection of information from a large, geographically dispersed population that would be too costly to do

Table 7.1 Survey Delivery Methods

Location of Interaction	Human/Electronic Involvement			
	Telephone	*Mail*	*Personal*	*Computer*
Home	WATS or IVR	Self-administered or panels	Door to door	Internet or disk by mail
Work	WATS or IVR	Self-administered or lock box	Executive Interview	Internet
Malls	--	--	Mall intercept	Internet
Central Location Research Facility	--	--	On-site	Computer assisted or Internet

in person; when eligibility is difficult (necessitating many contacts for a completed interview); when the questionnaire is relatively short; or when face-to-face contact is not necessary.

From the Home

In this case, interviewing is conducted directly from the interviewer's home. The interviewer has all the materials that will be needed to complete an assignment in his or her home and use the specified period (per instructions) on the telephone contacting respondents and conducting interviews.

From Central Location Phone Banks

A research firm may conduct interviewing from its facilities equipped with wide area telephone service (WATS). Central location interviewing has many advantages. It allows for constant monitoring and supervision. If an interviewer has a problem or question, it can be handled on the spot. Mistakes can be corrected; respondents can be called back immediately if the supervisor finds that the interviewer's information is not complete. Interviews can be monitored to ensure correct interviewing procedures and techniques, and that quotas are being filled. Since telephone interviewing is the most commonly used method of data collection, a detailed discussion on the specific procedures of telephone interviewing is located in Chapter 8.

Most market research companies now use some form of computer-assisted telephone interviewing (CATI) system. The survey instrument or questionnaire is programmed into a computer, and the "pages" of the questionnaire appear on the terminal screen in front of the interviewer. The interviewer can input the results either through the keyboard or in some cases by using an electronic light pen that can touch the appropriate response on the screen. The CATI System also provides for automatic skip patterns, immediate data input, and in some cases automatic dialing. This system promotes flexibility and simplification. In addition, increased speed and improved accuracy of the data are accomplished. Various programs of random-digit dialing can be attached to the CATI system. The computer-generated random-digit numbers can eliminate the sampling bias of unlisted numbers.

Predictive dialing is another important feature that makes telephone interviewing more effective. With predictive dialing, the technology does the dialing, recognizes a voice response, and switches to the caller so fast that the interviewer virtually hears the entire "hello." The system predicts how many dials to make to keep the interviewing staff busy without spending over half of their time just making contact. The system automatically redials no-answer and busy numbers at specified intervals. Some predictive dialing systems can be set to identify answering machines

Table 7.2 Advantages and Disadvantages of Telephone Interviewing

Advantages	Disadvantages
• Provides ease of making a contact (callback) with a respondent • Administration and close supervision is provided by professional staff at a central telephone center • Drawing representative samples of persons with telephones is relatively easy • Sequential disclosure, and questionnaire flexibility with skip patterns, refer backs, etc., is possible • Speed in gathering information • Simplicity at conducting a pretest • Access to hard-to-reach people	• Exhibits cannot be shown unless a mail/phone or phone/mail/phone methodology is used • Question limitations such as limited scales • Long interviews are difficult to administer by telephone

automatically and reschedule those calls as well. This results in more efficient calling and higher penetration of the sample list.

Increasingly, research firms are turning to interactive voice response (IVR) systems to conduct surveys by phone. In this approach respondents dial a toll-free number and respond to recorded questions either with a limited set of voice responses indicated (e.g., "Please answer by saying home, work, or both."), or by using the designated buttons on a touch-tone phone. Respondents may be members of a major panel (e.g., Market Facts, National Family Opinion, or Home Testing Institute), or just responding to a one-time survey. The use of IVR, or computer assisted telephone surveys (CATS), has been used to get quality data very quickly and has the advantage of letting respondents call anytime to answer the survey.

The advantage of having an interviewer ask questions of a respondent using a WATS line is, of course, the ability to ask open-ended questions where probing for response is needed and answer respondent questions or provide clarification when necessary. These needs may sometimes be greater than the needs for the speed and cost savings of the IVR approach.

Telephone Communication

As compared to personal or mail interviewing, telephone interviews have the advantage of speed and relative economy. Interviews of this type are also easily validated and the personal interaction of a qualified interviewer maintains a relatively high degree of control. The proper sequencing of question response also can be maintained. While not as flexible and productive as a personal interview, a well-designed questionnaire administered by a skilled interviewer can gather relatively comprehensive information. The interviewer also is in a position to probe at appropriate times and follow appropriate skip patterns. Weaknesses of the telephone interview are its inability to be as long or as detailed as personal interviews and its inability to show the respondent any products, pictures, or lists. Respondents sought at home may use caller ID to screen calls and not answer calls when they don't recognize the caller's number or see and "unknown name/unknown number" appear. Specific advantages and disadvantages of telephone interviewing are listed in Table 7.2.

Mail Surveys

Mail surveys are commonly used in either ad hoc (one time) or mail panel research. In ad hoc research projects a sample of respondents is chosen to be representative of the population of

Table 7.3 Advantages and Disadvantages of Mail Surveys

Advantages	Disadvantages
• Cost-effective • Efficiency in reaching large samples • Access to hard-to-reach people • Self-administered/no interviewer bias • Limited use of exhibits is possible	• Low return rate • Nonreturn bias; those who return a mail questionnaire may not represent the sample as a whole • No control of who fills out the questionnaire • No ability for sequential disclosure of information • Slow response • Hard to pretest • Question limitations

interest and a questionnaire is sent by mail. The mail questionnaire may be preceded by and/or followed by a telephone call intended to encourage participation. The combination of telephone and mail is an attempt to reduce the high rate of nonresponse that plagues ad hoc, and to a lesser degree, panel mail surveys.

When mail is used in surveying people at work a *lockbox* approach is sometimes used to avoid secretaries or assistants completing a survey intended for an executive. Here an accompanying letter tells the respondent the purpose of the survey and that the box is a gift, but the combination will be provided at the time of a phone interview. The respondent opens the box at a scheduled interview time, completes the interview and, in some instances, returns the survey by mail.

Mail surveys are sometimes dropped off at homes or work sites with the intent of having the respondent complete the questionnaire and return it by mail. Such an approach has been shown to increase response rates and has the advantage of allowing the person dropping off the questionnaire to explain the purpose of the interview.

Mail questionnaires allow for wide distribution. Also, the lack of interviewer/respondent interaction can give the feeling of anonymity that can encourage accurate response to relatively sensitive questions. In theory, the respondent has time to check records or even confer with someone else to make sure reported information is accurate. Disadvantages include a low response rate that results in nonresponse error. Control of the sample is minimal. Knowing the difference in results between those who participated and those who did not is not possible. Too often participants are those who are either more interested in the subject area or who have more free time to fill out questionnaires. Also, a mail survey is slow, less flexible, and does not allow for probing. Control is lost with a mail questionnaire and sequencing is difficult. Furthermore, researchers never actually know who completed the questionnaire. Many of these problems can be overcome through the use of mail surveys conducted by consumer panel organizations (see Chapter 2). Table 7.3 lists the advantages and disadvantages of mail surveys.

Personal Interviewing

This face-to-face method is employed when the survey may be too long to conduct over the telephone or there might be material to show the respondent. Personal interviews are effective when the interviewer is placing a product in a home or office; the respondent is tasting a product; or the sample necessitates contacting homes in a specific manner, such as every fourth home or going to every home until an interview is conducted, then skipping a specified number of homes before attempting the next contact as well as other applications.

Personal interviews allow for more in-depth probing on various issues and are the most productive, accurate, comprehensive, controlled, and versatile types of communication. There is ample opportunity for a well-trained interviewer to probe and interpret body language, facial

Table 7.4 Advantages and Disadvantages of Personal Interviewing

Advantages	Disadvantages
• Exhibits such as ads, packages, pictures can be shown • Flexibility and versatility • Speed can be accomplished with multiple interviews being completed in multiple locations • Sampling can be done in a very representative way • Observation of the respondent allows for viewing behavior as well as asking questions	• High cost • Interviewer bias • Administration/execution problems

expression, and other nuances during the interaction. Rapport can be developed that would put the interviewee at ease and gain his or her cooperation. The interviewer can explain any misunderstanding the respondent might have and keep the respondent on track and in sequence in responding to the questionnaire. In spite of the advantages of greater depth and productivity, the personal interview does take more time and money to administer. The advantages and disadvantages of personal interviewing are listed in Table 7.4.

There are several varieties of personal interviews. The most common are:

Door-to-Door Interviewing

In door-to-door interviewing, the client or field-service director will assign an interviewing location and often the exact address at which to begin. The interviewer then takes a specific direction in order to contact respondents according to the sample pattern that is specified to be followed. The interviewer will ask the questions and record the respondent's answers either during the interview or immediately afterward.

Central Location/Mall Interviewing

The use of a central location or mall area is effective in instances where respondents will taste a product, look at a package design, view a commercial, or listen to a recording or view a videotape and report their impressions. Shopping malls are frequently used because of their high volume of traffic. Other central locations such as a church meeting hall, hotel, or other facility might be used to conduct a large number of personal interviews. When this method of personal interviewing is used, the respondents are generally recruited in advance. Shopping malls may be used as locations for prearranged interviews or involve "intercepts" where shoppers are recruited in the mall for the interviews.

Vendor/Dealer/Executive/Professional Interviewing

Interviewing of executives at their places of business is the business-to-business marketing research equivalent to consumer door-to-door interviewing. Locating people of interest to the researcher by title or name can be expensive and time-consuming if an accurate list is not available from a list vendor. Once identified, respondents must be contacted, an appointment scheduled for the interview, and then the survey can be administered in person at the workplace. Highly trained interviewers who are appropriately dressed and knowledgeable about the topic are much more likely to be successful in obtaining response, so this type of interviewing can be costly.

Table 7.5. Strengths and Weaknesses of Methods of Data Collection

	Interviewing		Questionnaire		
	Personal	*Telephone*	*Self-administered*	*Mail back*	*Internet*
Response rate	Moderate to high	Moderate to high	High	Low to high	Low to high
Timing	Slow	Fast	Moderate	Slow	Fast
Cost/coverage	High	Moderate	Low	Low	Low
Interviewer Impact (bias)	High	Moderate	Low	Low	Low
Ability to handle complex questions	High	Low	Moderate	Moderate	High
Control	High	High	Low	Low	Low
Length	Long	Short	Long	Long	Moderate to long
Sample Control	High	High	Moderate	Low	Moderate

See Table 7.5 for the strengths and weaknesses of the "traditional" means of surveying respondents.

Computer Assisted and Internet Surveys

It is not uncommon for the computer to be used in telephone (CATI) interviewing, personal interviews conducted at shopping malls, or at a central location. See Table 7.6 for a summary of the various ways the computer may be used in survey research. See Table 7.7 for benefits achieved through the various computer-assisted survey methods.

Table 7.6 Methods of Computerized Data Collection Available to Marketing Researchers

Survey Methods	Characteristics
Computer-assisted personal interviewing	A method in which the researcher reads questions to the respondent off a computer screen, and keys the respondent's answers directly into the computer.
Computer-assisted self-interviewing	A member of the research team intercepts and directs willing respondents to nearby computers. Each respondent reads questions and keys his or her answers directly into a computer.
Computer-assisted telephone interviewing	Interviewers telephone potential respondents, ask questions of respondents from a computer screen, and key answers directly into a computer.
Fully automated telephone interviewing	An automated voice asks questions over the telephone, and respondents use their touch-tone telephones to enter their replies.
Electronic mail survey	Researchers send e-mail or web-based surveys to potential respondents who use electronic mail. Respondents key in their answers and send an e-mail reply or submit the complete web survey.

Source: Adapted from V. Kumar, David A. Aaker, and George S. Day, *Essentials of Marketing Research* (New York: John Wiley and Sons), 1999, p. 258.

Table 7.7 Computer-Assisted Data-Collection Methods

Benefits	Personal	On-Site		Telephone		Mail	Internet
	Computer-Assisted Personal Interviewing	*Computer Assisted Self-Interviewing*	*Fully-Automated Self-Interviewing*	*Computer Assisted Telephone Interviewing*	*Fully-Automated Self-Interviewing*	*Computer Disks by Mail*	*Electronic Mail Survey or Web-based*
Respondents need not have any computer-related skills	Y			Y	Y		
Allows respondent to choose own schedule for completing survey		Y	Y			Y	Y
Can easily incorporate complex branching questions throughout the survey	Y	Y	Y	Y	Y	Y	Y
Can accurately measure response times of respondents to key questions	Y	Y	Y	Y	Y	Y	Y
Can easily display a variety of graphics and directly relate them to questions	Y	Y	Y			Y	Y
Eliminates need to encode data from paper surveys	Y	Y	Y	Y	Y	Y	Y
Errors in data less likely, compared to equivalent manual method	Y	Y	Y	Y	Y	Y	Y
Speedier data collection and encoding, compared to equivalent manual method	Y	Y	Y	Y	Y	Y	Y

Source: Adapted from Scott G. Dacko, "Data Collection Should Not be Manual Labor," *Marketing News*, August 1995, p. 31. Reprinted with permission from Marketing News, published by the American Marketing Association, August 28, 1995, p. 31.

Internet Research

Earlier in this chapter we discussed the use of the Internet for doing exploratory research in the form of Internet focus groups. We will now discuss the use of the Internet for conducting survey research.[4] Some of the newer-based approaches will be discussed here. Several reasons have been suggested for explaining the rise in the use of the Internet for conducting surveys. First, the questionnaire can be created, distributed to respondents, and electronically sent to the researcher very quickly. Since data are electronically delivered, statistical analysis software can be programmed to analyze and generate charts and graphs summarizing the data automatically. Second, Internet surveys are less expensive than using interviewers or printing, mailing, and tabulating mail surveys. Third, it is possible to create panels of respondents on the Internet and longitudinally track attitudes, preferences, behaviors, and perceptions over time. A fourth reason is that other methods are not as cost effective as is the Internet for asking just a few questions. Another reason is the ability to reach large numbers of people globally very quickly and at low cost. Finally, Internet surveys can be made to look aesthetically pleasing and can add audio and video to the questionnaire.

Internet surveys can either be e-mail or Web-based approaches. E-mail surveys are simple to compose and send and allow for visual presentations (e.g., photos or video based stimuli) and interactive capabilities, and may not incorporate complex skip patterns. Most companies routinely collect email addresses from customers giving them access to using email related surveys of customers. Accessing noncustomer email addresses is a more difficult task and purchasing email addresses may yield mixed results due to spam protection programs used by hosting companies and changes in email accounts.

Web surveys, in comparison, are in HTML format and offer much more flexibility to the researcher, providing opportunity for presentation of complex audio and visual stimuli such as animation, photos, and video clips; interaction with respondent; skip patterns; use of color; pop-up instructions to provide help with questions; and drop-down boxes to allow respondents to choose from long lists of possible answers (e.g., "In which state do you currently reside?"). Based on answers to a set of screening questions, Web-based Internet surveys can direct respondents to customized survey questions specifically designed with those respondent characteristics in mind. These types of HTML format surveys can also be downloaded to the respondent's computer for completion and then either mailed or electronically sent to the researcher. Of course differences in monitor screen size, computer speed, use of full or partial screen for viewing questionnaire, etc., may result in different presentations of the questionnaire for different viewers. Also, computer navigation skills still vary widely across the population and must be taken into account when designing a Web-based survey. Designing Internet surveys adds another set of challenges to the researcher using questionnaires to collect data, and those researchers interested in using this medium should consult one of the recent publications addressing this topic.[5] Vovici (http://www.vovici.com/index.aspx) provides the ability for researchers to create customized surveys and collect data from variety of media for customer feedback.

A more recent source of marketing data for research is social media such as Facebook, YouTube, blogs, etc. One source indicates social media as a way to tap into authentic customer voices expressed in social media to help you understand what they love (and hate) about brands, categories, issues they are concerned about, and trends in buying products. (http://www.netbase.com/social-media-monitoring/social-media-research-workbench/)

Some of the movement toward the use of the Internet for survey research is due to the increasing number of people with access to and amount of time devoted to being on the Web. Set-up time can be as fast or faster than CATI, with faster survey execution (often the targeted number of completed surveys can be reached in a few days). Also, the ability of the respondent to choose the time for completing the survey gives it an advantage over personal or telephone interviewing.

Not everything about the use of the Internet for survey research is positive, however. At present one of the issues of greatest concern is the degree to which respondents to Internet surveys are representative of a target population. If the survey is meant to be projectable to a population with a high percentage of access to and usage of the Internet (e.g., university faculty, businesses, groups of professionals, purchasers of computer equipment), then this issue is of less concern. But when the survey is meant to be projectable to the "mass market" (i.e., U.S. population in general or a large portion of it cutting across ages, occupations, income levels, etc.), then conducting research by using the Internet exclusively is problematic. Descriptive research requires the use of probability sampling methods and use of the Internet may violate the "known and equal probability" random sample selection requirement, it is also true that email address directories do not provide all addresses with a known probability of being sampled. "In sum, e-mail and Web surveying of the general public is problematic and may be inadequate as a means of accessing random samples of defined populations of households and/or individuals."[6]

In comparison, the sampling frame for telephone interviews is well defined and its coverage biases are documented. With phone interviewing it is much easier to verify that the respondent is the person you targeted than it is with Internet surveys. Voluntary response at a Web site is particularly troublesome as a means of sampling a specified population with particular parameters (e.g., geographic, demographic, experience, etc., characteristics). Based on these problems, many researchers restrict Internet surveys to nonprobability-sampling based exploratory research. However, there are researchers who claim it is just as valid to use the Internet for probability-sampling based descriptive research as it is to use mall interviews or mail surveys. As previously mentioned, these claims for projectability are more valid when almost the entire target population has Internet access.

Another computer-based survey method is to put the questionnaire on a computer disk and send it by mail to the home or work location of the respondent. The computer disk contains the skip patterns for the questionnaire in its software. For example, if the question is, "Do you have a pet?" and the answer is no, the next question asked is different than if the answer was yes. Some of the same advantages and disadvantages regarding the use of graphics and other visuals, and ease of tabulating and statistically analyzing e-mail surveys are also true for computer disk by mail surveys.

A code of conduct providing guidelines for conducting research over the Internet has been developed by the Market Research Society and can be found at www.mrs.org.uk/standards/internet.htm. These standards, published in January, 2012, include the following sections:

- Definition of Internet research
- Co-operation is voluntary
- Respondents must not be inconvenienced
- Respondents must give their informed consent
- Researcher's identity must be disclosed
- Respondent's anonymity must be safeguarded
- Safeguarding data
- Client-supplied data
- Research with children and young people
- Privacy policy statements

Internet Research Suppliers

Some companies specialize in, or at least provide support for, conducting research online. Some of the better known suppliers are listed below along with their areas of specialization.

- Full service Internet research: Greenfield Online
- Designing questionnaires: Websurveyor(Vovici); freeonlinesurveys; SurveyMonkey
- Distributing questionnaires online and processing data: Harris Interactive; Knowledge Networks; Socratic Technologies
- Obtaining samples for online research: Survey Sampling Incorporated
- Analyzing data and distributing results: SPSS
- Reporting results and additional interactive analysis: ConsumerMetrics, Inc.; Burke Digital Dashboard
- Online panels: Lightspeed Research; Greenfield Online

Table 7.8 Examples of Data-Collection Methods Used for Generating Exploratory, Descriptive, or Causal Research Information

Data collection form	Research design types		
	Exploratory	Descriptive	Causal
Secondary			
Communication	Previous industry studies help to define what "customer service" means to consumers.	Annual survey revealing the number of times during the week people wash dishes by hand.	A journal article that reports on testing the hypothesis that public service advertising changes peoples' attitudes toward donating blood.
Observation	A Wall Street Journal article reporting that there are a growing number of magazines devoted to Internet usage.	Syndicated data indicating the market shares of various brands of coffee.	A report by a marketing research firm on the use of test marketing by different industries in the past year.
Primary			
Communication	A focus group of distributors that discusses tends in package handling technologies.	A survey of salespeople to determine the frequency with which competitors have given free goods to dealers.	Running two advertisements in matched markets and determining which ad resulted in greater recall and positive attitudes toward the company.
Observation	Watching production line workers using a handheld grinder and gaining insights on product design changes.	Recording license plate numbers in store parking lot and getting R.L. Polk to generate a map showing trade area and distribution of customers.	Doing a test market for a new product and determining if sales reached objectives.

Observation Methods

Observation involves the process of physically or mechanically recording some specific aspect of a consumer's activity or behavior. Some research designs call for this type of data. Some contend that observation is more objective than communication. However, observation, whether in a field setting or a laboratory, is not very versatile. Observation cannot answer questions concerning attitudes, opinions, motivations, and intentions of consumers. Observation works well when measuring specific behavioral variables but is less effective measuring attitudinal variables. Often a design that starts with unobtrusive observations followed by communication to obtain information about motives, attitudes, etc., behind the observed behavior, is an effective approach. *Direct observation* involves actually watching an individual's behavior. Their purchase behavior is watched or they are viewed while using a specific product. Sometimes this behavior is monitored in a natural setting or real-life situation. Observations can also be made in an artificial setting that is developed by the researcher to simulate a real-life situation. Quite often a contrived store setting is established to simulate consumers' responses to products in an "actual" purchase situation. A major advantage of artificial or simulated observation is the greater degree of control offered researchers to alter specific variables.

An observation may be accomplished with or without the knowledge of the subject. Obviously, the advantage of disguised observation is that the subject has no motivation to alter his or her behavior. *Mechanical observation* is sometimes appropriate to meet the study objectives of the research design. When this is the case various mechanical devices such as cameras and counting instruments are used to make observation. Eye motion, galvanic skin response, perspiration, pupil size, and various counting devices are examples of mechanical methods of measuring and recording activity. Eye tracking equipment can be used to measure where the eye goes in viewing an advertisement, a product package, or promotional display. A specific application of this technology would be to determine the impact of color in advertising and copy on a newspaper page. The tracking equipment records not only where the eye goes on the page, but also how long it focuses on a specific area. People meters are designed to measure both the channel that is being watched as well as which person in the household is doing the watching.

Summary

So far, we have discovered that the pursuit of answers to research objectives necessitates both a research design and data-collection methods that permit the execution of that design. "Good research" in any particular case could involve collection of information using one or more of the combinations of research design type and data-collection method. Table 7.8 illustrates that all combinations are possible. Which cell(s) a researcher should be in is a function of the research objectives, research budget, time available, and the decision maker's preferred data form for making decisions.

Discussion Questions

1   What things do you consider when choosing whether to use communication or observation in your research?
2   What differences exist between doing exploratory, descriptive, or causal observation? Use examples to illustrate your points..
3   What is the relationship between the 3 types of research designs, the 2 forms of data, and the 2 methods of data collection?
4   Do you use communication or observation when you are trying to understand someone's motives? Behaviors? Explain.

8 Designing the Data-gathering Instrument

Learning Objectives

Upon completing this chapter, you should understand:

1 the goals of a data collection instrument;
2 the basic components of a well-designed instrument;
3 the different types of questions that can be used in a data collection instrument;
4 the steps involved in designing a questionnaire;
5 how pre-testing can be used to improve the data collection process.

When we use the term data-gathering instrument, we typically are referring to using a descriptive research design data-collection method. That is because we do not think of collecting data per se in exploratory research (i.e., we are generating hypotheses, ideas, insights, clarifying concepts, prioritizing objectives for the next phase of research, etc.), and although we do generate data in causal research, we tend to think in terms of putting together an experimental design rather than designing a data-collection instrument.

The quality of the information gathered is directly proportional to the quality of the instrument designed to collect the data. Consequently, it is extremely important that the most effective data-gathering instrument possible be constructed.

As mentioned in Chapter 5, it is necessary to anticipate the total information needs of the project so the data-gathering instrument can be designed in such a way that it will provide answers to the research questions. The instrument must also gather the data in a form that permits processing it using the analytical techniques selected. As a result of its importance, the data-gathering instrument is the "hinge" that holds the research project together and must be done well.

A questionnaire is the main type of data-gathering instrument in descriptive-research designs. A questionnaire is defined in *Webster's New Collegiate Dictionary* as "a set of questions for obtaining statistically useful or personal information from individuals." Obviously, an effective questionnaire is much more than that. Since poor questionnaire design is a primary contributor to nonsampling errors, specifically response errors, the questionnaire should be well designed. The questions should minimize the possibility that respondents will give inaccurate answers. The questions that are asked respondents are the basic essence of a research project. Inquiring by way of interrogation through specific questions forms the basic core of survey research. The reliability and validity of survey results are dependent on the way the specific questions are planned, constructed, and executed.

Constructing a questionnaire that generates accurate data that is relevant to solving the management problem is not a simple matter. It is quite possible to construct a questionnaire that flows well from part to part, containing questions easily understood by respondents, addressing the issues identified in the study's research objectives, and lending itself to the appropriate analytical techniques, but totally failing to present an accurate picture of reality conducive to making decisions that lead to a solution of the management problem. How is this possible? As Patricia Labaw notes, a questionnaire is more than just a series of well-worded questions. "It is a totality, a gestalt that is greater than the sum of its individual questions. A questionnaire is organic, with each part vital to every other part, and all parts must be handled simultaneously to create this whole instrument."[1]

A questionnaire must provide data that allows the researcher to determine the information contained in Table 8.1. Without these contextualizing components, it is not possible to extract meaning from the answers respondents give to the questions in a questionnaire.

We need to include questions that reveal respondent consciousness, knowledge, behavior, and environmental situation so that we can know how to interpret, or extract meaning from the answers to those questions that are derived from our research objectives. While our research objectives provide guidance for what questions we will ask respondents, fulfill the research purpose, and permit selection from among our decision alternatives, thereby solving our management problem, those research objectives are not the only source of our questionnaire questions. We will only be able to derive meaning from the answer to those questions by using responses to the four components discussed in Table 8.1 as a "filter." For example, we can imagine grouping respondents, based on their answers to some factual questions, into two groups, those knowledgeable about the topic and those not knowledgeable about the topic, and then analyzing the responses by the knowledgeable group in our attempt to make meaningful conclusions from the data. In fact, answers to well-worded, relevant questions may lack meaning for several reasons:[2]

1   Respondents may not respond truthfully to the question, either to protect their ignorance or true feelings.
2   The questions were understandable, but failed to allow respondents to reveal how they really thought, felt, or behaved because of inadequate response options.
3   Respondents may answer without really being in touch with their own thoughts or emotions (this is a consciousness problem).
4   Respondents provide meaningful answers but they only provide a piece of the total picture. Other questions that could have completed the picture were not asked.
5   Respondents may answer the questions honestly, but the answers were based on incomplete or faulty knowledge. More knowledge might have changed the answers.
6   Researchers may impute meaningfulness to the answers when, in fact, the issues have no importance or salience to the respondents. They just answered because we asked, they really do not make their decisions by thinking about the issue. It is vitally important to us but not at all important to them.

Goals of a Questionnaire

Researchers therefore should take great care in designing a data-collection instrument that it is perceived in the gestalt sense—more than just a well ordered series of questions resulting from our research objectives. A good questionnaire should accomplish the following goals:

Contextualize the Information Collected

This is what we mean by collecting meaningful information, as outlined in Table 8.1. The researcher should include any questions that will aid in the interpretation of those questions

Table 8.1 Necessary Components of Questionnaires to Allow for Meaningful Analysis

Component	What it means	Evidence of it	Why it is needed	Example
1. Determination of levels of respondent consciousness	Does the respondent see or understand the implications of his or her answers to the questions?	Unconscious answers that are inconsistent, not based on objective reality, purely emotional, ignorant, or misleading	If data from answers reflect low level of consciousness, no amount of statistical analysis can help us to predict behavior	Respondent says in answer to one question that they don't believe in abortion "under any circumstances," then say in another answer that abortion is OK to save a mother's life
2. Delineation of the structures or environments affecting behavior	The physical determinants surrounding the respondent's behavior	Such things as age, sex, health, race, locale, mobility, etc., which impinge on respondents ability to behave in certain ways	People, despite their attitudes toward an object, may behave in ways different than their attitude would suggest because of environmental or situational constraints	While a respondent's attitude toward mass transit may be quite favorable, the key determinant of whether he or she will use it is whether it exists in his or her environment
3. Determination of levels of respondent knowledge	Does the respondent really have an understanding of the topic of the questions?	Ability to answer factual questions correctly	Lack of knowledge colors respondent attitudes and behaviors and makes decisions based on such responses very risky	Respondents may answer questions about the positioning of a product relative to its competition without possessing any knowledge of the product, making interpretation of the positioning map impossible
4. Determination of present respondent behavior in specific situations	Respondents reporting what they have already done	Responses to questions asking for the frequency with which specific behaviors are performed	Behavior acts as a measure of experience (or knowledge) with the topic as well as importance of the topic	Someone who smokes reveals more in that behavior than what might be revealed from answering attitudes about smoking (e.g., believing smoking is deleterious to your health)

Source: Adapted from Patricia Labaw, *Advanced Questionnaire Design,* 1980 (Cambridge, MA: ABT Books).

that are directly related to the research objectives. In other words, include questions such as those indicated in Table 8.1 and others, which can be used by the decision maker in the decision-making process, even if those additional questions are not directly related to the research objectives. A questionnaire is more than merely a conversion of research objectives into questionnaire questions.

Express the Study Objectives in Question Form

The questionnaire must capture the essence of the study objectives and ask questions that will provide the information needed to answer the various research questions. Quite often, a set of study objectives are adapted to an existing questionnaire that has been effective in the past. Care must be taken that one does not compromise the achievement of the current research study's objectives by trying to "force" a previous study's questionnaire questions into use in an attempt to economize time and effort. Each project with its unique set of study objectives should have a custom-made questionnaire designed especially for that project. The design of the questionnaire is the wrong place to try to economize during the research process. Judicious selection of questions from previous studies is appropriate in some cases, however.

Measure the Attitude, Behavior, Intention, Attributes, or Other Characteristics of the Respondent

The questions must be specific and reported in a form that will allow for comparisons to be made and results to be analyzed. The responses to the questions must provide the information that is necessary to answer the research questions and in a format that can be subjected to the appropriate analytical technique (techniques of analysis will be discussed in Chapters 11 and 12).

Create Harmony and Rapport with the Respondent

A well-designed questionnaire targeted at the correct population sample should provide an enjoyable experience for the respondent. The frame of reference of the respondent must be considered in the design, wording, and sequencing of a questionnaire. Occupational jargon, cultural background, educational level, and regional differences can alter the effectiveness of a questionnaire if they are not taken into consideration. Not only should the questionnaire appeal to the respondent, it should be designed so the respondent can easily understand it, be able to answer it, and be made willing to answer it.

Provide Just the Right Amount of Information: No More, No Less

This is a trite statement, but it has much truth to it. There are often honest differences of opinion on just how much information is needed to answer a set of research questions. However, in designing a questionnaire the two basic mistakes are leaving an important question unasked, which makes the survey incomplete, and asking too many irrelevant questions, which makes the survey too long and unwieldy. A researcher must learn to economize in asking questions to avoid respondent burnout, which leads to early terminations, and incomplete and inaccurate information. However, care must be taken in the design process to be sure the proper quantity of information is gathered to accomplish the research objectives.

Classification of Questions

Questions can be classified in terms of their degree of *structure* and *disguise*. By structure we mean the degree to which the question and the responses are standardized at some point in the data-collection process. When a questionnaire is classified according to disguise, it depends on how evident the purpose of the question or questionnaire is. An undisguised questionnaire is one in which the purpose of the research is obvious to the respondent because of the questions asked. A disguised questionnaire obscures the purpose of the research and tries to indirectly get at a respondent's point of view. Of course the sponsor of the research may or may not be revealed to the respondent before he or she answers the questions, but this is not what is meant by "disguise."

Based on the classification of questions according to structure and disguise, the following general types emerge.

Structured-Undisguised Questions

Structured-undisguised questions are the most commonly used in research today. Every respondent is posed the same questions in the same sequence, with the same opportunity of response. In most cases the purpose of the research is clearly stated in an introductory statement or is obvious from the questions asked. This type of instrument has the advantages of simplicity in administration, tabulation, and analysis; standardized data collection; objectivity; and reliability. The disadvantages include lack of flexibility in changing questions "on the fly."

Structured-Disguised Questions

Structured-disguised questions are probably the least used questions in market research. They maintain the advantages of structuring while attempting to add the advantage of disguise in eliminating possible bias from the respondent's knowledge of the purpose of the survey. The main advantages of this type of questionnaire are ease of administration, coding, and tabulating. An additional advantage is to gain insight on a sensitive issue without "tipping" your hand to the respondent. The problem with this type of research is the difficulties encountered in interpreting the respondent's answer. An example of a structured-disguised question would be:

> Which of the following types of people would eat a lot and which would eat a little hot cereal?

	Eat a lot	Eat a little
Professional athletes	_____	_____
Wall Street bankers	_____	_____
Farmers	_____	_____
College teachers	_____	_____

The structure is obvious. The disguise is related to the purpose of the questions, which is to use the responses to determine the image people have of hot cereal. It is easy to tabulate the responses but considerably more difficult to interpret what the responses mean with regard to the respondents' image of the product (e.g., What does it mean that 23 percent of respondents said professional athletes eat a lot of hot cereal, while 18 percent said they eat only a little compared to 31 percent and 22 percent respectively for college teachers?).

Unstructured-Undisguised Questions

Unstructured-undisguised questions are appropriate for in-depth interviews and focus group interviews. They allow the interviewer or moderator to begin with a general question or series of questions and allow the discussion to develop following a general series of questions in a discussion guide. Because of the nature of these types of questions, the effectiveness of the depth or focus group interview depends largely upon the skills of the interviewer or moderator. Advantages of this method are that more in-depth and accurate responses can be obtained, particularly for complex and sensitive issues, and greater cooperation and involvement can be obtained from the respondent. The unstructured-undisguised interview is well-suited for exploratory research, gaining background, and generating and clarifying research questions.

Unstructured-Disguised Questions

Unstructured-disguised questions are often used in motivation research to determine the "whys" of an individual's behavior. Projective methods are often used to get at the subtle issues that are not easily explored by direct questioning. Word association, storytelling, and sentence completion are methods that can be used to try to gain information about a subject without revealing the actual purpose of the research (see Chapter 5).

Descriptive-research questionnaires largely consist of structured-undisguised questions. They are highly structured data-gathering instruments, compared to the less structured instruments used in focus groups or in-depth interview guides. In the descriptive-research questionnaire each respondent hears (or sees) the same question, and has the same response options. This is obviously true with questions such as:

> Would you say you eat away from home more often, less often, or about the same as you did three years ago?
>
> More _____   Less _____   Same _____

Here, both the question and the response categories are highly structured. Open-ended questions are structured but the response is not, at least at the point of gathering the data. An example of an open-ended question:

> [If said "less"]
> Why do you eat away from home less often than you did three years ago?
> _____
> _____

The respondent could give any explanation to the interviewer or write in any response if the respondent were completing the questionnaire alone. The responses become structured when the researcher develops categories of the answers based on the type and frequency of the responses (e.g., the number of times the researcher sees an answer such as "I work at home now whereas I used to eat lunch out every day at work" or "Our household income has decreased and we cannot afford to eat out as often"). The researcher may establish a number of different categories of responses after considering all the responses and then tabulate the responses for all completed questionnaires by categories. Thus, what appears to be an unstructured question is in fact structured as a question before asked and as an answer after it has been asked (i.e., open-ended questions are still structured-undisguised).

Another way of collecting information is when the respondent hears what appears to be the same open-ended question in a phone or personal interview, but the interviewer categorizes the response into predetermined categories at the time the question is asked, such as:

[If "less often" indicated in previous question asked]
Why do you eat away from home less often than you did three years ago? [CHECK ALL THAT APPLY]

___ Economics/less money/lower income
___ Change in household members/circumstance
___ Changed jobs, etc.
___ Other [WRITE IN VERBATIM]

_____

_____

Instructions to the interviewer are in brackets and upper case or capital letters. In this example the interviewer exercises the judgment in categorizing the response (the respondent hears only the questions, the responses are not read). Response categories may have been established based on exploratory research or previous descriptive studies. If a response does not fit any of the given categories the interviewer is to record the verbatim response, allowing the researcher to later establish new categories to capture the unanticipated responses. The researcher must balance the ease of tabulating and lower expense of having structured responses with the flexibility and "richness" of the more expensive open-ended responses that must later be structured.

Designing a Questionnaire

There is no single generally accepted method for designing a questionnaire. Various research texts have suggested procedures ranging from four to fourteen sequential steps. Questionnaire design, no matter how formalized, still requires a measure of science and a measure of art with a good dose of humility mixed in. In designing a questionnaire, presumption must be set aside. Although for simplicity of format, the sequence for developing a questionnaire is given on a step-by-step basis, rarely is a questionnaire constructed in such a routine way. Quite often it is necessary to skip from one step to another and to loop back through a previous series of steps.

The following steps represent a sequential procedure that needs to be considered for the development of an effective survey instrument.

- *Step 1:* Determine the specific information needed to achieve the research objectives.
- *Step 2:* Identify the sources of the required information.
- *Step 3:* Choose the method of administration that suits the information required and the sources of information.
- *Step 4:* Determine the types of questions to be used and form of response.
- *Step 5:* Develop the specific questions to be asked.
- *Step 6:* Determine the sequence of the questions and the length of the questionnaire.
- *Step 7:* Predetermine coding.
- *Step 8:* Pretest the questionnaire.
- *Step 9:* Review and revise the questionnaire.

Remember that a questionnaire is a "measurement" device, and all the procedures discussed in Chapter 6 on how to develop more scientific measures apply here as well (see Figure 6.2). A brief discussion of each of the questionnaire development steps follows.

Determine the Specific Information Needed

The initial step to be taken in the design of a questionnaire is to determine the specific information needed to achieve the research objectives—answer the research questions and test the hypotheses. Or, another way of thinking of this step is that you are specifying the domain of the constructs of interest and determining the constructs' attributes (Chapter 6). This task can be made much easier if the earlier phases of the research process have been precisely accomplished. Clear study objectives facilitate this important decision. One of the most common and costly errors of research is the omission of an important question on the data-gathering instrument. Once the questionnaire is fielded, it is too late to go back for additional information without significant delay and additional cost.

The researcher must determine all of the information required before the questionnaire is developed. Sometimes the articulation of research objectives into specific questions by setting up dummy tables to be used when analyzing the results will trigger a new idea or research question that should be included in the survey. Every effort needs to be marshaled at this point of the design process to ensure relevant results for the analysis phase of the research process. In some cases it is advisable to conduct exploratory research to ensure that all of the relevant variables are identified. Focus groups, reviews of secondary sources of information, and some selected personal interviews are good ways of making sure that the pertinent variables are identified. Also, contextualizing information such as is listed in Table 8.1 should be determined.

Identify the Sources

Step 2 involves the important aspect of identifying the sources of the information requirements determined in Step 1. Sample selection will be discussed in more detail in Chapter 9; however, the characteristics of the sample frame are extremely important in designing the data-gathering instrument. The sophistication, intelligence, frame of reference, location, ethnic background, and other characteristics of the potential respondents are vital to determining the type of questionnaire, the wording of questions, the means of administration, as well as other aspects of the questionnaire. Consider, for example, the difference in the design of a questionnaire if the questions are asked of ten-year-old children or twenty-year-old college students.

Choose the Method of Administration

Step 3 involves utilizing the results of Steps 1 and 2 to decide whether the Internet, or a personal interview, telephone survey, or mail questionnaire is most acceptable. Issues such as whether a stimulus is required, the length of the questionnaire, the complexity of the questions, and the nature of the issue being researched must be considered in choosing which type of survey is best. These decisions should be made with respect to the information required and the nature of the sources of the information. Other considerations that affect this decision are the cost and time constraints placed on the research project (see Chapter 7).

Determine the Types of Questions

Step 4 involves choosing the types of questions to be used in the questionnaire. To accomplish this the researcher must look both backward and forward. The researcher looks back to review the information required and the nature of the respondents. This can dictate various decisions concerning the types of questions selected. The researcher must also look forward to the analysis stage of the research process to ensure that the right form of data is obtained to accommodate the proper analytical techniques.

There are four basic types of questions that might be used in a questionnaire: (a)open-ended, (b) dichotomous, (c) multichotomous, and (d) scales. Most questionnaires have more than one type of question.

Open-Ended Questions

Open-ended questions such as "What did you like about the product?" provide an unlimited range of replies the respondent can make. The major advantages and uses of this type question are that they can be used when the possible replies are unknown, when verbatim responses are desired, and when gaining deep insight into attitudes on sensitive issues is needed. Open-ended questions are also useful to break the ice with the respondent and provide background information for more detailed questions. As discussed earlier, these questions are good for providing respondents with maximum flexibility in answering questions regarding motivations (why they behave as they do), or in explaining attitudes, behaviors, or intentions in greater depth. Their responses can be categorized by the researcher after the questionnaire has been completed, but the extra time for collecting and categorizing responses may add to the expense of the study (thousands of dollars for each open-ended question).

Dichotomous Questions

Dichotomous questions give two choices: either yes or no, or a choice of two opposite alternatives. They are preferred for starting interviews, are easy to tabulate, and can be used as a lead-in for more specific questions to a particular group. A weakness of dichotomous questions is that they can force a choice where none exists or lead to bias (such as the classic "Do you still cheat on your taxes?"___ Yes ___ No). Another weakness is that few questions can be framed in terms of a dichotomy, particularly more complex questions.

Multichotomous Questions

Multichotomous questions provide several alternatives to respondents. In some cases they may be asked to select only one from a list or asked to select as many as are applicable. The advantages of the multichotomous question are: ease of administration, ease of tabulation, and flexibility for factual as well as attitudinal responses. Some disadvantages exist in the length of the list of alternative responses, response alternatives may not be mutually exclusive, or reading the list may lead the respondent to a particular response.

Scales

Although a scale can be considered a multichotomous question, it deserves separate consideration. (Scaling was discussed and examples provided in Chapter 6.) The benefit of a scale is that it permits the objective measurement of attitudes and feelings. This allows for the identification of segments who are more favorably inclined toward a product, service, or issue. Scaling is somewhat subject to various frames of reference differences and to the halo effect. Some debate exists concerning whether scales should be balanced or unbalanced. Balanced scales have the same number of responses on the positive side of the scale as on the negative side of the scale. Unbalanced scales have more possible responses on one side of the scale than the other, usually the positive side. Some debate also exists over whether to have a neutral response. Those who feel there should be a "neutral" option believe so because they think that this is a legitimate response category and for the sake of accuracy the respondent should have that "ground to stand on." People against having a neutral response category argue that most individuals are unlikely to be authentically neutral on an issue. They consider the neutral as an easy way out or a "polite negative." Consequently, they feel that it is much better to frame the issue so that the respondent is "forced" to indicate a preference, however slight.

The "don't know," or "no opinion" response should always be available to respondents. An honest expression of a lack of awareness, experience, or thought given to an issue should be allowed so that these responses are not lumped together with those people who have considered the issue and find their position is the neutral point on the scale.

Earlier we mentioned that the researcher must look ahead to the analysis stage of the research process when determining the types of questions in order to ensure that the right levels of data are obtained to accommodate the planned analytical techniques. By this we mean that the researcher who plans to use specific analytical techniques (e.g., multiple regression, multidimensional scaling, conjoint analysis, analysis of variance, etc.) to test hypotheses or determine the relationship between variables of interest (such as between sales volume and various attributes of the target market), must have collected data in the form required by the analytical technique. In other words, one cannot just use any data as an input to these techniques. They require "raw data" in very specific forms before they can be run, just as a production process requires raw material to be in a very specific form to be able to produce a product. It must be determined how to analyze the data even before questions are written that will generate the data. In the interest of simplifying things somewhat, we will confine our questionnaire design suggestions to address analytical procedures no more complicated than cross-tabulation. As will be seen in Chapter 11, that technique is the most widely used and useful approach to getting managerial answers to the research objectives.

Develop the Specific Questions

Step 5 of the process of constructing a questionnaire is to actually write the specific questions that will be asked (i.e., the operational definitions of our constructs' attributes discussed in Chapter 6). The previous steps regarding the information required and the choices made relative to the types of questionnaire and questions will, to a large extent, control the content of the questions. The wording should be understandable and as explicit as possible. Questions should be worded in ways that avoid leading, pressuring, or embarrassing the respondent. The questions should avoid ambiguous words. Six basic rules for wording questions are:

1 Keep the questions short, simple, and to the point. Reasons for keeping the questions as brief as possible are that longer questions make the response task more difficult, are more subject to error on the part of both interviewers and respondents, cause a loss of focus, and are less likely to be clear. One question should not ask more than one thing at a time.

2 Avoid identifying the sponsor of the survey. In some cases, such as customer satisfaction surveys, the researcher may want to identify the sponsor of the survey. In most cases, however, it is best to not identify the sponsor so more objective responses may be gathered.

3 Keep the questions as neutral as possible. Unless a question can be worded objectively, it should not be asked. Nonobjective questions tend to be leading because they suggest an answer.

4 Do not ask unnecessary questions. Always ask yourself, "Is this question necessary?" Each question should relate or add meaning to a specific research objective. If the question falls in the "nice to know" but "not necessary" category, leave it out.

5 Avoid asking questions the respondent either cannot answer or will not answer. Since respondents will answer most questions, it is important to determine if a respondent can be expected to know the information desired. On other occasions, respondents will have the information required but may not be willing to divulge it. If a question appears to be

sensitive it may be best to leave it out. If it is crucial to the research objective, then it is best to ask the sensitive question later in the survey after a degree of trust has been established with the respondent.

6   Avoid asking leading or overly personal questions. Words or phrases that show bias are emotionally charged and will lead to inaccurate results. When sensitive questions must be asked, they should be asked after a warm-up period and/or hidden within a series of less personal questions.

Researchers should refer to some of the standard texts on how to word questions.[3]

Determine Question Sequence and Length of the Questionnaire

Step 6 can be extremely important in the completion rate of the survey. Excessive length may deter some respondents from completing the survey. This step can be equally important to the quality of the results acquired. The sequence of the questions should follow a logical pattern so it flows smoothly and effortlessly from one section to another. Another important consideration is to ensure that questions building on previous questions are placed properly in the questionnaire. Generally, questions will flow from the general to the specific. This warms up the respondents and lets them reflect appropriately before being asked specific questions that require good recall and some degree of detail. Skip patterns for branching questions need to be carefully designed. Quite often, a respondent must be directed to a specific location in the questionnaire based on a previous question such as, "Have you baked brownies in the past three months?" "Yes" respondents go on to answer specific questions about the baking occasion while "No" respondents "skip" to a different part of the survey. Personal, telephone, and Internet surveys lend themselves more to branching than do mail questionnaires.

Most questionnaires have three basic sections: (a) introduction, (b) body/content, and (c) classification section.

Introduction

The introduction tells the respondent who the researcher is, why he is requesting the respondent's information, and explains what is expected of the respondent. The introduction should explain the purpose of the questionnaire and enlist the cooperation of the respondent. In the case of a mail survey this may take place in an attached cover letter. On the phone this is accomplished with a positive tone without sounding like a polished sales pitch. Most people want to express their opinion as long as they know it is not a sales gimmick. The introduction should promise to keep the respondent's identity anonymous and his information confidential. Often the introduction will qualify the respondent in a special way to make sure that the interviewer is talking only to the right respondents. Qualification questions may include brand usage, age/sex categories, security issues such as whether the respondent or any member of his or her household works for a competitor of the client, an advertising agency or a marketing research company.

Body/Content

The body or main content of the questionnaire provides basic information required by the research objectives. This is usually the most substantial portion of the questionnaire. If the respondent has not been qualified in the introduction, the first question of this section should identify the proper respondents and have instructions to end the survey for all others. This section should begin with easy, direct questions. Place questions that are personal or reflect a sensitive issue well toward the end of the body. Once respondents have become interested in the survey, they are more likely to respond to personal or sensitive issues.

Classification Section

The final section is designed to obtain cross-classification information such as sex, income, educational level, occupation, marital status, and age. These demographic data allow for comparisons among different types of respondents. Certain market segments may emerge through the use of this cross-classification data. Many of these questions address the situational or environmental questions described in Table 8.1.

Predetermine Coding

In step 7, questionnaires should be pre-coded so that any difficulties encountered in entering data into computer tabulation and analysis programs may be solved before the data are gathered. Once the questionnaires are completed and returned, the responses can be quickly entered into the database and results generated.

Pre-test the Questionnaire

The eighth step is an essential step that should not be ignored. Following the maxim, "the proof is in the pudding," a questionnaire should be pre-tested before it is administered. A questionnaire may be too long, ambiguous, incomplete, unclear, or biased in some way. Not only will a thorough pre-test help overcome these problems, but it will help refine any procedural problems a questionnaire might have. Some of the procedural problems might be improper skip patterns and misunderstanding the interviewer. A pre-test will evaluate and fine-tune the questionnaire, estimate the time required for completion of the interview, and allow for setup of coding refinements for tabulations. The pre-test should be administered under actual field conditions to get an accurate response. If significant changes result from an original pre-test, it is advisable to conduct a second pre-test after appropriate revisions have been made. A relatively small number of interviews are sufficient to pre-test a normal questionnaire. Once they have been completed, all interviewers who participated should report their findings. They will be able to determine whether the questions work and be able to make suggestions for revision.

Review and Revise the Questionnaire

Based on the pre-test and a thorough review of all the previous steps, in the last step, the questionnaire should be revised. The bottom line for an effective data-gathering instrument is the accuracy of the data collected. Everything that can possibly be done in advance should be done to ensure the accuracy of the instrument.

The steps used to design an effective data-gathering instrument need to be viewed as a dynamic outline and not a sequential step-by-step process. Each step should be applied with a sharp eye on the research objectives and the data needs they require. The finished questionnaire is the result of rearticulating the study objectives into a set of effective questions for extracting the required information from the pertinent set of respondents.

> **Research Project Tip**
>
> Developing a good questionnaire requires both creativity and highly structured, disciplined thought. You will go through numerous drafts of the questionnaire, so allow plenty of time for this part of the research. Pretest each version of the questionnaire. Refer to the books listed in this chapter's notes for more on questionnaire design.

Summary

Good questionnaire design is both an art and a science. The questionnaire is a gestalt—more than the sum of its parts—and must be designed in such a way that it generates meaningful data. Questions that provide answers to our research questions and test our hypotheses are necessary, but not totally sufficient to the construction of the questionnaire. We must also contextualize the information gained from our research objective-related questions if we are to gather meaningful data that leads to better decision making.

Discussion Questions

1 Why will good questionnaires collect information beyond that identified in the research objectives (i.e., research questions and hypotheses)?
2 Discuss when you would typically use structured-undisguised questions and when you would use unstructured-disguised questions.
3 How are dummy tables (discussed in Chapter 5) used to help design the questionnaire?
4 What is meant by saying that a questionnaire is a "gestalt." In what ways does thinking of a questionnaire in this way impact the quality of information obtained from the use of a questionnaire?

9 Sampling Methods and Sample Size

Learning Objectives

Upon completing this chapter, you should understand:

1 the difference between a sample and a population or universe;
2 why sampling is preferred over a census;
3 what is meant by sampling error, sample bias, and nonsampling error;
4 the difference between probability and nonprobability sample designs;
5 the steps involved in selecting a sample;
6 how sample size is calculated;
7 factors influencing sample size.

In the course of most research projects, the time usually comes when estimates must be made about the characteristics or attitudes of a large group. The large group of interest is called the *population* or *universe.* For example, all of the registered Republicans in Jefferson County or all of the heads of households in Madison, Indiana, would each constitute a universe. Examples of a population are all people in the United States, all households in the United States, or all left-handed Scandinavians in Biloxi, Mississippi. Once the determination of the study universe is decided, several courses of action might be taken. First, the decision might be made to survey all of the entities in the universe. If all of the members of the selected universe are surveyed, this is called a census. With a census, direct, straightforward information concerning the specific universe parameters or characteristics is obtained. A second course of action would be to survey a sample of the universe (population). A sample is the term that refers to the group surveyed any time the survey is not administered to all members of the population or universe. The process of selecting a smaller group of people who basically have the same characteristics and preferences as the total group from which it is drawn is called sampling.

What is Sampling?

Sampling is something everyone has some experience with. Anyone who has taken a bite of fruitcake and decided "never again!" or any child who after a quick taste, has tried to hide their asparagus under the mashed potatoes has experienced sampling.

A famous quote from Cervantes states, "By a small sample we may judge the whole piece." Most of our everyday experiences with sampling are not scientific. However, our satisfaction with the results of our decisions, based on sampling, depends on how representative they are. In marketing research the goal is to assess target segments efficiently and effectively by designing and executing representative sample plans.

Sampling consists of obtaining information from a portion of a larger group or population. While making estimates from a sample of a larger population has the advantages of lower cost, speed, and efficiency, it is not without risk. However, fortunately for researchers, this risk can be set very low by using probability-sampling methods and appropriate estimating techniques, and by taking a sufficiently large sample. Thanks to the European gamblers of several centuries ago who were eager to establish the odds on various games of chance, some of the best mathematical minds of the day were dedicated to the task. This effort led to the fascinating branch of mathematics known as probability theory. Development in this area laid the foundation for modern scientific sampling.

Why Sampling?

There are many reasons for selecting a sampling technique over a census. In most cases the study objects of interest consist of a large universe. This fact alone gives rise to many advantages of sampling. The most significant advantages of sampling are:

1 *Cost savings*—Sampling a portion of the universe minimizes the field service costs associated with the survey.
2 *Time economy*—Information can be collected, processed, and analyzed much more quickly when a sample is utilized rather than a census. This saves additional monies and helps ensure that the information is not obsolete by the time it is available to answer the research question.
3 *More in-depth information*—The act of sampling affords the researcher greater opportunity to carry the investigation in more depth to a smaller number of select population members. This may be done in the form of focus group, panel, personal, telephone, mail, or Internet surveys.
4 *Less total error*—A major problem in survey data collection comes about as the result of nonsampling errors. Greater overall accuracy can be gained by using a sample administered by a better trained, supervised field-service group. In fact, the Bureau of the Census used sampling (as opposed to a census) in the year 2000 to improve the accuracy of their data.
5 *Greater practicality*—A census would not be practical when testing products from an assembly line, when the testing involves the destruction of the product, such as durability or safety tests or when the population is extremely large. The U.S. government has great difficulty accomplishing the U.S. Census every ten years.
6 *Greater security*—This is particularly true if a firm is researching a new product or concept. Sampling would be preferred to keep the product or concept a secret as long as possible.

Sampling Error, Sample Bias, and Nonsampling Error

It may be somewhat disconcerting to the novice researcher to discover that even with all the attention to developing a valid and reliable data-collection instrument (Chapter 6), there are still numerous ways error can contaminate the research results. We can divide the sources of error into three categories: sampling error, sample bias, nonsampling error.

Sampling Error

Sampling error occurs when the sample does not perfectly represent the population under study. Sampling error occurs either from flaws in the design or execution of drawing the sample, causing it to not be representative of the population, or from chance, the random error that is introduced into any sample that is taken from a population. Design or execution errors can be minimized by careful attention to sample selection procedures. Random error cannot be avoided, but can be calculated and can be reduced by increasing the size of the sample. Convention restricts the definition of sampling error to that calculable error which occurs when a sample is drawn from a population. We will follow that convention by discussing the calculation of sampling error in this chapter and discussing other errors introduced in the sampling process (e.g., such as the selection of a sampling frame) and nonsampling error in Chapter 10.

Sample Bias

Sample bias is introduced into a sample when the sample varies in some systematic way from the larger population. Examples are using the Internet to do a survey that is supposed to represent the entire population. Those who do not have Internet access may vary in a number of ways from those who do. The same is true for calling people at home during the day—they are different from people who are not at home, asking only people who ride mass transit about their opinions of mass transit funding and believing you have measured the general public's opinions, and so on. Obviously unlike sampling error, you can not reduce sample bias by increasing sample size. In fact, increasing sample size merely increases the bias of the results. Controlling sample bias is achieved by careful attention to the sampling process—defining a population of interest, carefully selecting the sample from the population that is representative, and having success in obtaining responses from the sample group.

Nonsampling Error

Nonsampling error is introduced into the research results from any source other than sampling. It can occur whenever research workers either intentionally (e.g., cheating, leading respondent) or unintentionally (e.g., by belonging to an ethnic group, sex, age category, etc., which elicits a particular response from respondents; misunderstanding a response; being tired and missing a response, etc.) introduce errors into the data-gathering process; or can occur whenever respondents intentionally (e.g., lying or not responding) or unintentionally (e.g., misunderstanding a question, guessing or answering with a response when "don't know" is more accurate, becoming distracted or fatigued, etc.) introduce error into the responses. Other errors can enter the research at the recording, coding, tabulating, editing, or analysis stages of data management.

Sampling Decision Model

Sampling involves several specific decisions. This section briefly discusses the steps of a sampling decision model (see Figure 9.1).

Step 1: Define the Population or Universe

Once the researcher has decided to apply sampling techniques rather than a census, he or she must make several important sampling decisions. The first decision is to define the population or universe. Since sampling is designed to gather data from a specific population, it is extremely important that the universe be identified accurately. Often this universe is called a target population because of the importance of focusing on exactly who the study objects are and where they are located. Usually any effort expended to do a first-rate job of identifying the population pays generous dividends later in terms of accurate and representative data.

The definition of the population of interest should be related directly back to the original study objectives. Clues to identifying the target population can be found in the statement of

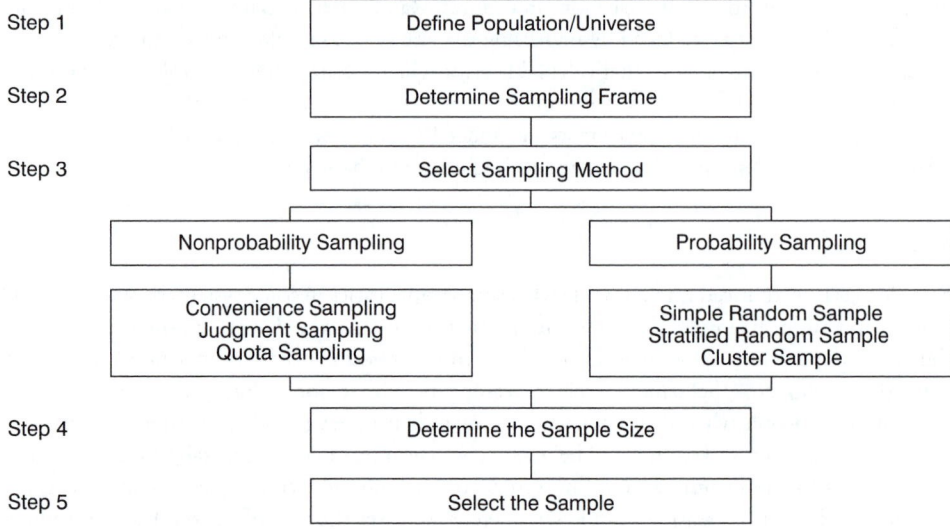

Figure 9.1 Sampling Decision Model

research purpose. The research questions and research hypotheses generated from the research purpose should refine the definition of the target population. The sample must be reduced to the most appropriate common denominator. Do the research questions require selecting as sample elements individuals, households, purchase decision makers, or product users? Defining a population improperly can introduce bias into the study. Professional staff experience and insight are required to properly specify the target population.

The definition of a population consists of four parts: element, sampling unit, extent, and time. A slight change in any one of these parts can have a significant impact on the results of the research. For example, consider the impact on a research study whose purpose is to understand the eating habits of single adults when we make changes in two of the four parts.

Population Definition #1
Element: All unmarried persons 18 years of age or older who are shopping in
Sampling unit: Supermarkets
Extent: In Los Angeles
Time: During the week of January 18–24.
Findings: "Single adults do not eat meals away from home as frequently as previously thought."

Population Definition #2
Element: All unmarried persons 18 years of age or older who are eating in
Sampling unit: Restaurants
Extent: In Los Angeles
Time: During the week of January 18–24
Findings: "Single adults eat meals away from home more frequently than previously thought."

Obviously, great care must be given to the definition of the population from which a sample will be drawn. In fact, contrary to popular belief, the first Step and Steps 2 and 3 of the sampling *process* will have a greater impact on the findings of the research than determination of the sample *size*. Reviewing the management problem, research purpose (including decision alternatives and criteria, time frame, and budget), and research objectives (questions and hypotheses) is an important prerequisite to establishing the four parts to the definition of the population.

Step 2: Determine the Sampling Frame

The second step in the sampling decision model is to determine the sampling frame. The *sampling frame* is a listing of the members of the target population that can be used to create and/or draw the sample. It might be such things as a directory, subscribers list, customer list, or membership roster. In some cases, the sampling frame consists of a process instead of a list (e.g., random-digit dialing, or asking every tenth person passing the interviewer in a mall to complete a questionnaire). The sampling frame might include everyone in the target population defined in Step 1 without duplication.

This ideal situation seldom exists in actual experience, however. Sample lists or frames can be purchased from third-party companies specializing in sample preparation, or they can be put together by combining several sources. Because of the incompleteness of sampling frames, several discrepancies develop. In some cases, the sample frame is made up of the subjects of interest but is smaller than the total population. As a result, certain elements of the population are omitted from the survey. In other cases, the sample frame includes all members of the population but is larger than the population. Duplications or inappropriate units are included in the survey in these situations. A third situation occurs when some elements of the population fall in the sampling frame and some elements of the sampling frame are not of the population. In this case, both omissions and undesired inclusions occur.

For general population surveys, a traditional sample frame has been the telephone directory. In the United States, 95 percent of potential respondents can be reached by telephone. However, the telephone directory is an incomplete sample frame because in some metropolitan areas almost two-thirds of the telephone subscribers have unlisted numbers. Not only does this condition cause a large number of people to be left out of the directory, the omission of elements is not proportional across geographical areas. As a result, random digit designs, where phones are programmed to dial random digits, are often used to overcome the exclusion bias inherent in directory-based sampling designs. There are numerous sources of computer-generated, random-digit sample frames for commercial use.

The goal of developing an appropriate sample frame is to get a listing of elements of the target population that is as inclusive and proportionally representative as possible with a minimum of duplication. Survey Sampling, Incorporate (SSI) provides computer software that allows researchers to order very specific sampling frames (e.g., females aged 25–30, living in Indiana, with MBAs). SSI can then send this sampling frame to the researcher over the Internet.

Step 3: Select the Sampling Method

The third step in the sampling decision model is to select the sampling method. This decision logically follows the decisions to determine the target population and to define the sampling frame. The initial consideration in the selection of a sample is whether or not to employ a probability-sampling procedure or a nonprobability-sampling procedure.

Probability Sampling

Probability samples are simply those samples where each element has a known chance to be included in the sample. "Known" in this case simply refers to the theoretical ability to calculate the likelihood of inclusion in the sample, rather than actually knowing with precision the probability of inclusion. With nonprobability samples there is no known way of estimating the probability of any given element being included in the sample. With probability sampling a random or a systematic, chance-based procedure is utilized to select the study elements. The researcher preselects the respondents in a mathematical way so that persons in the universe have an equal or known chance of being selected. From a statistical point of view, probability sampling is preferred because it allows a calculation of the *sampling error*. Probability-sampling procedures tend to be more objective and allow the use of statistical techniques.

Nonprobability sampling introduces certain biases, from an operational perspective, and offers the advantage of being less expensive and quicker to implement. However, the fact that a sample is a nonprobability sample does not mean that the sample must be less *representative* than a probability sample. The problem is, with nonprobability samples we cannot compute the degree to which they are representative, and therefore they cannot be used to generate such desirable statistics as confidence intervals (i.e., we cannot say such things as "We are 95 percent confident that 45 percent ± 2 percent of the respondents say they will definitely buy formulation A.").

The most commonly used probability samples are simple random samples, stratified samples, cluster samples, and systemic samples.

SIMPLE RANDOM SAMPLE

A simple random sample is a technique that allows each element of the population an *equal* and *known* chance of being selected as part of the sample. The implementation is often accomplished by the use of a table of random numbers. Computer and calculator random numbers can also be generated to assist in selecting random samples. A common analogy for a random sample is the traditional drawing of a sample from a fishbowl containing slips of paper with the names of the elements of the sampling frame.

STRATIFIED SAMPLES

When subgroups of the population are of special interest to the researcher, a stratified sample may serve a better purpose than a simple random sample. A stratified sample is characterized by the fact that the total population is (1) divided into mutually exclusive subgroups (strata) (e.g., different age or income groups) and that (2) a simple random sample is then chosen from each subgroup. This is a modified type of random sample. The method of creating a stratified sample ensures that all important subgroups are represented in the sample. The stratified random-sampling technique is good for classifying consumers by various demographic factors. Stratified samples can be divided into proportionately stratified samples or into disproportionately stratified samples. A proportionately stratified sample allows for a breakdown where the number of items randomly selected in each subgroup is proportionate to their incidence in the total population. A disproportionately stratified sample is a sample where the allocation of sample elements is not established according to relative proportion. This may result in an equal number of elements per subgroup or it may result in the greater sampling of the subgroups that have the greater potential for variability. This, however, requires prior knowledge of the characteristics of the population. Just as with a simple random sample, there can be no stratified sample if there is no available sampling frame of elements of the population that breaks down the population into the appropriate subgroups. Also, choosing a variable for stratification (e.g., age or income) means that you believe people *within* the strata are similar along some dimensions of interest to the decision maker (e.g., attitudes or behaviors) that ultimately will influence marketing decisions, and different *between* strata (e.g., people in different income categories differ in some behavior of interest to marketers).

Some specific reasons for choosing to stratify a population sample include:

1   A desire to minimize variance and sampling error or to increase precision. If a population is segmented into strata that are internally homogeneous, overall variability may be reduced. The required sample size for a well-designed stratified sample will usually be smaller than for a well-designed unstratified sample.
2   A desire to estimate the parameters of each of the stratum and have a "readable" sample size for each one.
3   A desire to keep the sample element selection process simple.

CLUSTER SAMPLES

In some cases when stratified sampling is not possible or feasible, cluster sampling can be utilized. The first step in selecting a cluster sample is the same as in a stratified sample: the population is divided into mutually exclusive subgroups. However, the next step involves the selection of a random sample of subgroups rather than a random sample from each subgroup. Cluster sampling may not be as statistically efficient as a stratified sample; however, it is usually more procedurally efficient in terms of cost and time. Cluster sampling is often associated with area sampling. In area sampling, each cluster is a different geographic area, census tract, or block.

SYSTEMATIC SAMPLES

A fourth technique of probability sampling is called systematic sampling. In this method of cluster sampling, every element has a known but not equal chance of being selected. Systematic sampling is an attempt to increase the efficiency of the sample at favorable costs. A systematic sample is initiated by randomly selecting a digit, *n,* and then selecting a sample element at every *n*th interval, depending on the size of the population and the sample size requirement. This method is often used when selecting samples from large directories. Some loss of statistical efficiency can occur with systematic samples, particularly if there are hidden periodic sequences that cause some systematic variances to occur at the intervals selected. A systematic sample may be more representative than a simple random sample depending on the clustering of objects within the sample frame. The ideal list will have elements with similar value on the key defining characteristics of the sample close together and elements diverse in value in different locations of the list.

Nonprobability Samples

Nonprobability samples are defined as any sampling techniques that do not involve the selection of sample elements by chance. The most commonly utilized nonprobability sampling techniques are convenience sampling, judgment sampling, and quota sampling.

CONVENIENCE SAMPLE

The least expensive and least time-consuming of sampling techniques is generally considered to be convenience sampling, which is any process that quickly and easily selects sample elements. The sample element close at hand is chosen and surveyed in the application of this technique. Man-on-the-street interviews are examples of this type of sampling. The greatest problem with convenience sampling is the inability to know if the sample is representative of the target population. Consequently, one cannot generalize from the sample to the target population with a high degree of confidence.

Since the convenience sampling technique follows no predesignated method, the sampling error cannot be calculated and specific precision and confidence level estimates cannot be made. Even with the drawbacks of convenience sampling, it is frequently used, particularly for exploratory research.

JUDGMENT SAMPLE

The representativeness of a judgment sample depends on the skill, insight, and experience of the one choosing the sample. Although a judgment sample is a subjective approach to sampling, the knowledge and experience of a professional researcher can create a very representative sample. This is particularly true in industrial studies where a knowledge of the industry dynamics and decision-making procedures is necessary in identifying the correct respondents. In the area of polling "expert opinion," judgment samples can be very effective. Even though judgment samples are more restrictive and generally more representative than convenience samples, they have the same weakness that does not permit direct generalization of conclusions derived to a target population. In the final analysis, representativeness of a judgment sample depends on the experience, skill, knowledge, and insight of the one choosing the sample. Focus group recruitment is an example of a judgment sampling process.

A particular kind of judgment sample is the "snowball sample." The snowball sample relies on the researcher's ability to locate an initial group of respondents with the desired characteristics. Additional respondents are identified on a referral basis, relying on the initial set of respondents to identify other potential respondents.

QUOTA SAMPLE

Quota sampling is the third type of nonprobability sampling; it is similar in some respects to stratified and cluster sampling. In quota sampling, the researcher divides the target population into a number of subgroups. Using his or her best judgment, the researcher then selects quotas for each subgroup. The quota method takes great effort to obtain a representative sample by dividing the population and assigning appropriate quotas based on prior knowledge and understanding of the characteristics, of the population. Quite often the subgroups of the population are divided into categories such as age, sex, occupation, or other known characteristics. Usually quotas are assigned based on known proportions for these characteristics, such as provided by the U.S. Census. In this way, a quota sample can be drawn to represent the population based on the defining characteristics selected. An example could be to establish quotas based on age/sex proportions provided by the census and known product-usage patterns. While this would not ensure a representative sample, the researcher would know that the respondents come in the same proportion as the total population among product users and nonusers.

The difference between quota sampling and stratified sampling is that quota samples do not use random sampling from the categories as we do in stratified sampling. Also, in stratified sampling we must select the strata based upon a correlation between the category and the respondent behavior of interest (e.g., expenditures on furniture vary by age of head of household). In quota sampling researcher judgment is used in establishing the categories and choosing the sample from the categories.

The problems with quota sampling are the same as for other nonprobability-sampling methods. The sampling error cannot be calculated and projection to the total population is risky. A quota sample might be very representative of the quota-defining characteristics; however, there may be some other characteristic that is supremely important in defining the population that is not used to establish quotas. Consequently, this characteristic may be disproportionately represented in the final sample. It is impractical to impose too many cell categories on a quota sample. Despite some of its drawbacks, quota sampling is often used in market research projects.

Probability Versus Nonprobability Sampling

The reader by now realizes that probability-sampling methods are the methods of choice for descriptive research and nonprobability methods for exploratory research. This fits our discussion in Chapter 5, when we said exploratory research is best described as "flexible," while descriptive is best described as "rigid." It also makes sense when we remember the goal of exploratory research is to generate ideas, insights, better focus the problem, etc.—all of which are best done by using a nonrandom-respondent selection process, and choosing a smaller number of people than we would choose if our goal is to measure or describe a population in terms of frequencies and covariations as we do in descriptive research. For example, if we are screening people for inclusion in in-depth interviews or for focus groups, we want to use a nonprobability (i.e., nonrandom) method of selection so we can talk to those people whose experience puts them in the best position to provide us with the insights, ideas, etc., we are looking for.

In contrast, when we do descriptive research we are ultimately measuring the frequency with which something occurs, or the extent to which two variables co-vary (e.g., consumption rate varies with respondent age), which means we want to be able to report results using statistics (e.g., "We are 95 percent confident that the average of our heavy users age is 35.2 ± 3 years."). The only sampling method that allows us to report statistical results in this way is probability sampling, and hence, since we want to "describe" our population in this way when doing descriptive research, we want to use probability-sampling methods.

It is worth remembering that we previously mentioned that exploratory research sometimes uses surveys, as does descriptive research. But the results of an exploratory-research survey using nonprobability sampling could not be reported the same way as descriptive-research results. Whereas the descriptive research/probability survey results of a sample of 200 respondents might be stated as: "We are 95 percent confident that the average age of our heavy users is 35.2 ± 3 years;" our exploratory/nonprobability survey results for a sample of 400 (i.e., sample size twice as large) could only be reported as: "Our heavy users are about in their midthirties."

Our nonprobability sample may be as representative as our probability sample, but because it was chosen using a nonprobability method we are not able to calculate the sampling error, and therefore will never know if it was as representative. But again, such a limitation is of no consequence if we are merely looking for ideas, insights, generating hypotheses, etc. It is of considerable consequence if we are testing hypotheses, trying to establish frequencies, co-variation, etc.

Step 4: Determine Sample Size

The size of the sample will be a function of the accuracy of the sample. Two criteria are used in measuring accuracy: the margin of error and the level of confidence. The first is determined as the tolerated-error range (also known as sample precision) and the second is the probability that the sample will fall within that tolerated-error range. A margin of error of 3 percent, for example, means that out of all possible samples of a certain determined size of coin flips, 95 percent will differ from the actual population by no more than three percentage points.

Sample-size determination ultimately is a reflection of the value of the information sought. Scientific journals require that reported results must fall in the 95 to 99 percent confidence levels. When the risk involved in the decision alternatives is high, then 95 to 99 percent confidence levels will be required. However, a sampling of well-known television ratings is at the 66 percent confidence level. Even though the margin of error in these ratings is far greater than most scientific research, many advertising decisions are based on this result. Even low-budget studies, with low-risk decision alternatives that serve as a glimpse into the market environment, should usually not consider a confidence level of less than 80 to 90 percent. The 95 percent confidence level is suggested for most research. Sample sizes may be selected by using either statistical calculations or non-statistical methods. Each of these will now be discussed.

Statistical Sampling Concepts

THE STATISTICAL SIDE OF SAMPLING

The sample size for a probability sample depends on the standard error of the mean, the precision desired from the estimate, and the desired degree of confidence associated with the estimate. The standard error of the mean measures sampling errors that arise when estimating a population from a sample instead of including all of the essential information in the population. The size of the standard error is the function of the standard deviation of the population values and the size of the sample.

$$\sigma_{\bar{x}} = \frac{\sigma}{\sqrt{n}}$$

where $\sigma_{\bar{x}}$ = standard error

σ = standard deviation

n = sample size

The precision is the size of the plus-or-minus interval around the population parameter under consideration, and the degree of confidence is the percentage level of certainty (probability) that the true mean is within the plus-or-minus interval around the mean. Precision and confidence are interrelated and, within a given size sample, increasing one may be done only at the expense of the other. In other words, the degree of confidence or the degree of precision may be increased, but not both.

The main factors that have a direct influence on the size of the sample are:

1   *The desired degree of confidence associated with the estimate.* In other words, how confident does the researcher want to be in the results of the survey? If the researcher wants 100-percent confidence, he or she must take a census. The more confident a researcher wants to be, the larger the sample should be. This confidence is usually expressed in terms of 90, 95, or 99 percent.

2   *The size of the error the researcher is willing to accept.* This width of the interval relates to the precision desired from the estimate. The greater the precision, or rather the smaller the plus-or-minus fluctuation around the sample mean or proportion, the larger the sample requirement.

The basic formula for calculating sample size for variables (e.g., age, income, weight, height, etc.) is derived from the formula for standard error:

$$n = \frac{\sigma^2}{\sigma_{\bar{x}}^2}$$

The unknowns in the formula above are $\sigma_{\bar{x}}$ (standard error), σ (standard deviation), and n (sample size). In order to calculate the sample size, the researcher must:

1   select the appropriate level of confidence;
2   determine the width of the plus-or-minus interval that is acceptable and calculate standard error;
3   estimate the variability (standard deviation) of the population based on a pilot study or previous experience of the researcher with the population;
4   calculate sample size (solve for n).

For example, a researcher might choose the 95.5 percent confidence level as appropriate. Using the assumptions of the Central Limit Theorem (that means of samples drawn will be normally distributed around the population means, etc.), the researcher will select a standard normal deviate from the following table:

Level of Confidence	Z Value
68.3%	1.00
75.0	1.15
80.0	1.28
85.0	1.44
90.0	1.64
95.0	1.96
95.5	2.00
99.0	2.58
99.7	3.00

This allows the researcher to calculate the standard error ($\sigma_{\bar{x}}$). If, for example, the precision width of the interval is selected at 40, the sampling error on either side of the mean must be 20. At the 95.5 percent level of confidence, $Z = 2$ and the confidence interval equals $\pm Z\sigma_{\bar{x}}$.
Then the standard error is equal to 10.

$$CL = \bar{x} \pm Z\sigma_{\bar{x}} \qquad CI = \pm Z\sigma_{\bar{x}}$$

$Z = 2$ at 95.5% level

$2_x\sigma_{\bar{x}} = 20$

$\sigma_{\bar{x}} = 10$

CL = Confidence limits

CI = Confidence interval

Having calculated the standard error based on an appropriate level of confidence and desired interval width, we have two unknowns in the sample size formula left, namely sample size (n) and standard deviation (σ). The standard deviation of the sample must now be estimated. This can be done either by taking a small pilot sample and computing the standard deviation or it can be estimated on the knowledge and experience the researcher has of the population. If you estimate the standard deviation as 200, the sample size can be calculated.

$$\sigma_{\bar{x}} = \frac{\sigma}{\sqrt{n}}$$

$$n = \frac{\sigma^2}{\sigma_{\bar{x}}^2}$$

$$n = \frac{(200)^2}{(10)^2}$$

$$n = \frac{40,000}{100}$$

$$n = 400$$

The sample size required to give a standard error of 10 at a 95.5 percent level of confidence is computed to be 400. This assumes that assumptions concerning the variability of the population were correct.

Another way of viewing the calculation of sample size required for a given precision of a mean score is to use the following formula:

$$\sigma_{\bar{x}} = \frac{\sigma}{\sqrt{n}}$$

$$n = \frac{Z^2 \sigma^2}{h^2}$$

where $Z =$ value from the normal distribution table

for the desired confidence level

$\sigma^2 =$ standard deviation

$n =$ sample size

$h =$ desired precision $\pm$

Using the same information as used in the previous example, the same result is obtained:

$$\sigma_{\bar{x}} = \frac{\sigma}{\sqrt{n}}$$

$$n = \frac{(2)^2 (200)^2}{(20)^2}$$

$$n = \frac{(4)(40,000)}{(400)}$$

$$n = \frac{160,000}{400}$$

$$n = 400$$

Tables in most statistical books are provided to allow you, at several given confidence levels, to select the exact sample size given an estimated standard deviation and a desired width of interval.

Determining sample size for a question involving proportions (e.g., those who eat out/don't eat out, successes/failures, have access to internet/don't have access, etc.) or attributes is very similar to the procedure followed for variables. The researcher must:

1   select the appropriate level of confidence;
2   determine the width of the plus-or-minus interval that is acceptable and calculated the standard error of the proportion $\sigma_{\bar{p}}$;
3   estimate the population proportion based on a pilot study or previous experience of the researcher with the population;
4   calculate the sample size (solve for n).

The basic formula for calculating sample size for proportions or attributes is derived from the formula for standard error of the proportion:

$$\sigma_{\bar{x}} = \frac{\sigma}{\sqrt{n}}$$

$$\sigma_{\bar{p}} = \sqrt{\frac{pq}{\eta}}$$

where $\sigma_{\bar{p}}$ = standard error of proportion

p = percent of sucesses

q = percent of nonsuccesses $(1 - p)$

Assume that management has specified that there be a 95.5 percent confidence level and that the error in estimating the population not be greater than ± 5 percent (p ± 0.05). In other words, the width of the interval is 10 percent. A pilot study has shown that 40 percent of the population eats out over four times a week.

$$\text{CI} = \pm Z\sigma_{\bar{p}} \qquad \sigma_{\bar{p}} = \frac{0.05}{2}$$

$$2\sigma_{\bar{p}} = \frac{\pm\text{CI}}{2} \qquad \sigma_{\bar{p}} = 0.025$$

Substituting in:

$$\sigma_{\bar{p}} = \sqrt{\frac{pq}{n}} \qquad n = \frac{(0.40)(0.60)}{(0.025)^2}$$

$$n = \frac{pq}{\sigma_{\bar{p}}} \qquad n = \frac{0.24}{0.000625}$$

$$n = 384$$

Another way to view calculating the sample size required for a given precision of a proportion score is to use the following formula:

$$n = \frac{Z^2(pq)}{h^2}$$

where Z = value from normal distribution table

for desired confidence level

p = obtained proportion

$q = 1 - p$

h = desired precision ±

Using the same information as used in the previous example, the same result is obtained:

$$n = \frac{(2)^2(0.40 \times 0.60)}{(0.05)^2}$$

$$n = \frac{(0.40)(0.24)}{0.0025}$$

$$n = \frac{0.96}{0.0025}$$

$$n = 384$$

The sample size required to give a 95.5 percent level of confidence that the sample proportion is within ±5 percent of the population proportion is 384.

Tables in statistics books provide a simple method for selecting sample size at several alternative confidence levels given an estimated value of the proportion (p) and a desired confidence interval.

Since sample size is predicated on a specific attribute, variable, proportion, or parameter, a study with multiple objectives will require different sample sizes for the various objectives. Rarely is a study designed to determine a single variable or proportion. Consequently, to get the desired precision at the desired level of confidence for all variables, the larger sample size must be selected. In some cases, however, one single variable might require a sample size significantly larger than any other variable. In this case, it is wise to concentrate on the most critical variables and choose a sample size large enough to estimate them with the required precision and confidence level desired by the researchers/clients.

Nonstatistical Determination Of Sample Size

While the formulas previously listed are used to calculate sample size, frequently in marketing research studies one of the following nonstatistical approaches is used to establish the sample size for a research study.[1] Recall that our determination of sample size is a separate step in the sampling process from determination of sampling method (i.e., probability versus nonprobability). Therefore, using one of these nonstatistical approaches to establish the size of the sample does not change the way in which we would report our findings from the sampled respondents, it merely affects the ultimate selection of sample size (and hence, with a probability sample, it affects the sampling error). So, using one of these nonstatistical approaches to setting sample size might change a reported result using a probability sampling method from

> "We are 95 percent confident that the average age of our heavy consumers is 35.2 ± 3 years." (Sample of 200)

to

> "We are 95 percent confident that the average age of our heavy consumers is 35.7 ± 1.8 years." (Sample of 350)

but using the nonstatistical approach does not alter our ability to report statistical results as shown here.

USE PREVIOUS SAMPLE SIZES

Companies that do repeated studies over time to gather similar information to compare data and determine trends might automatically use the same sample size every time the research is

Table 9.1 Typical Sample Sizes for Consumer and Institutional Population Studies

Number of subgroups	Consumer or households		Institutions	
	National	Regional or special	National	Regional or special
0–4	850–1,500	200–500	50–500	50–200
5–10	1,500–2,500	500–1,000	350–1,000+	150–500
Over 10	2,500+	1,000+	1,000+	500+

Source: Adapted from Seymour Sudman, *Applied Sampling*, (Academic Press, New York,) 1976.

conducted. Also, if the same type of study is done (e.g., concept tests of new product ideas), companies will often use the same sample size. Researchers are cautioned against using the same sample size for all research studies—it is possible to be spending too much or too little money compared to the value of the information.

USE "TYPICAL" SAMPLE SIZES

"Common wisdom" has led to an accepted sample size based upon the number of subgroups which might be used to analyze the data (see Table 9.1). Another typical sample size determination based on the number of subgroups is that major subgroups should have 100 or more respondents (e.g., males and females = 2 major subgroups), and less important subgroups should have approximately 50 respondents (e.g., males under 35 years old, 35–50 years old, 51+ years old, plus females under 35 years old, 35–50 years old, 51+ years old = 6 subgroups). Using this rule-of-thumb, the analysis of males versus females would mean a minimum sample size of 200 (i.e., 2 × 100), while males versus females by age categories would mean a minimum sample size of 300 (i.e., 50 × 6).

USE A "MAGIC" NUMBER

Decision makers unaccustomed to reviewing research findings before making decisions may be skeptical of research findings that reveal unexpected results or that go against conventional wisdom. In such cases, researchers should say something like "It is possible this research will produce findings which may be unexpected. What size sample would you need to see the results as legitimate representations of the market and not a fluke?" Sample sizes should then exceed the number given by the decision makers who will review findings in making their decisions.

USE RESOURCE SIMULATIONS

Perhaps the most common method of selecting a sample size is "whatever the budget will allow." An example of determining sample size using this method:

Total amount allocated for research	$30,000
Minus fixed costs (research company fees, data analysis costs, overhead, etc.)	−$16,000
Amount available for variable costs	$14,000
Divide by cost of completed interview	÷ $15
Equals number of interviews that can be conducted within the budget (i.e., the sample size)	933

Such an approach to determining sample size has appeal because it is expressed in a language managers understand—dollars and cents. Of course, a sample size determined in this way should be checked against the other research information needs to see if the size is satisfactory and efficient.

ASK AN EXPERT

A final nonstatistical approach is to ask an expert in research for advice on appropriate sample size. The expert will probably use one of the statistical or nonstatistical approaches described here, but at least you will feel better about determining the sample size.

Step 5: Select the Sample

Once the target population has been identified, an appropriate sampling frame determined or compiled, all sampling procedures selected, and a sample size determined, it is time for the final step in the sampling-decision mode. The sampling process should be executed in an efficient and professional way. Whether a sample is a probability sample or a nonprobability sample, the important aspect is to obtain as much representative information and eliminate as much sampling and nonsampling error as possible. Generally speaking, the sample size should be increased whenever the population exhibits high variability or whenever high levels of confidence and precision are required.

What Is A "Significant" Statistically Significant Difference?

Henry Clay once said, "Statistics are no substitute for judgment." Just because two values can be adjudicated as statistically different does not mean that they are substantively different, and the reverse is also true. Substantive significance refers to the strength of a relationship or the magnitude of a difference between two values. Does the difference imply real-world practicality? If a very large sample is used, very small differences may be concluded to be statistically different; however, they may not be different in any substantive way. On the other hand, the difference between two values in a research project may not test as being statistically significant at a given level of confidence, but if the difference holds up in the real world it could be substantively significant.

Research Project Tip

You should address how you will select a sample(s) in your research, whether your research is exploratory, descriptive, causal, or any combination of these designs. You might, for example, be using a nonprobability sample to conduct in-depth interviews in the exploratory phase of your research, and a probability approach for the descriptive phase. Describe the process you will use in each case, following the five-step process covered in this chapter.

Summary

Chapter 9 has presented the important aspects of sampling. The nature of the research project determines the type of sample, the sample size, the sample frame, and the method necessary to correctly draw/select the sample. In some projects, sampling consideration is a critical decision area because of the impact on costs and the need to draw inferences about the population from which the sample is drawn.

Discussion Questions

1   Discuss the thought process that a marketer of home furniture would go through in deciding whether or not to use a stratified sample for research being done to select target markets and set positioning strategies.
2   Give an example of the definition of the population of the business students at your college.
3   Define sampling frame. What would be the sampling frame if the population of interest were the business students who eat lunch in the school cafeteria at least once a week on average?
4   What considerations go into a decision whether to use probability or non-probability sampling? How does selection of a sample size differ between probability and non-probability sample (e.g., when do you use statistical calculations for determining sample size vs. non-statistical methods)?

10 Fielding the Data-gathering Instrument

Learning Objectives

Upon completing this chapter, you should understand:

1 the importance of careful planning of the data collection process;
2 the different types of interviews and requirements of each type;
3 the importance of identifying "qualified respondents" and probing;
4 the errors of omission and commission of data collection;
5 the sources of error in the research process and in data collection.

Once the questionnaire has been completed, it is ready for the field. The field-operation phase of the research process is the occasion that the data-collection instrument is taken to the source of the information. The planning of the field work is closely related to the preparation of the questionnaire, and the sample selection. All three of these aspects of data gathering must be well conceived, planned, and executed in order to achieve the objectives of a study. Error can occur in all three phases, and the field collection portion is no exception. The results of any excellently conceived questionnaire drawn from a scientifically selected representative sample can be nullified by errors in the fielding of the questionnaire. Consequently, the data-collection phase of the marketing research process is extremely important. A poorly executed data-collection effort can nullify the impact of a well-designed sampling scheme and data-collection instrument.

Planning

To minimize total error and to gather accurate information as efficiently as possible, the field service of a questionnaire should be well planned. Time, money, and personnel must all be budgeted appropriately. Time for the field portion of a research project is extremely important, since it must fit into the overall time frame of the entire research project. The field service portion should have a realistic completion date with a little leeway built in. This will allow for timely and accurate completion. Since the field work must be done before analysis can occur, good sequencing is necessary.

Budgets

Money must be appropriately budgeted for the field service effort. Cost must be assigned to all the component activities of the field-service phase. Cost estimates must be made for:

- wages of interviewers, supervisors, and general office support;
- telephone charges;
- postage/shipping;
- production of questionnaire and other forms;
- supplies.

Staffing

Personnel are the key to successful field-service operations. Care must be taken to have the best possible personnel to accomplish the research task. There is no substitute for well-trained, experienced interviewers. Consequently, the personnel must not only be selected and scheduled for a project, they must have been trained in the techniques of interviewing. Some of the basic rules of interviewing are discussed later in this chapter. Another important part of preparing the personnel for a specific study is to ensure they are thoroughly briefed on the specific aspects of the questionnaire that will be administered. The personnel must have a clear understanding of the data-gathering instrument and what information is desired.

Guidelines for Interviewers

The field-service operation should include the following responsibilities to be carried out by the interviewer:

1   Cover the sample frame in accordance with instructions to ensure representative data. The proper areas and/or persons must be contacted.
2   Follow study procedures and administer the questionnaire as written. Be familiar with the questionnaire before beginning.
3   Write down open-ended responses verbatim. Record all other responses according to instructions in the proper terms of measurement.
4   Probe, but do not lead. If a person does not understand the question, read it again, verbatim, perhaps more slowly or with more inflection.
5   Establish rapport with the interviewee. Be confident in what you are doing and assume people will talk to you. Most people love to have the opportunity to say what they think. Reflect enthusiasm in the questonnaire, but do not lead the respondent.
6   Accomplish a field edit to ensure that the data are being collected in appropriate form.

Types of Interviews

Personal Interviews

The requirement of personal interviews creates special problems from the field-service point of view. As discussed in Chapter 7, personal interviews may be done through door-to-door, mall intercept, central location interviewing, or executive interviewing. Interviewers must be located, screened, hired, trained, briefed, and sent out in the proper geographic areas called for in the sampling plan in order to execute a door-to-door survey. A company will often hire outside field-service organizations to conduct this type of interviewing. If a company has subcontracted the entire project to an outside consultant firm, it would be wise to make sure that the research firm has its own in-house field-service personnel or at least has a good network of field services that it subcontracts to. Interviewers must also be well trained in the art of interviewing, but quite often they must also understand technical terms and jargon, particularly in industrial marketing research. This high degree of competence and preparation of interviewers, as well as the time and travel involved, make this door-to-door interviewing quite expensive.

Mall-intercept interviewing is a very popular way to execute personal interviews across a wide geographic area. This method of survey research intercepts shoppers in the public areas of shopping malls and either interviews them on the spot or executes a short screening survey and, if respondents qualify, they are invited to a permanent interviewing facility in the mall to participate in a research study. Many different types of studies may be conducted in shopping malls: concept studies, product placement/home use tests, taste tests, clipboard studies (short, simple surveys), simulated controlled-store tests, and focus groups.

Another method of questionnaire administration that involves a personal interview approach is a recruited central location test (CLT). A CLT usually involves the need for a probabilistic sample plan or a category of respondent that has a low incidence that cannot be conveniently located by other approaches. In this type of study, respondents are screened ahead of time and invited to a location at a pre-set time for the actual interview. These locations may include an office, church, school, private facility, hotel/motel, or even a mall research facility.

In-store intercepts are sometimes done to personally interview survey respondents. These studies are usually accomplished in a retail establishment central to the project's objectives (e.g., in a tire store for discussion of tire purchases).

Executive interviewing is the industrial equivalent of door-to-door interviewing. This type of interviewing requires very skilled interviewers who are well versed on the subject matter of the project. Consequently, this type of research is very expensive.

Telephone Interviews

Some of the same considerations involved with the development and management of a group of personal interviewers applies to telephone interviewers. However, greater control of a telephone interviewing staff can be maintained, particularly if the work is accomplished from a central telephone location. The entire interviewing effort can be monitored by a trained supervisor. On-the-spot questions can be answered and field editing can be accomplished to allow for quick correction of any problems with the data-gathering instrument. Computer-assisted interviewing systems have greatly automated telephone survey research and allow for better supervision, sample administration, and quality control. Currently, telephone interviewing is one of the most widely utilized types of survey communication, due to the time and financial advantages of the method. Callbacks can be made much more easily and many people will talk on the phone when they would not open their door to talk with a stranger. In addition, telephone interviewing can execute a study design that requires a probability sample that would be too costly to do in a door-to-door manner.

Mail Surveys

Mail surveys eliminate the problems of selecting, training, and supervising interviewers. They are convenient, efficient, and inexpensive. However, they create some of their own problems such as lack of response and coverage, inability to control the sample responding, time lags in response, inability to handle lengthy or complex material, and potential for misinterpretation of questions.

The procedure for mail-survey administration is the same for questionnaire development, pre-testing, finalization, and production. However, the mail survey eliminates the field-service worker. In place of the personal or telephone interview, there is a mailing or series of mailings of the questionnaire. Postcard reminders, incentives, tokens, and follow-up questionnaires could be sent at appropriate times to encourage return of questionnaires.

Internet Surveys

The Internet is increasingly being used as a means of conducting marketing research. Internet surveys can take various forms and target different groups of respondents. One of the most common uses of Internet surveys is to gather data from existing customers/clients. Most companies systematically gather email addresses from customers for their files and then use these email addresses to deliver Internet surveys they design themselves or the email addresses are provided to a marketing research company that does Internet surveys. These surveys may cover topics such as purchase/service satisfaction, sales/service personnel evaluations, and future buying/shopping intentions. Typically, socio-economic data such as age, gender, income, education, geographic location, occupation, etc. is also collected to develop profiles of customers which can later be analyzed to determine differences in levels of satisfaction by customer type, gender, location, and may be used to profile prospects for future marketing effort.

A second commonly used type of Internet survey is one that is linked to the company's website. This could be a "pop up" link or a permanent link on the website. This enables the company to gather information from website visitors who may or may not be customers/clients of the company—basically anyone who visits the website and decides to complete the survey. Such surveys can determine how the visitor learned about the website, the company's products/ services, and may also be used to collect additional data about the visitor such as email/mailing address, telephone numbers, and socio-economic data. These types of surveys may also ask questions about the website itself in terms of layout, finding needed information, and ease of using the website navigation tools.

A third type of survey is an email delivered survey that ask the recipients to click on a link to take a survey. The email addresses may be purchased or they may be developed by the company by going to various websites to collect email addresses of those targeted in the survey. A typical email is shown in Figure 10.1

Note that this survey was approved by the University's Human Subjects Committee. This is usually necessary for surveys done by university personnel and is based on a university's human subjects research policies. Also note that the recipient is given an approximate time for completing the survey which may encourage them to participate.

The Interviewing Relationship

Cooperation

The first step in the interviewing process requires the interviewer to obtain the cooperation of the potential respondent to be interviewed and then to develop rapport with the respondent. If the interview is on an informal, conversational basis, the respondent will be at ease, and he or she will be less hesitant to voice real opinions. To be conversational and informal, an interviewer need not lose control of the situation. A balance should be sought between the stiff, formal inquisition, in which questions are grimly read and answers methodically checked, and the situation where the interviewer is too friendly and is out of control. An interview in which twenty minutes is spent on the actual questions and twenty minutes more is devoted to irrelevancies and "conversation" is inefficient.

Rapport

The second step of the interviewer is to develop appropriate rapport with the respondent. Rapport is the term used to describe the personal relationship of confidence and understanding between the interviewer and the respondent; rapport provides the foundation for good interviewing. A prerequisite to good rapport is that the respondent knows where he or she stands in the

Dear IT Resource Manager,

Would you please help us? We are conducting a survey of university IT resource managers to get their input on monitoring employee and student uses of a university's IT resources. Your cooperation in clicking on the link below and completing the short Internet survey will be greatly appreciated. Your choice to participate is strictly voluntary and your responses are confidential and anonymous. Please understand that there is no correlation between survey responses and e-mail addresses. You can withdraw from the survey at any time. You should understand that by agreeing to take this survey, as with all surveys, you are accepting any potential risks associated with taking surveys. This survey has been approved by the University's Human Subject Research Review Committee. Your responses will remain confidential and combined with other respondents. You will not receive any promotional material or other emails in connection with this survey. The survey should take about 5-7 minutes to complete.

If you would like a summary of the results, you can send us a separate email to request the summary.

To participate in the survey, simply click on the link below.

Survey

Thanks for your help,

Dr. Robert Stevens
John Massey School of Business
Southeastern Oklahoma State University
1405 N. 4th Ave., PMB 4176
Durant, OK, 74701

Figure 10.1 A Typical Survey Invitation Email

interview. The interview is actually a new situation for most people, and, when it begins, the respondent does not know what is expected or how far he or she can safely go in expressing opinions. Obviously, a respondent will react more favorably and openly in a situation he or she understands and accepts. The respondent should understand that the interview is confidential, that the interviewer is a friendly person ready to listen, that he or she can discuss the interview topics in detail, and that the information being provided is important. Throughout the interview, and especially in its early stages, the interviewer should make a careful effort to establish the tone of the interview in the respondent's mind. The respondent will then have a clear idea of where he or she stands, and what roles he or she and the interviewer have. The respondent should be made to understand that there are no right or wrong answers, that the interviewer is only interested in unbiased responses to the questions. Most people like to share their opinions. Good rapport, coupled with a well-designed data-gathering instrument, should serve the goal of making the interview a very positive experience for the respondent.

The Interviewing Situation

The Approach

The approach an interviewer takes in executing a survey is extremely important. In order for the sample to be representative, it is important that potential respondents are not "lost" or passed by because of something an interviewer may do or say to cause the potential respondent to refuse to participate or be excluded from the sample.

How To, How Not To

The method of approach will vary a great deal according to circumstances. As a general rule, the following scripted approach works well:

> Hello. I'm *(name)* from *(agency)*. We're conducting a survey in this area on *(subject),* and I'd like your opinion.

Notice the introduction does not ask, "May I ask you some questions?"; "Are you busy?"; "Would you mind answering some questions?"; or "Could you spare a couple of minutes?" These are approaches that allow the respondent to say "No" easily and should be avoided.

Qualified Respondent

The interviewer should make sure that the respondent qualifies for the survey. If only certain types of people are specified for in the study, no compromise can be made.

In most surveys, only one member per household should be interviewed. Including more than one interview per household will bias the survey. The exception, of course, is when the study itself seeks to collect data from multiple members of the same household, such as hearing from both husband and wife regarding a purchase decision.

Time Factor

The respondent should not be misled about how long an interview might take. An accurate answer should be given if asked, or in long interviews it is helpful to state the time required before an interview begins. However, the interviewer need not call attention to time or the length of the interview unless the respondent asks or appears to be in a hurry. For most respondents, time passes very quickly while they are engaged in responding to a survey.

Declines, "Too Busy"

Should a respondent initially decline to be interviewed, the interviewer should not give up too easily. He or she should be patient, calm, and pleasantly conversational. Often a potential respondent who has initially refused will then agree to participate. If a person is completely opposed to being interviewed, the interviewer should go on to find another respondent.

In some cases, the selected respondent *is* actually too busy or is getting ready to go out so that an interview at that time is impossible. The interviewer should give a general introduction and try to stimulate the respondent's interest to the extent that he or she will be willing to be interviewed at a later time. The interviewer may need to suggest several alternate times before a convenient time for the interview can be agreed upon. If the survey is being done by telephone, an excellent technique to obtain later cooperation is to offer the respondent the option of calling back on a toll-free, 800 number at his or her convenience. Callback appointment times can be noted on the screening questionnaire/introduction page of the questionnaire.

Respondents may ask why they were selected. The interviewer should explain that they were selected as one of a very small number of people in the area to take part in the survey. The respondent should be told there are no right or wrong answers; the interviewer is only interested in candid opinions. The respondent should be told that responses are confidential, and that his/her identity will not be disclosed since responses will be grouped or tabulated as part of a total with hundreds of other interviews.

The Actual Interview

If at all possible, the respondent should be interviewed alone. The presence of other persons may influence the respondent's answers. From time to time, the respondent may be accompanied by a friend who may begin to answer the questions with or for the respondent. The interviewer should remind them that he or she is interested in only the opinions of the respondent.

The Questionnaire

The interviewer should be completely familiar with the designed questionnaire and all survey materials before conducting an interview. Practice interviews should be conducted to assure that the interviewer will not be awkward with his or her first respondents.

The interviewer should know and follow instructions that are actually printed on the questionnaire or on the screen in all capital letters or enclosed in parentheses. They will indicate:

1 Skip patterns (tell which questions to ask next when a specific answer to a question is given).
2 When to read or not read possible answer sets.
3 When only one answer may be recorded or when multiple answers are acceptable.

Legibility

This issue arises when interviewers are unable to input responses directly into the computer. Legibility is of paramount importance in filling out such questionnaires. Often a lot of time is wasted in the tabulation process by trying to decipher just what was written. The interviewer should always take time at the end of the interview to scan the work and rewrite any words that may be difficult to read by someone else. Each interview should be checked to see that it is entirely legible and understandable.

The interviewer should always use a lead pencil with sufficiently dark lead to be easily read. They should not use colored pencils or any form of ink: a number 2 lead pencil is preferable. Some forms to be scanned require blanks to be filled in with a number 2 pencil.

Asking the Questions

Each question on a questionnaire has been designed for a specific purpose. If an interviewer were to record or put the questions into his or her own words, a bias would be introduced and the interviews would no longer be like those of fellow interviewers who are asking the questions as stated on the questionnaire.

In the case where a respondent does not seem to understand the question, the interviewer should repeat the question to the respondent slowly, but again, not explain it in his or her own words. If the respondent cannot answer or refuses to answer a question, the circumstances should be noted in the margin and the interviewer should go on to the next question.

Do Not Lead the Respondent

The interviewer must not "lead" the respondent. By this we mean that the interviewer should not ask the respondent anything that would direct the respondent to answer the way he or she thinks the interviewer would like. The interviewer should never suggest a word, phrasing, or idea to the respondent. An example of leading would be:

Respondent: It tasted good.
Interviewer: By good, do you mean fresh? Respondent: Yes.

The interviewers' correct clarification to a "It tasted good" response should be "What do you mean by 'good'?"

Do Not Be Negative

It is human nature to ask a question in a negative way. By this we mean that instead of asking, "What else do you remember?" as he or she should, the interviewer may ask inappropriately, "Don't you remember anything else?" or "Can't you remember anything else?" By asking a question in a negative way, the interviewer may put the respondent on the defensive, and continued negative questioning may lead to irritation and termination. In addition, the normal reply to a negative probe is a negative response ... No.

Record the Response Verbatim

Not only should the questions be asked verbatim; the interviewer is to record the answers verbatim. The interviewer will usually be able to keep up with the respondent. If the answer rushes on, the interviewer may have to repeat each of the respondent's words as he or she writes. The respondent usually slows down when this is done. Or, the interviewer may have to say, "You were saying something about ..." The respondent will usually go back and cover the point again.

Another way of slowing down the respondent is by explaining that his or her answer is very important and the interviewer wants to be sure to get every word down.

The exact words of the respondent capture more of the "flavor" of the response and the respondent than through the use of pet phrases and words. The interviewer must not edit or rephrase the respondent's answer. Responses are recorded in the first person, exactly as the respondent states his or her answer.

"X" or Circle, Not a Check

Unless otherwise specified by specific survey instructions, closed-end responses should be noted with an "X." An "X" has been proven to be more legible than a check.

If the instructions indicate that the interviewer is to circle a specified number on the questionnaire to indicate a respondent's answer to a question, it should be neatly circled and should not extend around a second word or number. When a questionnaire uses a grid format for responses, care should be taken to circle the answer in the column number corresponding to the question number.

Interviewer Attitude

The interviewer must remain completely neutral. A respondent's answers can easily be biased by the interviewer interjecting improper voice inflections, biasing comments, or making facial gestures.

The respondent should not be rushed. Some people just do not think or converse as rapidly as others. It should be recognized that the respondent is being asked for an opinion without prior preparation and about which he or she has had very little time to think.

When interviewing, the interviewer does not have to have an expressionless face. He or she should develop the habit of encouraging the respondent to talk, without leading, and then listen carefully to what is said. There are many ways to indicate that the interviewer is following the respondent's remarks. Sometimes the nod of the head is sufficient; sometimes unbiased remarks such as "I see what you mean," "I understand," or "That's interesting," will keep the respondent expressing ideas and thinking further about the topic without leading or biasing the data.

Closure

After completing the interview, the respondent should be thanked. Before the interviewer leaves a respondent, he or she should review responses to all questions to be certain that they have been answered correctly and the answers are clear, meaningful, and legible. The interviewer should then leave as quickly and pleasantly as possible.

Classification, Demographic, and Statistical Information

Generally, questionnaires include some classification questions such as income, age, education level, occupation, number of children in household, etc. Most people answer such questions willingly. Refusals will be rare if these questions are asked properly in an unapologetic fashion. Respondents may also be told that the answers are tabulated by a computer and that no one answer will be looked at individually.

Validation

A validation questionnaire should be prepared for every project. This questionnaire should include the original screening questions plus standard questions on method of recruitment, acquaintance with the interviews, and participation in other studies. Validation should be completed within one to two days of the end of fielding the real survey. This important quality check on the fieldwork ensures that the interview has actually taken place. Ten to 15 percent of all respondents who were reportedly interviewed are recontacted to verify their participation. If a respondent cannot answer the verification questions satisfactorily, then the interview that he or she allegedly completed is declared "invalid" and those results are not included in the aggregated tabulations. If more than one invalid survey is attributed to a specific interviewer, all of that interviewer's work is discarded.

Fielding a Research Project

Security of the Survey

The questionnaires, the responses, and all materials used in conjunction with the survey are confidential and should be returned to the supervisor at the completion of interviewing. Respondents generally are not told for whom the study is being conducted. The interviewer should not discuss interviews with family, friends, other interviewers, or anyone else. Confidentiality of the client and survey content and results is of utmost importance.

Briefings

Briefings, or training sessions, will be held before each project is initiated. The entire job will be discussed, giving both the supervisor and the interviewers an opportunity to carefully study job specifications and instructions and to ask any questions pertaining to the job. Field instructions will be reviewed and practice interviews will also be conducted to familiarize interviewers with the questionnaire. Individuals will be assigned quotas or specific duties involved with the job.

Supervisor Assistance

Each research project must have adequate supervision. If a question or problem arises, the interviewer should ask the job supervisor and not another interviewer for assistance. Once called to the supervisor's attention, any questions or problems can be remedied for all interviewers on the job or can be referred to the client for resolution.

Do Not Interview Friends or Acquaintances

A friend or acquaintance of the interviewer should never be interviewed. He or she might answer the questions in a manner that he or she thought would "please" the interviewer, rather than give a candid response.

Adhere to the Study Specifications

The specifications of a study have been set forth for very definite reasons, and the specifications must be adhered to, to the letter. Therefore, if the interviewing method is personal, the interviewer cannot interview a respondent on the telephone; if the interviewer is to contact only one person in the household, he or she cannot interview other family members; if the interviewer is to interview one person at a time, he or she cannot interview a group of respondents. The interviewer cannot interview the same respondent on multiple studies at the same interview. By doing any of these things, the interviewer would not be following the specifications, and the interviews would be rendered useless.

Follow All Study Procedures and Instructions

It is very important that each interview be conducted in the same manner by all interviewers. Instructions about showing exhibit cards, posters, or keeping products concealed must be obeyed the same way in all interviews. Detailed field instructions are designed to reiterate to supervisors and interviewers the technical aspect of executing the specific study, and are usually provided for each project. These instructions come in many forms. A simple study may require an administrative guide, an interviewer's guide, a tally sheet, and sample questionnaire. More complicated tests may require quota sheets, test plans, preparation instructions, product-handling procedures, exhibits, concept statements, and/or sorting boards.

The administrative guide is designed for the field supervisor of the study. It provides useful background information, a start and end date, quotas, respondent qualifications, procedures for conducting the study, personnel requirements, briefing instructions, and many other special instructions.

The interviewer guide is provided for each interviewer. The interviewer guide usually has some of the same information as the administrative guide as well as specific step-by-step, question-by-question instructions on how to administer the survey questionnaire.

Accurate Record Keeping

It is the interviewer's responsibility to keep accurate records of all information required by the supervisor or the survey's client. If the addition of columns of numbers is required, it is the interviewer's responsibility that the addition be correct. Information collected through use of a tally sheet is often just as important as information collected in the actual interview.

Complete Assignments on Time

An interviewer is responsible for completing assignments on time. Should unforeseen circumstances arise, or if the interviewer anticipates that the assignment will not be completed within the specified time, the supervisor should be notified immediately.

Work Efficiency

Two factors can affect the efficiency of work performance: speed and quality. Conducting interviews at a reasonable speed is important. However, speed for the sake of numbers should never sacrifice quality. On the other hand, gaining desired information from the respondent is critical and can be done without spending undue time on any one area or by undue conversation with the respondent.

Probing

Many questions, particularly in in-depth interviews, are open-ended and require the interviewer to coax the answers from the respondent. Getting as much information as possible from open-ended questions often requires skillful probing. The interviewer should never assume anything about what the respondent is implying, but he or she should probe to get clear and complete answers to all parts of the question in the respondent's own words. The two basic purposes of probing are to clarify and develop additional information.

Clarify

The interviewer should get as much information as possible from open-ended questions. An answer that tells something specific is much more valuable than getting several answers that are vague. The interviewer's objective should be to clarify why the respondent gave a particular answer to one of the questions. The more concrete and specific these reasons are, the more valuable the information becomes. For example, a respondent is talking about a car that he or she believes would be "economical." What does he or she mean by economical? He or she means that it is not very expensive to buy, that it gets good gas mileage, that it is not very expensive to maintain, that it has a high trade-in value, or something else. It is up to the interviewer to find out precisely what the respondent means by "economical."

The following is an example of how to probe for clarity.

Respondent: It's not my kind of movie.
Interviewer: Why do you say that?
Respondent: It doesn't look interesting.
Interviewer: What do you mean by "interesting?"
Respondent: The thread of the picture seems difficult to follow and the action is slow and drawn out. I enjoy fast-paced, action-packed movies.

Develop Additional Information

An interviewer must often get respondents to expand on an answer. "It would be true to life" or "It makes you think" and other general answers should be probed by saying "Why do you say that?" or "Tell me more about that." Many of the best probes are on key words and the interviewer may repeat the key words from the respondent's answer as a question: "True to life?" or "Makes you think?"

The following is an example of probing for additional information.

Respondent: They showed a bowl of soup.
Interviewer: What kind of soup was it?
Respondent: It looked like vegetable soup.
Interviewer: What else did they show?
Respondent: A little boy eating the soup and smiling because he liked it.
Interviewer: What did they say about the soup?
Respondent: They said this soup makes a warm and nutritious meal in itself.

Technical Aspects of Probing

1   When key words are probed, the word in the respondent's answer being probed should be underlined, e.g., "I thought the soup looked <u>tasty</u>."
2   Probing questions asked that are not tied to key words should be indicated by prefacing those questions with a "p" with a circle around it, signifying an interviewer probe.
3   Answers should always be recorded verbatim in the respondent's own words. The interviewer should not edit, try to improve his or her English, or put things in complete sentences for him or her. Abbreviations may be used when possible as long as they are obvious to anyone who might see them. If they are not, the interviewer should go back after the interview and write them out.
4   The interviewer should begin writing the minute the respondent begins to speak. Responses are much more easily recorded if started before the respondent gets underway.
5   If necessary, the interviewer may ask the respondent to stop for a minute, or to repeat something he or she missed.
6   The interviewer should never lead the respondent. Legitimate probes must be distinguished from leading questions. A leading question would be "Was it a bowl of vegetable soup?" or "Do you remember the little boy that was in the ad?" Anything that suggests something specific about the subject is inadmissible.

Summary

The interviewer should get specifics, and ask "what else" only after probing the original response. They should not accept an adjective or a thought—but find out why the respondent feels that way and get the respondents to expand on their answers. Details, whether positive or negative about the subject, are very important. Figure 10.2 illustrates words to clarify and questions to help probe and clarify.

Sequencing of Contact Methods

It is not unusual in survey research to use multiple mediums in a sequence to ensure a higher rate of response. For example, a research project might use the following sequence:

Words to Clarify

All right	Different	Good/Bad	Rich
Appealing	Difficult	Homemade	Satisfying/Satisfied
Appearance	Dislike	Tastes	Service
Attractive	Easy/Hard	Interesting	Shape
Better/Best	Effective	Lighting	Size
Cheap	Expensive	Like	Smell/Odor
Cleanliness	Feel/Soft/Hard/Stiff	Many	Smooth
Color	Few	Material	Spicy/Spicier
Comfortable	Fine	Neat	Stayed in Place
Consistency	Fit	Nice	Better
Convenient	Flavor	Okay	Sweet/Sweeter
Cost	Food	Price	Taste/Flavor
Crisp/Crunchy	Frequently	Protection	Texture
Decor	Fresh	Quality	Variety
Design	Funny	Quick	Worse/Worst

Questions to Help Clarify

Why do you feel that _____ ?
What do you mean by _____ ?
Would you explain that more fully?
Would you be more specific?
Where does that occur?
When did you notice _____ ?
How is it ?
What makes it _____ ?
What about _____ ?
In what way is it _____ ?

Probe Phrases

What else can you tell me?
What other reasons do you have?
What else can you remember/recall?
Your ideas/opinions are so helpful; can you tell me more?
What (specific wording in question)?

Final Probe

Are there any other ideas/opinions/brands/types/reasons, etc.?

Tell respondents their responses will be written down. This will eliminate long uncomfortable pauses.

Figure 10.2 Clarifying and Probing

1   Select respondents, obtain their phone number, mailing address, email address.
2   Contact respondents by mail or email telling them they have been selected for the study, asking them to go to a website or call an 800 number to arrange a time for a phone interview, or tell them a questionnaire will be mailed soon.
3   Phone interview conducted or questionnaire mailed or emailed.
4   Phone, mail, or email follow-up to ask for completion of survey if response not received.

Errors In Data Collection

The accuracy of any data provided in a research project depends on several interrelated things. First of all, there must have been clearly articulated research objectives. Second, correct design must have been accomplished. Third, correct sampling techniques and procedures must have been used. Fourth, the data must have been collected well, and finally, the data must be analyzed correctly. Mistakes or errors at any point can negate excellent design sampling, survey technique, and questionnaire design. Figure 10.3 illustrates the relationship between sampling and nonsampling error.

There are many types of errors generally classified as sampling and nonsampling errors. Sampling error was discussed in Chapter 9. However, nonsampling error, which results from some systematic bias being introduced during the research process, can be a bigger problem

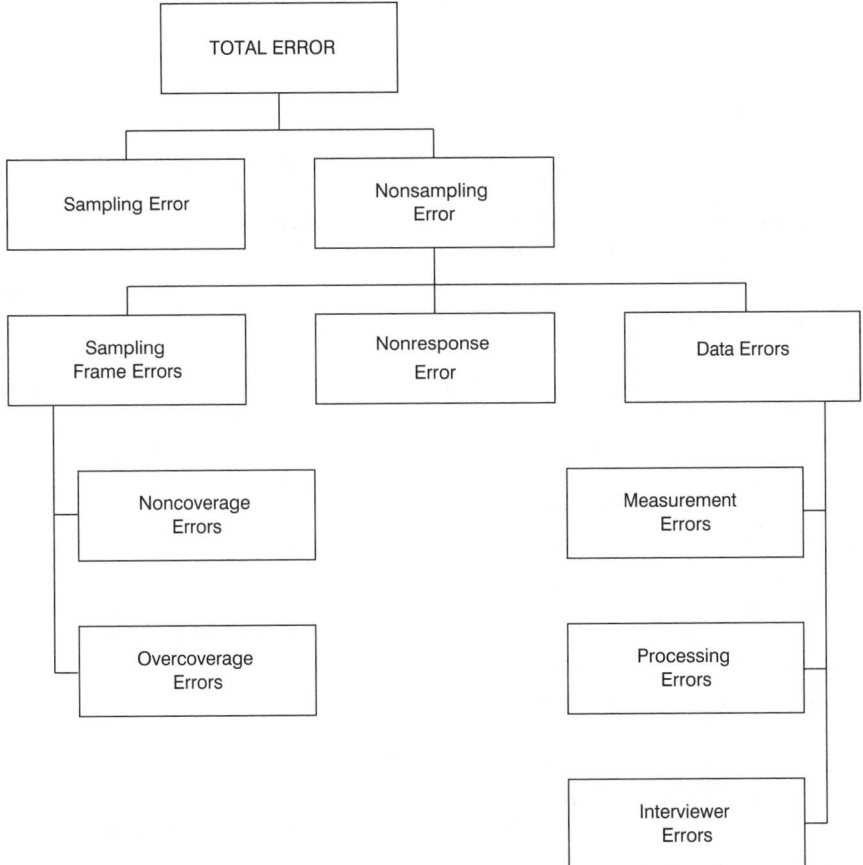

Figure 10.3 Sources of Research Error

than sampling error.[1] Nonsampling errors are not a result of sampling. They include mistakes that come from sampling frame errors, nonresponse errors, and data errors.[2] Nonsampling errors commonly arise from errors in design, logic, interpretation, field service, or presentation.

Nonsampling errors are a numerous breed. They are pervasive in nature and are highly arbitrary. Nonsampling errors, unlike sampling errors, do not decrease with sample size. In fact, they tend to increase as sample size increases. While sampling errors can be estimated, the direction, magnitude, and impact of nonsampling errors are generally unknown. As a result of this, nonsampling errors are frequently the most significant errors that arise during a research project. Their reduction is not dependent on increasing sample size, but on improving methods and procedures dealing with the handling of the data itself.

Types of Nonsampling Errors

There are three basic types of nonsampling errors: sampling frame error, nonresponse error, and data error. Sampling frame errors occur when certain parts of the survey population are not represented or are overrepresented in the study. Nonresponse errors result when there is a systematic difference between those who respond and those who do not respond to a survey. Data errors occur because the information gathered is inaccurate or because mistakes are made while the data is being processed. Quite often nonsampling errors are made without the researcher being aware of them. This makes them potentially dangerous to the outcome of the project. An understanding of these types of errors will help the researcher prevent or correct them.

Sampling Frame Errors

Sampling frame errors generally consist of noncoverage and overcoverage errors. Noncoverage errors occur when some elements of the original population are not included in the sample. The bias from this type of error is the difference in characteristics, attributes, and opinions between those who are included and those who are not included. This is a very troublesome problem in marketing research because researchers do not know if there are significant and strategic differences between the ones who did not respond and the ones who did when there is no information on the noncovered potential respondents. Noncoverage is basically a problem with the sampling frame. The sampling frame is simply a listing of all the possible members of the population being studied. All of the basic survey methods depend on a listing of the members of the population under study. Telephone directories are not complete frames of a city's population because not every household has a number. Furthermore, of those that do, many are unlisted, and many people are in transition at any given time. Mail surveys have the same noncoverage problems, because there is rarely a list that exactly includes the total population under study.

The noncoverage of sample members is as important as the noncoverage that results from not including all possible respondents in the sample frame.

This occurs when the listed sample units are not contacted and happens with both personal and telephone surveys. Quite often this situation arises when interviewers do not follow instructions or do not make the appropriate callbacks.

The most effective ways to limit the extent of noncoverage error is to recognize its existence and to take conventional measures. These measures are: (1) improve the sample frame; (2) establish clear instructions concerning who to interview, when to interview, and where to interview; (3) specify callback requirements; and (4) when possible, verify or monitor interviews.

Overcoverage errors occur when there is duplication or overrepresentation of certain categories of sampling units in the sampling frame. In many cases, noncoverage of certain portions of the sample frame leads to overcoverage of other portions. Overcoverage can also occur when certain sample units are listed more than once. This leads to double counting and study bias.

Nonresponse Errors

Nonresponse errors occur when some of the elements of the population selected to be part of the sample do not respond. This happens most frequently in Internet and mail surveys, but can also occur in telephone surveys and personal interviews. The people originally chosen to be interviewed might not respond because they are not at home or because they refuse to participate. Incorrect email addresses are a continuing problem for Internet surveys.

"Not at homes" result because the potential respondent is not at home when the interviewer calls. This source of nonresponse error tends to be on the increase. Included in the "not at home" category of respondents are those who are literally not at home and those who cannot be located. This includes those who use their answering machines or caller ID to screen their calls while they are out for the day, gone on an extended trip, or even those who have recently moved. There is some evidence that the "not at home" categories of respondents tend to have different characteristics than those who are more easily located. Dual-career households tend to aggravate the problem. Care must be taken to account for the "not at home" factor or survey results will be incomplete and biased. The segments less likely to be home will be underrepresented and the results skewed toward the more commonly at home respondents.

Refusals occur when some respondents decline to participate or terminate prematurely after beginning the survey. The actual rate of refusal will depend on the nature of the respondent, the subject of the research, the ability of the interviewer, the length and design of the questionnaire, and the personal situation of the respondent. Mail surveys are particularly susceptible to the refusal nonresponse error. Personal, telephone, and Internet interviews are also plagued with refusal nonresponse. Overall, the refusal rate appears to be increasing. More and more people are being interviewed and the novelty of being surveyed is wearing off. Because of fraud and crime, people are wary of having interviewers come into their homes. The use of the phone for telemarketing sales pitches disguised as surveys has also made legitimate surveys more difficult to complete.

Fortunately, there are many effective methods of reducing nonresponse problems. Some of the most common ones are:

1 sell the respondent on the importance of his or her opinion and the value of the research;
2 notify the respondent in advance and make an appointment for a callback at a mutually agreeable time;
3 ensure confidentiality;
4 maintain contact with a callback or a follow-up mailing;
5 include return postage and envelopes for mail surveys;
6 use tokens or money incentives;
7 provide a toll-free number so the respondent can call back at his or her convenience.

Careful use of these techniques will increase the response rate of surveys and help avoid the problems associated with nonresponse error.

Data Errors

Data errors consist of interviewer errors, measurement errors, and processing errors. Usually these errors occur because inaccurate information is gathered from the respondent or the wrong information is recorded. This can result from measurement instrument bias resulting from a

Research Project Tip

If your research project involves descriptive or causal research you must describe in detail how you will obtain the desired information from the "field." That is, you must describe the experimental design and the details of its implementation for causal research (see Chapter 5), or how the descriptive research will be carried out. Use the following checklist to ensure you have a plan for taking the descriptive research questionnaire to the field:

1. Budgets—Has money been appropriated for the following?
☐ Wages of interviewers, supervisors, and general office support
☐ Telephone charges
☐ Postage/shipping
☐ Production of questionnaire and other forms
☐ Supplies

2. Guidelines for interviewers—Have the following been done?
☐ An introduction been written
☐ Interviewers know how much time the interview will take when asked by respondent
☐ Provision has been made on the interview form for second callback appointment
☐ Interviewer is thoroughly familiar with questionnaire
☐ Interviewer has been trained as to the proper way to ask questions and probe for responses
☐ Interviewer records answers verbatim in legible handwriting
☐ Interviewer uses proper attitude in conducting interview

3. Validation
☐ Validation questionnaire has been designed
☐ Validation questionnaire has been used

4. Administrative Guide—The field supervisor has a guide that includes the following:
☐ Background information on purpose and objective of the research
☐ Start and end dates
☐ Quotas for interviewers
☐ Respondent qualifications
☐ Procedures for conducting the study
☐ Personnel requirements
☐ Briefing instructions

5. Interviewing—Probing
☐ Interviewers are familiar with when and how to probe to clarify or obtain additional information

6. Nonsampling Errors—Have the following nonsampling errors been addressed through preplanned procedures to prevent or overcome the problems?
☐ Sampling frame errors
☐ Noncoverage
☐ Overcoverage
☐ Nonresponse errors
☐ Not at home
☐ Refusals
☐ Data errors
☐ Interviewing errors
☐ Coding
☐ Tabulating
☐ Processing

poorly designed questionnaire. In some cases processing error is also introduced during the editing, coding, tabulating, and processing of the data. Interviewer bias occurs due to interaction between the interviewer and the respondent. Respondents may overstate or understate certain behaviors, either consciously or unconsciously. In some ways these types of errors are the most dangerous because, unlike nonobservational errors, researchers have no idea when and how observational errors might arise. Careful training, supervision, monitoring, and editing are required to minimize this type of error.

A final type of data error that should be mentioned is cheating. Cheating is the deliberate falsification of information by the interviewer. To avoid this problem, adequate control and supervision must be exercised.

Summary

Once a data-gathering instrument is designed and the appropriate sample frame and size selected, it is time to field the instrument and execute the data-gathering process. To accomplish this smoothly and with a minimum of error, preplanning is a necessity. Proper budgeting and personnel recruitment lead the list of planning activities for the well-executed field-service effort. Interviewers should be trained, briefed, and well supervised to obtain optimum results.

The interviewing relationship requires special attention to ensure proper rapport and understanding between the interviewer and respondent. Specific guidelines should be followed by interviewers depending on the type of interview being conducted.

General rules of interviewing must be maintained at all times. They include: insuring security of the survey, providing proper training and briefing sessions, having close supervision, adhering to specific study specifications, following all study procedures and instructions, keeping accurate records, completing assignments on time, working efficiently, probing appropriately, and achieving clarity.

Discussion Questions

1   Why is it important to focus on reducing "total error" in a research project and not just on sampling error? What else, besides sample size, are potential contributors to total error?
2   Discuss the correct way to probe during interviewing.
3   Discuss the three types of non-sampling errors.

Part IV
Data Analysis and Reporting

11 Analyzing and Interpreting Data for Decisions

Learning Objectives

Upon completing this chapter, you should understand:

1. the relationship between data analysis and decision making;
2. the importance of planning the data analysis procedures to be used on the collected data;
3. how frequency distributions, measures of central tendency and dispersion help in summarizing and understanding data;
4. the usefulness of cross tabulations in data analysis to understand underlying differences in responses.

Hamlet:	Do you see yonder cloud that's almost in shape of a camel?
Polonius:	By the mass, and 'tis like a camel indeed.
Hamlet:	Methinks it is like a weasel.
Polonius:	It is backed like a weasel.
Hamlet:	Or like a whale?
Polonius:	Very like a whale.

Hamlet, Act III, Scene ii

Data, like cloud formations, can be made to appear to support any number of conjectures. The fertile mind of the analyst can "see" conclusions to the data that may be more the creation of the imagination than an objective reading of the information generated by the research. This gives pause to the researcher/analyst, because it implies that, while there may be an ultimate truth, the analyst's personal agenda, perceptual inclinations, experience, and even personality can influence the interpretation of the research study's results. Nevertheless, we must use all the means at our disposal to arrive at the most objective, concise, but also thorough analysis possible of the data generated by the research. However, the same observation of objective data may be subject to multiple interpretations. Consider the following apocryphal story.

An American shoe company sent three researchers to a Pacific Island to see if the company could sell its shoes there. Upon returning they made a presentation to management. The first researcher summed up the findings this way. "The people here don't wear shoes. There is no market." The second researcher said: "The people here don't wear shoes. There is a tremendous market!" The third researcher reported: "The people here don't wear shoes. However, they have bad feet and could benefit from wearing shoes. We would need to redesign our shoes, however, because they have smaller feet. We would have to educate the people about the benefits of wearing shoes. We would need to gain the tribal chief's

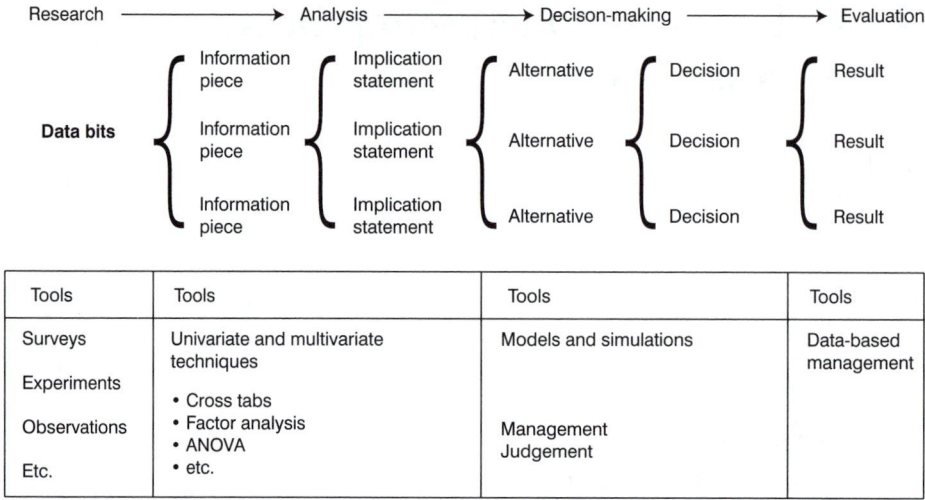

Figure 11.1. Overview of the Data Analysis/Management Decision-Making Relationship

cooperation. The people don't have any money, but they grow great pineapples. I've estimated the sales potential over a three-year period and all of our costs including selling the pineapples to a European supermarket chain, and concluded that we could make a 30% return on our money. I say we should pursue the opportunity."[1]

Here the three analyses reported the same results, but with different implications. The term "data analysis" covers a huge number of techniques, statistical programs, and processes that can be applied to the results generated by the data-collection instrument(s) used in our research. These can range from interpreting respondents' reactions to projective research, or the conclusions drawn from conducting focus groups (for both see Chapter 4), to sophisticated multivariate statistical techniques used to manipulate large databases. It is beyond the scope of this book to address these extremes of the data analysis continuum. The reader interested in such analytical processes should read material that specifically addresses those topics.[2] The discussion in this chapter will be limited to data analysis "basics" that will permit the researcher/analyst to successfully draw useful information out of the types of data generated via a descriptive research survey format.

From Data To Decisions

The manipulation and analysis of data generated by research becomes a "value-added" management activity when it takes place within a series of tasks leading to management decisions and, ultimately, to a market's reaction to those decisions. Figure 11.1 suggests that the output of the data analysis process is to always lead to better decision making than could have been done without having conducted the research. This is consistent with the philosophy about the value of research presented throughout this book.[3]

An example may help to elucidate the process shown in Figure 11.1.

Worthington Foods, now owned by Kellogg, a company that markets egg substitutes (e.g., Scramblers, Better 'N' Eggs) conducted survey research which in part, sought answers to these research objectives:

1   Why do people control their cholesterol?
2   How did people who use egg substitutes first hear about them?
3   What is the trial-to-usage ratio for those cholesterol controllers who have tried a brand of egg substitute?

A phone survey of a demographic cross-section of the adult U.S. population was conducted (2,000 respondents). Once respondents passed a set of screening questions identifying them as cholesterol controllers they were asked to respond to these and other relevant questions:

1   What is the primary reason you are controlling your cholesterol intake? (check one response)
2   Which of the following brands of egg substitutes have you ever tried? Which do you currently use?
3   From which of the following sources did you first hear about egg substitutes?

Table 11.1 shows a sampling of the data bits generated from these questions:

Each of the numbers listed in Table 11.1 represents a "data bit." Obviously, even a short phone survey can generate thousands of these bits of data. Although interesting by themselves, they become of even greater value when combined with each other to generate "information." For example, if we know the number of people who have tried a particular egg substitute brand (*a data bit*) and which of these same people currently use that brand (another data bit), we can determine that brand's retention ratio, the percentage who have tried and still use, or the brands rejection ratio, the percentage who tried and no longer use (i.e., *information pieces*).

Moreover, when multiple *pieces of information* are combined, some important *implications* can be drawn. Consider, for example what is learned when information is combined about the primary reason for controlling cholesterol with usage or nonusage of egg substitutes:

Table 11.1 Data bits generated by survey

1.	Reason for controlling cholesterol		
	On doctor's orders	36%	
	Family history of cholesterol problem	11%	
	Concerned about future levels	53%	
2.	Percentage of all cholesterol controllers trying and using egg substitutes brands:		
		Tried	*Currently Use*
	Egg Beaters	72%	25%
	Scramblers	12%	7%
	Second Natures	4%	1%
	Eggs Supreme	1%	—
3.	Source of "first heard" for egg substitute triers:		
	TV ad	13%	
	Physician	10%	
	Friend or relative	26%	
	Magazine ad	24%	
	Hospital	2%	
	Saw product in store	7%	

	Egg Substitute	
Reason for controlling cholesterol	*Users*	*Nonusers*
On doctor's orders	61%	32%
Family history	12%	11%
Concerned about future levels	27%	57%
Total	100%	100%

Here, the *implication* may be drawn that users of egg substitutes are much more likely to be under physicians' orders to control cholesterol than are nonusers. Looking at the data from another angle, of all the cholesterol controllers under physicians' orders to control cholesterol, the vast majority are users of egg substitutes (74% of all those under physicians' orders to control cholesterol are users of egg substitute brands).

	Egg Substitute		
Reason for controlling cholesterol	*Users*	*Nonusers*	*Total*
On doctor's orders	74%	26%	100%
Family history	20%	80%	100%
Concerned about future levels	31%	69%	100%

Another related implication comes from combining information about how respondents first heard about egg substitutes with their retention/rejection information.

	% of Egg Substitute Triers		
First heard of egg substitutes from:	*Rejectors*	*Continuing to Use*	*Total*
TV ad	58%	42%	100%
Magazine ad	45%	55%	100%
Friend or relative	38%	62%	100%
Physician	18%	82%	100%

The implication from this table is that those who first hear about egg substitutes from a physician are more likely to continue using them after trial than those who first hear of them from other sources.

Combining these and other implications about usage and information sources leads to *decision alternatives* regarding the allocation of resources among TV media, magazine ads, coupons, in-store promotions, and calling on physicians. When the company conducting this research did a subsequent cost-benefit analysis of promoting directly to physicians, they determined that it was to their advantage to begin to pursue that course of action.

This illustration shows how data bits are combined into pieces of information which are combined into implications, which suggest decision alternatives, which lead to *decisions.* In this case, the decision to make physicians aware of the egg substitute brand and give their high-cholesterol patients a coupon for a free package of that brand was based on research findings which demonstrated that getting trial usage from that source was much more likely to result in continued usage than if trial was gained from other sources. Monitoring the *results* of this change in the allocation of promotional resources showed that the efforts with physicians were very cost-effective in increasing sales. Thus, these decisions led to results that became data bits which ultimately resulted in future decisions (continued promotion to physicians).

This example also demonstrates that data analysis goes beyond merely determining answers to research questions. The analytical aspects of this case did not stop with reporting answers to the original three research objectives, but rather sought to reveal the *association* that might exist between the three questions. That is, the *implications* drawn between the information pieces were what added real, significant value to the research findings. The research analyst is acting as more than a reporter of findings; he/she is seeking to know the answer to such provoking questions as:

- What does it mean that *this* (e.g., why they control cholesterol) and *this* (e.g., a difference in retention rate) are both true simultaneously? and
- What does it matter that the researcher has discovered this association? *Answer:* It suggests physicians could play an important gatekeeping role in generating product trial for people who may prove to be brand-loyal heavy users. Not reported in this example, but true for the research, was the discovery of a direct correlation between egg substitute usage rate and physician involvement.

Therefore, the researcher/analyst's job is only half over once the research is finished. The real value-added activities come with the data-analysis tasks performed on the gathered data.

We will now discuss the means by which such data analysis can be conducted.

Data Summary Methods

Developing a Plan of Analysis

For the purposes of this discussion we will assume that the researcher/analyst has successfully coded and entered data into the computer and now desires printouts that can be analyzed and interpreted.

The first step in generating summary data to be analyzed is to prepare a plan of analysis. Actually, the genesis of such a plan was started in the discussion in Chapter 1 concerning how to state research questions and hypotheses, and was further developed in the Chapter 5 discussions of dummy tables. Therefore, the heart of a plan of data analysis consists of:

- how to obtain answers to research questions;
- how to test hypotheses to determine if they are supported by the data or must be rejected;
- the execution of the dummy tables that were used early in the research design process to alert the researcher to the type and form the descriptive survey data should take.

However, as demonstrated by the egg substitute research example at the beginning of this chapter, it may be necessary to go beyond obtaining answers to the research questions, testing existing hypotheses, and filling out dummy tables. In that example, a new hypothesis was generated during the data analysis. The new hypothesis was that retention rates of egg substitute usage would vary by reason for controlling cholesterol and by source of first mention of egg substitutes. Such a hypothesis could very well have been generated at the time the research purpose and objectives were stated at the very start of the research process. However, it is inevitable that some hypotheses or specific tabulations or analytical outputs will be initiated during the data-analysis process and not before.

Frequency Distributions

It is common for researchers to generate a set of frequency distributions which indicate how respondents answered the survey questions. For example:

Q: What is the primary reason you are controlling your cholesterol intake?

	Number	*Percentage*
On doctor's orders	651	36%
Family history	199	11%
Future concern	959	53%
	1,809	100%

Note that of the 2,000 respondents surveyed, only 1,809 answered this question. The remaining 191 were omitted for the usual reasons (spoiled questionnaire, refusal to answer, etc.). The percentage is best computed as 100 percent for those respondents who did answer the question, rather than based on the full 2,000 respondents. However, the researcher may wish to know why the 191 subjects were not included. If many could not easily choose a primary reason (they were controlling cholesterol for two or three reasons), or were controlling cholesterol for reasons not given as a response option (e.g., because their spouse was controlling and prepared meals with reduced cholesterol), then the researcher would want to know this so he/she could revise the question in the future to make provision for such problems. Hopefully, exploratory research done before the survey would reveal most or all of the response categories needed. Also, offering a fourth option:

Other [Record]: _____

is an expensive, but effective, means of learning of other reasons respondents control cholesterol. Nevertheless, if the analyst is primarily concerned with how the target population is distributed among these three reasons, then the percentages should be computed based on the 1,809 respondents instead of 2,000.

If the question had been phrased differently a different-looking frequency distribution might result:

Q: Why are you controlling your cholesterol intake? [Check all that apply]

	Mentions	
	Number	*Percentage*
On doctor's orders	702	39%
Family history	295	16%
Future concern	1,120	62%
	2,117	117%

Here it is obvious we have multiple reasons given by some of the 1,809 respondents and the percentages are computed based on the number of respondents instead of number of responses. The percentages may be interpreted as follows: "39 percent of the respondents mentioned that they controlled their cholesterol because of a physician's orders; 16 percent mentioned controlling ..." We might be interested in asking this question both ways, with "check all that apply" asked first, followed by the "primary reason" question. Researchers should be cautioned to carefully consider why they are asking such questions and how they plan to analyze the results before assuming automatically that it would be best to always ask both questions. Time is valuable and only a limited amount of it will be given by respondents. If the researcher uses it up by asking these two questions it means he/she will not be able to ask some other important question within the time frame.

Before leaving percentages as a topic, two important aspects of their use should be mentioned:

1 *Percentages cannot be averaged unless the percentage is weighted by the size of the sample responding to the question.*

For example, consider the following frequency distribution:

	Egg Beaters			Scramblers	
Usage rate	Number of users	Percent		Number of users	Percent
High	250	50%		75	37.5%
Medium	100	20%		100	50.0%
Low	150	30%		25	12.5%
	500	100%		200	100%

It would be incorrect to say that an average of 35 percent of users of these two brands are medium users (i.e., 20% + 50% = 70% ÷ 2 = 35%) when actually medium users represent 28.6 percent of the two brands' usage rate (i.e., 100 + 100 = 200 ÷ 700 = 28.6%).

2 *Do not refer only to percentages when the base of their computation is very small.*

For example, while the following percentages may be accurate, be careful not to misrepresent the data by referring to just the percentages:

	Male Respondents	
Reason for controlling cholesterol	Number	Percentage
On doctor's orders	7	70%
Family history	2	20%
Future concern	1	10%
	10	100%

3 *Dealing with "don't know," "no opinion" responses is a matter of analyst judgment.*
Usually it is best to include them as a legitimate answer to knowledge or attitude-type questions and record the response rate such as:

Q: Which do you believe would be higher priced, Egg Beaters or Scramblers?

Egg Beaters	65%
Scramblers	30%
Don't know	4%
No opinion	1%
	100%

Researchers should be aware that it is standard operating procedure for marketing research firms using phone or personal interviewers to push for responses other than "don't know" or "no opinion" when asking a knowledge or attitude question, and recording a "don't know" response only when, after unsuccessful prodding, the respondent insists on maintaining that answer. Therefore, the "don't know" and "no opinion" responses will almost always be underrepresented in the final data. While in many cases that is desirable, in some cases it may grossly distort the truth.

As an illustration of such a danger, consider results generated by research which asked triers of multiple brands of egg substitutes which brand had a higher fat content. The results (simplified here for discussion purposes) were as follows:

	Percent Mentioned as High Fat
Brand A	17%
Brand B	13%
Don't know	70%
	100%

This distribution actually was a test of the researcher's hypothesis that the low involvement of people in purchasing a product such as an egg substitute brand would be reflected in their lack of knowledge about such attributes as fat levels for the brands they had purchased. Consequently, interviewers were instructed to record the first response of the subjects and not to use standard operating procedure (SOP) to push for an answer other than "Don't know." The results supported the hypothesis and suggested that altering some product attributes would have a limited effect on brand demand. Therefore, researchers should consider how they wish to deal with the "Don't know" and "No opinion" response percentages.

Central Tendency and Dispersion Measures

As seen in the discussion in Chapter 6 on measurement, the measures of central tendency that can be used to describe the data depend upon the type of data we have generated (nominal, ordinal, interval, ratio). The frequency distribution discussion in the previous section is pertinent to each of these four types of data.

Additionally, Figure 11.2 displays the measures of central tendency and dispersion which can be computed for the data types.

Nominal   Mode

Ordinal   Mode, Median

Interval   Mode, Median, Mean , Standard Deviation

Ratio   Mode, Median, Mean , Standard Deviation

- Mode = The most frequently occurring response.
- Median = The response that separates the top half of response frequencies from the bottom half.
- Mean = The average of the responses computed by summing all responses and dividing by the number of responses.

Figure 11.2. Measures of Central Tendency and Dispersion

Table 11.2 Calculation of Mean

(1) *Number of times eat at fast food restaurants/week*	(2) *Number of respondents*	(1) × (2)
Less than once a week (coded as .5)	100	50.0
Once or twice a week (coded as 1.5)	250	375.0
Two or three times a week (coded as 2.5)	175	437.5
More than three times a week (coded as 4)	50	200.0
Total	575	1062.5
Mean = 1.85 times per week (1062.5 ÷575)		

The most commonly used measures in Figure 11.2 are defined below and will be discussed in this section of the chapter.

When the question involves indicating the frequency with which something occurs (e.g., the number of times a person eats at a fast food restaurant in a typical week) the frequency is multiplied by the number of respondents checking that answer, those numbers are summed, and the mean is computed by dividing that sum by the number of total respondents. For an example see Table 11.2.

Here, a judgment was made regarding how to code a range of responses. Since people are being asked to give an estimate of their behavior instead of requiring them to keep a diary or an accounting of their actual behavior, researchers are dealing with approximate responses instead of documented frequencies. Consequently, the coded midpoint of the range (e.g., two to three times per week coded as 2.5) is an estimate, and the mean of 1.85 times per week is also an approximation. Researchers should not forget this fact later when they are using this number in calculations and when drawing implications from such calculations.

It is important to assess the mean's ability to accurately reflect the sample respondents' responses by calculating a standard deviation for the responses.

> *Standard Deviation:* Representing the degree of "spread" of responses among the response categories, it tells us the range of answers which includes roughly 70 percent of the sampled respondents.[4]

So, for example, if the mean is 1.85 times per week and the standard deviation is 0.32, then roughly 70 percent of respondents (and hence the population universe) eat at fast food restaurants between 1.53 and 2.17 times per week (1.85 − 0.32 = 1.53; 1.85 + 0.32 = 2.17). Obviously, the smaller the standard deviation is, the closer are the actual responses to the mean. If the standard deviation is large relative to the range of responses, then the mean is not a very good measure to use in understanding the data. For example, if in the illustration above the standard deviation is 1.70, it is almost half of the range (4 times per week minus .5 time per week = 3.5). The mean of 1.85 is relatively meaningless, since answers in this case are spread widely throughout the range of responses, and few people are actually near the mean. This could be an important observation when dealing with a highly segmented population. Consider Figure 11.3, which illustrates this idea.

In this case the market in question consists of five market segments. Graphically depicted is a mean which is the computation of the responses from the segment members, but, as seen here, there is no segment of respondents which actually is at the mean. The mean in this hypothetical example represents no one and is therefore highly misrepresentative of the data. Consequently, considering the standard deviation along with the mean as a measure of central tendency helps inform the analyst of the dispersion of the data and what precautions to take when reporting the results.

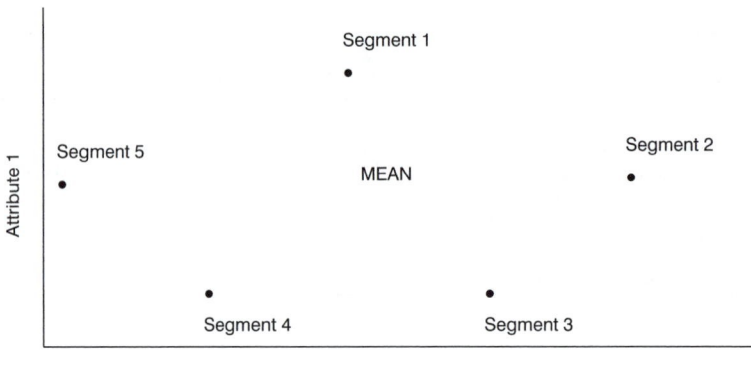

Figure 11.3 Segmented Populations

Cross-Tabulation

It is almost certainly true that virtually all sets of marketing data will reveal only a fraction of the possible significant findings if viewed only in terms of frequency distributions and measures of central tendency and dispersion. As seen in the egg substitute market data, more is revealed about the underlying relationship between variables of interest when two or more variables are considered simultaneously. Cross-tabulation, probably the most often used analytical technique in marketing research, involves examination of one variable "crossed" by one or more other variables. In the egg substitute example trial-to-usage or retention rates were examined for egg substitutes crossed by reasons for controlling cholesterol. Several observations about the use of cross-tabulations will help the analyst achieve maximum benefit from the use of this analytical tool.

Setting Up Cross-Tabulation Tables

We usually think of a cross-tabulation table as looking at two or possibly three variables simultaneously. This is most often the case when a firm conducts the research project itself, including processing the data and using some software program such as SPSS or Mini-Tab to run each cross-tabbed table. If the researcher has contracted with an independent marketing research firm to do the survey (i.e., send out and receive the mail questionnaires or do the phoning of respondents), they will likely be doing the data processing, including setting up the cross-tabs per the researcher's instructions. If they are responsible for the data collection and processing, then they will probably include as part of the contracted price what will be referred to as an "18-point" or "20-point" (or some other number) "banner" (see Figure 11.4 as an example).

This means they will provide a set of computer printout pages that are 18 or 20 columns wide for every question in the survey. Each question in the survey would appear down the side of a page, called the "stub." For example, in a series of Likert-scaled attitude questions, demographic questions, and other types of questions, each question would have a separate printout as shown in Figure 11.4

The appeal of banners is obvious—they provide a simple way to look at survey questions crossed by the most important variables the researcher is interested in exploring (e.g., gender and region in this example).

An 18-point banner means any combination of column headings that total 18 can be used. It is usual practice to devote the left-most column to "Grand Total," which in effect gives the frequency distribution for each question. So, this column on Page 1 of the example in Figure 11.4

Page 1 I like the taste of the egg substitute brand I usually eat	Grand Total	Gender		Region				
		M	F	S	N	E	W	Etc.
Strongly Agree 5								
Agree 4								
Neither Agree nor Disagree 3								
Disagree 2								
Strongly Disagree 1								
Page 2 Household Income	Grand Total	Gender		Region				
		M	F	S	N	E	W	Etc.
More than $80 K								
$60,0001 - $80,000								
$40,001 - $60,000								
$20,000 - $40,000								
Less than $20 K								
Page 3 Control Cholesterol	Grand Total	Gender		Region				
		M	F	S	N	E	W	Etc.
Yes								
No								

Figure 11.4 Sample Printouts

indicates the total number and percentage of people who answered Strongly Agree, Agree, etc., for that question. The remaining 17 columns may be divided in any combination of columns desired. In Figure 11.4 a set of two columns is devoted to gender, followed by four columns for region of the country. How are the column headings selected? In a single cross-tabulated table such as education level by income the "independent" variable would normally be placed across the top and the "dependent" variable down the side (see Figure 11.5).

We are maintaining that income "depends upon" education, so income is the dependent variable and education is the independent variable. An easy way to identify the independent and dependent variables in any situation is to ask the question:

Does *A* depend upon *B*?
A = Dependent variable
B = Independent variable

So, if the researcher is wondering about the relationship between age and attitude toward pop music, it makes sense to ask:

Does *your attitude toward pop music* depend upon *your age?*

The converse question:

Does *your age* depend upon *your attitude toward pop music?*

is obviously illogical—I cannot expect that my attitude will influence what my age is.

Income	Grand Total	Education Level						
		<HS	HS	Some Coll	Col Grad	Some Grad	Grad Degree	Etc.
$60 K+								
$40-60 K								
$20-40 K								
< $20 K								

Figure 11.5 Single Cross-Tabulations

It is customary to have the banner headings consist of *independent* variables that the research purpose, questions, and hypotheses suggest are most likely to be influencing the dependent measures of interest (such as attitudes, consumption rate, likelihood of purchase, membership or nonmembership, etc.). However, this is not an inviolate rule since the researcher may wish to examine some categories of dependent variables for numerous questions in the survey. The researcher may want to see how heavy users, light users, and nonusers differ from each other in terms of their attitudes, demographics, behaviors, etc., and would therefore use those three categories of a dependent variable (rate of consumption) as a set of three columns in a banner. If it is decided to include some dependent variables as banner points it is suggested that two banners be used—one 18- or 20-point banner with all independent variables and a second 18- or 20-point banner with dependent variables. This will help prevent confusion of what the data are revealing, as will be shown shortly.

Another common practice in setting up a banner heading or single cross-tabbed table is to consistently move from low to high moving from left to right in the banner, and from high to low moving down the stub. Therefore, a banner heading for income would look like this:

< $20K $20–40K $40–60K $60K+

and a stub heading for income would look like this:

Income
$60K +
$40–60K
$20–40K
< $20K

An easy way to remember this structure is to envision a graph, which is set up the same way as Figure 11.6

If the variable is not a quantifiable number but is rather one of an expressed intensity of feeling, the same rule holds, such as in Figure11.7 (i.e., more positive as move left to right or bottom to top).

Choosing Variables for Cross-Tabulations

It might be tempting to ask the data processors to "cross everything by everything" so that a cross-tabled table for every combination of two questions in the survey is available. That way, no matter what the issue, one or more tables are available to look at to help the researcher determine the relationship between the variables of interest. Such a temptation should be resisted because

Figure 11.6 Axes

Agreement with Statement	Attitude Toward Product		
	Unfavorable	Neutral	Favorable
Strongly Agree			
Agree			
Neither			
Disagree			
Strongly Disagree			

Figure 11.7 Cross-Tabulations of Nonquantifiable Values

it both fails to recognize all the valuable thinking about the project prior to this point, and it also generates a surprising number of tables (e.g., 50 variables generates 1,225 two-way cross-tab tables, 100 variables generates 4,950 two-way tables). Having a request for "everything crossed by everything" delivered as a four-foot stack of computer printouts is a sure way to dissuade the start of an analysis of the data! Considerable thought has already been given to the variables of interest as delineated in the research questions, hypotheses, and dummy tables. In fact, a cross-tabbed table is merely inserting data into a dummy table, so the plan of analysis primarily consists of determining which variables (i.e., questionnaire questions) should be simultaneously examined for possible relationships to get answers to questions, test hypotheses, or fill in dummy tables. While, as previously mentioned, the researcher will think of relationships he/she wishes to examine during the analysis and not before, there is also a point at which the researcher must get on with the implications and alternative decision suggestions, which is the purpose of the research and its analysis. It is easy to become distracted by the almost infinite number of possible relationships so that one avoids drawing the conclusions necessary to move through the process shown in Figure 11.1. Finding some balance between focusing only on the original objectives of the research and adding to those objectives as the analysis progresses must be achieved if conclusions are to be reported in a timely fashion.

Interpreting Cross-Tabulations

To this point, tables have been set up and a determination made concerning some finite number of relationships between variables to explore. It is now necessary to discuss some important

Table 11.3 Two-Way Cross Tabulation

I will pay up to 25¢ more to get my favorite brand of egg substitute.	Egg Substitute Consumption Rate					
	Low		Medium		High	
	#	%	#	%	#	%
Strongly agree or agree	113	34%	239	54%	308	67%
Neither agree nor disagree	107	33%	108	24%	101	22%
Strongly disagree or disagree	108	33%	98	22%	54	11%
T O T A L	328	100%	445	100%	463	100%

considerations involved with their interpretations. First, if the tables have been set up as suggested, it is possible to analyze the pattern of percentages from left to right to see if there is a positive or negative relationship between the independent and dependent variables. If the percentages increase moving left to right, there is a positive relationship between the variables. If the percentages decrease, then the relationship is negative. For example, in Table 11.3 there is a positive relationship between willingness to pay more to get the favorite brand of egg substitutes and consumption rate.

Note that in this case it is merely being observed that a positive relationship exists between a willingness to pay more to get the favorite brand and consumption rate without trying to make a claim that one variable *causes* the other. In fact, causal relationships cannot be determined from cross-tabulated data, even if the demonstrated relationship is statistically significant (to be discussed shortly). That is true even if computing a correlation coefficient that determined a very strong positive relationship between two intervally scaled variables. While too involved to discuss in depth here, the reader should understand that evidence of a positive *relationship* between variables does not provide evidence that the variables should be thought of as *causally* related. This is not necessarily a major problem in the analysis, however, since it may in many cases be sufficient for managers to know that a relationship exists to choose among alternative decisions (see discussion in Chapter 3). Evidence of causality does not necessarily alter the conclusions drawn nor the resulting decision. Knowing that high consumers of our brand of egg substitutes believe it is worth paying more to get our brand has managerial significance apart from the issue of whether consumption rate causes attitude or attitude causes consumption. One additional conclusion that might come from such an observation is that it is necessary to look more closely at the way the variables are related. This leads to the next issue in analyzing data via cross-tabulations.

Three-Way Cross-Tabulation

Researchers who see a positive relationship between two variables of interest, such as shown above, might wonder if there is a third variable that is possibly related to both of these two variables and that may actually explain more about the existence of this relationship. In this example, the researcher might wonder if household income explains both attitude (willingness to pay more to get their brand) and usage rate (low, medium, high). These suspicions may be explored by conducting a three-way cross-tabulation (see Table 11.4).

It appears that both agreement with the statement (see percentage of agreement varies by consumption rate) and consumption rate (see column totals for number or respondents) vary with income, which mitigates the conclusion that agreement is related to consumption rate (i.e., there is a stronger relationship between income and agreement than consumption rate and agreement, or, the relationship between consumption rate and agreement depends upon income). These observations reveal an important caveat to analysts using cross-tabulations as their primary analytical tool—sometimes cross-tabulations may in fact be showing a *spurious*

Table 11.4 Three-Way Cross Tabulation

I will pay up to 25¢ more to get my favorite brand of egg substitute.	Income											
	Low Consumption Rate						High Consumption Rate					
	Low		Medium		High		Low		Medium		High	
	#	%	#	%	#	%	#	%	#	%	#	%
Agree	84	30	62	32	20	32	29	60	177	71	288	72
Neither agree nor disagree	98	35	54	28	21	34	9	19	54	22	80	20
Disagree	98	35	78	40	21	32	10	21	20	8	33	8
T O T A L	280	100	194	100	62	98	48	100	251	101	401	100

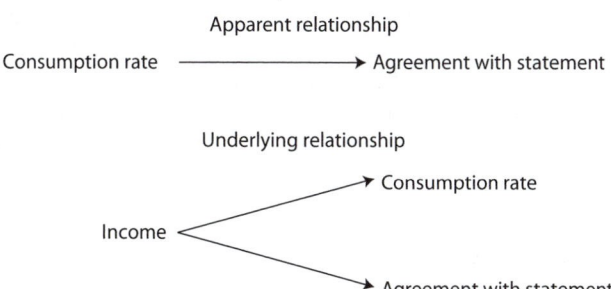

Figure 11.8 Spurious Versus Real Relationships

relationship between variables. A spurious relationship disappears when another variable enters the analysis. Figure 11.8 graphically illustrates this.

How can the researcher avoid basing conclusions, and ultimately decisions, on spurious relationships? The only real answer is that the savvy analyst maintain a certain skepticism about what he/she can legitimately conclude from the data and comes to an implication only after carefully examining the data from several angles. There is no single procedure or tool of analysis which will avoid all erroneous conclusions. A healthy dose of skepticism is the analyst's best defense against future regret and recrimination. As Thomas Huxley said: "Skepticism is the highest of duties, blind faith the one unpardonable sin."

One sure way to fall prey to spurious relationships and at the same time become distracted from the objectives of the analysis is to indiscriminately generate cross-tabulations and begin to examine them for "meaningful relationships." The danger is that the analyst might encounter some table where there is a strong relationship between two variables that he/she would not ordinarily examine or predict to have such a relationship. Fertile imagination then takes hold and very plausible-sounding explanations are devised for what is in reality a spurious and meaningless association between variables. This leads to the sort of fanciful conclusions that Hamlet and Polonius engaged in as quoted at the beginning of the chapter. The analyst's best "friend" in this case is the "theories" (research questions, hypotheses, relationships of interest) that originated at the beginning of the research. Analysts would do well to remember that logic should drive data, not data drive logic (i.e., let hypotheses, which are based on logical expectations, be tested by the data; do not let a "blind empiricism" of indiscriminate data analysis determine what is "logical.") This is not to say that data that is not consistent with presuppositions should be ignored. Rather, it argues that our "theories" of how consumers behave and the market operates, etc., are altered only after multiple findings consistently and persuasively suggest our old theories are wrong and new ones must be developed to explain the findings.

Statistical Significance in Cross-Tabulation

Analysts of cross-tabulated data do not have to wonder whether they are looking at relationships that might or might not be statistically significant. A statistical test called *chi-square* will reveal whether the differences noted in the table are "real" or could be merely due to chance. Readers interested in how chi-squares are calculated are referred to relevant works on the subject.[5] For our purposes here, most software programs such as SPSS that perform cross-tabulations will print chi-square statistics indicating whether the relationship between the table's variables is "statistically significant" or could have occurred by chance due to sampling variations. It should be noted here that chi-square tests require data that are categorical rather than continuous (i.e., low, medium, high consumers instead of one, two, three, four, five, etc., times per week) the numbers analyzed must be counts and not percentages, and there must be at least five or more "counts" in each cell. (Other requirements are necessary, but these are the ones likely to be of primary interest to readers of this book.) While useful in helping to determine if the observed relationship is statistically significant (e.g., there really is a difference in the rate of agreement with the statement between high, medium, and low egg substitute consumers), the chi-square statistics will not inform the analyst if the statistically significant relationship is spurious or not. The use of statistical tests *increases* rather than *decreases* the need for theory, predetermined hypotheses, and common sense.

Advanced Analytical Techniques

Cross-tabulations are a very useful and commonly used place to begin an examination of data beyond what can be done by frequency distribution and measures of central tendency. However, as has been seen, they are not trouble free as an analytical technique. Moreover, they cannot reveal all that there is to know about the relationship between variables in the data set. It is beyond the scope of the following discussion to describe these other techniques in any depth, but other techniques will be briefly explained that may be useful when analyzing research results.

Correlation

Correlations establish a relationship between any two intervally scaled variables. Variables can be negatively and positively correlated. Correlation scores range from +1.00 to –1.00 with 1.00 (or –1.00) indicating a perfect relationship and 0 indicating no relationship at all. Generally (depending on sample size), two variables are said to be slightly correlated when the correlation scores are between 0.21 and 0.35. Moderate degrees of correlation are generally associated with scores of 0.36 through 0.55. High degrees of correlation would be 0.56 through 0.75. Extremely high degrees of correlation would be associated with the scores 0.76 through 0.99. When two variables are positively correlated, it means that when one variable tends to increase in value (importance, preference, etc.), the other will likewise tend to increase. When two variables are said to be negatively (or inversely) correlated, it means that when one variable tends to increase in value, the other decreases and vice versa. One example might be that the purchase selection factor of the importance of product quality is inversely correlated to the importance of cost savings. This would mean that as the quality of the product increased, the importance of cost savings to the consumer would decrease.

Summary

Up to the point of data analysis the research that has been conducted to address a management problem has merely generated costs, with no return. It is only with the advent of data analysis that research begins to generate a return against those costs. Therefore, it is critically important to the success of the project that the researcher/analyst use all appropriate means of extracting valuable insights from the data. While a "tool chest" of sophisticated statistical programs may be necessary in getting the most from a data set, it is also true that many of the research objectives and hypotheses which drove the research can be addressed with techniques as simple as cross-tabulation. Another valuable "tool" of data analysis is the analyst's reluctance to draw implications and make decisional recommendations until he/she is convinced, by looking at the data from a variety of perspectives, that the information truly suggests the validity of those implications and recommendations.

Discussion Questions

1   Discuss how the process of analyzing data leads to solving management problems.
2   What is a "plan of analysis" and why is it important to have a plan before beginning the analysis of research data?
3   In your own words, describe how to analyze a cross-tabulated table.

12 Advanced Data Analysis

Learning Objectives

Upon completing this chapter, you should understand:

1. the difference between statistically significant differences and managerially significant differences;
2. what it means to say we are testing hypotheses;
3. how to explain the difference between a "null" and "alternative" hypothesis;
4. how to explain the different types of error that may occur when we test hypotheses;
5. how to explain the purpose of ANOVA and the two commonly used forms;
6. how to describe the different types of bivariate association;
7. how to describe various multivariate techniques and how they are used.

Once you have collected data through descriptive or causal research, and have run descriptive statistics and cross tabulations, you may wish to conduct some of the statistical analyses described in this chapter. But first we will discuss how marketing researchers approach the use of statistical tests in analyzing data.

Marketing Research and Statistical Analysis

Marketing research, as we well know by now, is conducted to help reduce the uncertainty in decision making. If we could be certain of making the correct decision without conducting research, why would we ever want to do research? Marketing research in such cases would not reduce uncertainty because there would be no uncertainty. You would always know which decision would be best. However, we all know that managers are often unsure which decisional alternative is best. Consequently, we conduct research to help determine which alternative should be selected, given what we discover is the nature of the market from conducting the research.

Statistics help us to better understand the significance of marketplace characteristics. We should distinguish between statistical and managerial differences, however:

- *Statistically significant differences:* when a difference (e.g., between two market segments, attitudes, likelihood of purchase between two products, etc.) is big enough that it is unlikely to have occurred due to chance.
- *Managerially significant differences:* when any observed difference in findings is considered significant enough to influence management decisions. For example, some statistically significant differences are considered inconsequential to management, while some that do not cross a certain statistical threshold to be considered statistically significant may influence management decisions.

Marketing researchers run statistical analyses on the data they have collected in order to be able to reduce the uncertainty of management decisions by identifying those measured variables that are managerially significant and also statistically significantly different from one another. For example, statistical analysis of marketing research data may reveal that a market consists of five consumer segments that differ from one another in ways significant to marketing managers making targeting and positioning decisions. Without the use of statistical analysis we would not have been able to identify or define these segments or the important differences among them upon which marketing decisions will be based.

Before we begin a discussion of the kinds of statistical analytical procedures of value to researchers, let us briefly review how we arrived at this point of the research process, for we arrive at this point because of the research decisions we previously made.

Readers will remember that in Chapter 1 we devoted considerable time and effort to the development of a statement of management problem/opportunity; identification of the research purpose (which required stating the decision alternatives and criteria); and the research objectives (research questions and hypotheses), which have driven all of our subsequent research decisions. Our research design, data-collection methods, measurement tools and methods, and data-collection instruments were all selected and developed as the most effective and efficient means possible of answering our research questions/testing our hypotheses, which allow us to achieve our research purpose and thereby solve our management problem or capitalize on our management opportunity. The statistical process we use at the analysis stage is merely another step along this same path, leading from management problem to data to decisions to problem solution. We emphasize this interconnectedness of the steps because it is easy for the novice researcher to become so overwhelmed by the variety and complexity of the statistical procedures that he or she fails to keep the "big picture" in mind. We are analyzing data for a reason—to allow us to choose the best among the decisional alternatives that helps solve our problem. Statistical analysis merely aids in that choice. Our discussion of statistics in this chapter is no substitute for the kind of coverage you get in a statistics course, but rather covers the main topics of interest to marketing researchers seeking to reduce the uncertainty of management decision making.

Hypothesis Testing

As we noted in Chapter 1, hypotheses are speculations regarding specific findings of the research. When researchers refer to "hypothesis testing" they are referring to any means used, such as the use of cross-tabulated tables (see Chapter 11), to determine if the hypotheses we stated at the early stages of the research are supported by the evidence. For example:

> **H**: First-time home buyers spend more time researching how to determine construction quality than people buying for the second, third, etc. time.

When researchers speak of "Hypothesis Testing" they are referring to a particular process and set of statistical tools used to determine the probability of observing a particular result from the research if the stated hypothesis were actually true. This formal statistical process (i.e., "Hypotheses Testing") is what we are describing.

We have hypotheses because we *suspect* our results will reveal some characteristic of the population under study. If we already *knew* the results would be a particular way we would not need to do the research. So, we approach the testing of an hypothesis the same way we do research in general: we are not out to prove (or disprove) anything, but rather seek to discover, test, and learn the "truth." We are testing our hypotheses to determine whether they should be accepted as statements accurately portraying the population's characteristics, or rejected because the observed difference is likely due to sampling error and there really is no difference as we hypothesized.

The underlying rationale for testing the hypothesis is that we will make different decisions based upon whether the results of the statistical tests lead us to conclude the hypothesis is supported or not. For example, if our hypothesis is that there is no difference between males and females in their preference for product design A or B, and that hypothesis is rejected (i.e., the results indicate the preferences for males versus females are "real" and unlikely due to chance), then we would make different decisions on which product design to introduce and how to target our marketing programs for the product.

Hypothesis testing involves five steps:[1]

1   The hypotheses are stated, with decisions identified for the outcome of the hypothesis test.
2   The "costs" are determined in relation to the two types of error that may result from your decisions (the concept of error is discussed below).
3   Select the significance level (the alpha) you will use to determine whether to reject or fail to reject (FTR) the null hypothesis (significance is discussed below).
4   Collect the data and conduct the appropriate statistical tests.
5   Compare the results to your null hypothesis and make your decision

The following example illustrates how marketing researchers could use these steps to help marketing managers make better decisions. Assume you work for a company that manufactures light bulbs. Your R&D (research and development) department has developed a new light bulb (named the Longlast bulb) that they claim lasts much longer than traditional bulbs, but could sell for only a 50 percent premium over traditional bulbs. The marketing manager believes this bulb could have a competitive advantage in the market, but to attract consumers the company will need to provide a money back guarantee for the minimum life expectancy of the bulb—if it does not last at least 36 months the consumer gets a full refund. The company will refund if the bulb doesn't last 36 months, that the average life of a bulb is significantly more than 36 months at the .01 level of significance; and the following sections discuss testing the hypothesis that the mean life is 36 months. The decision is then to either market the bulb with the guarantee or not market the bulb.

Step 1: Stating the Hypotheses and Decisions

Hypotheses are stated in two forms:

- *Null hypothesis* is stated in terms that indicate you expect to find "no difference" or "no effect."
- *Alternative hypothesis* states that you expect to find a difference or effect.

In our Longlast light bulb case these hypotheses and the resulting decisions would be:

- *Null hypothesis*: The unknown mean (average) life of our Longlast bulb population is less than or equal to thirty-six months.
- *Decision NH:* If we accept (or more appropriately fail to reject) the null hypothesis we will not market the bulb.
- *Alternative hypothesis:* The unknown mean life of our Longlast bulb population is greater than thirty-six months.
- *Decision AH:* If we accept the alternative hypothesis we will market the bulb.

The statement of a null hypothesis is in keeping with the "healthy skepticism" mentioned in Chapter 11. That is, while our R&D people claim the Longlast bulb will last more than 36 months ("Oh, no problem. Piece of cake. Easily last more than 36 months," as they put it.), you retain a healthy dose of skepticism and the null hypothesis reflects that skepticism. We assume the null hypothesis is true until evidence suggests otherwise. The alternative hypothesis says what you hope will be true, that the R&D claims are correct. These are competing hypotheses—only one can be true.

Step 2: Determine the Costs of Decision Errors

Since we are going to collect a sample of light bulbs and determine the average life of the light bulbs in the sample instead of testing every light bulb produced (which would not leave us any to market!), we are going to draw inferences from our research sample to the entire Longlast bulb population. These inferences can either be right or they can be wrong. Table 12.1 illustrates the possible combinations of inferences made about the null hypothesis.

- *Type 1 Error*: We reject the null hypothesis when it is actually true.
- *Type 2 Error*: We accept the null hypothesis when it is actually false.

When testing a hypothesis in any particular study we can make either a Type 1 error or a Type 2 error (or no error), but not both a Type 1 and Type 2 error. Table 12.2 shows how this table looks for our Longlast example.

We all know (or at least suspect, if we have not had personal experience) that making the wrong marketing decisions incurs costs. In the Longlast case both Type 1 and Type 2 errors are costly, but in different ways. If we decide to market the bulb because the average life of our sample (which we thought would also be true of the population) was longer than 36 months, but its life was actually shorter than 36 months (a Type 1 error), we will discover our error when people begin to return expired bulbs and get their money back in perhaps 24 or 30 months from when they were first marketed. Lots of Longlast bulbs have been sold in the past 24 to 30 months. The *Wall Street Journal* runs a front-page story of how we are flooded with returned bulbs and requests for refunds, consumer confidence in our other products begins to slip, we have trouble recruiting good marketing people who do not want to be associated with such "losers," and other unpleasantness occurs.

A Type 2 error would occur when we decide not to market a bulb whose actual life is more than 36 months, but the lifetime of our sample was less than 36 months. We had a winner on

Table 12.1 Possible Inferences About the Null Hypothesis

Based on the sample evidence we decide to	The truth about the population parameter	
	Null is true	*Null is false*
Accept the null (FTR the null)	Correct decision	Type 2 error
Reject the null	Type 1 error	Correct decision

Table 12.2 Longlast Example

Based Upon the Sample Evidence We Decide to	The Truth About the Longlast Bulb				
	36 months or less			*Over 36 months*	
Not market the bulb	Correct Decision	1	2	Type 2 Error	
Market the bulb	Type 1 Error	3	4	Correct Decision	

our hands but did not capitalize on the opportunity. Depending on the number of people who would have been interested in our competitive advantage, we might have missed out on a golden opportunity.

Step 3: Setting a Significance Level

No one wants to have significant bad decisions on their career track record, but there always is the possibility that when we make decisions based on inferring from a sample to our population, we were wrong. In hypothesis testing the significance level is the maximum risk you will accept of making a Type 1 error (marketing the light bulb when you should not have). It now becomes clear why Step 2 is so important:

> We must consider how significant the costs are to making a mistake by marketing the light bulb when we should not have in order to know how low to set our *maximum* risk of making such an error of judgment.

or

> The greater the costs associated with a Type 1 error, the lower we should set our maximum risk.

Some guidelines help us determine how to set the level of significance:

1   If costs associated with a Type 1 error are high and a Type 2 error is not costly, set the level of significance (i.e., the chance of making a Type 1 error) very low—at 0.05 or below.
2   If costs associated with a Type 1 error are not very high, but making a Type 2 error is costly, set the level of significance much higher (perhaps at 0.25 or above).
3   If both Type 1 and Type 2 errors are costly, set the level of significance very low and increase the sample size, reducing the chance of a Type 2 error (however, this does increase the costs of the research).

In the Longlast light bulb case the potential costs associated with making a Type 1 error are of sufficient magnitude to justify setting the level of significance very low (say, 0.01). This means if you reject the null hypothesis (i.e., decide to market the light bulb) the chance that you made a Type 1 error (decided to market it when you should not have because the average life expectancy was actually less than 36 months) is only one chance in a hundred. In other words you can be 99 percent confident that you made the right decision.

Step 4: Collect the Data and Conduct Statistical Tests

This is the step where the research is designed, data are collected, and the appropriate statistical tests are used to analyze the data. Our research design in this case would involve descriptive research since exploratory is not used to collect data per se, and our hypothesis does not involve cause–effect relationships. The research could run internal (within the company) tests of a sample of light bulbs, or we could conduct in-home tests, where consumers agree to try the product in typical consumer-usage situations. This approach provides researchers with information about the product's performance under actual market conditions and the subsequent research that tests consumers' opinions, perceived benefits received, problems, future purchase intent, and the like provides valuable marketing targeting and positioning information.

In this case we will assume we select a random sample of 1,000 light bulbs (we use *probability* sampling since we are doing descriptive research) for an internal test and use a special testing technology that "speeds up" time so that we do not have to wait thirty-six months for the results of our test of the bulbs' lifetime. So, we run our test of 1,000 light bulbs and determine the average simulated lifetime of the bulbs in months. We discover the following:

Sample mean (written as $\bar{x}$) = 37.7 months

Standard deviation (written as *s)* =0.42 months

The t Test

A frequently used statistical test is the *t* test. We use a *t* test in this case to determine if the null hypothesis should be rejected or accepted (FTR) because we do not know the population's standard deviation. However, because the sample size is so large, the *t* value is the same as the *Z* value.

A *t* test is constructed as follows:

$$t = \frac{\text{Sample value} - \text{Hypothesized population value}}{\text{Stand deviation of the sample value}}$$

In the Longlast light bulb case the calculation would be

$$t = \frac{37.7 - 36.0}{0.42} = 4.05$$

Analysis of Variance (ANOVA)

Another frequently used test is analysis of variance. The purpose of analysis of variance (ANOVA) is to determine if samples come from two or more populations with equal means. In the lightbulb example, we may have more than two samples of bulbs we want to test at the same time. We could run multiple *t* tests, but this will inflate the overall Type I error rate. ANOVA does not inflate the Type I error, especially when we are comparing a number of groups. Basically, ANOVA determines the probability that differences in group means are due to sampling error and not Type I error. ANOVA is used when there is a true experimental design with random assignment of subjects to each group. Below is a discussion of the two of the most used ANOVA designs. The purpose is to familiarize the student with the design. The statistical analysis of ANOVA is beyond the scope of this text.

One-way ANOVA is based on one independent and one dependent variable. The researcher assumes that the populations from which the samples were drawn are normally distributed, have equal variances, and that the samples are randomly and independently drawn. The null hypothesis (H_0) is that the means of all the groups are equal.

$$H_0 = \mu_1 = \mu_2 = \mu_3 \ldots = \mu_n$$

The alternative hypothesis is that they are not all the same;

$$H_1: \mu_1 \neq \mu_2 \neq \mu_3 \neq \cdots \mu_n$$

Two-way ANOVA examines: (1) two factors of interest on the dependent variable, and (2) the interaction between the different levels of the two factors. For example, our two factors of interest may be the percent of sugar in boxes of children's cereal and the line speed of the boxing process. The interaction between these two factors would involve attempting to understand if the level of sugar per box of cereal depended on the level of the line speed. The same assumptions

Table 12.3 Statistical Tests for Hypothesis Testing

Types of hypotheses	Number of subgroups or samples	Scale of data	Test	Requirements
Hypotheses about frequency distribution	1	Nominal	Chi-square (χ^2)	Random Sample
	2 or more	Nominal	Chi-square (χ^2)	Random, independent samples
	1	Ordinal	Kolmogorov-Smirnov	Random
Hypotheses about proportions (percentages)	1 (large sample)	Interval or ratio	Z-test for one proportion	Random sample of 30 or more
	2 (large sample)	Interval or ratio	Z-test for two proportions	Random sample of 30 or more
Hypotheses about means	1 (large sample)	Interval or ratio	Z-test for one mean	Random sample of 30 or more
	1 (small sample)	Interval or ratio	t-test for one mean	Random sample of less than 30
	2 (large sample)	Interval or ratio	Z-test for two means	Random sample of 30 or more
	3 or more (small sample)	Interval or ratio	One-way ANOVA (one independent variable)	Random sample

Source: Adapted from Carl McDaniel and Roger Gates, *Contemporary Marketing Research* (Cincinnati, OH: South-Western, 1999), pp. 516–517.

apply to two-way ANOVA as to one-way ANOVA (populations are normally distributed, populations have equal variances, and independent random samples are drawn). Hypotheses for a two-way ANOVA are as follows:

For Factor A

$$H_0 = \mu_1 = \mu_2 = \mu_3 \ldots = \mu_n$$

$$H_1 : \mu_1 \neq \mu_2 \neq \mu_3 \neq \cdots \mu_n$$

For Factor B

$$H_0 = \mu_1 = \mu_2 = \mu_3 \ldots = \mu_n$$

$$H_1 : \mu_1 \neq \mu_2 \neq \mu_3 \neq \cdots \mu_n$$

For the interaction effect:

H_0: the interaction of A and B equals zero

H_1: the interaction of A and B is not equal to zero

See Table 12.3 for the appropriate statistical tests for the different forms of hypotheses.

Table 12.4 Statistical Software Sites on the Internet

Software	Web Site	Description
SPSS	www.ibm.com	A popular, comprehensive statistical package with links to other sites and data sets.
STATA	www.stata.com	STATA software for Windows, Apple, DOS, and UNIX operating systems.
UNISTAT	www.unistat.com	Comprehensive package compatible with Windows Excel. Data handling, analysis, and graphic presentation.
StatSoft	www.statsoft.com	Presents the STATISTICA range of statistical analysis products. Easy to use yet powerful statistical package.

Step 5: Compare Results to the Null Hypothesis and Make a Decision

Looking at a *t* distribution table we see that the *t* value for *n*–1 degrees of freedom (999 in our case, but "infinity" on the table) and for an alpha (the level of significance, which was 0.01 in our case) in a "one-tail" test (on a normal curve, the area under the curve at only one end of the curve rather than both ends) was 2.326. Since our *t* value of 4.05 exceeded this 2.326 value we can say we are *more than* 99 percent confident that our sample mean of 37.7 months is drawn from a population whose mean is more than 36. Or, in other words, the chances that our sample mean would be 37.7 when the actual population mean is 36 months is very, very unlikely (less than one in a hundred). Because the odds of the null hypothesis being true (i.e., that our population mean is 36 months or less) are so small, it is much more reasonable to assume that the reason our sample mean was 37.7 months is that the null hypothesis should be rejected and our alternative hypothesis should be accepted (i.e., that the population mean is greater than 36 months).

In Step 1 we established a decision rule that said if we reject the null hypothesis and accept the alternative hypothesis we will market the Longlast light bulb, so that is what we should do. Referring to Table 12.2, this decision means we either will make the correct decision (cell 4), or will be making a Type 1 error (cell 3). The actual chance that we are making a Type 1 error is called the "*p* value," which in this case would be the likelihood of getting a sample mean of 37.7 months if the null hypothesis were true. This is very remote (less than 1 chance in 100), which is very reassuring of the correctness of our decision.

While our null hypothesis was stated as a test of means (i.e., was our sample's average of 37.7 months statistically significantly different from the hypothesized population's average of 36 months?), we could state hypotheses as frequency distribution, differences between subgroups (e.g., men versus women), or proportions (e.g., percentages of college educated versus noncollege graduates intending to buy our product). Table 12.3 shows the appropriate statistical tests for different forms of hypotheses. Once you set up the hypothesis and go through the steps outlined here, a statistical software program such as SPSS can be used to conduct the appropriate statistical tests. Otherwise, the same process (the five steps) are followed to arrive at a decision based on the marketing-research results. See Table 12.4 for a list of statistical software sites on the web.

Concluding Thoughts on Hypothesis Testing

Hypothesis testing is very decision oriented, as demonstrated in this discussion. In fact, the underlying reason for testing hypotheses is to get to the point (Step 5) where you can determine how confident you can be in choosing between two previously identified decision alternatives (e.g., to market or not to market the Longlast light bulb). Some other thoughts on hypothesis testing are:

1   As described in Chapter 4, we use exploratory research to *generate* hypotheses, we use descriptive or causal research to *test* hypotheses. While the exploratory research "detective work" may allow us to "check out our hunches" by looking at secondary data and doing exploratory communication or observation, and even provide us with enough information that we are willing to make a decision without further research, we can not claim we have "tested hypotheses" by doing exploratory research. This is true even if we conduct an exploratory survey of thousands of people. The reason is that true hypothesis tests, as described here and listed in Table 12.3, all demand probability samples that are the province of descriptive and causal research. If we have not obtained our sample using a probability sampling approach (simple random, stratified, systematic, or cluster sampling methods), the plain fact is that we can not conduct these hypothesis tests, no matter how large our sample. This is not to say that we can not use exploratory survey results to make decisions. We simply cannot arrive at those decisions through statistical tests of our hypotheses.

2   There are two types of errors possible when conducting tests of hypotheses. We must determine their respective costs and then set the level of significance consistent with the costs of making a Type 1 error. In doing this we must understand that we do not want to automatically set the significance level very low (e.g., 0.05 or less) so we will not make a Type 1 error. The fear of making a Type 1 error is only justified when the costs of a Type 1 error are very high. Sometimes the costs of a Type 2 error (e.g., *not* marketing the Longlast bulb when we should have in our example) may be high as well and must be factored into our decision. As described in Step 3, when Type 2 error costs are high relative to Type 1 error costs, we should set our level of significance much higher (e.g., 0.25 or higher).

3   Doing causal research also may involve hypothesis testing. Although beyond the scope of our discussion, one typical statistical test used in determining the difference between experimental treatments is the ANOVA test (analysis of variance, see Table 12.3). For example, we can use an ANOVA test to determine if there is a statistically significant difference in the sales of a cereal brand that was tested in an experimental design with three coupon levels: 35¢, 50¢, and 75¢. ANOVA is not used exclusively with experimental data (it can be used with descriptive survey results), nor is it the only way to analyze experimental data, but it is a commonly used statistical test for experimental data.

Measures of Association

Marketers frequently want to know how variables are associated with each other. For example, Levi's may want to know what types of people are interested in a more formal, dressy line of pants. Target may want to know the lifestyle characteristics of the women who visit their website so they can change its content to satisfy customer needs, and IBM may want to know which characteristics best describe their top salespeople. In such cases marketers are interested in using statistical analysis to determine the degree to which two or more variables are associated with each other. Our discussion of cross-tabulation in Chapter 11 was an example of looking for associations. In this chapter we will examine other statistically measurable means of determining association among variables. We will examine bivariate (association between two variables) and multivariate (between three or more variables) techniques.

Bivariate Association

The association between two variables can be graphically described in a variety of ways (see Figure 12.1):

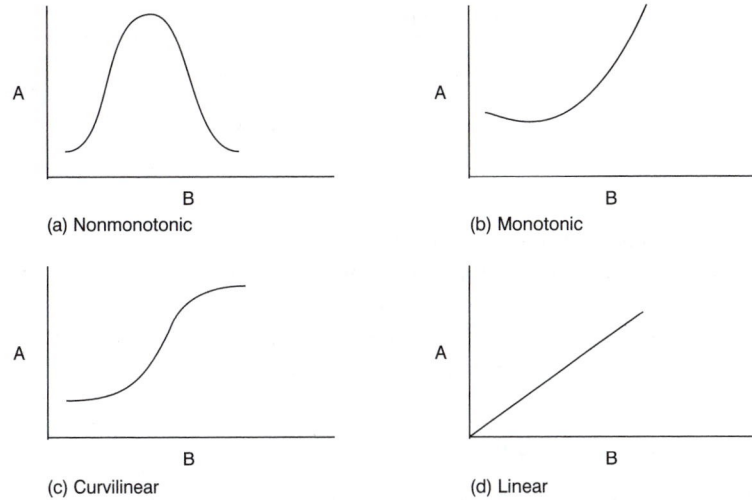

Figure 12.1 Graphic Representation of Bivariate Association

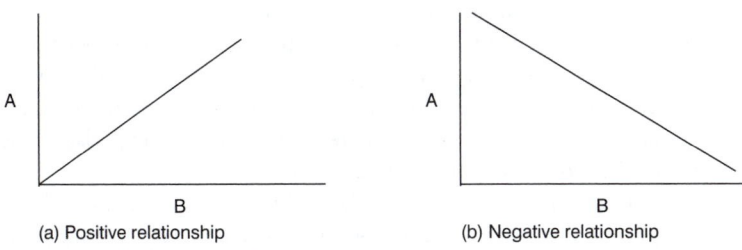

Figure 12.2 Relationship Between Variables

- *Nonmonotonic:* there is no discernable direction to the association or relationship between the two variables, but the relationship exists.
- *Monotonic:* there is a general direction to the association between the two variables.
- *Curvilinear:* the association between the variables can be described by a curved line.
- *Linear:* a straight line can be drawn to describe the relationship between the variables.

We will restrict our discussion to associations between variables that can be described as linear. Linear relationships may either be positive or negative in nature. In Figure 12.2(a) we see a positive relationship: as variable A increases (e.g., education) so does B (e.g., income). This association does not have to be perfect. There are examples of people with little education but very high income, and people with very high education but modest incomes (your instructor, for an unfortunate example), but in general the relationship is positive.

In Figure 12.2(b) we see a negative relationship: as variable A increases (e.g., price), variable B declines (e.g., sales of cellular phones).

Marketers are very interested in determining the association between variables so they can use this information in making decisions. If buyer loyalty for a personal computer manufacturer as measured by repeat purchase behavior is associated with a buyer's satisfaction with the company's toll-free help line, and satisfaction with the help line is associated with the number of trained customer service agents, the company may decide to hire and train more customer service agents. If the association between two variables is strong, you can predict one variable by knowing the other one, but first you must be able to measure the degree of association. We will

Table 12.5 Bivariate Measures of Association

Type of Data	Measures
Interval or ratio	Pearson product moment correlation
Ordinal	Spearman rank-order correlation
Nominal	Chi-square analysis

discuss the primary statistical procedures used for measuring association. Readers wishing for a more comprehensive discussion of these and other statistical measures of association should consult one of the standard works on the subject.[2]

The choice of bivariate measures of association depends upon the scale of the data being analyzed. Table 12.5 describes several common measures.

Pearson Product Moment Correlation

The Pearson product moment correlation is used to measure the degree to which two variables are correlated or associated with each other when both of those variables are *metric (i.e.,* either intervally or ratio-scaled data). The output of running this statistical analysis on two variables is a single number called a correlation coefficient, which can range from −1.00 to +1.00. The closer the correlation coefficient is to −1.00 or +1.00, the stronger the association is between the variables. Two variables are perfectly inversely correlated when the coefficient is −1.00 and perfectly positively correlated when it is +1.00. A correlation coefficient of 0.00 indicates there is no statistical association between the two variables. Statistical software packages such as SPSS will compute both the Pearson product moment correlation coefficient (referred to as the r) and the statistical significance statistic (referred to as the p) for two sets of metric-scaled data. The r measures the strength of the association on the −1.00 to +1.00 scale, while the p indicates the likelihood that the association is due to chance (i.e., that the null hypothesis of no association between the two variables is supported).

A $p = 0.05$ says that the chance we would be seeing the strength of the r (i.e., the association or correlation between the two variables) as what we see it for our sample data, when in fact there is no association (i.e., $r = 0.00$) between the two variables is only 5 chances in 100. So, a p of 0.05 or lower would indicate that the degree of association between the variables as measured by the r is "real" and unlikely due to chance. Once we see that the p indicates that we are looking at a statistically significant association, we can look at the r to determine the strength of the association. Physicists expect to see perfect (or very near) correlations between the physical materials they study. Marketers, as behavioral scientists, realize that people are far from "perfect" and so the correlations we measure between variables related to the behavior of consumers are not going to be −1.00 or +1.00. Marketers measuring and correlating such variables of interest as:

consumption rate   correlated with   satisfaction with product

Table 12.6. Correlation Coefficient and Strength of Association

Range of Correlation Coefficient	Strength of Association
Greater than .80	Very strong
.61 to .80	Moderate to strong
.41 to .60	Weak to moderate
.21 to .40	Weak
.00 to .20	Nonexistent to very weak

attitude toward product	correlated with	intention to buy
household size	correlated with	frequency of usage

and many other correlations involving metric data of interest, are looking at correlations revealing various degrees of less-than-perfect association. Table 12.6 suggests some general rules of thumb for correlation coefficients and implied strength of association.

Spearman Rank-Order Correlation

Marketing researchers may find that they seek to know the association between two variables that are ordinally (i.e., rank ordered) rather than intervally or ratio scaled. In such cases we should use the Spearman rank-order correlation rather than the Pearson product moment correlation. For example, we might want to know if there is any association between the way people rank ordered brands of automobiles based on "sportiness" and "like to be seen driving." The resulting correlation coefficient, r_s, and the measure of statistical significance are interpreted in the same way as we do for the Pearson product moment correlation. That is, a higher r_s indicates higher degrees of association (or stronger inverse association if the coefficient is a negative value).

Chi-Square Analysis

As shown in Table 12.3, chi-square tests are run when we are conducting hypothesis tests for nominally scaled variables. Chi-square tests are run on cross-tabulated data when we want to determine if the frequencies we see in each cell of a cross-tabbed table fit an "expected" (i.e., hypothesized) pattern. Since the null hypothesis states that we expect not to find an association between the two variables, the chi-square tests tells us whether we should accept the null hypothesis or not. So, for example, if we want to know whether there is an association between the preferences of males versus females for new product concept A or B, our cross-tabulated data may look like this:

Preference for new product concept	Males	Females	Total
A	199	18	217
B	40	43	83
Total	239	61	300

The decision we want to make is whether or not to target the two new products to consumers on the basis of gender. The question of the statistical analysis then becomes, "Is there a statistically significant difference in the preferences between males and females for the two new product concepts?" The null hypothesis for the chi-square test is then

H_o: There is no relationship between gender and new product concept preference.

And our alternative hypothesis is

H_a: There is a significant relationship between gender and new product concept preference.

When you enter the data in the cross-tabulated table (which must be in "counts" not percentages, and at least five or more counts must be in each cell of the table) into a statistical program such as SPSS, the program then calculates the probability you would find evidence in support of the null hypothesis if you repeatedly collected independent samples and got these results. So, if the chi-square test showed a 0.01 probability for the null hypothesis, the conclusion would be that you would get these results only 1 time in 100 occasions if the null hypothesis were true. That is highly unlikely, so the null is rejected and the alternative hypothesis is accepted: There is a relationship between gender and product concept preference. Chi-square does not tell the researcher the nature of the association (e.g., whether males prefer A and females B), only that the association exists by telling you the probability of seeing such results if the null hypothesis were true. Researchers would then need to study the association between the variables more closely to discern the nature of the association between the variables and ultimately, along with other research findings, what decisions should be made about marketing the new products.

Multivariate Association

Multivariate (multiple variable) association refers to the statistical methods that simultaneously analyze multiple measurements of attitudes, attributes, or behavior. Multivariate techniques are simply extensions of univariate (analysis of single variable distributions) and bivariate techniques (two variable methods such as cross-tabulations, correlations, and simple regression). For a research project to terminate prior to employing multivariate techniques assumes that the purpose of the research was only to identify the variables, or that the importance of the results for the decision information required would need no more than the establishment of the associations between two variables. Multivariate techniques serve to determine the relationships that exist between multiple sets of variables. Multivariate methodologies are clearly sometimes needed to examine the multiple constraints and relationships among pertinent variables to obtain a more complete, realistic understanding of the market environment for decision making.

Description and Application of Multivariate Techniques

The satisfactory utilization of multivariate methods assumes a degree of understanding of the market dynamics or market behavior in order to conceptualize a realistic model. The identification of the variables whose relationships are to be measured is foundational to an incisive multivariate approach. The nature and number of variables to be examined will determine what type of multivariate method will be utilized.

The first commonly used method is known as *multiple regression.* Multiple regression allows for the prediction of the level or magnitude of a phenomenon such as market size or market share. Multiple regression has as its objective the identification of the optimum simultaneous relationship that exists between a dependent variable and those of the many independent variables. For example, frequency of listening to a particular radio station may well be a function of a number of marketing mix variables such as the type of programming, listener loyalty, community promotionals, billboard advertising, disc jockey personality, and tastefulness of the commercials.[3]

Another method is *multiple discriminant analysis.* Multiple discriminant analysis has as its objective the identification of key descriptors on which various predefined events will vary. It might be learned from a discriminate analysis that middle-income families who work in a downtown area and who have school-age children might be expected to be the first to move into a new, rural, totally planned community housing development.

Canonical correlation analysis allows for the establishment of a predictive model that can simultaneously forecast or explain several phenomena based on an understanding of their correlates. The canonical correlation analysis differs from multiple regression analysis in that there is more than one dependent variable. Whereas family income and family size might be used to predict the number of credit cards a family might have (by using a multiple regression technique), the canonical correlation analysis would also be able to predict the average monthly charges on all of their credit cards.[4]

One of the more popular of the multivariate techniques is *factor analysis*. Fred Kerlinger states[5] that the factor analysis might be called the queen of analytic techniques because of its power and elegance. He describes factor analysis as a method for determining the number and nature of underlying variables among larger numbers of measures. It also serves to reduce large groups of complex variables to their underlying and predictive entities. Factor analytic techniques first gained prominence in psychological and psychiatric studies. For example, verbal ability, numerical ability, memory, abstract reasoning, and spatial reasoning have been found to underlie intelligence in some studies.[6]

The applications for factor analysis have been used extensively for behavioral and attitudinal studies used in the marketplace. For example, a study[7] that measured a large group of variables related to job satisfaction and morale among a certain group of engineers revealed the ability to grow professionally was the most important factor in morale and job satisfaction. This was followed closely by self-esteem as it related closely to the type of firm they work for. The analysis revealed five central factors, which in general terms, fit closely to Maslow's hierarchy of organizational needs, except that the order of prominence for each of Maslow's needs was found to have a different sequence for the engineers surveyed. Factors identified by this technique, therefore, have served as a new dimension of segmentation that focuses on shared agreement among respondents as the differentiation among the segments.

Multidimensional scaling addresses the problem of identifying the dimensions upon which customers perceive or evaluate phenomena (products, brands, or companies). Multidimensional scaling techniques result in *perceptual maps* that describe the "positioning" of companies or brands that are compared relative to the "position" they occupy in the minds of customers according to key attributes. These "maps" allow the decision maker to examine underlying criteria or dimensions that people utilize to form perceptions about similarities between and preferences among various products, services, brands, or companies. The question of positioning, as viewed by multidimensional scaling (MDS) and perceptual mapping, deals with how a firm compares to its competitors on key attributes, what the ideal set of attributes sought by the customer might be, or what positioning or repositioning strategy should be developed for a specific sector of the marketplace.[8] A medium-sized bank might learn, for example, that the most effective way to compete for commercial loan business with larger, more prestigious banks with a wider range of services, is by focusing on the genuine concern communicated by loan supervisors as well as the expertise they develop in their knowledge of their client's subsector of industry (see Figure 12.3).

Cluster analysis allows for the classification or segmentation of a large group of variables into homogeneous subgroups based on similarities on a profile of information. Cluster analysis enables the description of topologies or profiles according to attitudes toward preferences, appeals, etc., that might also include psychographic data. For example, this analysis might be used to describe psychographic profiles and interest in new transactional services among savings and loan customers.

The last major technique to be explained is *conjoint analysis*. Conjoint analysis, also known as trade-off analysis, is used for evaluating judgmental data where choices between attributes are involved. It is more commonly used in measuring the trade-off values of purchase selection factor attributes. Specifically, conjoint analysis is concerned with the joint effect of two or more independent variables on the ordering of a dependent variable. In essence, this method allows a determination of how consumers value various levels of purchase criteria and the extent to which they might tend to forego a high level of one attribute in order to obtain a high level of another. For example, the trade-off values of holding power, scent, nonstickiness, brand name, and price for hair spray might be cause for a conjoint evaluation.[9]

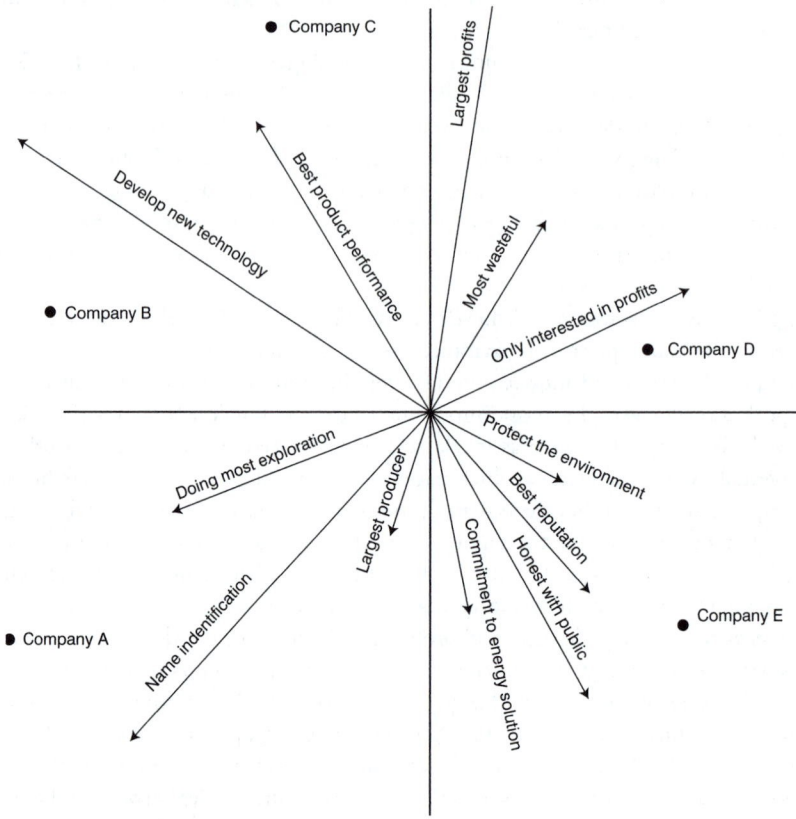

Figure 12.3 Perceptual Map

Research Project Tip

Make sure that your plan for analyzing your data conforms to the "rules" for use of the statistical techniques described in this chapter. If you plan to use statistical tests, particularly multivariate tests, use the references for this chapter for more information on how to use them correctly before actually analyzing the data.

Summary

Marketing researchers use statistical analysis of association to know how to interpret data describing the relationship between two or more variables. Ultimately, as suggested in Chapter 11, such analysis of data needs to provide us with answers to our research questions and lead us to choices among our decision alternatives. Statistical analysis gives us a window with which we can view the results of our research and see which decisions would be best. It is very important that we use the appropriate statistical-analytical procedures, or the window we are looking out of can give us a distorted view of reality and our decisions based on that distorted view could be ill-chosen.

Discussion Questions

1   Which is more important, statistically significant differences or managerially significant differences? Explain.
2   What do we mean when we say we are testing the hypotheses of our research?
3   Explain why we state hypotheses as "null hypotheses."
4   Does rejecting a null hypothesis mean the results have no real meaning for the researcher? Explain.
5   What is the difference between univariate and multivariate analysis?
6   Explain decision error. What are the costs associated with each type of error?
7   Why are multiple *t* tests not appropriate for determining the differences in means across a number of populations? What statistical method can be used to solve this problem?
8   Describe the different types of bivariate association.
9   Discuss the uses of various multivariate techniques.

13 The Research Report

Learning Objectives

Upon completing this chapter, you should understand:

1 the importance of a clearly written report and the make up of the audience in communicating the findings of the research;
2 the basic components of a written report;
3 how the use of charts and graphs can improve the communication value of the results of the study;
4 the need for preparing and trouble-shooting oral reports.

This chapter discusses the essentials of preparing the research report. The basic purpose of the research report is to communicate the results, conclusions, and recommendations of the research project. (If a project encompasses several phases or a long period of time, progress reports are normally sent to the purchaser or user of the research to inform them of the progress to date on a given project.) The key word in the preceding statement of purpose is *communicate*. The report must be an effective tool of communication not only to accurately present the findings and conclusions, but also to stimulate the reader to some managerial action. The research project was predicated on the need for information to aid in the decision-making process. Now the cycle has been completed and the report must address that decision and recommend a course of action in view of the research findings. The user or purchaser of the information must decide whether or not to heed the advice given in the recommendation of the report, but the actions recommended by the researcher must be communicated.

As with any other instance in which you wish to communicate effectively, the marketing researcher should understand the target audience—its objectives for studying the research report, its tendencies for selective perception (selectively choosing to see what they want to see and ignoring what they do not), the time they will devote to the report, etc. Marketers and marketing researchers are trained to look at what they do through the eyes of the "target market," and it is particularly important that those skills be applied to the development of the research report.

In writing the report, the marketing researcher should keep two audiences in mind: the decision makers who commissioned the research in an effort to reduce the uncertainty of their decisions, and those people, unacquainted with the genesis of the research, who will pick up the report sometime in the future and want to use the findings to help them better understand something about the market. The report should serve as a guide to those interested in immediately implementing the recommendations cited in the report, but it must also be an archival document, able to "tell its story" to someone unacquainted with the study's background (i.e., management problem or opportunity initiating the need for research, the research purpose, etc.). It is possible that sometime in the future, decision makers may feel the need to duplicate the study in order to track market trends or changes in the decisional environment. In such cases a report originally written with an eye toward it becoming an archival document would contain all the information needed to duplicate the study in the absence of the original researchers and decision makers.

Report Format

While there is no standardized reporting format used in all research reports, the following outline gives the elements commonly included. Each of these elements of the report will be discussed, using an actual research report written by one of the authors as an example (with changes in individual and company names to respect confidentiality).

- Title Page
- Tables of Contents
- Introduction
- Research Objectives
- Research Methodology
- Executive Summary
- Findings
- Conclusions and Recommendations
- Supporting Documentation (Appendixes)

Title Page

The title page (see Figure 13.1) should tell the reader four things: (1) the subject of the study, (2) who it was prepared for, (3) who it was prepared by, and (4) the date of the study. This title page may also bear the logo of the preparing organization, if applicable. If the report has been revised, this revision should be noted on the title page.

Table of Contents

A good rule to follow for including a table of contents, charts, and illustrations is to base the decision on the length of the report (see Figure 13.2). If the report is only ten to twelve pages in length, then a table of contents is not necessary. For longer reports, a table of contents, charts list, and illustrations list are usually included to enable the readers to locate the sections or illustrations in the report which they want to refer to at a given time. The table of contents should be detailed enough to serve as a guide to locating specific sections in the report. Thus, subheadings should be listed if the sections are long and contain many different subsections. This is especially true of the "findings" section.

Introduction and Research Objectives

The introduction to the report should refer the reader to the basic purpose of the research and the specific objectives that were agreed upon in the research proposal (see Figure 13.3). In most cases it is advisable to list the statements of management problem, research purpose (including decision alternatives and criteria), along with your research objectives and hypotheses. This material should represent your latest thinking on these topics. If the research study (particularly the exploratory research) has caused you to change the objectives or list new hypotheses not

Pilot Study of Financial Institutions

Prepared for:
Bill Berry, President Financial Institution

by
Marketing Research Associates

101 Anystreet
Anytown, State
(800) 555-1212
Date

Figure 13.1 Title Page

TABLE OF CONTENTS

Introduction	1
Research Objectives	2
Research Methodology	3
Executive Summary	4
Findings	5
Sample Characteristics	6
Primary Institution/Services Utilized by Respondents	7
Services Utilized at Secondary Financial Institution	8
Changes in Primary Financial Institutions	9
Images of Financial Institutions	10
Advertising Awareness	11
Conclusions and Recommendations	12
The Sample	13
Primary Financial Institution	14
Services Utilized at Primary Financial Institution	15
Services Utilized at Secondary Financial Institution	16
Changes in Primary Financial Institutions	17
Images of Financial Institutions	18
Advertising Most Remembered and Media Survey	19
Retail Banking Survey	20

Figure 13.2::Table of Contents

identified in the original research proposal (see Chapter 1), these changes should be noted here (e.g., state both original and new objectives).

Research Methodology

This section should include a brief summary of the research methods (see Figure 13.4). Remember the audience for the report—executives are not (or at least, rarely) interested in the small details of how the research was conducted. This description should be limited to mention of the primary means of data collection (e.g., focus groups followed by a telephone survey, or the series of experiments conducted, etc.); who were the respondents, how many were contacted and where they were located; the type of instrument used to collect the information (e.g., structured or unstructured surveys or interview guides); and a *general* discussion of the analysis process

Executive Summary

The executive summary of the report presents the highlights of the research report in a straightforward and precise manner (see Figure 13.5). This summary is usually organized by topics investigated or by questions that must be answered before a decision is made.

This may be the only section read by some executives, so enough detailed statements of major issues must be given to arm them with the basic facts that emerged in the study. It should be strong enough to permit the reader to get the essence of the findings without assuming that careful reading of the entire report will be made by *every* reader.

The summary should take the form of a detailed abstract in describing purpose, methodology, and findings. Usually two to three pages is the maximum length for a good summary. It is best

INTRODUCTION

The following study was conducted to assist local financial institutions with the planning necessary to determine future courses of action in response to changing market conditions. This involves developing a database from which conclusions can be drawn about positioning strategy, market share goals, and promotional strategy. The purpose of this present study was to analyze the retail banking market in the City area. The study analyzed market share by primary financial institutions, services utilized by primary and secondary institutions, images of financial institutions, and advertising awareness.

RESEARCH OBJECTIVES

The specific research objectives of this study were as follows:

I   Determine the market share for primary institutions for the major financial institutions in the area.
II   Evaluate the utilization of various services at both primary and secondary institutions.
III Identify the level of satisfaction with primary institutions and the reasons for any dissatisfaction.
IV   Determine changes in primary institutions by respondents and the reasons for any changes.
V   Assess respondents' image of various financial institutions on a series of image characteristics.
VI   Measure advertising awareness and media exposure of respondents.
VII Analyze responses by socioeconomic characteristics such as age, sex, income, education, etc.

RESEARCH METHODOLOGY

To accomplish these objectives, telephone interviews were conducted with 299 area residents who used the services of local financial institutions. Respondents were randomly selected from the City area telephone book to assure a representative sample was used as the basis of data analysis.

The respondents were surveyed using a structured questionnaire designed to respond to the project's specific research objectives. The questionnaire was thoroughly pretested before being administered to improve the quality of the measuring instrument. the resulting data were edited, entered into computer files, and processed by a statistical-analysis program to provide a comprehensive set of tables and cross-tabulations for the study. The tables included number of respondents and percentages by response to each question and chi-square analysis of the cross-tabulations of the data by primary financial institution to identify differences in response patterns to the questions contained in the questionnaire.

Figure 13.3 Introduction and Research Objectives

Figure 13.4: Research Methodology

to photocopy the executive summary on colored paper so it can easily be located by the busy executive who may ignore the rest of the report.

Findings

This section of the report contains the detailed findings of the study (see Figure 13.6). A great deal of detail is given in this section with supporting graphs and charts included as both references and sources of support for the statements that are made in the narrative of this section. This section is normally the largest section of the report and should be organized in a logical way. A topically organized format lends itself to both ease of preparation and reading. The major topics related to each research objective are presented so that the reader is taken in a step-by-step progression through all of the findings of the study. This also ensures that all the objectives are covered in the write-up of the findings.

Conclusions and Recommendations

As mentioned earlier, the culmination of the research deals with the statements given in reference to the decisions to be made based on the results of the research (see Figure 13.7). This material could be given in the summary but it will have more impact on the readers if it is separated into a new section. The researcher's role is not just to present the facts, but to draw conclusions on the basis of the findings and to make recommendations on the basis of the conclusions. The reader should be presented a set of conclusions and recommendations for managerial action. While no researcher can force a manager to act on a set of recommendations, he or she should know

EXECUTIVE SUMMARY

- A survey of 299 City area respondents was completed during the months of April and May. The survey involved the use of a structured questionnaire administered by telephone to randomly selected area residents who had an account with a local financial institution. The questionnaire was pretested to assure the completeness and accuracy of responses. A typical respondent could be described as follows: married; male; between the ages of 35-44; lived in the area for 6-12 years; median income of between $35,000-$49,999; attended or graduated college.

- Each respondent was asked to identify his or her primary financial institution. City Bank was by far the most frequently mentioned financial institution (47 percent), followed by The First National Bank (14 percent) and Public Bank (11 percent).

- The services utilized most frequently at the primary financial institution were checking accounts, savings accounts, ATMs, and investment instruments. Fifty-one percent of the respondents had done business at their primary institution for 6 or more years and 52 percent were highly satisfied with their primary financial institution.

- Thirty-eight percent of the respondents reported having an account at a secondary institution. The most frequently utilized services were savings (18 percent), checking (14 percent), and investment instruments (13 percent). The majority of the respondents have done business with their secondary financial institution for over 6 years. The high proportion of respondents with secondary institutions may indicate a preference for multiple financial relationships or a lack of cross-selling by primary institutions.

- Sixty-two (20.7 percent) of the respondents stated they had changed their primary financial institution since living in the area and of this group 62.9 percent had done so in the last 5 years. This indicates the volatility of the market with major changes (Public and The First National) during that time period. Based on this study and supplemental sources on deposits, it appears that City Bank and The First National Bank have both gained market share at the expense of Public Bank. Most respondents who reported switching financial institutions changed from one bank to another bank.

- Respondents were also asked to respond to 17 image characteristics to measure the image of several different institutions. City Bank was the most frequently mentioned institution on every item except "the one you would never recommend." City Bank was followed most closely by The First National Bank, while Public Bank was a distant third.

- The main reason respondents gave for switching primary financial institutions was poor service. This theme was echoed in responses to another question on dissatisfaction with their current primary institution. Poor service was named by 55 percent of the respondents who expressed dissatisfaction with their current primary financial institution. Keeping current customers satisfied with the service received appears to be a safeguard against dissatisfaction and ultimate switching from one financial institution to another.

- Respondents appear to see City Bank, the First National Bank, and to some extent Public Bank as well-managed, progressive, innovative, customer-oriented institutions with a strong financial base, local, and involved in community activities. They were viewed as providing the best service, leaders among local financial institutions with friendly, knowledgeable employees—the one they would recommend to others and best for people like themselves.

- Respondents were also asked questions to determine advertising awareness and media exposure for financial-institution advertising. When the three financial institutions with the most active promotional campaigns (The First National Bank, Public Bank, and Premier Homestead) were compared, 29 percent remembered seeing or hearing an ad for the First National Bank, 22 percent remembered Public Bank, and 17 percent remembered Premier Homestead. Media exposure for these campaigns was: (1) saw/heard TV ad—43 percent; (2) heard radio ad—27 percent; and (3) saw newspaper ad—16 percent. All other media accounted for only 14 percent.

Figure 13.5 Executive Summary

enough about the decision and the data collected to recommend a course of action. That is what the researcher is being paid for! To simply "present the facts" and offer no recommendations is to lose the advantage gained by having someone who is not responsible for making the decision to at least suggest *some* alternative actions. The decision maker still has to "drive the car," but the one who just reads the "road map" can surely offer some suggestions about which direction to go! (Actual recommendations were removed in the banking study in the example in Figure 13.7).

Supporting Documentation (Appendixes)

The appendixes can be used to present copies of questionnaires used in the study, more detailed secondary data, or any other type of data or material that might be helpful to the user of the report (see Figure 13.8). In one study of a new outdoor recreational concept, articles on innovative recreational concepts that had been previously introduced were given. This is only one example of how appendixes can be used. The researcher should avoid any attempt to "pad" or build up the size of a report through the use of appendixes. This only takes away from the communicative force of the body of the report. However, detailed statistical analysis or even computer printouts can be included in an appendix. It is also possible to provide this material in a separate volume for those who will make a detailed study of the report.

FINDINGS

This section presents the findings of the study. The first part shows the characteristics of the respondents who participated in the project. This is followed by a question-by-question analysis of the results of the study.

Sample Characteristics

FIGURE E-1
LENGTH OF TIME RESPONDENTS HAVE LIVED IN AREA

Length of Time	Frequency	Percent
0-2 years	40	13
3-5 years	67	23
6-12 years	52	17
13-20 years	41	14
Over 20 years	92	31
Don't Know/Refused	7	1
Total	299	100

FIGURE E-2
MARITAL STATUS OF RESPONDENTS

Marital Status	Frequency	Percent
Single with No Children	74	26
Married with No Children	50	17
Married with Children at Home	86	30
Single with Children at Home	12	4
Married with No Children at Home	53	18
Single with No Children at Home	11	4
Refused	4	1
Total	290	100

FIGURE E-3
AGE CATEGORY OF RESPONDENTS

Age Category	Frequency	Percent
18-24	44	15
25-34	84	29
35-44	55	19
45-54	44	15
55-64	28	10
65 and older	20	7
Refused	13	5
Total	288	100

FIGURE E-4
TOTAL FAMILY INCOME OF RESPONDENTS

Total Family Income	Frequency	Percent
Under $15,000	22	7
$15,000-24,999	44	15
$25,000-34,999	48	16
$35,000-49,999	49	17
$50,000-64,999	33	11
$65,000-79,999	7	2
$80,000-94,999	–	–
$95,000-110,000	–	–
Over $110,000	8	3
Don't Know/Refused	88	29
Total	299	100

FIGURE E-5
EDUCATIONAL LEVEL OF RESPONDENTS

Educational Level	Frequency	Percent
High School Graduate	52	17
High School Graduate with Some College	88	30
College Graduate	102	34
College Graduate with Some Graduate School	15	5
Graduate Degree Holder	18	6
Don't Know/Refused	24	8
Total	299	100

FIGURE E-6
SEX OF RESPONDENTS

Sex	Frequency	Percent
Male	150	52
Female	140	48
Total	290	100

FIGURE E-7
AVERAGE MONTHLY BALANCE IN CHECKING ACCOUNT
OF RESPONDENTS

Monthly Balance	Frequency	Percent
Under $250	24	8
$250-500	43	14
$501-1,000	63	21
$1,001-2,000	27	9
Over $2,000	51	17
Don't Know/Refused	91	31
Total	299	100

FIGURE E-8
AMOUNT RESPONDENTS HAVE INVESTED IN CDs, MONEY
MARKET DEPOSIT ACCOUNTS, INDIVIDUAL RETIREMENT
ACCOUNTS, OR OTHER HIGH-YIELD INVESTMENTS

Amount Invested	Frequency	Percent
None	82	28
Under $10,000	41	14
$10,001-25,000	38	13
$25,001-75,000	27	9
Over $75,000	7	2
Don't Know/Refused	103	34
Total	298	100

FIGURE E-9
TYPICAL MONTHLY BALANCE FOR NONCHECKING
SAVINGS ACCOUNT OF RESPONDENTS

Monthly Balance	Frequency	Percent
None	32	11
Under $2,500	38	13
$2,501-5,000	37	12
$5,001-7,500	32	11
$7,501-10,000	19	6
Over $10,000	37	12
Don't Know/Refused	104	35
Total	299	100

Primary Institution/Services Utilized by Respondents

Each respondent was asked to identify his or her Primary Financial Institution. The results revealed the following statistics.

FIGURE E-10
RESPONDENT'S PRIMARY FINANCIAL INSTITUTION

Financial Institution	Frequency	Percent
City Bank	136	47
First Bank	25	9
The First National Bank	39	14
Premier Homestead	13	4
City Homestead	19	7
Public Bank	33	11
Other	24	8
Total	289	100

Of the 289 customers interviewed, 136 or 47 percent stated that City Bank was their primary financial institution. The First National Bank was the primary financial institution for 39 or 14 percent of the respondents. Of those surveyed, Public Bank was preferred by 11 percent or 33 of the respondents as their primary financial institution.

The following figure shows the services utilized by respondents at their primary financial institutions.

FIGURE E-11
SERVICES UTILIZED BY RESPONDENTS AT
PRIMARYFINANCIAL INSTITUTION

Services	Frequency	Percent
Automatic Teller Machine	162	54
Personal Loan	48	16
Automobile Loan	47	16
Home (Mortgage) Loans	28	9
Telephone Bill Paying Service	7	2
VISA/MasterCard Service	85	28
Safe Deposit Box	58	19
Checking Account	286	96
Savings Account	229	77
Trust Account	11	4
Money Market Deposit Account	23	8
CDs and Investment Instrument	116	39
Individual Retirement Accounts (IRAs)	54	18
Overdraft Protection	69	23
Educational Loan	17	6
Other	14	5

Figure 13.6 Findings

Of those surveyed, 286 or 96 percent have a checking account with their primary financial institution. A savings account was the second largest service utilized by 229 respondents or 77 percent. The automatic teller machine was used by 162 respondents or 54 percent. CDs and other investment instruments were used by 116 or 39 percent of those surveyed at their primary financial institution. Only 7 or 2 percent of those surveyed used th telephone bill paying service at their primary financial institution. Another infrequently used service by respondents is the trust account, used by 11 or 4 percent.

FIGURE E-12
LENGTH OF TIME RESPONDENTS HAVE DONE BUSINESS WITH
THEIR PRIMARY FINANCIAL INSTITUTION

Length of Time	Frequency	Percent
Less than 1 Year	34	12
1-2 years	30	10
3-5 years	79	27
6-12 years	82	28
Over 12 years	67	23
Total	292	100

Of those surveyed, 28 percent or 82 respondents have done business with their financial institution for 6 to 12 years. Seventy-nine respondents or 27 percent have done business with their primary financial institution for 3 to 5 years. Of those surveyed, 51 percent have done business with their primary financial institution for 6 or more years.

Services Utilized at Secondary Financial Institution

Of those respondents interviewed, 112 or 38 percent have accounts at a secondary financial institution. The following figure outlines the services used by the respondents at their secondary financial institution.

FIGURE E-13
SERVICES UTILIZED BY RESPONDENTS AT SECONDARY
FINANCIAL INSTITUTION

Services	Frequency	Percent
Automatic Teller Machine	8	3
Personal Loan	11	4
Automobile Loan	17	6
Home (Mortgage) Loans	25	8
Telephone Bill Paying Service	1	–
VISA/MasterCard Service	15	5
Safe Deposit Box	5	2
Checking Account	42	14
Savings Account	53	18
Trust Account	3	1
Money Market Deposit Account	3	1
CDs and Investment Instrument	38	13
Individual Retirement Accounts (IRAs)	17	6
Overdraft Protection	1	–
Educational Loan	6	2
Other		

Those respondents who have a secondary financial institution use a savings account as the primary service (53 respondents or 18 percent). A checking account as a service at a secondary financial institution was used by 42 of the respondents or 14 percent. Of those surveyed, 38 or 13 percent utilized CDs and investment instruments at their secondary financial institution. The services utilized least by respondents at their secondary financial institution were telephone bill paying service, overdraft protection, and trust accounts.

FIGURE E-14
LENGTH OF TIME RESPONDENTS HAVE DONE BUSINESS WITH
THEIR SECONDARY FINANCIAL INSTITUTION

Length of Time	Frequency	Percent
Less Than 1 Year	5	4
1-2 Years	14	12
2-5 Years	28	25
6-12 Year	32	8
Over 12 Years	36	31
Total	115	100

Of those surveyed who have secondary financial institutions, the majority (59 percent) have done business with their secondary institution for over 6 years.

This indicates that either respondents prefer to have more than one financial institution or that primary institutions are not doing a good job of cross-selling their services.

Changes in Primary Financial Institutions

Respondents were asked if they had changed primary financial institutions while living in this area. Of those surveyed, 62 or 21 percent had changed primary financial institutions. The following figure shows how long ago the change was made.

FIGURE E-15
HOW LONG AGO RESPONDENTS CHANGED PRIMARY
FINANCIAL INSTITUTIONS WHILE LIVING IN THIS AREA

How Long Ago Change Was Made	Frequency	Percent
Less Than 1 year	13	21
1-2 Years	8	13
3-5 Years	18	29
6-12 Years	10	16
Over 12 Years	13	21
Total	62	100

Of those surveyed who changed primary financial institutions while living in this area, 18 or 29 percent made that change 3 to 5 years ago. This indicates a great deal of volatility in the customer base of financial institutions in the area. In the last 5 years, 63 percent have changed their primary financial institution.

The following figure states what type of change was made when respondents changed primary financial institutions.

FIGURE E-16
TYPE OF FINANCIAL INSTITUTION CHANGE MADE
BY RESPONDENTS

Categories	Frequency	Percent
A Bank to a Savings and Loan	3	5
A Bank to a Credit Union	2	3
A Savings and Loan to a Bank	5	8
A Savings and Loan to a Credit Union	–	–
A Credit Union to a Bank	–	–
A Credit Union to a Savings and Loan	–	–
A Bank to Another Bank	50	84
Total	60	100

FIGURE E-17
MAIN REASON RESPONDENTS CHANGED PRIMARY FINANCIAL
INSTITUTIONS

Reason for Change	Frequency	Percent
Poor Service at Old	22	34
Better Location at New	14	22
Unsure of Stability/Felt Safer at New	9	14
Interest Rates Higher at New	5	8
Other	14	22
Total	64	100

According to those surveyed, the most frequent reason to change primary financial institutions was poor service. Twenty-two percent of respondents also stated that a better location was the reason they changed. Of those surveyed who have changed primary financial institutions, 14 percent changed because they were unsure of the stability of their current bank and felt safer at another institution, 8 percent changed to get a higher interest rate, and 22 percent stated some other reason for their decision to change primary financial institutions.

The following figure will look at respondents' level of satisfaction with their current primary financial institution. Respondents were asked to rank their financial institution on a scale of 1 to 5, where 1 is strongly dissatisfied and 5 is very satisfied.

FIGURE E-18
RESPONDENTS' SATISFACTION WITH THEIR PRIMARY
FINANCIAL INSTITUTION

Categories		Frequency	Percent
Strongly Dissatisfied	–1	2	1
	–2	9	3
	–3	31	11
	–4	97	33
Very Satisfied	–5	152	52
Total		291	100

Figure 13.6 continued

The overall level of satisfaction with the primary financial institution of respondents was fairly high. Of those surveyed, 52 percent or 152 respondents were very satisfied with their primary financial institution. A satisfaction rating of "4" was given to primary financial institutions by 97 respondents or 33 percent. Of those surveyed, 31 or 11 percent gave their primary financial institution a satisfaction level of "3." Only 2 respondents or 1 percent were strongly dissatisfied with their primary financial institution with a rating of "1" and 9 respondents or 3 percent gave a rating of "2."

Respondents that rated their overall level of satisfaction with their primary financial institution as "Strongly Dissatisfied –1 or –2" were asked to specify why they were dissatisfied. The findings are in Figure E-19. This figure reinforces the earlier findings that poor service causes dissatisfaction and eventual departure from a particular financial institution.

FIGURE E-19
RESPONDENT'S REASON FOR DISSATISFACTION WITH
PRIMARY FINANCIAL INSTITUTION

Categories	Frequency	Percent
Poor Service	6	55
Bad Location	–	–
Unsure of Stability	5	45
Interest Rates are Low	–	–
Other	–	–
Total	11	100

Of those surveyed, only 11 expressed dissatisfaction with their primary financial indicated by 55 percent of the respondents. Respondents' second major reason for dissatisfaction was "Unsure of Stability," indicated by 5 respondents or 45 percent.

Images of Financial Institutions

Respondents were asked to express their initial impression or opinion about financial institutions in the area. Those surveyed were asked to mention what financial institution came to mind when the interviewer mentioned each factor about financial institutions. The results are listed in the following figure.

FIGURE E-20
RESPONDENTS' PERCEPTION OF LOCAL FINANCIAL
INSTITUTIONS

Factor	City Bank	First Bank	First Nat.	Premier Home	City Home	Public Bank	Other
Best managed	51%	6%	20%	4%	2%	12%	5%
Friendliest, most personal service	47	8	16	6	5	12	6
Most customer-oriented	46	10	19	5	3	12	5
Most progressive and up-to-date	39	5	33	5	2	13	3
Best for investment-oriented customers	38	8	30	6	4	10	4
Most innovative in the market	43	5	32	4	1	12	3
The financial institution most involved in community leadership and activities	66	6	14	2	2	6	4
Strongest financial base	37	7	31	5	2	14	4
Best reputation for being successful, reliable, and honest	53	8	16	4	2	12	5
The one you would recommend	45	9	21	4	2	13	6
The one you would never recommend	10	21	6	9	30	12	12
Has the best advertising	59	5	17	4	2	12	1
The leader among local financial institutions	49	7	26	3	1	10	4
Has the best service	43	9	21	5	3	12	7
Makes fewest errors on accounts	43	10	18	5	6	11	7
Friendliest, most knowledgeable employees	44	10	17	7	5	11	6
Is the best place for people like you	46	9	21	5	2	11	6

Of those responding, Figure E-20 shows the percentage of respondents that chose each of the banks for the various factors. In all the categories, City Bank was the number one choice, except on the question that asked respondents to name the "One financial institution they would never recommend."

The respondents' perceptions on City Bank were highest when asked to name the financial institution "Most involved in community leadership and activities," with 66 percent of those surveyed choosing City Bank. When respondents were asked to name the financial institution with the "Best reputation for being successful, reliable, and honest," "Best managed," and "The leader among local financial institutions," City Bank was clearly the favorite choice. City Bank was the dominate choice in several other categories as well. When respondents were asked which financial institution has the "Friendliest, most personalized service"; the "Most customer-oriented"; "Most innovative in the market"; "Has the best service"; and "Makes fewest errors on accounts," City Bank has the highest percentages in each of these categories.

In several of the categories City Bank and The First National Bank were the 2 obvious favorites. When respondents were asked to name the financial institution that is the "Most progressive and up-to-date," 39 percent chose City Bank and 33 percent chose The First National Bank. When asked to name the financial institution with the "Strongest financial base," 37 percent chose City Bank and 31 percent chose The First National Bank.

Advertising Awareness

Respondents were asked if they remembered recently seeing or hearing advertising for any of the local financial institutions. The following figure states which financial institutions were remembered by respondents for advertisements.

FIGURE E-21
RESPONDENTS' RECOLLECTION OF RECENT ADVERTISEMENTS
BY LOCAL FINANCIAL INSTITUTIONS

Financial Institution	Frequency	Percent
Public Bank	47	22
The First National Bank	61	29
Premier Homestead	37	17
All Others	67	32
Total	212	100

Sixty-one respondents (29 percent) remembered recently seeing or hearing advertisements for The First National Bank. Of those surveyed, 67 or 32 percent remembered advertising for "All others," which would include any of the financial institutions in the area except the ones mentioned above (Public Bank, the First National, and Premier Homestead). The following figure outlines the media source remembered by respondents as advertising for a local financial institution.

FIGURE E-22
MEDIA SOURCE REMEMBERED BY RESPONDENTS IN
ADVERTISEMENTS FOR A LOCAL FINANCIAL INSTITUTION

Media Source	Frequency	Percent
Heard TV Advertising	98	43
Heard Radio Advertising	62	27
Saw a Newspaper Ad/Article	36	16
Saw a New Sign Going Up	8	3
Billboards	21	9
Someone Told Me About It	3	1
Other	2	1
Total	230	100

Ninety-eight respondents (43 percent) cited TV as the media source remembered for advertisements for a financial institution. Radio was the second largest media source remembered, cited by 62 respondents or 27 percent. Advertising through the paper was remembered by 16 percent of the respondents.

Figure 13.6 continued

CONCLUSIONS AND RECOMMENDATIONS

The Sample

The sample consisted of interviews with residents in the City area who had an account with a local financial institution. Of the 299 area residents who were surveyed, 52 percent were male and 48 percent were female. A typical respondent is described as a married male between the ages of 35-44, who has lived in this area for 6 to 12 years, with a median income of between $35,000 and $49,999, and has attended or graduated from college.

Primary Financial Institution

Of the 299 residents who were surveyed, 47 percent named City Bank as their primary financial institution, followed by The First National Bank, named by 14 percent of the respondents.

FIGURE E-23
PRIMARY FINANCIAL INSTITUTION

Financial Institution	Frequency	Percent
City Bank	136	47
First Bank	25	9
The First National Bank	39	14
Premier Homestead	13	4
City Homestead	19	7
Public Bank	33	11
Other	24	8
Total	289	100

Services Utilized at Primary Financial Institutions

Once the primary financial institution of respondents was established, respondents were asked which services they utilized at their primary financial institution. The following figure lists those services used most by residents who were surveyed.

FIGURE E-24
SERVICES UTILIZED AT PRIMARY INSTITUTION

Services	Frequency	Percent
Checking Account	286	96
Savings Account	229	77
Automatic Teller Machine	162	54
CDs and Investment Instruments	116	39
VISA/MasterCard Service	85	28

Of those surveyed, 96 percent utilize a checking account at their primary financial institution, and 77 percent utilize a savings account. Fifty-one percent of the respondents have done business with their primary financial institution for 6 or more years.

Services Utilized at Secondary Financial Institution

Of those surveyed, 38 percent have accounts at a secondary financial institution. The following figure shows those 4 services used most frequently by those with secondary financial institutions

FIGURE E-25
SERVICES UTILIZED AT SECONDARY INSTITUTION

Services	Frequency	Percent
Savings Account	53	18
Checking Account	42	14
VISA/MasterCard Service	36	13
Home (Mortgage) Loan	25	8

Of those respondents with secondary financial institutions, 59 percent have done business with their financial institution for 6 or more years.

Changes in Primary Financial Institution

Of those surveyed, 21 percent had changed primary financial institution while living in this area. Respondents were asked what type of change they made, and 84 percent changed from one bank to another. The main reason respondents changed primary financial institutions while living in this area was due to poor service.

This finding coincides with respondents' level of satisfaction or dissatisfaction with their primary financial institution. Fifty-two percent of those surveyed were very satisfied with their primary financial institution, while 4 percent of those surveyed were strongly dissatisfied. Those respondents who stated they were dissatisfied were then asked why they were dissatisfied. Fifty-five percent of those stated their main reason for dissatisfaction was poor service.

Images of Financial Institution

Respondents were asked to express their initial impression about financial institutions in the area to determine the image of several local financial institutions. The overall favorite in all of the categories (except for "the financial institution you would never recommend"), was City Bank. Some of the characteristics respondents were asked about were: which local financial institution is well managed, progressive, innovative, customer-oriented, with a strong financial base, and involved in the community. The local institution mentioned first by the majority of the respondents was City Bank. The First National Bank was the respondents' second most frequently mentioned, and Public Bank came in a distant third.

Advertising Most Remembered and Media Source

To determine advertising awareness and media exposure for local financial institutions, respondents were asked to identify financial institutions for which they recalled seeing or hearing advertising. When The First National Bank, Public Bank, and Premier Homestead (the three local financial institutions with the most active promotional campaigns) were compared, 29 percent remembered seeing or hearing an ad for The First National Bank, 22 percent remembered Public Bank, and 17 percent remembered Premier Homestead. Those who did recall seeing or hearing ads for financial institutions were also asked to identify the media sources where they saw or heard the ads. The media source most frequently remembered was TV (43 percent), radio ads (27 percent), and newspaper ads (16 percent).

Figure 13.7 Conclusions and Recommendations

Retail Banking Survey

[1-3] Hello. Am I speaking with the man/lady of the house? (IF NO, ASK TO SPEAK TO THAT PERSON.)

Hello, I'm _____. We're conducting a marketing research project with area residents. This study deals with financial institutions and we need your help in this project. Your answers will be confidential and used only in combination with the responses of other people.

1a. Do you, or does a member of your household, work for a bank, savings and loan, credit union, advertising, public relations, or market research firm?
___YES (Terminate)
___ NO

1b. Do you have a checking or savings account with a local financial institution?
___ YES
___ NO (Terminate)

[4] 2. How long have you lived in this area?
___ 0-2 Years[1]
___3-5 Years[2]
___ 6-12 Years[3]
___ 13-20 Years[4]
___ Over 20 Years[5]

[5] 3. What is the name of your primary financial institution?
___ City Bank[1]
___ First Bank[2]
___ The First National Bank[3]
___ Premier Home Bank[4]
___ City Home Bank[5]
___ Public Bank[6]
___ Other[7]

4. What services are you currently utilizing at your primary financial institution? (READ)
[6] ___ Automatic Teller Machine
[7] ___ Personal Loans
[8] ___Automobile Loans
[9] ___ Home (Mortgage) Loans
[10] ___ Telephone Bill Paying Service
[11] ___ VISA/MasterCard Services
[12] ___ Safe Deposit Box
[13] ___ Checking Account

[14] ___Savings Account
[15] ___ Trust Account
[16] ___Money Market Deposit Account
[17] ___CDs and Investment Instrument
[18] ___Individual Retirement Accounts (IRAs)
[19] ___Overdraft Protection
[20] ___Educational Loans
[21] ___Other

[22] 5. How long have you done business with your primary financial institution?
___ Less than 1 year1 ___ 1-2 years[2]
___ 3-5 years[3]
___ 6-12 years[4]
___ Over 12 years[5]

[23] 6. Do you also have accounts at other institutions?
___ YES[1] ___ NO[2]

7. What services do you currently utilize at this institution?
[24] ___Automatic Teller Machine
[25] ___Personal Loans
[26] ___Automobile Loans
[27] ___Home (Mortgage) Loans
[28] ___Telephone Bill Paying Service
[29] ___VISA/MasterCard Services
[30] ___Safe Deposit Box
[31] ___Checking Account
[32] ___Savings Account
[33] ___Trust Account
[34] ___Money Market Deposit Account
[35] ___CDs and Investment Instrument
[36] ___Individual Retirement Accounts (IRAs)
[37] ___Overdraft Protection
[38] ___Educational Loans
[39] ___Other

[40] 8. (If secondary financial institutions) How long have you done business with your secondary financial institution? ___
___ Less than 1 year[1]
___ 1-2 years[2]
___ 3-5 years[3]
___ 6-12 years[4]
___ Over 12 years[5]

[41] 9. Have you changed your primary financial institution while living in this area?
___ YES[1]
___ NO[2] (Skip to question 13)

[42] 10. ___ How long ago did you make that change?
___ Less than 1 year[1]
___ 1-2 years[2]
___ 3-5 years[3]
___ 6-12 years[4]
___ Over 12 years[5]

[43] 11. Did you change from:
___ A bank to a savings and loan[1]
___ A bank to a credit union[2]
___ A savings and loan to a bank[3]
___ A savings and loan to a credit union[4]
___ A credit union to a bank[5]
___ A credit union to a savings and loan[6]

[44] 12. What was the main reason you changed financial institutions?
___ Poor service at old[1]
___ Better location of new[2]
___ Unsure of stability of old/felt safer at new institution[3]
___ Interest rates higher at new[4]
Other, specify[5] _____

[45] 13. On a scale of one to five, where "one" is strongly dissatisfied and "five" is very satisfied, how would you rate your satisfaction with your primary financial institution?
Strongly dissatisfied 1 2 3 4 5 Very satisfied
[46] If dissatisfied (1 or 2), ask Why are you dissatisfied?
___Poor service at old[1]
___Better location of new[2]
___Unsure of stability of old/felt safer at new institution[3]
___Interest rates higher at new[4]
Other, specify[5] _____

14. Now I would like you to think for a moment about financial institutions in this area. As I mention several factors about financial institutions, please tell me which one comes to mind first for each factor. It does not matter if you have ever done business with them or not. This is simply your initial impression or opinion.

		City Bank	First Bank	First Nat.	Premier Home	City Home	Public Bank	Other
[47]	a. Best managed	1	2	3	4	5	6	7
[48]	b. Friendliest, most personalized service	1	2	3	4	5	6	7
[49]	c. Most customer-oriented	1	2	3	4	5	6	7
[50]	d. Most progressive and up to date	1	2	3	4	5	6	7
[51]	e. Best for investment-oriented customers	1	2	3	4	5	6	7
[52]	f. The most innovative in the marketplace	1	2	3	4	5	6	7
[53]	g. The financial institution most involved in community leadership	1	2	3	4	5	6	7
[54]	h. Strongest financial base	1	2	3	4	5	6	7
[55]	i. Best reputation for being successful	1	2	3	4	5	6	7
[56]	j. The one you would recommend	1	2	3	4	5	6	7
[57]	k. The one you would never recommend	1	2	3	4	5	6	7
[58]	l. Has the best advertising	1	2	3	4	5	6	7
[59]	m. The leader among local financial institutions	1	2	3	4	5	6	7
[60]	n. Has the best service	1	2	3	4	5	6	7
[61]	o. Makes fewest errors on accounts	1	2	3	4	5	6	7
[62]	p. Friendliest, most knowledgeable employees	1	2	3	4	5	6	7
[63]	q. Is the best place for people like you	1	2	3	4	5	6	7

Figure 13.8 Supporting Documentation

15. Do you remember recently seeing or hearing advertising for local financial institutions? If yes, which ones?
[64] ___Yes, Public
[65] ___Yes, First National
[66] ___Yes, Premier
[67] ___Yes, Other
[68] ___No (Skip to question 17)

16. On what media did you hear the advertising? (Mark all that apply)
[69] ___Heard TV advertising
[70] ___Heard radio advertising
[71] ___Saw a newspaper ad/article
[72] ___Saw new sign going up
[73] ___Billboards
[74] ___Someone told me about it
[75] ___Other

[76] 17. Now just a few more questions about you. Are you:
___ Single with no children[1]
___ Married with no children[2]
___ Married with children at home[3]
___ Single with children at home[4]
___ Married with no children at home[5]
___ Single with no children at home[6]
___ Refused[7]

[77] 18. Which age category do you fit into?
___18-24[1]   ___ 56-64[5]
___25-34[2]   ___ 65 and older[6]
___35-44[3]   ___ Refused[7]
___45-54[4]

[78] 19. What is the category that includes your total family income? (READ)
___ Under 15,000[1]   ___ $65,000 to $79,999[6]
___ $15,000 to $24,999[2] ___ $80,000 to $94,999[7]
___ $25,000 to $34,999[3] ___ $95,000 to $110,999[8]
___ $35,000 to $49,999[4] ___ Over $110,000[9]
___ $50,000 to $64,999[5] ___ Don't know/refused[10]

[79] 20. Are you: (READ)
___ A high school graduate[1]
___ A high school graduate with some college[2]
___ A college graduate[3]
___ A college graduate with some graduate school[4]
___ A graduate degree holder[5]
___ Refused[6]

[80] 21. Sex: (Do not ask unless necessary)
___ Male1 ___ Female2

[81] 22. Which of the following most closely approximates your average monthly balance in your checking account(s)? (READ)
___ Under $250[1]
___ $251–$500[2]
___ $501–$1,000[3]
___ $1,001–$2,000[4]
___ Over 2,000[5]
___ Refused[6]

[82] 23. Which is the approximate amount you have invested in CDs, money market deposit accounts, Individual Retirement Accounts, or other types of high-yield investments with financial institutions? (READ)
___ None[1]
___ Under $10,000[2]
___ $10,001–25,000[3]
___ $25,001–75,000[4]
___ Over $75,000[5]
___ Refused[6]

[83] 24. Finally, what would be a typical monthly balance for your nonchecking savings accounts? (READ)
___ None[1]
___ Under $2,500[2]
___ $2,501–5,000[3]
___ $5,001–7,500[4]
___ $7,501–$10,000[5]
___ Over $10,000[6]
___ Refused[7]

Thank you very much for your time and cooperation

Figure 13.8 continued

Presentation

We also recommend that the final report be bound. This is a relatively inexpensive way to add value to the report and at the same time provide evidence of professionalism and pride. Copies of such reports may be used for years and binding ads protection to the contents. In general, a good rule of thumb to use when considering what to say and where to say it in the written report is to ask this question: "If someone totally unfamiliar with this research project were to take this report out of a file a month from now, would the report be complete enough to give them enough information to make decisions in this area?" Supply a sufficient number of copies for everyone attending the oral presentation of findings, plus at least two copies for the files of the primary recipient of the report and two copies for the researcher's file.

Guidelines for the Written Report

There are two methods used to present statistical data: tables and graphs. Both of these methods are commonly used in research reports. The type of data or the emphasis the researcher wishes to put on a given set of data determines which method to use.

Tables

A statistical table is a method of presenting and arranging data that have been broken down by one or more systems of classification. Analytical tables are designed to aid in a formal analysis of interrelationships between variables. A reference table is designed to be a repository of statistical data. The distinction between these two types of data is their intended use and not

Table 13.1 Preferences for Motel-Related Restaurants by Age of Traveler*

	Prefer Motel Restaurants		*Prefer Nonmotel Restaurants*		
	Number	*Percent*	*Number*	*Percent*	*Totals by Age*
Under 25	7	5.5	130	45.3	137
25–34	13	10.3	62	21.6	75
35–44	29	23.0	38	13.2	67
45–54	33	26.2	35	12.2	68
Over 55	44	34.9	22	7.7	66
Total	126	99.9**	287	100.0	413

Source: Survey data.
*Preference was defined as where they would eat if they were traveling and staying at a motel with a restaurant.
**Does not add up to 100 percent due to rounding

Table 13.2 Sex of Travelers

	Number	*Percent*
Male	294	71.1
Female	119	28.9
Total	413	100.0

Source: Survey data.

their construction. Table 13.1 is an example of an analytical table and Table 13.2 is an example of a reference table.

Table 13.1 was prepared to analyze differences in preferences based on the age of the respondents—an analytical table. Table 13.2 was prepared to report to the reader the number of respondents of each sex that were interviewed—a reference table.

Care should be taken in preparing tables to include proper headings, notes about discrepancies (percentages that add to more or slightly less than 100, for example), and sources of data. This helps the reader interpret the data contained in the tables and avoids obvious questions such as "Why don't the figures total 100 percent?"

Graphs

Many types of graphs can aid in presenting data. Three of the most commonly used are bar charts, pie charts, and line charts. These three add a visual magnitude to the presentation of the data. Graphics software packages offer a wide variety of options and are easy to use in creating a report with more visual impact.

A bar chart is easily constructed and can be readily interpreted even by those not familiar with charts. They are especially useful in showing differences between groups. Consider, for example, how much more clear and impactful the bar chart shown in Figure 13.9 is for communicating the findings of the data presented in Table 11.2. Here it is possible to visually represent in a clear and convincing fashion our interpretation of the relationship between the variables. Recall that in our Chapter 11 discussion we used Table 11.2 to identify a possible relationship between consumption rates and agreement to pay more to get your favorite brand of egg substitutes. The use of graphics to tell your analytical story can not only communicate your message more effectively, but also may leave more lasting recollection of the point you are making compared to use of tables full of numbers.

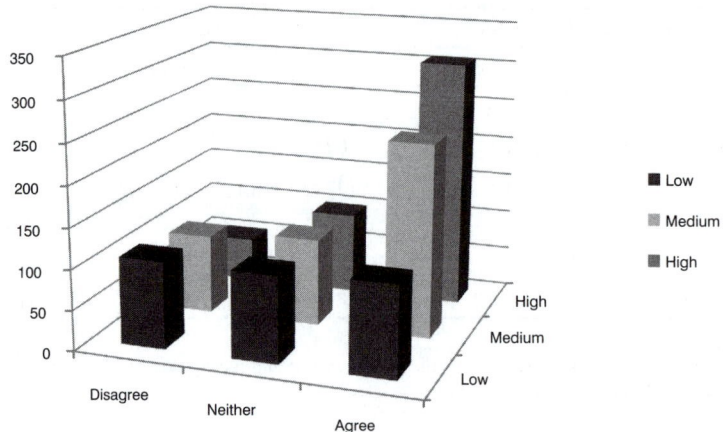

Figure 13.9 Bar Chart of Table 11.2 Data

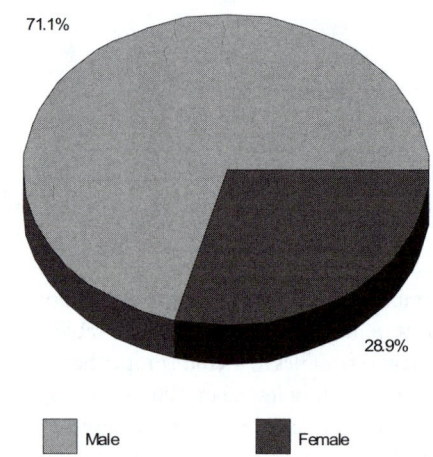

Figure 13.10 Sex of Travelers (Pie Chart)

A pie chart is a useful graph in marketing studies especially when showing market share or market segments. Figure 13.10 presents a sample pie chart. Adding color to highlight certain sections increases visual impact in pie charts. This permits identifying different shares held by different competitors also.

Figures 13.11 and 13.12 are line charts that are especially useful in showing trends in data and comparing trends for different products, customers, and market areas.

General Advice

Some general advice for preparing the written report is:

1   The written report represents you and your work. Make certain it leaves the impression you desire people to have about you as a professional by ensuring the report is well written, with proper grammar, no errors, correctly labeled tables, page numbers in table

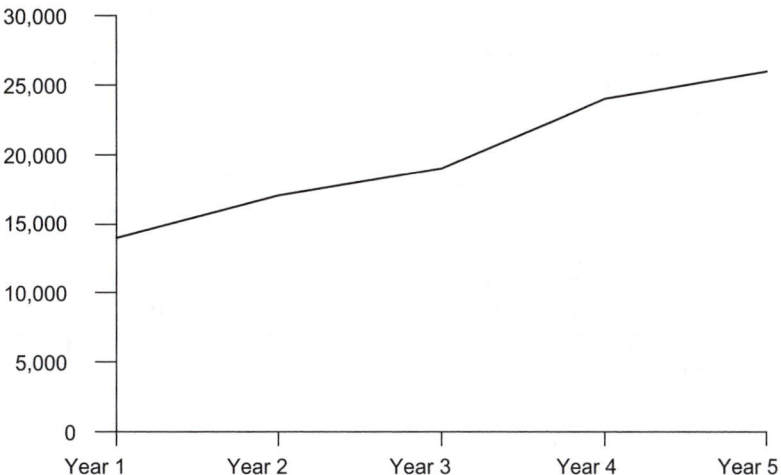

Figure 13.11 Sales by Year

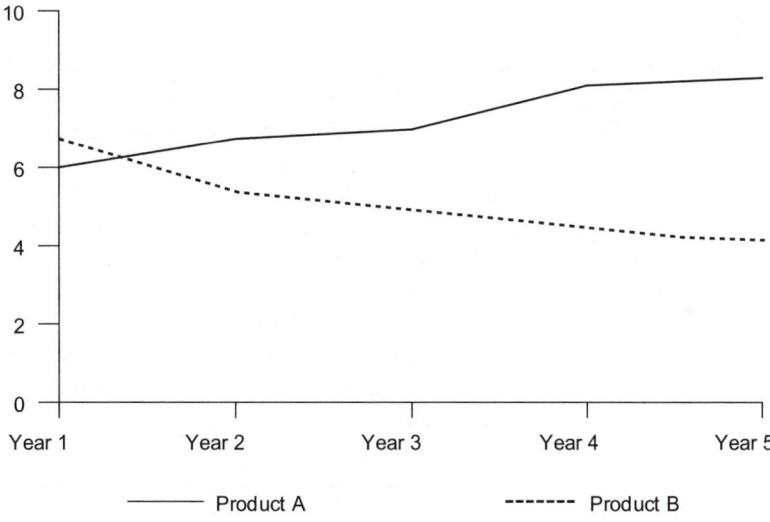

Figure 13.12 Sales by Product

of contents matches text, and so on. Be obsessive about getting every detail correct and people will believe the report was written by the kind of true professional you are striving to become.

2   Do not organize the report by the stages of the research (e.g., a heading of "Literature Review Results, Case Analysis Results," etc.). The decision makers reading the report do not want you to tell them what you discovered in each phase of the research (e.g., "In the literature review we found . . .," "In the in-depth interviews we discovered . . ."). They want you to put all the pieces together and discuss the overall findings, conclusions, and recommendations. Therefore, organize the report by key decisional areas and combine all the findings from all sources and all stages of the research in your discussion of that key decisional area. For example, if part of the research objectives related to making decisions about packaging, you might title this section of the report "Packaging Decisions" and report findings on industry trends discovered in your literature search, what inventory-management personnel of your

key customer accounts said in in-depth interviews, the results of a descriptive-research sample survey of customers, and the findings of an experiment testing the sales of two different package designs in this section, along with your conclusions and recommendations for packaging decisions.

3 Write for your audience. Some managers are interested in knowing that you used factor analysis to determine the underlying attributes people use to evaluate coffee brands, other managers perceive your telling them this as "showing off," irrelevant, and evidence that you are not part of the team.

4 Do not discuss exploratory reports using statistics (e.g., "42 percent of focus group participants liked this idea"). It is best to avoid heavy use of statistics even when reporting the results of a large sample size exploratory survey. It is better, for example, to report a finding as "about a third of the males said they would be willing to try the product," rather than

Would you be interested in trying this product?

	Male	Females
Yes	31%	27%
No	60%	70%
Not Sure	9%	3%

Reporting the results of an exploratory survey in the same way you would for a descriptive research study will result in the reader of the report attributing the same degree of precision and confidence in the exploratory as he or she did to descriptive research. Remember, the purpose of exploratory is to provide insights and ideas, and not measure frequencies and covariation with calculable amounts of precision and confidence intervals as in the case with descriptive research. Make sure the reader of the report understands how the type of research you conducted is reflected in the way you report the findings, and correct someone (tactfully) when he or she misstates a finding by suggesting it is something it was never intended to be (e.g., a statistic instead of a general observation).

5 Do not perform mathematical calculations on interval scaled data that can only be legitimately performed on ratio data. For example, let's say you were comparing your new brand of car wax to the market leader and asked people to indicate from their observation how shiny each wax made a car's hood look on the following scale:

Very shiny	*Shiny*	*Neutral*	*Not very shiny*	*Not at all shiny*
5	4	3	2	1

If the average response for your brand of wax was 4.2 on the scale and your competitor's was 3.3, you could *not* claim your wax is "27 percent shinier than the leading competitor."

$4.2 - 3.3 = .9 \div 3.3 = 27\%$

Why not? Because you are performing a calculation on intervally scaled data, which is permissible only with ratio data. If the scale had looked like this

Very shiny	*Shiny*	*Neutral*	*Not very shiny*	*Not at all shiny*
+2	+1	0	−1	−2

Your wax is neither 27 percent nor 300 percent shinier than your competitor's product because you can not use an interval scale to compute a ratio such as was done here.

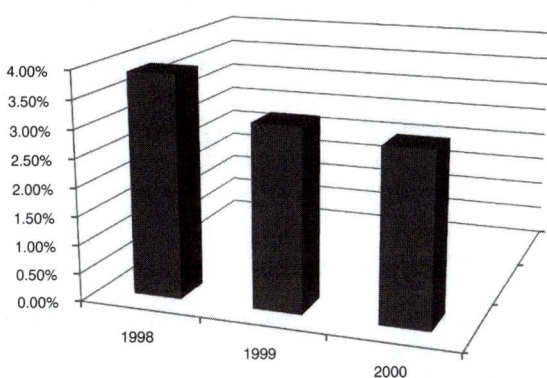

Figure 13.13 Advertising as a Percent of Sales

6   Do not manipulate your graphs to mislead a reader in his or her interpretation of the research findings. Consider, for example, the impression left by the bar chart in Figure 13.13. The impression is that there has been a significant downward trend in the percentage of sales dollars allocated to advertising, when actually the decline is less than one percentage point of sales. This misrepresentation would be even more egregious if actual advertising dollars had risen or remained the same from 1998 to 2000. Intentionally misleading the reader of your report is not only unethical, it brings all of your findings, conclusions, and recommendations into question. Do not do it.

7   Unless you are divinely inspired, do not think your first draft of the report will be your last. Allow enough time before the report is due to make several drafts. Have someone with good editing skills edit your work (expect to pay them for this job). Have someone unfamiliar with the research study read the report. If someone without a background in this particular project can read and understand why you needed to do the research, what you did, what you found, and sees the conclusions and recommendations as legitimate outcomes of the findings, then you probably have written a report that will actually influence decision making.

8   Quote respondents verbatim at appropriate points to "put a face on" your statistics. These quotes may be from statements made in the exploratory research phase, such as in a focus group, or from an open-ended question in a descriptive survey. For example, you may have just reported that only 13 percent of people found the graphics in a print ad attractive. You then might include some verbatim statements to illustrate the problem with the ad:

> "I give up. What is it supposed to be?"
> "Looks like one of those Rorschach tests."
> "I'd tell you what I think I see but my mother would wash my mouth out with soap."
> "You can't be serious!"

Judicious use of concrete examples to illustrate abstract points makes your findings more memorable.

9   If 12 out of 17 people responded yes to a question, do not report the results as Yes = 70.59 percent. Inevitably someone will ask for the sample size and when you tell them you will at best look idiotic if not untrustworthy. Do not give results an aura of precision they do not deserve.

10 Make liberal use of headings and subheadings to aid the reader's navigation through the report.

11 Use headings that communicate findings of interest to the decision makers. "Consumers Demand Quality" is better than "Findings Regarding the Importance of Quality."

12 Do all the other things you know you are supposed to do (e.g., use active instead of passive voice, say "we" instead of "I," use present tense as much as possible, begin paragraphs with topic-revealing sentences, avoid researcher jargon, use short words (e.g., "now" instead of "currently"), avoid clichés, do not use six words when two will do, etc.). Refer to one of the standard works on how to write well.[1]

Oral Reports

Another effective way to present the results of a study is in an oral presentation. The authors *do not* recommend this as a substitute for a written report, but as a supplement to the written document. The written report should be seen as an archival document, and not just a cryptic written presentation for those people thoroughly familiar with the project. If the oral presentation is effectively done, it becomes a communication tool to reinforce what is given in the written report. In many cases it becomes a technique to communicate results to key executives who might not otherwise have interest or access to those who have been collecting data outside the organization.

With today's audiovisual technology, no researcher should fail to use these aids in an oral presentation. Plenty of evidence suggests that we remember more of what we see and hear than of what we read only. Transparencies can be prepared at modest costs for most research budgets and greatly add to the impact of the presentation. Again, computerized presentation graphics are easy to use and enable the researcher to customize the graphics used in the oral presentation by including company logo, industry symbols, etc. Short excerpts from videotaped focus group sessions can be very effective in demonstrating with a specific example the broader finding and conclusions that tape segment is intended to illustrate. Remember, people are more likely to recall and use in formulating their own conclusions those bits of information presented in graphic or visual form rather than as tables or numbers. The following is some general advice for preparing and presenting an oral report:

1 There is increasing use of computerized presentation software such as PowerPoint, Adobe Persuasion, Astound, Harvard Graphics, and IBM Lotus Freelance when making oral presentations. The use of such programs may be expected by your audience, and use of "low-tech" presentation material such as overhead transparencies or flip charts may, unfortunately, label you as unsophisticated, inexperienced, or hopelessly behind the times. Check to see what is the common practice for presentations to this audience. If you use a computer software presentation package, ensure that you will be able to run your presentation software, even if it means bringing your own hardware.

2 Do not assume optimal conditions and equipment for your presentation. In fact, do not assume anything except that you will get to the room and none of your requests will have been met. Get there far enough ahead of the scheduled presentation that you can rearrange the seating, set up the screen and projector/computer that you brought in case your request for equipment was not met, ensure everything operates as it should, etc.

3 Practice your presentation at least three times before making it in front of the audience. Know your material in great detail. Be comfortable with your material. Plan your presentation to take up only about two-thirds of the allotted time. Know where you need to be in your presentation by specific points in time (e.g., each fifteen minutes). If you are behind schedule, skip less important material rather than rushing through everything.

4 Make sure you present your findings in an order that is consistent with the way people draw connections between pieces of information and construct meaning for information. Have your presentation "tell the story" that you have identified in the findings.

5   When appropriate, use visual aids (e.g., product packages, story boards, etc.) to help the audience better relate to the research and findings. A good idea, for example, is to at different points in the presentation play a few minutes of videotape from a focus group session to demonstrate how actual consumers feel about the topic. This could also be done when discussing descriptive research results when a few consumers on the videotape express in a more visceral way what the emotionless data are revealing.

6   As with the written report, use charts and graphs whenever that method of displaying the results communicates the findings more effectively than tables.

7   Provide the audience with an outline of the presentation and paper copies of the key visuals (graphs, tables, conclusions, recommendations, etc.).

8   Do all the other things common sense tells you you should do in a presentation (e.g., tell them what you are going to tell them, tell them, tell them what you told them; face the audience when describing a visual; make eye contact; do not make extravagant gestures, but do not seem stiff either; do not play with your pointer; make text on your visuals large enough to read by the person farthest away from you; do not read from a script; make sure everyone hears a question from the audience before answering it; etc.).

Summary

This chapter has presented a brief overview of the steps involved in preparing a research report. The research report is not only a communication tool, but is also a source document for future reference. The preparation of the report provides the researcher with the major vehicle to communicate findings to management and to display the results of the work that went into completing the project.

Discussion Questions

1   What are the objectives you want to achieve when writing a research report and making a presentation of research results?

2   What are the researcher's responsibilities in writing conclusions and recommendations?

3   Describe how "thinking like a marketer" will influence how you write the report and make the presentation

Part V
Cases

The SPSS files mentioned in the following cases are available from this book's companion website at www.routledge.com/cw/stevens

Case 1   Lone Pine Kennel Club

Jack Thornton leaned back in his chair and scratched Blue, his favorite bird dog, behind the ear. Jack was the president of the Lone Pine Kennel Club (LPKC) and a great believer in animal causes. In fact, Jack had taken the lead in moving the club beyond its primary mission of training hunting and show dogs to putting together a foundation to raise financial support for the local animal shelter. This Basic Animal Relief Foundation (BARF), however, was struggling with its fund raising efforts.

LPKC is a voluntary organization made up of dog enthusiasts. The club is located in a metropolitan area with a population of about 75,000 in an otherwise largely rural, southern state. Given the rural nature of the area, outdoor recreation activities including hunting and fishing are a major pastime for residents. Pickup trucks with a dog in the back are an everyday sight.

Unfortunately, being rural also means that the socio-economic status of the local population was not particularly high, despite the club being located in a metropolitan area. And there were always plenty of good causes seeking donations from the populace at any given time.

Jack wondered how and to what extent these factors played into his current concerns about raising money for animal care. He believed that residents probably had a soft spot in their hearts for dogs and other pets needing a proper home. But with money tight for many people and given the competing demands for the charitable dollar, Jack despaired that BARF would not be able to reach its financial goals in support of animal relief.

BARF's last fundraiser produced modest results at best. Intuitively Jack believed that there were just not enough people who really new enough about the Lone Pine Kennel Club and BARF to give to its cause. He was willing to bet that while a great many people owned pets, this was their main focus as far as animals were concerned. If true, this meant that not many had ever been to the local animal shelter, much less adopted a pet from there or given any thought to its support.

While Jack harbored his suspicions about the situation, he truly believed that taking care of derelict animals was a cause worth pursuing. But he also knew that his personal commitment to LPKC and his love of dogs might be coloring his expectations about BARF and its fundraising. He now believed that a more objective view and analysis would be necessary to get to the bottom of the problems behind BARF. So he wanted to bring in a market research firm to do a study of the local situation as it relates to BARF's efforts in support of the animal shelter.

To get his money's worth out of the study, Jack knew he had some planning to do. With pen in hand he began to jot down his thoughts. Jack saw the fundamental purpose of the study as improving donations to local animal relief efforts by determining the public's awareness of the local animal shelter and BARF, and the populace's willingness to contribute to animal control and care.

To more tightly focus the study, Jack next developed some goals for the research team to pursue. He believed they should uncover public opinions on the following:

1   concern over stray animals;
2   knowledge of animal shelter locations;
3   condition and treatment of animals at the shelter;
4   interest in adopting animals housed by the shelter;
5   BARF's role in raising funds to support the shelter.

And from the above, the research should: develop conclusions and recommendations to improve BARF's performance.

As Jack finished writing these notes, he felt like he was on the right track with the market research idea and that he now had the plan basics that he could talk to a research firm about and let them take it from there. He looked over at Blue and smiled. As the dog stirred, Jack knew it was time for them to enjoy a walk together in the cool night air.

Discussion questions/assignments

1   Prepare a two to three page proposal outlining the major management issues, research objectives, and a research methodology.
2   Prepare a questionnaire to respond to the objectives you listed in your proposal.

This case was prepared by Dr. Stanley G. Williamson, University of Louisiana Monroe, Dr. Robert Stevens, Southeastern Oklahoma State University, and Dr. David Loudon, Samford University Names, selected data, and corporate identities have been disguised

Case 2   Silver Jewelry Stores

John Thomas, a recent computer information systems (CIS) graduate, sat at his desk looking at some of the data sets provided to Silver Jewel Stores by other businesses owned by the parent company, ONG Holdings. These data sets provided detailed profiles of customers, complete with names, addresses, phone numbers, and email addresses plus psychographic profiles for those customers who had participated in the subsidiaries' surveys. The data also provided lists of purchases for each customer by type of product, date purchased, how it was paid for, use of the store's credit card (which is now administered by a bank), store pickup or delivery, in store purchases and internet purchases.

Thomas's assignment was to mine these data sets to develop lists of existing and potential customers who could be targeted by Silver Jewelry Stores, as well as other subsidiaries, for marketing specific types of products through different media. The parent company had followed standard statements in their privacy policy statement about what the storage mechanism's use of and sharing of customer data were and a statement about not selling lists to third parties. However, the privacy statement did mention that the company would, from time to time, use the data provided to market their own products and services to customers. Several customers had complained to store managers that since opening their account with the stores, there had been a big increase in the amount of mail from other companies and they were questioning store managers about whether their information was being sold to other companies.

Thomas knew, based on the number of "hits" on the company's website and surveys which ask about the company's privacy that had been mailed to them, that most customers did not read the privacy statement and treated it as "junk" mail. The website and the mailed statements all use ONG Holdings as the originator of the statement so it would apply to all subsidiaries' customers. He also knew that while his company did not sell it's data to other companies, data was freely shared by all the subsidiaries and therefore any subsidiary could use the data for marketing products and services to other subsidiaries.

Thomas wondered about whether or not it was ethical to share data between subsidiaries even though the company's attorney assured him that they were legally protected. He decided to ask the marketing team to get input from customers about this practice. The marketing team felt this was important enough to hire a research company to do two focus groups on this topic.

The two focus groups yielded a lot of insight into the company's operations in general and the privacy policy specifically. Some the of excerpts of the focus group research report are shown below:

1 As expected, most participants had not read the privacy policy statement but were aware the company had one.
2 Most were not aware that Silver Jewelry Stores was a part of the parent company, ONG Holdings.

After copies of the privacy policy were distributed and read by participants, all agreed that the policy seemed fair.

However, one of the participants who had had a store credit card for some time stated that since the card was now offered through a major bank and could be used at other stores, he had started getting all sorts of offers in the mail and by emails for a travel club, discounts on mail order/Internet purchases, and mail order/Internet offers in his monthly statement from the bank.

Then the discussion got heated as one participant said it looked like they were letting personal data be used by the bank to market products to card holders. Others quickly joined in the discussion and said this was a violation of the privacy statement they had just read.

The discussion leader stated that Silver Jewelry Stores had not sold their personal data to the bank but that the bank now had access to it because they were processing all their transactions. However, participants continued to discuss how every company wanted all their information and then they were inundated with mail, emails, and even phone calls from companies they had never heard of or done business with in the past.

Several participants stated that they were considering cancelling accounts with companies that appeared to follow that practice. Apparently, participants had a lot of anger about such practices and were venting that anger at the focus group discussions.

1   Based on the results of the two focus groups, the research team recommended that the company and its banking partner give all customers an "opt out" of some or all of the solicitations.

2   The bank also had a privacy policy statement that was included in each customer's credit card statement at least once a year. This statement complicated the situation even more because the statement gave a list of why personal data was shared and what customers could prohibit and not prohibit. A partial list is show below:

Personal Data Use

Purpose	Customer can limit	Customer can't limit
Everyday business		X
For our marketing purposes		X
For joint marketing efforts with other financial companies		X
For our affiliates business purposes		X
For nonaffiliates marketing purposes	X	

What this indicates is that in addition to ONG sharing data with all its subsidiaries, the bank that processed Silver Jewelry Stores' credit cards could also share customer data with all its affiliates. The affiliates were not listed in the insert but customers were given a number to call to "opt out" of direct marketing efforts of nonaffiliates.

Thomas wondered if the bank's sharing of information with its affiliates would enable the affiliates to share Silver Jewelry Store customers' data with their own affiliates. This would create a "snowball" effect of data sharing with many other companies who could then use direct marketing to the stores' customer base. The bank's privacy statement was not brought up at the two focus groups interviews and Thomas wondered what participants reactions would be to this new information.

This case was prepared by Dr. Robert Stevens, Southeastern Oklahoma State University, Dr. Lawrence Silver, Southeastern Oklahoma State University and Robert Howard, Southeastern Oklahoma State University.

Case 3   Select Hotels of North America

To gain experience in the hospitality industry, the sector of the economy Janet Huff wanted to enter after graduation, she applied for and was accepted to the Select Hotels of North America summer internship program. This program is run by one of the premier hotel organizations in the field, managing seven different brand chains.

Over the last seven weeks she has experienced all phases of operations at a medium-size hotel in one of the company's brand chains: maintenance, front desk operations, food preparation, housekeeping, banquet service, and reservations. With two weeks left in her internship she has been assigned to the company's headquarters. The goal of this portion of the internship is to expose her to the strategy and operation of the organization in a larger sense. One the first day of this stage of her internship, she was sent the following numerical data and memo:

Room breakdown by brand

	Jan.	Feb.	Mar.	Apr.	May	Jun.
Sleep Well	10,547	10,547	10,652	10,797	10,797	10,797
Welcome	44,150	44,150	44,150	44,150	44,250	44,250
Our Guest	84,415	84,415	84,612	84,612	85,095	85,695
Traveler	2,922	2,922	3,050	3,139	3,139	3,139
Homestay	42,831	42,831	42,831	42,831	44,220	44,220
Relaxation	6,140	6,140	6,140	6,240	6,240	6,240
Restful	4,175	4,175	4,340	4,670	4,950	4,950

Rooms in renovation[1]

	Jan.	Feb.	Mar.	Apr.	May	Jun.
Sleep Well	0	0	0	0	450	325
Welcome	0	365	120	558	620	55
Our Guest	785	750	1,200	850	800	0
Traveler	150	75	75	0	0	0
Homestay	2,000	2,500	0	0	0	0
Relaxation	0	600	0	0	0	0
Restful	0	0	250	200	200	0

Room Nights Rented[2]

	Jan.	Feb.	Mar.	Apr.	May	Jun.
Sleep Well	312,585	271,982	315,280	299,814	302,859	298,712
Welcome	1,289,870	991,574	1,125,996	1,158,798	1,222,819	987,456
Our Guest	2,358,205	2,002,596	2,157,991	2,254,073	2,045,377	2,459,700
Traveler	84,872	73,580	89,054	87,598	95,870	74,198
Homestay	988,785	894,050	1,211,459	974,566	1,125,987	1,165,805
Relaxation	172,589	129,478	160,589	157,498	175,098	175,874
Restful	110,341	105,983	107,983	98,114	112,588	128,419

Average Room/Rack Rate[3]

	Jan.	Feb.	Mar.	Apr.	May	Jun.
Sleep Well	$66	$66	$66	$66	$66	$66
Welcome	$62	$62	$62	$62	$62	$62
Our Guest	$54	$54	$54	$54	$54	$54
Traveler	$46	$46	$46	$46	$46	$46
Homestay	$39	$39	$39	$39	$39	$39
Relaxation	$42	$42	$42	$42	$42	$42
Restful	$30	$30	$30	$30	$30	$30

Average Room Rental Revenue Realized[4]

	Jan.	Feb.	Mar.	Apr.	May	Jun.
Sleep Well	$63.95	$63.95	$63.95	$63.95	$61.45	$62.10
Welcome	$50.88	$48.58	$48.95	$49.15	$50.88	$50.66
Our Guest	$45.15	$47.92	$39.85	$45.60	$43.25	$46.65
Traveler	$42.19	$43.25	$41.47	$42.81	$42.00	$39.87
Homestay	$38.16	$38.54	$38.00	$36.45	$35.79	$36.87
Relaxation	$41.11	$39.80	$40.25	$36.70	$41.75	$41.98
Restful	$29.65	$29.54	$28.57	$27.50	$28.31	$26.50

Average Total Room Revenue Realized[5]

	Jan.	Feb.	Mar.	Apr.	May	Jun.
Sleep Well	$72.26	$71.95	$70.81	$71.88	$64.27	$69.65
Welcome	$54.25	$51.88	$52.31	$52.48	$54.40	$54.19
Our Guest	$47.29	$50.20	$41.76	$47.68	$45.33	$48.71
Traveler	$42.19	$43.25	$41.47	$42.81	$42.00	$39.87
Homestay	$39.10	$39.46	$39.05	$37.28	$36.67	$37.54
Relaxation	$41.11	$39.80	$40.25	$36.70	$41.75	$41.98
Restful	$29.65	$29.54	$28.57	$27.50	$28.31	$26.50

Notes:

1 Number of room units not available for nightly rental for the month.
2 Summation of rooms rented each night across all nights in the month.
3 Posted nightly room rate.
4 Average room rate actually charged.
5 Average total revenue linked to room rentals (includes mini-bar, valet/dry cleaning services, and hotel portion of local and long-distance telephone charges as well as rack rate).

Select Hotels of North America
Serving the Traveler and Their Needs Yesterday, Today, and Tomorrow

To: Janet Huff
From: Carol Ortega
          Vice President for Operations
cc: Leon Thomas
          Coordinator, Summer Internship Program

Date: July 24, 2000

Regarding: Analysis of 1st and 2nd quarter performance data

Welcome to Select Hotels headquarters here in Scottsdale. Two months ago we were pleased that you decided to accept our offer for the summer internship program. Since then, you have done very well in the rotational assignments you have had. Your supervisors have made many favorable comments on your work ethic, enthusiasm, and customer service. Your formal evaluations have been similarly positive.

For this final portion of your experience you will be participating on a team undertaking several analysis projects that will have significant strategic consequences for all of the Select Hotels brands. More specifically, on the attached pages are operating data and other summary statistics for the first six months of this year. We would like to see what you can make of this information on your own, before you join the analysis team charged with the more detailed analysis that will follow. I am particularly interested in your appraisal (by brand) of how efficiently our operations are being run and the measures that you believe are appropriate to use. I suspect that spreadsheet analysis and/or selected graphing of the data (perhaps not in its original form) will prove more insightful than the raw data. I any case, I will leave those decisions to you.

Please get your memo to me by this Friday, July 28.

Discussion Questions

1 How well does each of the hotel chain brands perform if occupancy rate is used as the performance measure? Are there any drawbacks to using this as the sole performance measure?

2 How well does each of the hotel chain brands perform if average room rental revenue is used as the performance measure? Are there any drawbacks to using this as the sole performance measure?

3 Are there other issues or information not provided in this case that might affect your interpretation of the data? How could this additional information affect your conclusions?

This case was prepared by Dr. Michael R. Luthy, Bellarmine College. Brand names, selected data, and corporate identities have been disguised.

Case 4   River Pines School: A

Tom Sanders, headmaster of River Pines School, sat in his office one afternoon pondering the state of his school. Even though the school reportedly has the highest academic standards and a long list of distinguished graduates who have gone on to excel in college and life, enrollment was at dangerously low levels. It had been frustrating for Tom who had been hired four years ago to turn the school around. It seems that every time a positive step was implemented or positive recognition was achieved, it was met, at best, with community apathy and more often was ignored by the local newspaper and television stations.

River Pines is a private, not-for-profit college preparatory school located in the northeast-central quadrant of a county of 250,000 people. The school offers classes in pre-Kindergarten through the 12th grade. The school has suffered through declining enrollment over the past six to eight years, going from a high of approximately 550 students down to a low of approximately 200 students. Present enrollment is 235 students spread through 14 grades. River Pines' high school is one of four private high schools in the county and the only private high school not affiliated with a religious organization. A larger, religious-based private school is located five miles north of River Pines. Additionally, there are five large, public high schools in the county. The school offers a variety of extra-curricular activities in the middle and high school, including athletics (football, basketball, softball, baseball, track, tennis, cheerleading/drill team) and personal enrichment (drama club, quiz bowl, debate team, French and Spanish clubs, Fellowship of Christian Students, and choral competition). Academic requirements at River Pines exceed the requirements mandated by the state, and it is believed that academic standards and achievements of River Pines students (in all grades) exceed those of other private and public schools, due in part to a low student–teacher ratio. Over the past five years, the average dollar amounts of scholarships earned by River Pines graduating seniors has exceeded the average dollar amount earned by the graduating seniors at all other public and private high schools in the area.

While River Pines has suffered through major declines in enrollment, other private schools have enjoyed significant gains, sometimes at the expense of River Pines. While a number of possible causes of enrollment decline have surfaced, such as students wanting more social opportunities and different extra-curricular activities not offered by River Pines (e.g., band, boys and girls soccer), no one at the school has been able to determine a root cause of the enrollment decline. A troublesome problem has surfaced, however. Parents have been subjected to or have overheard negative rumors and other types of "character assassination" by members of a rival lower-middle private school. There appears to be some credible support for that claim. Over the last five to seven years, not one student completing that rival middle school's program has looked at or chosen River Pines as the high school of choice.

Tom knew that he and the school most likely needed a more focused marketing approach. It was obvious that word of mouth and internal recruiting efforts were failing. While the school was financially solvent—a minor miracle in view of the dramatic enrollment drops—there was very little money for extras, such as an expensive marketing campaign. He knew, however, that the school would have difficulty surviving and flourishing with the present enrollment level. Additionally, obtaining outside help was viewed as a necessity since Tom and members of the Board of Directors had no marketing expertise. The board gave Tom the approval to begin talks with outside groups.

One particular firm in the area, Conceptual Dimensions, Inc., seemed very interested and qualified to provide guidance and assistance to River Pines in this project. Becky Hutchinson, a senior marketing research professional, came to the school to meet with Tom and four key members of his staff. After touring the facilities, Becky asked the group some questions. She wanted to know what the school had done over the past few years to attract new students and to retain existing students. They described several attempts at attracting new students. These approaches included a 60-second video that aired on the local cable television channels, billboard advertising provided by a local bank which offered private school financing programs to families, and a program called Winterfest (held in January two years before). This program featured several academic contests between River Pines students along with a theme party. Students from schools of varying grade levels were invited (along with parents) to come and observe the academic competition and participate in the theme party. River Pines indicated that they added 3–5 students as a result of the Winterfest program.

Student retention programs were virtually non-existent. As mentioned earlier, students and parents stated that the reasons for leaving had to do with programs that were not available to them at River Pines. Tom suspected that the stated reasons were only superficial, but he had not been able to determine any other reasons. Becky Hutchinson suggested that obtaining more information about why students and families left River Pines for other schools would be critical information for the school to have in the development of marketing strategies. The committee agreed and asked Becky to put together ideas for them to review.

Discussion Questions/Assignments

1   Based on the information presented, what research objectives should Becky use to guide the study?
2   What methodology would be most appropriate for this project?
3   Develop a questionnaire that would support achieving the research objectives.

This case was prepared by Dr. Bruce C. Walker, University of Louisiana Monroe, Dr. Robert Stevens, Southeastern Oklahoma State University, and Dr. David Loudon – Samford University. Names, selected data, and cooperate identities have been disguised.

Case 5 River Pines School: B

Dr. Tom Sanders, headmaster of River Pines School, sat in his office one afternoon pondering results of a market research survey concerning attributes of competitive private schools in the area to better understand factors involved in private-school selection decisions by parents and students. These results were given to him by Becky Hutchinson, a senior marketing research professional with Conceptual Designs, Inc. (CDI), who came to the school to meet with Tom and four key members of his staff a few months back.

River Pines is a private, not-for-profit college preparatory school located in the northeast-central quadrant of a county of 250,000 people. The school offers classes in pre-Kindergarten through the 12th grade. The school has suffered through declining enrollment over the past six–eight years, going from a high of approximately 550 students down to a low of approximately 200 students. Present enrollment is 235 students spread through 14 grades. River Pines' high school is one of four private high schools in the county and the only private high school not affiliated with a religious organization. Additionally, there are five large, public high schools in the county. Even though the school reportedly has the highest academic standards and a long list of distinguished graduates who have gone on to excel in college and life, enrollment was at dangerously low levels. It had been frustrating for Tom who had been hired four years ago to turn the school around.

It seems that every time a positive step was implemented or positive recognition was achieved, it was met, at best, with community apathy and more often was ignored by the local newspaper and television stations. To make matters worse, River Pines was the only major private school in the county with declining enrollment. The other schools had been enjoying significant gains in their student body. River Pines had retained CDI to conduct market research to help the school attract and retain students.

River Pines currently provided students with a competitive variety of extra-curricular activities, including athletics (football, basketball, softball, baseball, track, tennis, cheerleading/drill team) and personal enrichment (drama club, quiz bowl, debate team, French and Spanish clubs, Fellowship of Christian Students, and choral competition). Academic requirements at River Pines not only exceed state requirements but also appear to be the highest in the county.

Tom and the board felt that a more focused marketing approach to attract and retain students was needed, since word of mouth, internal recruiting efforts, and other outside attempts at attracting students had either failed or were marginally successful, at best. CDI had been retained to assist in this process. CDI used both personal interviews and telephone surveys of the county's private schools to address the following objectives:

1 Analyze River Pines' current basic competitive position compared to the other area private schools. This would include identifying each school's offerings and evaluating how each

school is marketing their programs and services; and, Analyze River Pines' position compared to the other schools, and;

2   Use this information to make market share and enrollment recommendations.

Competitive information collected included levels of offered grades, primary geographic area of students, numbers of students and faculty members, fees and fee structures, extra-curricular activities, educational achievements (ACT, SAT scores), scholarship offers, and whether or not the schools were religious-or secular-based. From this information, CDI was able to develop a list of characteristics, including five-year enrollment trends, average student–teacher ratios, standardized test scores, performance-based or needs-based scholarship opportunities for existing and prospective students, to mention only a few. Results of the findings are included as Tables 1–10 below.

Table 1 Grades offered and enrollment for 1997

Grade	# of schools	Min	Max	Mean	Standard deviation	River Pines	RP vs. average
Pre-K	11	1	150	38.91	45.67	9	−29.91
Kindergarten	14	2	52	26.00	17.08	12	−14.00
First	13	2	61	28.54	17.21	32	3.46
Second	13	2	60	23.62	16.23	18	−5.62
Third	12	2	60	27.17	17.11	21	−6.17
Fourth	12	2	60	28.75	19.80	15	−13.75
Fifth	13	1	60	23.92	18.14	11	−12.92
Sixth	12	3	60	25.00	17.77	17	−8.00
Seventh	13	2	71	28.54	23.10	14	−14.54
Eighth	11	7	60	33.55	15.76	27	−6.55
Ninth	9	3	89	41.22	28.24	17	−24.22
Tenth	9	2	96	39.56	29.00	15	−24.56
Eleventh	9	6	97	40.11	28.73	16	−24.11
Twelfth	9	2	85	37.11	26.55	23	−14.11

Table 2 Enrollment for the past five years

Year	# of schools	Min	Max	Mean	Standard deviation	River Pines	RP vs. avg.
1992	14	30	589	269.71	172.76	364	94.29
1993	14	30	627	286.14	185.19	347	60.86
1994	15	30	627	281.40	197.67	323	41.6
1995	15	37	671	306.13	206.16	303	−3.13
1996	15	10	700	313.60	226.34	242	−71.6

Table 3 Geographical areas of students

	# of schools	Min %	Max %	Mean %	Standard deviation %	River Pines %
Area 1	11	20	98	62.00	27.37	96
Area2	12	1	100	33.67	30.83	1
Area 3	2	5	5	5.00	0.00	0
Area 4	3	2	80	29.00	44.19	2
Area 5	1	50	50	50.00	0.00	0
Area 6	2	1	54	27.50	37.48	1
Other	11	1	50	19.73	16.39	0

Table 4 Faculty size and student/teacher ratio

	# of schools	Min	Max	Mean	Standard Ddviation	River Pines	RP vs. Avg.
Faculty size	15	3	59	26.13	16.3	29	2.87
Student/ teacher ratio	14	6	20	12.50	4.03	9	−3.5

Table 5 Sports programs

	Is offered	Not offered	% offering	Standard deviation	River Pines
Softball	6	8	42.86%	0.4972	Offered
Baseball	6	8	42.86%	0.5136	Offered
Football	10	4	71.43%	0.4688	Offered
Basketball	12	2	85.71%	0.3631	Offered
Soccer	5	9	35.71%	0.1972	Not offered
Track	7	7	50.00%	0.5189	Offered
Tennis	4	10	28.57%	0.1688	Offered
Cross-country	3	11	21.43%	0.4258	Offered
Golf	7	7	50.00%	0.5189	Offered
Other	6	9	42.86%	0.5071	Offered

Table 6 Extracuricular activities offered

	# of schools	Percent	River Pines
Few	6	42.9	
Some	4	28.6	
Many	4	28.6	+
Total	14	100.0	

Table 7 Average test scores

	# of schools responding	Min	Max	Mean	Standard deviation	River Pines
SAT	3	1200	1201	1200.5	0.7071	1201
ACT	7	17.2	25	21.79	2.53	23.7
CAT	2	83	85	84.0	1.41	–
IOWA	2	75	98	83.6	12.55	–
Stanford Achievement	2	65	86	75.33	10.5	86

Table 8 Graduation, college, scholarships

	Min %	Max %	Mean %	River Pines
Graduation rates	98	100	99.75	100%
% who enter college	75	100	90.88	100%
% who receive scholarships	20	70	49.06	45–55%
Average dollar amount/scholarships	$4,000	$25,000	$13,236	$ 24,223

Table 9 Religious affiliation

	# of schools	Percent	River Pines
Not affiliated	3	20	+
Affiliated	12	80	
Total	15	100	

Table 10 Tuition, fees, scholarships

	# of schools	Min	Max	Mean	Standard deviation	River Pines	RP vs. avg.
Tuition	14	1400	3674	2471.93	682.231	2606	134.07
Other fees	14	0	897	231.79	251.816	897	665.21
Scholarships	14	6	8	43%	N/A	Yes	

Discussion Questions/Assignments

1   Prepare a written analysis of the information given in these tables
2   Based on your analysis of this information, what recommendations would you make to River Pines school?
3   What types of data and aids would you use to present the findings to River Pines?

This case was prepared by Dr. Bruce C. Walker, University of Louisiana Monroe, Dr. Robert Stevens, Southeastern Oklahoma State University, and Dr. David Loudon, Samford University. Names, selected data, and cooperate identities have been disguised.

Case 6   Gary Branch, CPA

During the last 5–10 years, business firms in the local area were finding it much more difficult to attract and retain qualified employees who had solid technical job skills. As such, companies have had to reassess and often modify their employment, compensation, and retirement packages to achieve these two goals. Additionally, Congress had passed legislation allowing different types of retirement programs for smaller businesses as well as modifying what constituted qualifying expenses under the tax code. For most of these companies, the changes in the tax codes and modifications to employee pay and benefit packages resulted in an overall increase in administrative and payroll costs. One major area of expense for employers related to retirement plans was the fee they were having to pay to third party administrators (TPAs) to manage and administer retirement programs and funds.

Gary Branch, CPA, has been in business as an independent certified public accountant for twenty years. Over that time, he had built up a respectable business portfolio. As with most CPA firms, the majority of his business was from preparing Federal and state income and related tax returns. While this business obviously has been lucrative for Branch, he recognized that resulted in a "feast and famine" business operation. With the majority of his business being related to taxes, this meant that he and his employees were extremely busy from November through mid-April, and somewhat bored from mid-April through October. As the business grew, both in terms of client size and employee size, Branch realized that he was finding it more and more difficult to keep up with the demands and responsibilities placed on him during the "feast" times. Therefore, he was looking for opportunities that might help increase his business and revenue opportunities in areas other than income tax preparation.

Branch for some time had been studying the role of TPAs and the demands placed on those providing those services. His basic research, garnered through readings and talking with his clients, was that there were three major types of firms fulfilling the responsibility of a TPA, each with major drawbacks. First, a number of commercial banks were marketing themselves as TPAs. Banks were able to provide the administrative services that were required; however, Branch's clients who used commercial banks were becoming more and more disappointed with their services because of the high variable service cost, charged as a percentage of plan assets. Additionally, brokerage firms and insurance companies also provided administrative services as well as investment services. The fees charged by these groups appear to be three to four times higher than those charged by the third major type of provider, the independent firm. Branch felt that the clients that he spoke with were not happy with these large firms because of the firm's inability to offer personal services that a small independent or local banking operation might provide. With this information, Branch suspected that his firm might be able to develop a niche market that could provide profitable, employee-friendly companies with value-added TPA services to his clients, resulting in a new major business and revenue source for his firm. Not only would he be able to provide additional services to existing clients, this might also generate new clients for both TPA and tax services. He was excited about these possibilities and concluded that the next step would be to conduct independent market research. To begin that process, he turned to a client and personal friend, Dr. Paul Creighton, a market research professor and author at the local university.

Since Creighton taught a senior-level marketing research course at the university, he felt this would be an outstanding project for a group of his students (with Creighton serving as the Project Director). Shortly after Branch and Creighton met for lunch to discuss the project, Creighton invited Branch to attend one of his market research classes and present his ideas and supporting information to the students. He met for approximately two hours with the group and the group was able to come up with three major research objectives. These objectives included:

1   Identify the continuing business needs of the firm in the area of administering retirement plans;
2   Identify the types of plans being offered and their level of satisfaction associated with the services being provided by the present TPA; and
3   Identify the potential target market through the use of NAICS (North American Industry Classification System) codes.

To accomplish these objectives, the students went through secondary data sources available to them to determine the NAICS codes with which they should be concerned. The students conducted a stratified proportional random sample of local industry and came up with the following codes and percentage of area businesses within each code. These results are listed in the table below

NAICS Codes and Percentages of Local Businesses

SIC Code	Industry	Percentage
7538	Automotive Repair, Services, and Parts	7.2%
1521	Building Construction	4.8%
5211	Building Materials	3.6%
7389	Business Services	7.2%
5191	Chemicals and Allied Products	1.2%
2899	Communications	1.2%
1629	Construction-Special Trade Contractors	1.2%
5812	Eating and Drinking Places	15.7%
8711	Engineering, Accounting, Research, Management, and Related Services	2.4%
3498	Fabricated Metal Products	1.2%
5411	Food Stores	7.2%
5712	Furniture and Fixtures	2.4%
8011	Health Services	22.9%
8041	Heavy Construction Contractors	1.2%
6411	Insurance Agents, Brokers and Service	13.3%
8099	Legal Services	1.2%
7699	Miscellaneous Repair Services	6.0%

Once this process was concluded, several interesting aspects surfaced. Three different NAICS codes were identified that contained more than 10% each of the local business establishments. The largest percentage of businesses categorized under one NAICS code was health services (22.9 percent). Most of the businesses in this category included individual doctors' offices and a few medical labs. Additionally, there were four major hospitals serving the immediate area. Of these four, only one was a locally owned, independent (not-for-profit) hospital. The other three included a state hospital (employees covered under the state employees benefit and retirement program), a not-for-profit Catholic hospital (one of three major catholic hospitals in a system), and a for-profit, national chain hospital. While these three hospitals represented a tremendous potential source of income and business, the reality was that being able to secure a contract with any of the three would be a very time-consuming process.

The second largest percentage of business represented by a NAICS code was found to be eating and drinking places (15.7 percent). Branch suspected that a large percentage of these businesses most likely did not offer retirement plans at all. Exceptions to this might involve two different organizations that owned a series of "fast-food" businesses. He suspected that those groups did provide a retirement package to senior level people and to restaurant managers. Those two groups might be potential client companies. Finally, the third largest percentage (13.3 percent) was made up of insurance agents, brokers, and service companies, potential competitors for TPA business.

Once the NAICS analysis was completed, the students developed a structured questionnaire that would be the basis for a telephone survey of local business establishments. The students decided to exclude from this survey businesses that were part of a franchise or chain, as well as Branch's existing clients. The questionnaire included questions concerning the type of retirement plan offered by a business, who administered these plans, and business satisfaction levels with their present TPA and plan. A copy of the questionnaire is shown below.

Gary Branch, CPA Survey Questionnaire
Retirement Plan Administration Survey

Company_____
Person Interviewed_____
Interviewer_____

This is a survey for the owner or manager of the business.

Hello, I'm_____, a student at the university and as a part of a class project we're conducting a market research project with the area businesses. This study deals with retirement plan administration. May I speak with the person in charge of making these decisions for your company. Would you take a few moments to answer a few questions for me? Your answers will be confidential and used only in combination with the responses of other people.

[1] 1. Does your company offer any type of retirement plan for employees?
　　　　_____Yes　　_____No (If yes, skip question two and continue)
[2] 2. Are you thinking about offering such a plan?
　　　　_____Yes　　_____No (If this question is answered, terminate)
[3] 3. What other types of retirement plans are offered to employees?
　　　　_____401K
　　　　_____Profit Sharing
　　　　_____Pension Plan
　　　　_____Other

[4] 4. Who administers the plan for your company?
     _____Self Administered (If so, terminate)
     _____Outside Administration Bank
     _____Outside Administration Brokerage Firm
     _____Outside Administration Consulting Firm or CPA Firm
     _____Other. Please Specify

[5] 5. What other services are you currently receiving from this firm?
     _____Retirement Plan
     _____Profit Sharing Plan
     _____Other

[6] 6. Are there other retirement plan services you would like to receive but are not available
     _____Yes _____No

7. Would you please rate the level of satisfaction you have with the form that administers your plan on each of the following characteristics using excellent, good, fair, or poor.

			Excellent	Good	Fair	Poor	NR
[7]	A.	Courtesy	1	2	3	4	5
[8]	B.	Product Knowledge	1	2	3	4	5
[9]	C.	Accuracy	1	2	3	4	5
[10]	D.	Speed	1	2	3	4	5
[11]	E.	Value for the Cost	1	2	3	4	5
[12]	F.	Convenience	1	2	3	4	5

[13] 8. What are the fees that your company is being charged for the administration of your retirement plan?_____

[14] 9. Given the number of available retirement plans to choose from, would you say that you are:
     _____Very Satisfied
     _____Somewhat Satisfied
     _____Not Satisfied At All

[15] 10. Given the administrators knowledge of alternatives, would you say you are:
     _____Very Satisfied
     _____Somewhat Satisfied
     _____Not Satisfied At All

[16] 11. How would you rate your likelihood of changing retirement plan administrator if a local firm, knowledgeable in retirement planning, offered this service at comparable rates? Would you say you would be:
     _____Very Likely to Change
     _____Somewhat Likely to Change
     _____Undecided
     _____Somewhat Unlikely to Change
     _____Very Unlikely to Change

[17] 12. What other plans have you been offered? _____

[18] 13. How many employees do you have?_____

[19] 14. Number of Full-time_____

[20] 15. Number of Part-time_____

[21] 16. SIC Code_____(To be filled in by the interviewer)

Questions

1 Analyze the questionnaire shown in the case. What changes should be made in the questionnaire?
2 The case points out that the group conducted a telephone survey and excluded franchise and chain operations, as well as Branch's clients. Develop an alternative methodology that could be used to accomplish the research objectives.
3 Should Branch's clients have been excluded in this survey? Why or why not?

SPSS Applications

Analyze the data found in the SPSS file and answer or complete the following questions or assignments.

1 Develop tables and/or charts that provide the following information:
   • Percent of firms in the area offering retirement plans.
   • Percent of firms not providing a retirement plan who might be interested in doing so.
   • The breakout of different TPAs presently serving the local market.
   • The likelihood that a business might be willing to change its present TPA.
2 What conclusions can be reached concerning respondent satisfaction levels of present TPAs with regard to courtesy, product knowledge, accuracy, speed, value, and client convenience?
3 Based on the data, what recommendations would you make to Gary Branch, CPA?

This case was prepared by Dr. Bruce C. Walker, University of Louisiana Monroe, Dr. Robert Stevens, Southeastern Oklahoma State University, and Dr. David Loudon, Samford University. Names, selected data, and corporate identities have been disguised.

Case 7 Juan Carlos' Mexican Restaurant

Juan Carlos Garcia, owner of Juan Carlos' Mexican Restaurant (JC), was faced with a problem faced by many small businesses. His idea of successfully operating a Mexican restaurant in a small- to medium-sized community had been largely successful up until six months ago. Since that time, he noticed a small drop in the average weekly number of customers and that profits were suffering from that drop. He had made it a point to spend more time on the floor during peak restaurant hours to observe how well and how effectively his employees were meeting the needs of the restaurant patrons. He also would visit with diners during their meal to make sure their needs were being satisfied. Not only did he not find any issues or problems, it seemed that his employees were exceeding his service expectations, a point that customers generally verified. It also appeared that the food quality was at the same level that it had been during the preceding three years. He also scanned the overall environment to try to determine if recently opened restaurants were hurting his business. Only one new Mexican restaurant had opened about a year before, but he concluded that the proximity of the restaurant did not negatively affect his business, at least during the first six months of the new firm's existence. The answer appeared to lie somewhere other than in the quality of food, quality of service, and outside competition. He was at a loss to figure out what it might be.

Juan Carlos Garcia had opened his restaurant about seven years before on a shoestring budget in a house that had been left to him through the estate of his uncle, Jose Gonzales Garcia. The house originally had been a single-family residential structure located in a residential neighborhood. Beginning in the mid 1970s, the neighborhood began to see zoning conversions from single family dwellings to zoning allowing for small commercial ventures. Jose saw future opportunities in the zoning change. He convinced the city planning commission to allow him to change his property's zoning restriction from single family to small commercial in order to operate a small commercial printing operation out of the structure. Before his dream could be realized, Jose passed away, leaving the house and a vacant lot across the street from the structure to Juan Carlos. Juan Carlos fulfilled a lifelong dream of opening a restaurant in the structure and had the vacant lot paved to provide approximately twenty parking spaces to be used exclusively by JC customers.

JC's Mexican Restaurant is located in a two and one-half square mile, older, restored residential area in the center of a community of approximately 75,000 people with average to above-average income levels. Being centrally located is advantageous to the restaurant because of the easy access. Several other small businesses are located within two blocks of the restaurant, including offices and a small nursing/medical supply company and a barbershop. There are several restaurants within this two-block area. These restaurants include a Chinese Restaurant, a somewhat trendy sit-down or take out "burger and fry" type restaurant, and a more upscale, sit-down restaurant named Jiving Java, which specialized in American cuisine. Jiving Java also held two or three fashion shows a month during the evening. The only time this seemed to hurt Juan Carlos' business was on those nights that Jiving Java had a women's lingerie fashion show.

He felt that there wasn't much he could do on those nights other than offer dinner specials. All of these restaurants, including Juan Carlos' served both lunch and evening meals.

Over the years, Juan Carlos had become a friend with Dr. Louise Gilmore, a frequent customer and a marketing professor at the local university. Juan Carlos invited Dr. Gilmore for dinner one night and visited with her during her meal. He explained in general terms the situation and asked if she might be able to help him or get him in contact with a group that could. Dr. Gilmore told Juan Carlos that she was teaching a marketing research class and that this would be an excellent project for the students. Juan Carlos felt very comfortable with Dr. Gilmore and felt sure that her research assistance would provide him with information that would help him correct his problem of declining profits. Dr. Gilmore committed to coming back next week with a student team to begin work on the research.

Dr. Gilmore and her team met with Garcia for approximately two–three hours the next week. During that time, Garcia gave the students the history of the restaurant and all financial statements during that time. The students asked Juan Carlos a number of questions about the area's restaurants, industry trends, and about any possible cyclical variations that might exist. For the most part, Garcia was able to provide the information that the team requested. One thing that he had not done, however, was to survey his customer base to see what type of appeal his restaurant and menu held for customers. The group then came up with the following objectives to guide the research for the restaurant:

1 To identify the most attractive features of JC's Restaurant in the areas of atmosphere, service, location, quality and quantity of food, and prices of the food;
2 To evaluate the importance of satisfaction in the areas of atmosphere, service, location, quality and quantity of food, and prices of the food;
3 To determine the factors involved in choosing Mexican restaurants in the areas of atmosphere, service, location, quality and quantity of food, and prices of the food;
4 To determine customer awareness and customers' most likely response to future dining at the restaurant;
5 To evaluate demographic and geographic profiles of the customers according to area and customer demographics (age, gender, marital status, income level, education); and,
6 To develop strategic implications of the results.

The team adopted a two-step sampling approach for these study areas. The first step involved sampling a group of restaurant employees. It was felt that the information that was gathered in this step would assist the team in preparing the questionnaire to be used in step two. The second step involved surveying a randomly selected group of restaurant customers using the questionnaire below

---

Juan Carlos' Mexican Restaurant Questionnaire>

Thank you for agreeing to participate in this survey. Our student marketing team is working to help Juna Carlos' improve the restaurant for you and others. Your response to this survey will help in that effort. Your responses will be confidential.

Check your answer to the following questions.

1. How often do you eat lunch (noon) at Juan Carlos' Restaurant?
    ____ once a month
    ____ 2–4 times a month
    ____ 5–8 times a month
    ____ First time at Juan Carlos'

2.   How often do you eat dinner (evening) at Juan Carlos' Restaurant?
     ___ once a month
     ___ 2–4 times a month
     ___ 5–8 times a month
     ___ First time at Juan Carlos'

3.   What other local Mexican restaurant have you eaten at in the last six months?
     (Mark all that apply)
     _____ El Charro
     _____ Pepe's
     _____ Chile Pepper
     _____ other, please specify _____

4.   How did you first **hear** about Juan Carlos'?
     ___ Friends
     ___ Family
     ___ Work
     ___ Advertisements
     ___ other, please specify _____

5.   Please rate Juan Carlos' on each of the following items using a scale from excellent to poor.

	Excellent	Good	Fair	Poor
Food Quality	1	2	3	4
Food Quantity	1	2	3	4
Food Taste	1	2	3	4
Value for the Money	1	2	3	4
Food Presentation	1	2	3	4
Speed of Service	1	2	3	4
Customer Satisfaction	1	2	3	4
Store Appearance	1	2	3	4
Store Atmosphere	1	2	3	4
Location	1	2	3	4
Parking	1	2	3	4
Overall Rating	1	2	3	4

6.   Considering all the characteristics above, please rank the following Mexican
     Restaurants with 1 being the best, 2 being the second best, 3 being the third best
     and 4 being fourth best.
     ___ Chile Pepper
     ___ Juan Carlos'
     ___ El Charro
     ___ Pepe's

7.   Based on what you receive at Juan Carlos', would you say their prices are:
     ___ lower than expected
     ___ about as expected
     ___ higher than expected

8.   What items would you like to see added to the menu at Juan Carlos'?

   _____

   _____

9.   What improvements could Juan Carlos' make to increase your satisfaction as a customer?

   _____

Now just a few more questions about you:

10.   Age :
   _____ Under 20
   _____ 21–30
   _____ 31–40
   _____ 41–50
   _____ 51 and Up

11.   Sex
   _____ Female
   _____ Male

12.   Marital Status Single
   _____ Married
   _____ Divorced
   _____ Single

13.   Education
   _____ High School
   _____ Some College
   _____ College Degree
   _____ Other

14.   Income
   _____ Under $10,000
   _____ $10,000 to $24,999
   _____ $25,000 to $34,999
   _____ $35,000 to $49,999
   _____ $50,000 to $69,9999
   _____ $70,000 or more

15.   What is your zip code? _____

16.   Occupation
   _____ Homemaker
   _____ Student
   _____ Laborer
   _____ Skilled craftsman
   _____ Business owner/manager
   _____ Retired
   _____ Other

Thank you for your time and cooperation.

The sample included randomly selected respondents on two different weekdays between the hours of 5p.m. and 7p.m. A total of 91 useful responses were received. The team first analyzed the data in general then cross-tabulated the results using SPSS to analyze specific questions related to specific demographic or individual characteristics. Frequencies, cross tabulations, and percentages were used to provide for systematic analysis of the data and to determine respondent differences based on demographic and individual difference characteristics.

Based on the information collected, the five following tables were developed.

Local Mexican restaurants visited in the last six months

Restaurant	Percentage
El Charro, Chile Pepper, Pepe's	16.9
Pepe's, Chile Picante	9.6
El Charro, Pepe's	9.6
El Charro	21.7
Chile Pepper	13.3
Pepe's	3.6
El Charro, Chile Pepper	13.3
None	8.4
Other	3.6

How Customers Rank Juan Carlos' Restaurant

Rank	Percentage
The Best	77
Second Best	8
Third Best	5
Fourth Best	4

Customers' Suggestions for Juan Carlos' Menu

Item	Percentage
Sopapilla	2.7
Desert	2.7
Chalupas	2.7
Chimichanga	5.4
Fajitas	56.8
None	29.7

Improvements Suggested for Juan Carlos'

Improvement	Percentage
Parking	34.5
Paint	17.2
Atmosphere	13.8
Kid's Menu	10.3
Location	6.9
Mexican Music	17.2

Satisfaction by Age

Age	Excellent	Good	Fair
Under 20	5	2	1
21–30	22	7	1
31–40	10	2	2
41–50	14	5	2
51 and Up	14	2	2

Questions / Discussions

1   Is the methodology appropriate for the research objectives? What are the disadvantages of the sampling plan and method of questionnaire administration?
2   Review the questionnaire. What are its good points? What areas or questions do you feel need improvement? Does it seem to capture the relevant information needed to meet research objectives?

SPSS Application

1   Using the SPSS file located on the disk, develop a profile of respondents.
2   Are customers satisfied with the restaurant's offerings?
3   Are there significant differences among respondents on their satisfaction with the restaurant based on age, sex, and inc.

This case was prepared by Dr. Bruce C. Walker, University of Louisiana Monroe, Dr. Robert Stevens, Southeastern Oklahoma State University, and Dr. David Loudon, Samford University. Names, selected data, and corporate identities have been disguised.

Case 8   Usedcars.com

Bill Spencer is interested in determining the feasibility of starting a business that provides a website designed for used car dealers in this area to display their cars on the Internet. Two keys to the success of the idea are current Internet users' interest in shopping for used cars on the Internet and the interest of used car dealers in the new advertising medium. Dealers would provide information about their vehicles such as model, accessories, mileage, etc., and Usedcars. com would take a photograph of the car.

The photograph and the information on the vehicle would be displayed on the Usedcars.com website. A local marketing consultant was hired to develop a survey to determine the following:

1   the most common uses of the Internet of residents who had access,
2   average time spent on-line,
3   their interest in shopping on-line, and
4   the likelihood that the consumer would shop for a used vehicle on-line.

This study would also determine the interest of used car dealers in advertising their vehicles on the Internet. The dealer study would specifically determine the following:

1   interest level of the dealers in such a service,
2   current advertising media of used car dealers, and
3   dealers' satisfaction with their current Internet provider's service if they are already using such a service.

The results of this survey would provide the basis for deciding whether or not to launch the new business.

Study Objectives

The following objectives and methodology were developed by the consultant to guide the research effort:

1   determine the consumer profile of Internet users in the studied area.
   - access to the Internet
   - time spent on-line
   - purchasing history
   - common uses of the Internet
   - business or personal time
   - likelihood of shopping for next used/new car on-line
   - other

2   determine dealers' interest in the Internet as an advertising medium
   - willingness to participate
   - current advertising media of used car dealers
   - payment options
     - monthly fee
     - annual fee
   - dealership involvement in maintaining web sites
3   evaluate the importance of concerns involved in shopping for a used car.
4   analyze results of the consumer survey based on socioeconomic characteristics such as age, sex, income, education, and occupation.

Methodology

Two samples were used for the study. The first was a random sample of metropolitan area residents who were screened to include only Internet users. The second was a random sample of used car dealerships from the area. The two samples included 100 Internet users and 20 dealerships.

The respondents were to be surveyed using a telephone survey designed to respond to the project's specific study objectives. The questionnaires are shown below.

Survey Questionnaires

Dealer Survey

Telephone Number _____
Dealership _____
Person Interviewed _____
Interviewer _____

Hi my name is…. Would you take a few moments and answer some questions for me? Any information you provide will be held in strict confidence and will be combined with the answers of others that participate in the survey.

1.   Do you have access to the Internet in your business
     __Yes[1]   __No[2]

2.   Do you have computer training or a computer specialist on staff with your company?
     ___Yes[1]   ____No[2]

3.   What forms of advertising do you currently use for your dealership?
     (mark all that apply)
     __ Newspaper   __ Car Magazine (News on Wheels)   __ Internet __Radio __ TV
     __ Other, please specify_____
     (If Internet is selected go to question 5. If Internet was not selected go to question 4)

4.   How interested would you be in a service that would allow you to advertise, on the Internet, your cars based on price, model, year, and make? The service would be sustained by a full-scale Internet savvy team that would create the website for you or allow you to maintain your own website. The service would entail a full color picture of cars chosen by the dealer with a detailed description and appraisal value of the car.

Rate your interest: (then skip to question 11)

1	2	3	4	5
No interest	Little interest	Somewhat interested	Very interested	Extremely interested

5. How satisfied are you with your current Internet advertising service provider? Rate your interest on a scale of 1 to 5 with 1 being very dissatisfied and 5 being very satisfied.

1	2	3	4	5

6. How are you billed for this service? Are you billed:
   _____ A flat rate[1]
   _____ An average per car[2]
   _____ A combination[3]
   _____ Not billed (if selected skip question 7)[4]
   _____ Other, please specify _____-

7. Is this a:
   ___ Monthly [1]
   ___ Annual fee[2]

8. Are there any services or features that you as a dealer would like added to your existing web site? (mark all that apply)
   __ Change vehicles more often
   __ Less down time
   __ More promotion of website to consumers
   __ More information about the company
   __ More information about employees
   __ No features need to be added
   __ Other, please specify _____

9. Since having the Internet service, what problems if any have you experienced with the service (mark all that apply)
   __ Downtime
   __ Slowness of search
   __ Not being able to access directly
   __ Poor consumer response
   __ No problems
   __ Other, please specify _____

10. What concerns would you as a dealer have with putting your dealership on-line?
   __ None
   __ Customers not coming to the lot
   __ Salespeople not interacting enough
   __ Other, please specify _____

11. Is your dealership
   _____ Privately owned[1]
   _____ Partnership[2]
   _____ One or more partners[3]

12. Does the dealership have
    ___ 1 location[1]
    ___ 2 locations[2]
    ___ 3 or more locations[3]

13. If one or more locations, where are they located?

    _____

    _____

14. Monthly sales volume of vehicles
    ___ Under 10[1]
    ___ 10 to 20[2]
    ___ 21 to 30[3]
    ___ 31 to 40[4]
    ___ 41 to 50[5]
    ___ 51 to 60[6]
    ___ 61 to 70[7]
    ___ 71 to 80[8]
    ___ more than 80[9]

Thank you very much for your time and cooperation

_____

Consumer Survey

Telephone number _____

Person Interviewed _____

Interviewer _____

Hi, my name is…….Would you take a few moments and answer some questions for me? Any information you provide will be held in strict confidence and will be combined with the answers of others that participate in the survey.

1. Do you have access to the Internet?
   ___ Yes[1]   ___ No[2] (If no, thank and terminate.)

2. If yes, do you have access at:
   ___ Home[1]   ___ Work[2]   ___ Both[3]

3. About how much time do you spend on the Internet each day?
   ___ Less than an hour[1]
   ___ 1–2 hours[2]
   ___ 2–3 hours[3]
   ___ 3–4 hours[4]
   ___ 4–5 hours[5]
   ___ 5 or more[6]

4. What are your most common uses of the Internet? (mark all that apply)
   ___ News
   ___ Weather
   ___ Sports
   ___ Information on products

___ Information on people
___ Chat
___ Adult entertainment
___ Research
___ Other, please specify _____

5. Have you purchased anything over the Internet?
    ____Yes[1]   ____ No[2] (If no, skip to question 7)

6. If yes, what products or services have you purchased? (mark all that apply)
    ____ Books
    ____ Airline tickets
    ____ Movie tickets
    ____ Clothes
    ____ Automobiles
    ____ Applied for credit card
    ____ Others, please specify _____

7. Assume that you were interested in buying a used car. How interested would you be in
    a service that would allow you to search on the Internet for a car, based on price, model,
    year, and make? The service would allow you to view a full color picture of the car, detailed
    description, with the appraised value of the car, but you would also be able to make an offer
    using email. The dealer would pay for this service.
    Please rate your interest in such a service on a scale of 1 to 5 with 1 being not interested at
    all and 5 being extremely interested.

    | 1 | 2 | 3 | 4 | 5 |

8. If a 4 or a 5 were selected ask. How would you probably use such a service to help you in
    shopping for a new car? (mark all that apply)
    ___ get information on specific cars
    ___ get information on what dealers have the cars
    ___ get information on both
    ___ get information prior to going to a dealership
    ___ purchase using the service
    ___ other, please specify _____

9. What would be your major concerns about the process of buying a car over the Internet?
    (mark all that apply)
    ___ Not seeing the car in person
    ___ No driving test
    ___ Not being able to get trader's information
    ___ Not getting a good deal
    ___Inaccurate information on the Internet
    ___Other, please specify_____

10. Now assume that you want to sell a used car, how interested would you be in an Internet
    service that would allow you to sell your used car by featuring your own web page? The
    service would include a full color picture of the car and an appraisal of your car based on
    current value, condition of the car, and options available.

Rate your interest on a scale of 1 to 5 with 1 being not interested at all and 5 being extremely interested.

1	2	3	4	5

11. (If a 4 or 5 were selected) How much would you be willing to pay for this service?
   ___ less than $50[1]
   ___ $51 to $99[2]
   ___ $100 to $149[3]
   ___ $150 to $199[4]
   ___ $200 to $249[5]
   ___ $250 to $299[6]
   ___ more than $300[7]

Now we would like to have some information about you.

12. Which of the following categories contains your age?
   _____18–34[1]
   _____35–49[2]
   _____50–64[3]
   _____65 and over[4]

13. What is your current family status?
   _____single [1]
   _____married[2] (married with no children)
   _____divorced[3] (with no children)
   _____widowed[4] (with no children)
   _____married with children at home[5]
   _____divorced with children at home[6]
   _____widowed with children at home[7]

14. Sex:
   _____male[1]
   _____female[2]

15. What is the highest level of education you have completed?
   _____completed elementary[1]
   _____completed middle[2]
   _____completed high school[3]
   _____completed some college[4]
   _____completed college[5]
   _____completed advanced degree[6]

16. What is your occupation?
   _____homemaker [1]
   _____student[2]
   _____laborer[3]
   _____skilled[4]
   _____professional[5]
   _____retired [6]

17. Which of the following categories contains your family's annual income?

     _____less than $10,000[1]

     _____$10,001–$30,000 [2]

     _____$30,001–$50,000[3]

     _____$50,001–$70,000[4]

     _____$70,001–$90,000[5]

     _____$90,001–$100,000[6]

     _____Over $100,000[2]

Thank you very much for your time and cooperation

Discussion Questions

1   Based on the information in the case, do the study objectives and methodology address management's information needs? Discuss.

2   Does the methodology fully describe how the research will be conducted? What needs to be added, if anything?

3   Provide a thorough evaluation of the questionnaires used in the research in terms of the research objectives, potential respondents, and data analysis needs.

SPSS Applications

1   Use the SPSS data file to analyze the data and answer the following questions:
- Does the data support consumer interest in using the Internet for used cars shopping?
- Does the data support dealer interest in this advertising medium?
- What conclusions would you draw on the basis of your analysis?

2   Are there significant differences in male and female respondents interest in using the internet to shop for a car?

This case was prepared by Dr. Henry Cole, University of Louisiana Monroe, Dr. Robert Stevens, Southeastern Oklahoma State University, and Dr. David Loudon, Samford University. Names, selected data, and corporate identities have been disguised.

Case 9   Welcome Home Church

Reverend Larry Love is pastor of the Welcome Home Church (WHC) located in a middle-class section of a city with a population of 50,000 people. Rev. Love was called as pastor of the church approximately four years ago. He had high hopes of increasing overall membership in the congregation, as well as expanding the church's outreach ministry. Unfortunately, highly successful ideas and programs that he had implemented in his previous churches had not achieved similar success levels, nor had the size of the congregation shown any measurable increases during his four-year tenure at the church. Rev. Love felt at this time that he would need to take a different approach in order to achieve his vision for the church.

Rev. Love contacted Ms. Jennifer Odom, a principal in Outsource Solutions, Inc., an independent marketing research company located in the area. When Love and Odom met, she began by asking Rev. Love a series of questions. First, she asked him to describe the church's mission, member profile, and to summarize the types of programs that the church had implemented in the past. WHC's mission was to reach as many people as possible in order to provide a church home in which members could grow in their faith, knowledge, and love of Christ. The types of programs that the church presently had in place could be described as the standard types of programs that many churches employ. Specifically, WHC has two services on Sunday (one at 9:30 a.m. and one at 6:00 p.m.), and one service on Wednesday evening (6:30 p.m.). Additionally, the church offers a Christian education program for children and adults on Sunday mornings, a Tuesday morning Bible study, and special preparatory classes as needed. The church has a very active Women's organization, a small, but dynamic youth program, and a good volunteer program to visit the sick and the elderly.

The typical adult member profile suggests that members tend to be either in their 20s or ages 45 and up (approximately 5 percent of adult members are retired). Many of the adult members could be described as "working class," and generally have high-school degrees with some education past high school (either vocational-technical training or a couple of years of college). Rev. Love indicated that the congregational population is somewhat racially diverse, a strength that the church had enjoyed for years.

Ms. Odom asked Rev. Love about unsuccessful programs that he had initiated during his four years that had been successful in other churches. He disclosed that he had tried to initiate a men's program that would allow male members to come together once a month and complete home improvement projects for less fortunate community and church members. This effort was met with only "luke-warm" enthusiasm, and was short-lived. Also, he had attempted to implement a "prayer buddy" program in which congregational members partnered with another church member to make contact each day (most often by phone) and spend approximately five minutes in prayer with each other. Only 7 out of 212 adult members expressed any interest in this program. Finally, Rev. Love attempted to engage the church members in a project to study the likelihood of building a youth hall, but this endeavor never got past the preliminary discussion stage.

Odom then asked Love if the church had ever engaged in any type of member satisfaction survey or any type of community market research study to determine if needs people had were being met by their present church. Also, if a community member was not associated with a church, what might be the reasons for non-affiliation? Love stated that he and his staff had conducted a small study of church members and that the responses of members indicated that they generally were happy with the present programs and that these programs tended to meet their personal needs. While Rev. Love was happy with the overall response level of members, the fact remains that the congregation level had remained somewhat constant, showing no upward or downward trends of membership in any of the major areas (youth, young families, singles, older members, etc.).

Odom made the observation that if Rev. Love wanted to see growth in his congregation, understanding the different factors and issues of both present members and non-members would be very useful to determine future church programs, initiatives, and direction. Additionally, she suggested to Love that sometimes churches (and businesses) fall into a trap of trying to be all things to all people. Having a database of information would allow the church to decide how to focus its programs to attract a desired group of new members (e.g., members between the ages of 30–45, members with children ages 10–20, etc.). Odom shared an example of a church in the Houston area which, after completing a market research project, began to target individuals, many of whom were homosexual, living in the area who were dying from AIDS. The church used the research to develop a target market, then made changes to its overall mission statement. A negative outcome of this, however, was that some of the established members left the congregation. Rev. Love agreed that the church might have to prioritize the type of members it wished to attract and that a database of information would be the most logical approach in addressing the growth issue. Rev. Love decided the market research idea was worth pursuing and that he asked Odom to begin the project.

Odom developed the questionnaire shown below and began the survey of area residents using a random sample from the telephone book. The completed questionnaires were edited and enter into a computer software program for analysis.

Survey Questionnaire

Telephone number_____

Person interviewed_____

Interviewer_____

Welcome Home Church Survey

Am I speaking to the man/lady of the household? (If not, ask to speak to that person.)

We are conducting a survey about churches in this area. "Would you like to take a few moments and answer some questions for me?" Your answers will be held in a strict confidence and combined with the answers of other respondents. If yes, go to question 1.

Questionnaire:

1. How long have you lived in this area?
    ___less than 5 years[1]
    ____6–10 years[2]
    ____11–20 years[3]
    ____more than 20 years[4]

2. Please rate how important each of the following items are to you personally on a scale of 1 to 5 with 1 being the most important and 5 being the least important.

	Most Important				Least Important
Health	1	2	3	4	5
Type of automobile you drive	1	2	3	4	5
Work	1	2	3	4	5
Where you live	1	2	3	4	5
Family	1	2	3	4	5
Church	1	2	3	4	5
Your appearance	1	2	3	4	5
Marital status	1	2	3	4	5
Income	1	2	3	4	5

3. What time of day do you prefer to attend church?
   ___Early service (8–8:30)[1]
   ___Mid morning service (9:30–10:30)[2]
   ___Regular service (11–12)[3]
   ___Evening service (6 or later)[4]
   ___No preference[5]

4. What style service would you say you enjoy most:
   (1) a traditional service with hymns and preaching or (2) a non-traditional service with contemporary music, preaching, drama, etc?
   ___Traditional'
   ___ Nontraditional[2]
   ___ No preference [3]

5. Do your children attend Sunday school?
   _____Yes[1]
   _____No[2]
   _____No children at home[3]

6. How would you rate your satisfaction with your current church? Would you say you are:
   ___Extremely satisfied'
   ___Satisfied[2]
   ___Neither satisfied nor dissatisfied[3]
   ___Dissatisfied[4]
   ___Extremely dissatisfied[5]

7. Do you prefer to attend a church where you are anonymous or and active participant?
   ___anonymous[1]
   ___active participant[2]
   ___No preference[3]

8. What sort of family or social services would you like to see your local church or organization perform above and beyond is usual services? (mark all that apply)
   _____Counseling
   _____Crisis Intervention
   _____Substance abuse
   _____Youth/family activities
   _____Other

9. If these services were available through a church other than your own, would you use them?
   _____Yes[1]   _____No[2]

10. Would you feel more comfortable in a church with a more relaxed dress style?
    _____Yes[1]
    _____No[2]
    _____No preference[3]

Now Just a few questions about you.

11. Are you:
    ___Single/divorced/widowed with no children[1]
    ___Single/divorced/widowed with no children at home [2]
    ___Single/divorced/widowed with children at home [3]
    ___Married with no children[4]
    ___Married with no children at home[5]
    ___Married with children at home [6]

12. Which age category do you fit into?
    ___18–24[1]
    ___25–34[2]
    ___35–44[3]
    ___45–54 [4]
    ___55–64[5]
    ___65 and older[6]

13. What is the category that includes your total family income?
    ___Under 15,000[1]
    ___$15,000 to $24,999[2]
    ___$25,000 to $34,999[3]
    ___$35,000 to $44,999[4]
    ___$45,000 to $54 '999[5]
    ___$55,000 to $64,999[6]
    ___$65,000 to $74 '999[7]
    ___$75,000 to $84,999[8]
    ___$85,000 to $94,999[9]
    ___$95,000 or over[10]

14. What is the highest level of education you have obtained?
    ___Did not complete high school'
    ___High School graduate[2]
    ___High School graduate with some college[3]

___College graduate[4]
___College graduate with some graduate work[5]
___Graduate degree holder[6]

15. What is the occupation of the chief wage earner in your household?
___Homemaker[1]
___Skilled craftsman[2]
___Business owner/managers[3]
___Retired[4]
___Student[5]
___Laborer[6]
___Other[7]

16. Sex: (Don't ask unless necessary)
___Male[1]   ____Female[2]

17. What is your race:
____Caucasian[1]
____Hispanic[2]
____Oriental[3]
____African-American[4]
____Other[5]

18. What is your zip code? _____

Thank you, very much for your cooperation. You have been very helpful.

Discussion Questions

1   What are the marketing management problems facing WHC?
2   What marketing research objectives would you propose?
3   Based on the information presented in the case, what types of information should Odom attempt to find?
4   Does the questionnaire contain the right type and number of questions to obtain the kind of information Reverend Love needs?

SPSS Applications

Use the SPSS file to analyze the data and answer the following questions:

1   What is the demographic profile of respondents surveyed?
2   What were respondents' preferences for style of dress for church services, style of services, and time preferences?
3   What did respondents rate as the most important things in their lives?
4   What percent of the respondents were aware of WHC? What percent had attended a service? Of those who had attended, what percent ranked the service as good?

This case was prepared by Dr. Bruce C. Walker, University of Louisiana Monroe, Dr. Robert Stevens, Southeastern Oklahoma State University, and Dr. David Loudon, Samford University. Names, selected data and organizational identity have be disguised.

Case 10 The Learning Source

The Learning Source's management is in the process of formulating a marketing plan to coincide with the relocation of the business to a new, larger facility. The Learning Source is a nine-month school for students in grades five through eight who are not successful in a traditional classroom setting. Many of the students suffer from attention deficit disorder (ADD), attention deficit hyperactivity disorder (ADHD), or dyslexia. With a five-to-one student–teacher ratio, children who are exceptional or learning-challenged have the ability to excel in a nontraditional setting.

The Learning Source provides other educational services, such as educational evaluations, homework labs, tutorials, study skills workshop, career mapping, computer training, test preparations, and summer programs. In addition, in-service training for teachers and workshops are also provided by The Learning Source. In conjunction with area school systems and local businesses, The Learning Source provides speakers to aid parents throughout the community in educating children.

The Learning Source is in the process of moving to a new location. The new facility is 7,500 square feet, almost tripling the size of the old facility. In its new location, The Learning Source hopes to expand from 21 students to a full capacity of 50 students. Also, The Learning Source wants to expand its tutoring services, ACT preparation classes, and homework labs.

To aid in the development of the marketing plan, a marketing research project was contracted through a local research firm. The firm's proposal included the objectives, methodology, and questionnaire shown below.

Detailed Study Objectives

The research objectives are to be as follows:

1   Determine any problems that respondents' children have experienced in school.
2   Determine the respondents' use of tutors and decision influences.
3   Determine the respondents' awareness of The Learning Source.
4   Determine awareness of the services provided by The Learning Source.
5   Identify the best way to advertise the services provided by The Learning Source.
6   Develop and evaluate demographic and psychographic profiles of consumers.

Methodology

The study will focus on awareness, interests, and attitudes of parents with children in the age range targeted by The Learning Source. A random sample of area residents will be used in the study. The sample will include 100 residents with school-aged children.

The information gathered from the structured questionnaire will be edited, tabulated, and processed by computer, providing a comprehensive set of tables. These tables include percentages, mean scores, and cross-tabulations where appropriate.

Study Questionnaire

The Learning Source

Hi, my name is …. "Would you please take a few moments of your time and answer some questions for me? Your answers will be held in strict confidence and combined with the answers of other respondents." (If the answer is yes, begin the survey)

1. Do you have any school-aged children in your household?
    ___Yes [1]   ___No[2] (*If no, terminate*)

2. Are your children in public or private school?
    ___Public[1]   ___Private[2]   ___Both[3]

3. What grade in school is/are your child/children?
    ___Prekindergarten
    ___Kindergarten
    ___Lower elementary (grade 1–3)
    ___Upper elementary (4–6)
    ___Middle School (7–8)
    ___High School (9–12)

4. Has your child experienced any problems at school in the classroom such as reading, math or attention span disorders? (mark all that apply)
    ___Reading
    ___ Math
    ___ Attention span
    ___ Other, please specify_____

5. If yes, please give a brief description of the problem(s)?
    _____

6. Have you ever used tutors for you child/children?
    ___Yes[1] (go to question 8)   ___No[2] (go to question 7)

7. If no, Why not? (mark all that apply)
    ___ No information
    ___ Too expensive
    ___ No big problems
    ___ Other, please specify_____

8. If yes, How did you first find out about the tutors?
    ___Newspaper[1]   ___Word of mouth[2]   ___Teacher[3]   ___Saw sign[4]
    ___Radio[5]   ___ Another parent[6]   ___Television [7]
    ___Other[8], please specify_____

9. Are the tutors used:
    ___More than 3 times per week[1]
    ___2–3 times per week[2]
    ___Once a week[3]
    ___Once every 2 weeks[4]
    ___Monthly[5]
    ___As needed for tests[6]

10. Have you ever heard of The Learning Source?
    ___Yes[1]   ___No[2] (go to question 18)

11. If yes, How did you first hear about the school?
    ___Newspaper[1]   ___Word of mouth[2]   ___Teacher[3]   ___Saw sign[4]
    ___Radio[5]   ___ Another parent[6] ___Television[7]
    ___ Other[8], please specify_____

12. Which of these sources would be most influential in your decision to use a school like The Learning Source?
    ___Newspaper[1]   ___Word of mouth[2]   ___Teacher[3]   ___Saw sign[4]
    ___Radio[5]   ___ Another parent[6] ___Television[7]
    ___ Other[8], please specify_____

13. What types of programs do you think they offer? (mark all that apply)
    ___School   ___ACT/SAT Participation
    ___Tutorials   ___Computer training   ___Homework Lab

14. Have you used any of the programs for your children?
    ___Yes[1]   ___No[2]

15. If yes, which ones?
    ___School   ___ACT/SAT Preparation
    ___Tutorials   ___Computer Training   ___Homework Lab

16. How frequently do you use these programs?
    ___More than 3 times per week[1]
    ___2–3 times per week[2]
    ___Once a week[3]
    ___Once every 2 weeks[4]
    ___Monthly[5]
    ___As needed for tests[6]

17. Do you know where The Learning Source is located?
    ___City[1]
    ___ Street[2]
    ___ No[3]

We would like to have some information about you.

18. Which of the following categories contains your age?
    _____ 0–17[1]
    _____18–34[2]
    _____35–49[3]
    _____50–64[4]
    _____65 and over[5]

19. What is your marital status?
    _____single[1]
    _____married[2]
    _____divorced[3]
    _____widowed[4]

20. Sex:
    _____male[1]
    _____female[2]

21. What is the highest level of education you have completed?
    _____completed elementary[1]
    _____completed middle[2]
    _____completed high school[3]
    _____completed some college[4]
    _____completed college[5]
    _____completed advanced degree[6]

22. What is your occupation?
    _____homemaker [1]
    _____student[2]
    _____laborer[3]
    _____skilled[4]
    _____professional[5]
    _____retired[6]

23. Which of the following categories contains your family's annual income?
    _____less than $10,000[1]
    _____$10,001–$30,000[2]
    _____$30,001–$50,000 [3]
    _____$50,001–$70,000[4]
    _____$70,001–$90,000[5]
    _____$90,001 or over[6]

Thank you for helping us with this survey.

_____

Discussion Questions

1   Evaluate the research objectives and methodology in relation to management's information needs.
2   Does the questionnaire appear to address all the research objectives? What should be added/deleted from the questionnaire to make it more effective?

SPSS Applications

Use the SPSS file to analyze the data and answer the following questions:

1   What is the profile of a respondent in this study?
2   What proportion of respondents use tutors? How did they find these tutors?
3   What is the level of awareness of The Learning Source? Programs? Location?
4   Based on your analysis, what major issues should be addressed in the marketing plan?

This case was prepared by Dr. Henry Cole, University of Louisiana Monroe, Dr. Robert Stevens, Southeastern Oklahoma State University, Dr. David Loudon, Samford University. Names, selected data, and corporate identities have been disguised.

Case 11 Madison County Country Club

Clint Streep, the General Manager of the Madison County Country Club (MCCC), placed his golf ball on the number one tee. He and board chairman Merrill Westwood were getting in a much-needed and well-deserved round of golf the day after a heated and brutal MCCC board meeting. The operating results for the MCCC had been disappointing for the second straight year, and there were a number of board members who blamed Streep for the results and were pushing for his termination. Fortunately, Westwood believed in Streep and was able to table, at least temporarily, the motion for Streep's dismissal. This round of golf provided the two gentlemen the opportunity to revisit the situation and, more importantly, explore ideas to turn the negative results around.

Madison County is located in the northeastern corner of a state known primarily for its rural economy and lifestyle. There is no large city within 75 miles of Barrington, the community where the MCCC is located. For years, the board felt that MCCC had some type of "monopoly" on the county's golfing and social situations. After all, everyone who was anybody in Madison County had been a member of the club for several generations. The fact that membership was declining was upsetting egos as well as bank accounts.

That operating results were down was not surprising. Membership in the MCCC had been declining for several years. Streep had been pushing the board to give him the authority to seek outside assistance to help define the issues and secure data to help drive future operating decisions. The board had denied the request in previous years, but grudgingly granted Streep limited authority to seek outside help. The stipulation by the board was that any decision to proceed with outside research had to be approved by Westwood and two other board members assigned to a special committee to oversee Streep's activities. The day's golf match allowed Streep and Westwood to brainstorm as friends and colleagues with a vested interest in the success of the club.

During the course of the round, Westwood suggested that Streep contact Progressive Marketing, Inc. (PMI) and have representatives from the firm come and visit with Streep and members of the board's special committee. Westwood spoke highly of the firm, having used their services in his insurance company a few years back. Westwood mentioned that one of PMI's partners, Steve Henry, had been especially resourceful in helping Westbrook's company identify its strengths and weaknesses, as well as market and industry opportunities and threats. Once these factors were identified (referred to as SWOTs), PMI was able to help the company develop an aggressive marketing strategy that resulted in major gains for the firm.

During the following week, Steve Henry and a young assistant, Rebecca Chance, met with Streep and the three board committee members. The country club members provided PMI with a short history of the club, as well as the confidential operating results from the previous five years of operation. Additionally, PMI was provided with the club's fee structure as well as a list of the club's member services and activities. PMI asked a number of questions related to member demographics (i.e., families, income levels, gender, educational levels, occupations, proximity to the club, age, etc.). Streep and the committee members were able to answer some of the inquiries; however, they admitted that the majority of this information was based on a "gut feel" as opposed to statistical data. The club also confessed that it had been years since any type of membership satisfaction survey had been conducted. Committee members felt that the services provided generally were quite frequently utilized, and they also felt that member pricing provided country club members with a good entertainment value. The club was unable to provide much in the way of specific data to back up their assumptions. MPI stated that a top priority would be to collect membership data that would provide MCCC with information that would allow them to make sound operating decisions.

Two weeks later, Henry and Chance returned to meet with Streep and the board's committee. They provided a four-page survey questionnaire that MPI claimed would capture the information needed to accurately assess member satisfaction, as well as member demographic information that would allow for more targeted program analysis. After discussing the questionnaire, minor modifications to the instrument were made, an appropriate fee structure was agreed upon, and completion timetables were established. At this point, the board committee authorized PMI to proceed with the membership survey.

PMI mailed a questionnaire and cover letter to all current MCCC members (373 members, total). One hundred sixty (160) questionnaires were returned, providing a 43 percent response rate.

Membership Response Survey
1. How long have you been a member of Madison Country Club?
    ___1–3 years
    ___4–7 years
    ___7–12 years
    ___12–16 years
    ___16–20 years
    ___over 20 years
2. What was the major reason you joined Madison Country Club?
    (Mark all that apply)
    ___Membership compatibility
    ___Location
    ___Service of club staff
    ___Highly recommended by friends
    ___Line of benefits offered
    ___Reputation of club
    ___Other (specify) _____
    _____
3. What do you consider the most attractive features of the Club?
    (Mark all that apply)
    ___Golf course
    ___Pro shop
    ___Eating facilities
    ___Swimming facilities
    ___Tennis facilities
    ___Club sponsored events
    ___Community events at the clubs
    ___Other (specify) _____
    _____

4. What do you consider the least attractive features?
   (Mark all that apply)
   ___Golf course
   ___Pro shop
   ___Eating facilities
   ___Swimming facilities
   ___Tennis facilities
   ___Club sponsored events
   ___Community events at the clubs
   ___Other (specify) _____

5. How important was the initiation fee in deciding your membership?
   ___Very important
   ___Somewhat important
   ___Not important

6. How important were the monthly dues in deciding your membership?
   ___Very important
   ___Somewhat important
   ___Not important
   ___No effect

7. On a scale of 1 to 8 (1 being most important and 8 being of least importance) what improvements do you feel need to be made to the Club in the future?
   ___Golf course quality
   ___Driving range quality
   ___Tennis facilities
   ___Swimming facilities
   ___Clubhouse quality
   ___Social events
   ___Tournaments
   ___Better management
   ___Others (specify)_____
   _____

8. Rank in order from 1 to 6 (1 being most frequent and 6 being least frequent) how often you use the club services.
   ___Golf course
   ___Driving range
   ___Tennis facilities
   ___Swimming facilities
   ___Club events
   ___Bar/Grill

9. How often do you use the club's facilities on a monthly basis?
   ___only once
   ___2–4 times
   ___5–7 times
   ___8–10 times
   ___over 10 times
   ___never

10. Are you currently satisfied with current club practices?
    ___Very satisfied
    ___Somewhat satisfied
    ___Not satisfied

11. Are you currently satisfied with club services?
___Very satisfied
___Somewhat satisfied
___Not satisfied

12. Have you ever considered moving your membership to another club?
_____ Yes, explain why _____
_____
_____ No

13. What changes do you feel need to be implemented? _____
_____

14   Are you:
___Female
___Male

15. What is the highest level of education you have completed ?
___Completed elementary school
___Completed middle school
___Completed high school
___Completed some college
___Completed college
___Completed advanced degree

16. Which of the following categories contains your family's annual income?

___Less that 10,000	___70,001 – 90,000
___10,001 – 30,000	___90,001 or over
___30,001 – 50,000	
___50,001 – 70,000	

17. Which of the following categories contains your age?
___18 – 24
___25 – 34
___35 – 44
___45 – 54
___55 – 64
___65 or older
___Refused

18. What is your marital status?
___Single
___Married with no children
___Married with children
___Divorced
___Widowed

19   What is your occupation?
___ Homemaker
___ Student
___ Laborer
___ Skilled worker (Computer operator, truck driver, etc…)
___ Professional (Doctor, Lawyer, etc…)
___ Retired

Discussion Questions

1   What general information do you feel would be needed for MCCC to make sound future operating decisions?

2 Does it appear that PMI's survey would capture this information? What changes or additions would you make?

3 Evaluate the methodology used in the study. What other methodologies are feasible? What about the response rate to the survey? What issues does this raise?

SPSS Application

1 What is the demographic profile of the typical respondent?

2 What club features appear to be the most desirable? Least desirable? What improvement recommendations should MCCC consider?

3 What conclusions might be reached concerning member use and satisfaction levels in view of the current pricing structure?

4 Are there significant differences between "younger" and "older" members in terms of needed improvements?

This case was prepared by Dr. Bruce C. Walker, University of Louisiana Monroe, Dr. Robert Stevens, Southeastern Oklahoma State University . Dr. David Loudon, Samford Universit. Names, selected data, and corporate identities have been disguised.

Case 12   Plasco, Inc.

Plasco, Inc. is a relatively new player in the plastic extrusion industry. Plastic extrusion companies use granular compounds to make plastic materials for fabrications such as plastic tubing and sheeting. The key to the production of extrusion products is expensive extrusion machinery used to convert the compounds into material, which can be used in subsequent production processes. Efficient production requires long production runs necessitating the need for a customer base of conversion companies (sometimes called fabricators) large enough to support long production runs.

Plasco, Inc. is preparing to aggressively expand over the next two years but needs additional financing for the expansion. They have approached several potential sources for funds, but all the financial sources want some evidence of Plasco's potential to attract new customers. Plasco engaged a local marketing firm to provide this necessary information on market potential. Excerpts from the marketing report and the questionnaire are shown below.

Study Objectives

The market research objectives were as follows:

1   Identify competitive suppliers of plastic extrusion products.
- Number of suppliers
- From which supplier do they make most of their purchases
2   Analyze strengths and weaknesses of these suppliers.
- Rate overall satisfaction
- Determine if any specific problems have been experienced
  - Quality of the goods
  - Cost
  - On-time delivery
  - Quality of service
  - Availability of goods
3   Determine what opportunities exist in the current plastic extrusion market for a new competitor.
4   Determine the likelihood of existing plastic conversion companies purchasing from a new plastic extrusion company.
5   Determine what quantities and products the plastic conversion companies are interested in purchasing.
6   Evaluate the importance of factors that have an influence over purchases.
- Service quality
- Cost

- Transportation availability
- Location of the supplier
- Number of products available
- Number of specialty products available
- Size of the supplier

7   Develop strategy implications of the results.

Methodology

A sample was prepared from two databases. The first sample came from a list of eight prospective companies provided by Plasco. The second sample came from an electronic database categorized by NAICS (North American Industry Classification System) codes. Only those NAICS codes pertaining to plastic companies were selected. A total of 100 companies were interviewed.

The prospective customers were surveyed using a telephone questionnaire. The questionnaire was administered using a trained interviewing staff.

Plasco personnel had final approval of the questionnaire. The information gathered from the structured telephone survey was edited, tabulated, and processed by computer to produce a comprehensive set of tables. This information provided percentages, mean scores, and cross-tabulations to understand relationships between variables.

Survey Questionnaire

Telephone number _____

Person interviewed _____

Interviewer _____

Am I speaking with the person responsible for purchasing? (If no, ask to speak to that person). Hello, my name is _____ Would you please take a moment to answer a few questions for me? Any information you provide will be held in strict confidence and will be combined with the answers of other participants in the survey.

1. Is your company primarily a:
    ___plastics conversion company [1]
    ___plastics extrusion company[2]
    ___combination[3]
    ___other[4], please specify _____
2. How many plastic extrusion suppliers are you currently using?
    ___one[1]   ____ five[5]
    ___two[2]   ____ six[6]
    ___three[3]   ____ seven or more[7]
    ___four[4] ____ none (skip to question 11)
3. From which plastic extrusion suppliers do you make most of your purchases?

    _____

4. How would you rate your overall satisfaction with your current suppliers?
    ___Very dissatisfied[1]
    ___Somewhat dissatisfied[2]
    ___Neither dissatisfied nor satisfied[3]
    ___Somewhat satisfied[4]
    ___Very satisfied[5]
5. Have you experienced any problems with your plastic extrusion suppliers?
    ____ Yes[1] ____ No[2] (skip to question 7)

6. If yes, what specific types of problems have you experienced? (mark all that apply)
    ___Cost
    ___Size of the company
    ___Quality of the goods
    ___Quality of the service
    ___Availability of goods
    ___On time delivery
    ___None
    ___Other, please specify_____

7. How likely would you be to purchase from another plastic extrusion supplier offering better quality and service?
    ___Very likely[1]
    ___Likely[2]
    ___Somewhat likely[3]
    ___Not likely[4] (go to question 10)

8. Are there any plastic products that you are interested in purchasing that are not currently being supplied?
    ___Yes[1] (ask what products) _____
    ___No[2] (skip to question 10)

9. What quantities would you purchase annually?
    _____

10. Please rate the importance of the following factors that may have influence over your choice of plastic extrusion suppliers using a scale from 1 to 5, with 1 being the least important and 5 the most important.

(a) Cost	1	2	3	4	5
(b) Size of the supplier	1	2	3	4	5
(c) Location of the supplier	1	2	3	4	5
(d) Transportation availability	1	2	3	4	5
(e) Service quality	1	2	3	4	5
(f) Number of products available	1	2	3	4	5
(g) Specialty products available	1	2	3	4	5

11. Is your company:
    ___privately owned[1]
    ___publicly owned[2]

12. What is your company's zip code? _____

13. How many plants does your company operate? _____

14. Which of the following categories most closely represents your company's annual sales volume?
    ___under $100,000[1]
    ___$100,000 to $500,000[2]
    ___$500,000 to $ 1,000,000[3]
    ___$1,000,000 to $5,000,000[4]
    ___$5,000,000 to $10,000,000[5]
    ___$10,000,000 to $50,000,000[6]
    ___$50,000,000 to $100,000,000[7]
    ___$100,000,000 and over[8]
    ___refused / don't know[9]

Thank you for your time and cooperation

Discussion Questions

1 Assuming a diverse market for extrusion products, does the sampling plan reflect the information needs of Plasco?

2 How will errors in the sampling plan affect results?

SPSS Applications

Use the SPSS file to answer the following questions:

1 Do most respondents use more than one supplier?

2 Are most respondents satisfied with their current suppliers? What types of problems have they experienced?

3 Are these respondents likely to purchase from a new supplier?

4 Which factors are most important/least important in selecting a supplier?

5 What is the profile of respondents in this study?

6 Are there significant differences between smaller and larger companies' ratings of the importance of factors involved in selecting a supplier?

This case was prepared by Dr. Henry Cole, University of Louisiana, Dr. Robert Stevens, Southeastern Oklahoma State University, and Dr. David Loudon, Samford University. Names, selected data, and corporate identities have been disguised.

Case 13　St John's School

St. John's Catholic Church wants to determine the market potential and viability of moving its private school when the church is relocated. The church has outgrown its current facility and has purchased land about 10 miles away. There is enough land and money to build a new school but the new school would need strong drawing power to increase enrollment by about 20 percent. This may mean attracting non-Catholic families as part of the new student base. A major input into the decision is the results of a survey of area residents. A survey was used to examine (1) the attitudes of the church members toward relocation, (2) the feasibility of beginning an early childhood program for age 2, and (3) awareness of a center-based approach to early childhood development. Consumers were also surveyed to determine (1) whether teacher certification and class size are influential in choosing a school for grades K through 6, and (2) the price sensitivity to the level of tuition.

Personnel from the Small Business Development Center at a local university helped develop the research objectives, methodology, and the questionnaire used in the study. These are shown below.

Research Objectives

The marketing research objectives were as follows:

1　Determine the factors involved in the choice of a private school
   - Early childhood program
   - Location
   - Tuition and fees
   - Class size
   - Teachers' education
   - Special needs of students' services
2　Evaluate the importance of
   - Size of school
   - New location
   - Tuition and fees
   - Class size (i.e., attention given to each child)
   - Advertising
   - Centered-based approach
3　Determine consumer awareness and likely response to future move.
4　Determine present customer satisfaction with present services and likelihood of switching to another school after move.

5   Evaluate results based on socioeconomic factors such as age, sex, income, education, and occupation.
6   Develop strategic implication of results.

Methodology

Random samples were drawn from two groups of residents. The first group was residents within a 10-mile radius of the new location and the second was a sample of the congregation. The total sample included approximately 70 respondents from each group, for a total sample of 140.

The respondents were surveyed using a telephone questionnaire. The questionnaire was pre-tested before being administered by a group of church volunteers. The information gathered from the survey was edited, tabulated, and processed by computer to provide a comprehensive set of tables, which included percentages. The SBDC personnel entered the data and prepared a report for the church.

Survey Questionnaire

Telephone number_____
Person interviewed_____
Interviewer_____

St. John's Survey

Am I speaking to the man/lady of the household? (If not, ask to speak to that person.)
Hi! My name is …. Would you take a few moments and answer some questions for me? Your answers will be held in strict confidence and combined with the answers of other respondents. (If the answer is yes, begin the survey with question one.)

1.   Are you or anyone else living in your home presently employed by a public or a private school?
     ____yes[1]   ____no[2] (if yes, thank and terminate)
2.   Do you have any school-aged children living at home?
     ____yes[1] (if yes, what age_____)   _____no[2] (if no, thank and terminate)
3.   Which school do your children attend?
     ___St. John's[1]
     ___Riverwood[2]
     ___Riverdale[3]
     ___Oaklawn[4]
     ___West Milton High[5]
     ___West Milton Elementary[6]
     ___West Middle School[7]
     ___St. Luke's[8]
     ___Other[9]
4.   Do you plan to keep them in this (these) school(s)? ____yes[1] _____no[2] ____undecided[3]
5.   Is this a public or a private school?
     _____public[1]   _____private[2]   ___both[3]

6. Please rate the following factors on how they would influence the decision to send your child to a private school. Please rate the factors on a scale of 1 to 3, with 1 being not at all important to 3 being very important

Cost	1	2	3
Size	1	2	3
Location	1	2	3
Religious affiliation	1	2	3
Extracurricular activities	1	2	3
Transportation availability	1	2	3
Quality of education programs	1	2	3

7. Would you be interested in starting your child at age 2 in a developmentally appropriate early childhood program?
____yes[1] ____no[2] ___undecided[3]

8. Do you think that your area needs a developmentally appropriate, early childhood program?
____yes[1] ____no[2] ____undecided[3]

9. Are you aware of what a center-based approach to early childhood development is?
____yes[1] ____no[2]

10a. If yes, ask if this is important to them. ____yes[1] ____no[2] ____undecided[3]

10b. If no, explain center-based approach and then ask if this is important to them.
____yes[1] ____no[2] ____undecided[3]

11. What do you think is the ideal number of students in a classroom?
___less than 15[1]
___15–25[2]
___more than 25[3]

12. Do you think schools should employ uncertified teachers?
___yes[1]
___no[2]
___DK[3]

13. Would you consider sending your child to a private elementary school in your area?
___yes[1] ____no[2] ___undecided[3] ___depends on cost[4] ___depends on location[5]
____depends on quality of school[6] ____other[7]

14. If you were to send your child to a private school early in their education, please rate how important is it that they remain within the private school system with one being unimportant and 5 being extremely important. (Circle one)
1   2   3   4   5

15. Do you think religion classes are helpful in raising children with strong values and morals?
___yes[1] ____no[2] ___undecided[3]

16. What is the maximum amount of tuition you could pay each month per child to attend a private school?   _____

17. If the school that your child is currently attending were to relocate at least 5 to 10 miles from the current location, would you want to continue sending your child there?
___yes[1] ___no[2]

Now just a few questions about you.

18. Which of the following categories contains your age?
___18–34[1]
___35–49[2]
___50–64[3]
___65 and over[4]

19. What is your marital status?
    ___single[1]
    ___married[2]
    ___divorced[3]
    ___widowed[4]

20. Sex:(don't ask unless necessary)
    ___male[1]
    ___female[2]

21. What is the highest level of education you have obtained?
    ___Did not complete high school[1]
    ___High school graduate[2]
    ___High school graduate with some college[3]
    ___College graduate[4]
    ___College graduate with some graduate work[5]
    ___Graduate degree holder[6]

22. What is the occupation of the chief wage earner in your household?
    ___Homemaker[1]
    ___Student[2]
    ___Laborer[3]
    ___Skilled craftsman[4]
    ___Business owner/manager[5]
    ___Retired[6]
    ___Other[7]

23. Which of the following categories contains your family's annual income?
    ___less than $15,000[1]
    ___$15,001–$30,000[2]
    ___$30,001–$50,000 [3]
    ___$50,001–$70,000[4]
    ___$70,001–$90,000[5]
    ___$90,001 or over[6]

24. What is your race?
    ___Caucasian[1] _____Hispanic[3] _____Other[5]
    ___African/American[2] _____Oriental[4]

25. What is your zip code? _____

26. What is your religious preference?
    ___Catholic[1]
    ___Protestant (Baptist, Methodist, Lutheran, Presbyterian, Pentecostal, Assembly of God, Church of Christ, Church of God, inter or nondenominational)[2]
    ___Other[3]
    ___None[4]

Thank you very much for your cooperation.
You have been very helpful.

Discussion Questions

1   Are the study objectives and methodology appropriate for management's information needs given in the case? Discuss.
2   Evaluate the questionnaire in relation to the research objectives.

SPSS Applications

Use the SPSS file to analyze the data and answer the following questions:

1   What is the demographic profile of respondents surveyed?
2   What factors appear to be most important in selecting a private school?
3   What is the average tuition respondents expect to pay per student?
4   Does moving the school appear to be a major problem for respondents keeping their children in the same school system?
5   Are there significant differences between male and female respondents on the ratings of the seven factors listed in Question 6.

This case was prepared by Dr. Robert Stevens, Southeastern Oklahoma State University and Dr. David Loudon, Samford University. Names, selected data, and corporate identities have been disguised

Case 14   The Webmasters

Two recent college graduates who majored in computer science have just launched The Webmasters as a business. They have developed a client base of 25 small businesses in a one-month period and are interested in expanding this base as quickly as possible. They charge a flat fee that varies from $100 to $250, depending on the complexity of the site, and a monthly service fee of $15 to $25 to maintain the site. They want to focus on small businesses, since such businesses are less likely to employ their own computer technicians. The young owners contracted with a consultant to provide data on potential growth of the market. They calculated that they needed at least 200 clients to get their monthly maintenance fees up to a level to support both of them in the business. There are about 8,000 small businesses in the area.

Excerpts from the consultant's report are shown below along with the questionnaire used in the study.

Project Purpose

This project focused on small business Internet usage in the metropolitan area. Local small businesses were surveyed to determine what percentages of businesses have access to the Internet, what percentage use the Internet, and how these businesses use the Internet. The study also sought information on website ownership, plans for a website, and characteristics of businesses surveyed.

Project Objectives

The project objectives were as follows:
1   Determine what proportion of area small businesses have access to the Internet.
2   Determine what ways these businesses use the Internet.
3   Determine what proportion of businesses have a web site or are planning on having a web site within the next year.
4   Determine how the company web site is used and with what level of success.
5   Identify characteristics of businesses which use the Internet.

Methodology

A random sample of 120 small businesses was surveyed using a telephone questionnaire. The questionnaire was pretested on a sample of 20 small businesses. A field service company was used to collect the data. The information gathered from the survey was edited, tabulated, and processed by computer to provide a comprehensive set of tables. These tables included percentages and mean scores, which were used to answer the research questions.

Project Questionnaire

The Webmasters

May I speak with the owner? Hello, my name is_____, This survey deals with the Internet usage of small businesses in this area. Your answers will be confidential and used only in combination with the responses from other businesses.

Computer Information:

1. Do you use a computer at your business?
    ___Yes[1]
    ___No[2]
2. If yes, Do you have access to the Internet at your business?
    ___Yes[1] (go to question 4)
    ___No[2]
3. If no, Why not?(mark all that apply)
    ____ No need
    ____ No interest
    ____Too expensive
    ____Other, please specify_____
4. Who is your Internet provider?
    ___ AOL[1]
    ___ AT&T[2]
    ___ Bayou Internet[3]
    ___ MCI[4]
    ___ Prodigy[5]
    ___ Other, please specify[6]_____
5. In what way(s) is the Internet used in your business? (mark all that apply)
    ___General information (news, weather)
    ___Supplier information
    ___Competitive information
    ___Entertainment
    ___Customer information
6. In what ways has Internet helped your company? (mark all that apply)
    ___ Information on products/services
    ___ Competitive information
    ___ Information about suppliers
    ___ Sales leads
    ___Other, please specify_____
7. Does your company currently have a webpage?
    ___Yes[1]
    ___No[2] (skip to question 12)
8. If yes, for how long?
    ___Less than 6 months[1]
    ___More than 6months but less than a year[2]
    ___ A year[3]
    ___ More than a year[4]
9. If yes, how is your webpage being used or how do you plan for it to be used? (mark all that apply)
    ___Selling over the Internet
    ___Advertise company products

___Display of general company or product information
___Dealers locations to buy your products
___ Other, please specify_____

10. As a result of your webpages, do you feel you have experienced?
    ___No change in sales[1]
    ___An increase in sales[2]
    ___ A decrease in sales[3]

11. If an increase in sales volume has been experienced, How much increase have you experienced?
    ___5%–10% [1]
    ___10%--15% [2]
    ___More than 15%[3]

12. If no, Do you plan on having a webpage within the next year?
    ___Yes[1] ___No[2]

13. If no, why not?
    ___ Too expensive[1]
    ___ No expertise[2]
    ___ Do not know how it would help[3]

Company Information:

14. Is your company primarily a:
    ___ Manufacturer[1]
    ___ Wholesaler[2]
    ___ Retailer[3]
    ___ Service organization[4]
    ___ Other, please specify[5]

15. How many employees do you have?
    ___Less than 5[1]
    ___5–15[2]
    ___16–25[3]
    ___26–35[4]
    ___36–45[5]
    ___46–50[6]
    ___ over 50[7]

16. How many years have you been in business?
    ___Less than 5 years[1]
    ___6–10 years[2]
    ___11–15 years[3]
    ___16–20 years[4]
    ___More than 20 years[5]

17. What is your annual sales volume?
    ___Less than $100,000[1]
    ___$100, 000–$249,000[2]
    ___$250,000–$299,000[3]
    ___$300,000–$349,000[4]
    ___$350,000–$499,000[5]
    ___More than $500,000[6]

Thank you for your time and cooperation

Discussion Questions

1   Evaluate the research objectives and questionnaire in relation to management's information needs.
2   Are the sample size and selection process appropriate for the objectives and methodology?

SPSS Applications

Use the SPSS file to answer the following questions:

1   What is the profile of respondents in this survey?
2   What proportion of businesses have Internet access?
3   How are respondents using the Internet in their business?
4   What proportion are planning to get a webpage within the next year?
5   Based on your analysis, does there appear to be sufficient market potential for developing this business? Why?
6   Is there a significant difference in the impact of having a web site on sales among respondents based on size or years in business?

This case was prepared by Dr. Henry Cole, University of Louisiana Monroe, Dr. Robert Stevens, Southeastern Oklahoma State University and Dr. David Loudon, Samford University. Names, selected data, and corporate identities have been disguised.

Case 15　House of Topiary

Maurice Bernard had what he felt was a great idea. After being in the floral arrangement business for years, he had ventured out to open a new venture, The House of Topiary (HT). He had started off rather modestly and was quite pleased at his results in his first two years of operation. He now was considering whether or not to expand his operation.

Bernard had to overcome some significant challenges to achieve the present success level. First, many people viewed this business as just another florist in a 60,000-population community; as such, product differentiation had been an uphill battle. He had been fortunate that his reputation as a florist and decorator provided him with opportunities that allowed him opportunities to market and sell his topiary designs. Convincing clients and the public that a small leafed plant pruned and shaped into a design of animals or other objects was in good taste had been quite challenging. He felt that the hard work and sleepless nights of the past two years had paid off; there had been a steady increase in demand for his topiaries during the past six months. Now, he was considering expanding his business by venturing out into a larger geographic area. This would require an increase in the size of his shop, as well as hiring more employees. What was lacking at this point was research that would support this decision. A good friend of Maurice's suggested that he contact the Center of Marketing Excellence (CME) at the local university. The CME had worked with many different small businesses by providing student labor to complete market research services at little or no cost to area small businesses. The students benefited from this arrangement by having the opportunity to conduct market research and provide valuable services for small businesses in the community.

Five students and their marketing professor, Dr. Bobby London, came out to visit with Maurice about his business. Maurice gave the researchers the history of the company and shared his vision and concerns about his anticipated expansion. After a 90-minute meeting, the researchers suggested three major study objectives. First, the group felt that determining overall consumer awareness and the likely response to HT's future expansion was very important. Second, the group felt that defining HT's target market (i.e., wholesalers, and residential customers) would be a critical factor. Finally, making a solid business decision would require a good understanding of the demographic profiles of consumers and area florists. Both parties agreed to allow the CME to conduct this research on behalf of Maurice and the House of Topiary.

The CME team developed a residential questionnaire targeted to mid- to upper-mid level income families. The purpose of this questionnaire was to determine consumer demographics, such as location, education level, marital status, occupations, income levels, age, and locations of potential customers. A survey of area florists also was conducted to assess the feasibility of HT's wholesale business potential. The survey sample was 100, including 80 consumers and 20 florists. All data was collected using a structured questionnaire designed to meet the project's specific research objectives. All information was collected by telephone.

After about two months, Dr. London and his students provided Maurice with a written report that included the following information, charts, and tables.

Consumer Responses (n=80)

- Lived in area 15 years or more;
- Between 35–44 years of age;
- Income range of $65,000–79,999;
- Had high school degree with some college;
- Female;
- Retired or homemaker;
- 18.8% of consumers had purchased a topiary at a cost of $5–$25.00;
- Of the consumers making a purchase, 16.3% were very satisfied with the purchase;
- Eleven out of 15 respondents who had previously purchased topiaries stated that they would do so, again.

Floral Responses (n=20)

- Located in area more than 15 years;
- Currently have one to five employees;
- Annual sales volume of $60,000 or more per year;
- One out of 7 florists who do not carry topiaries would be interested in carrying topiaries in their stores.

Table 1 How Respondents Became Aware of the House of Topiary

Comunication Method	Percentage
Drove by store	2.5%
Radio ad	5.0%
Newspaper ad	8.8%
Friends	6.3%

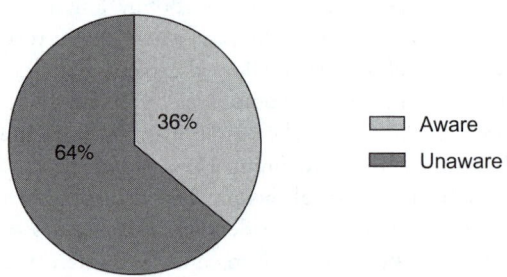

Figure 1 Awareness of House of Topiary

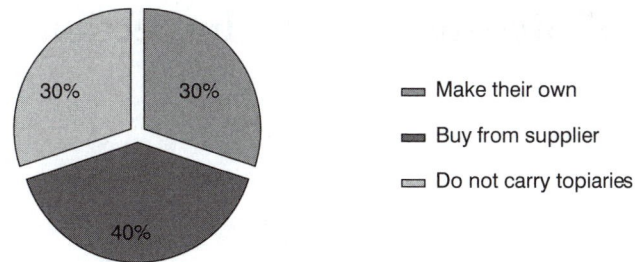

Figure 2 Business and Topiaries

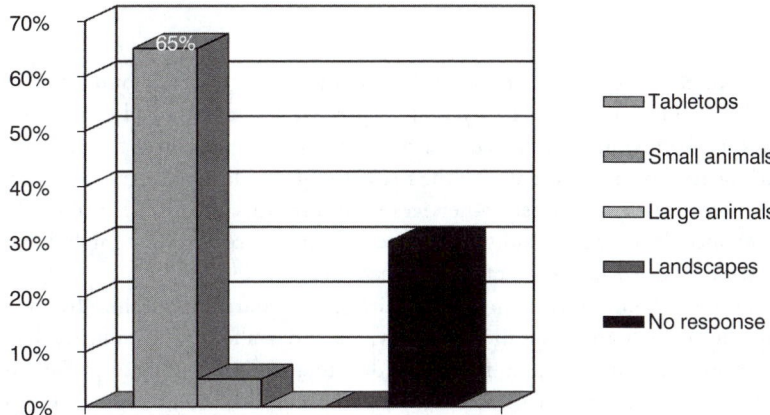

Figure 3 Types of Topiaries Preferred

Comunication Method	Percentage
Florists	1.3%
Other	5.0%

Questions/Assignment

1 Based on the information presented above, what different alternatives might be considered?
2 What recommendations would you make to the House of Topiary?

This case was prepared by Dr. Bruce C. Walker, University of Louisiana Monroe, Dr. Robert Stevens, Southeastern Oklahoma State University and Dr. David Loudon, Samford University. Names, selected data, and corporate identities have been disguised.

Case 16 Professional Home Inspection

Arthur C. Doyle, owner of Professional Home Inspection (PHI), found himself rather depressed. The community where he lived and operated his business had experienced a huge surge in existing home sales during the past five years, yet the success of his business had not approached the level commensurate with the market surge. Arthur had spent considerable time (and money) attempting to market his services to area realtors and the general public, yet his sales had remained flat over the past five years. He was very concerned what might happen to his business when the next major real estate slump occurred.

The professional home inspection industry in general and PHI specifically, specializes in conducting thorough home inspections for owners and realtors. The industry has enjoyed increased exposure during the past few years due to increased publicity about health and operational hazards that can surface in one's home. Specifically, recent negative health reports involving the area's water supply, radon and carbon monoxide levels in the home, as well as a Surgeon General's scathing report about the negative health consequences concerning indoor air pollution, had been widely reported. Additionally, traditional home problems, such as electrical, plumbing, heating and air conditioning unit efficiency, as well as structural problems related to shifting, were on-going concerns for homeowners. In spite of all of this, Doyle's business had not experienced the growth rate that he felt it should have experienced. He determined that he had to find out why if he was going to grow his business to the level he felt was appropriate.

PHI operated in Mason, Missouri, a city with a population of approximately 125,000 people. Additionally, Mason was the county seat, but the population that lived outside of the city represented approximately 10 percent of the total population of the county. Because of that, Doyle had focused most of his time and resources toward the Mason home market. The community was thriving with a solid industrial tax base and a small, but growing, university. According to the Mason Chamber of Commerce, the average per capita income in Mason was approximately $27,500 per year, up approximately 15 percent from about eight years ago. There had been a considerable number of new homes built during this time, and the sale of existing homes in the city had steadily increased.

In an attempt to determine whether or not he was using the right business model, Doyle decided to contact and employ his cousin, Oliver W. Holmes, to conduct market research on behalf of PHI. Holmes had graduated with a degree in marketing from a highly rated university about 15 years ago, and had operated his own market research firm for about ten years. This business, Market Research Institute (MRI), had a strong history and reputation for assisting small struggling businesses in developing market niches and strategies. After a lengthy phone conversation, Holmes and Doyle met in a two-hour lunch meeting to discuss specific issues related to Doyle's business and the role Holmes could play in assisting PHI.

Holmes asked Doyle to explain the various services that PHI offered. After hearing this, Holmes asked Doyle to describe his marketing strategy. Doyle explained that he used several different approaches to maximize exposure of his business and services provided. First, he used broadcast advertising on a limited basis. PHI was a co-sponsor on a weekly business review program on cable TV, and helped co-sponsor realtor business meetings and generally set up an exhibitor's booth at the annual homebuyers trade show held at the local civic center. PHI also was a member of the local chamber of commerce, and advertised in many of the commercial chamber reports, especially those related to real estate and economic development activities going on in the community. Doyle also had conducted continuing education seminars through the local university. Additionally, Doyle utilized a direct mail campaign geared to the local real estate brokers and agents to try to influence them to recommend PHI to potential buyers of existing homes. Since Doyle was not happy with the success of his business, he wondered to Holmes whether a different advertising strategy could help.

Holmes then asked Doyle to describe the typical user of PHI services. Doyle had to admit at that point that he had no idea, other than the fact that the typical user had a purchase contract pending, generally on an existing home (as opposed to new construction). Doyle rarely had been called to inspect new construction since the building requirements and the newness of the home's operating systems tended to negate issues that generally surfaced in older, existing dwellings (i.e., plumbing, electrical, structural, sewage problems). Doyle then questioned whether or not knowing a profile of his client was really that meaningful since PHI was inspecting homes as opposed to providing services to individuals, even though individuals were required to pay for such services, generally as part of the closing costs. Holmes explained to Doyle that having a customer profile might provide insight as to future company services as well as clues as to what type of advertising and promotions might be more effective. For example, if the typical decision maker for these types of services is a 35 year old male blue collar worker, advertising or sponsoring activities such as in hunting and fishing programs, might result in greater exposure to his potential customers. On the other hand, if the typical decision maker is a 50-year old female professional, PHI might become more involved in advertising or promoting through garden clubs or certain civic organizations. Doyle admitted that he had never really thought about that.

At the close of the meeting, Doyle and Holmes agreed upon the following market research questions and objectives:

1 What are the factors involved in the choice of a home inspection company?
2 How important is each of these factors?
3 What is the most feasible and effective means of reaching home buyers?
4 What are the most attractive features of each PHI service, and what are the selection considerations of consumers?
5 What is the level of realtor satisfaction with PHI services?
6 Develop and evaluate the demographic profiles of consumers according to areas and consumer classifications.
7 Determine the strategic implications of the findings.

MRI determined that the best and most cost-effective manner to capture the information needed to accomplish the above objectives would be through telephone surveys that targeted two different groups: area realtors and potential home buyers. It was felt that the responses of these two groups would provide insight as to how PHI services were actually sold and what factors were important in the buying decision. MRI professionals developed, pre-tested, and conducted a potential customer telephone survey and a realtor telephone survey. A total of 90 usable questionnaires were received, with 30 responses from area realtors and 60 responses from potential customers. The questionnaires are shown below.

Survey Questionnaire

Home Inspection Service

Telephone Questionnaire(Home owners)

Number called _____   Date of call _____   Time _____

Hello, am I speaking with man/lady of the house? (If no, ask to speak to that person.)
Hello, my name is _____. I'm with MRI, a marketing research company and we're conducting a marketing research project with area residents. This study deals with Home Inspection Services. Would you please help us by answering a few questions? Your answers will be confidential and used only in combination with the responses of other people.

1a.   Do you own or rent your home?
___Own (skip to 1c)[1]
___Rent (go to 1b)[2]
1b.   If rent, are you planning to buy a house in the next year?
___Yes[1]
___No (terminate)[2]
1c.   Do you or any members of your family work for a home inspection service or a realtor?
___Yes (terminate)[1]
___No[2]
1d.   Have you or any member of your family recently purchased a home?
___ Yes[1]
___ No[2]
2.   Are you aware of the availability of home inspection services?
___Yes[1]
___ No[2]
If yes, how found out? _____
If no (explain), in home inspection an inspector comes to a home you might purchase or sell and inspects it for damage or problem areas, such as, electric, plumbing, the roof, the foundation, insulation, in addition to many other minor areas.
3.   When choosing such a service, what factors would most influence your choice of inspectors?
___ recommended by realtor
___ referrals from friends
___ word of mouth
___ good reputation
___ cost of service
___ money-saving benefits
___ inspector credentials
___ other
4a.   (If yes to question 2) When you were planning to buy your home, which of the following would have been the most effective way to inform you of home inspection services?
___ realtor
___ television ads
___ referrals
___ newspaper ads
___ business cards

___ direct mail/brochures
___ car sign
___ yellow pages
___ billboards
___ real estate magazine
___ other

4b. (If no to question 2) If you were in the market to buy a home, which of the following would be the most effective way to inform you of home inspection services?
___ realtor
___ television ads
___ referrals
___ newspaper ads
___ business cards
___ direct mail/brochures
___ car sign
___ yellow pages
___ billboards
___ real estate magazine
___ other

5. Please rate your interest in the following home inspection services, using very interested, somewhat interested, or not interested:

a. Structure
___ very interested[1]   ___ somewhat interested[2]   ___ not interested[3]

b. Electrical
___very interested[1]   ___ somewhat interested[2]   ___ not interested[3]

c. Plumbing
___very interested[1]   ___ somewhat interested[2]   ___ not interested[3]

d. Foundation
___very interested[1]   ___ somewhat interested[2]   ___ not interested[3]

e. Heating and air conditioning
___very interested[1]   ___ somewhat interested[2]   ___ not interested[3]

f. Lot grading (sloping of yard away from home)
___very interested[1]   ___ somewhat interested[2]   ___ not interested[3]

g. Carbon monoxide testing
___very interested[1]   ___ somewhat interested[2]   ___ not interested[3]

h. Combustible gas testing
___very interested[1]   ___ somewhat interested[2]   ___ not interested[3]

i. MO home energy rating and evaluation
___very interested[1]   ___ somewhat interested[2]   ___ not interested[3]

j. 203k consulting (inspection of a home for a first time buyer. The expenses to fix are included into first mortgage)
___very interested[1]   ___ somewhat interested[2]   ___ not interested[3]

k. Radon testing
___very interested[1]   ___ somewhat interested[2]   ___ not interested[3]

l. Tap water testing
___very interested[1]   ___ somewhat interested[2]   ___ not interested[3]

m. Indoor air pollution testing
___very interested[1]   ___ somewhat interested[2]   ___ not interested[3]

6. Do you live in?
   ___ Mason[1]
   ___ East Mason[2]

7. How long have you lived in the area?
   ___ 0–2 years[1]
   ___ 3–5 years[2]
   ___ 6–12 years[3]
   ___ 13–20 years[4]
   ___ over 20 years[5]
   ___ refused[6]

8. Now just a few more questions about you. Are you:
   ___ single with no children[1]
   ___ married with no children[2]
   ___ married with children at home[3]
   ___ single with children at home[4]
   ___ married with no children at home[5]
   ___ single with no children at home[6]
   ___ refused[7]

9. Which age category do you fit into? (Read)

   ___ 18–24[1]   ___ 55–64[5]
   ___ 25–34[2]   ___ 65 and older[6]
   ___ 35–44[3]   ___ refused[7]
   ___ 45–54[4]

10. What is the category that includes your total family income? (Read)

    ___ under 15,000[1]   ___ $65,000 to $79,999[6]
    ___ $15,000 to $24,999[2]   ___ $80,000 to $94,999[7]
    ___ $25,000 to $34,999[3]   ___ $95,000 to $109,999[8]
    ___ $35,000 to $49,999[4]   ___ over $110,000[9]
    ___ $50,000 t0 $64,999[5]   ___ don't know, refused[10]

11. Are you: (Read)
    ___ a high school graduate[1]
    ___ a high school graduate with some college[2]
    ___ a college graduate[3]
    ___ a college graduate with some graduate school[4]
    ___ a graduate degree holder[5]
    ___ refused[6]

12. Sex: (Do not ask unless necessary)
    ___ Male[1]
    ___ Female[2]

13. What is the approximate amount you paid for your home?

    ___ less than $50,000[1]   ___ $150,001 to $175,000[6]
    ___ $50,000 to $75,000[2]   ___ $175,001 to $200,000[7]
    ___ $75,001 to $100,000[3]   ___ $200,001 to $225,000[8]
    ___ $100,001 to $125,000[4]   ___ $225,001 to $250,000[9]
    ___ $125,001 to $150,000[5]   ___ Over 250,000[10]

Thank you very much for your time and cooperation

Home Inspection Survey

Telephone Questionnaire (Realtors)

Number called _____   Date of call _____ Interviewer _____
Realtor _____

Hello, am I speaking to the owner/manager?
Hi, my name is _____. I'm MRI, a marketing research firm, and we're conducting a survey of area realtors. This survey deals with home inspection services. Would you please help us by answering a few questions? Your answers will be confidential and used only in combination with responses of other realtors.

1. Are you familiar with home inspection services?
    ___ Yes[1]
    ___ No (terminate) [2]
2. Have you ever recommended a home inspection service to a home buyer?
    ___ Yes[1]
    ___ No[2] if no, why _____(terminate)
3. If yes, which inspector do you recommend?
    _____
4. Is the cost of a home a factor in recommending home inspection services?
    ___ Yes[1]
    ___ No[2]
5. If yes, at what price level would you begin recommendations?
    ___ below $50,000[1]
    ___ $50,000 to $69,999[2]
    ___ $70,000 to $89,999[3]
    ___ $90,000 to $109,999[4]
    ___ over $110,000[5]
    ___ refused[6]
6. Have you ever used Professional Home Inspection Services? (ask if Doyle not mentioned in question 3)
    ___ Yes[1]
    ___ No[2] (Terminate)
    If they have not used PHI terminate. If they have used PHI, ask questions 7 and 8.
7. If PHI was mentioned on question 3, ask "On a scale of one to five, where "one" is very dissatisfied and "five" is very satisfied, how would you rate your satisfaction with Professional Home Inspections?
    very dissatisfied   1   2   3   4   5   very satisfied
8. If dissatisfied (1 or 2), ask why are you dissatisfied?
    ___ Poor service[1]
    ___ Too expensive[2]
    ___ Other,
    specify[3]_____
    _____
    _____

Thank you very much for you time and cooperation.

Questions:

1   Do you feel the consumer survey provided the information necessary to meet the study's objectives? Why or why not?
2   What major conclusions might be reached based on the realtor responses?
3   Based on the information received from the potential customer survey, what recommendations would you give to Doyle concerning marketing to this group?

SPSS Application:

1   What were the factors that influenced the choice of a home inspector? Were these factors the same for those who were aware of home inspection services as opposed to those who were unaware?
2   How interested were potential customers in inspection services related to carbon monoxide, indoor air pollution, and radon testing? Based on these findings, should PHI strongly market this type of inspection services?
3   Based on the information received from the survey, is PHI in a position to influence a realtor's willingness to recommend PHI over its competitors? Why or why not?

This case was prepared by Dr. Bruce C. Walker, University of Louisiana Monroe, Dr. Robert Stevens, Southeastern Oklahoma State University and Dr. David Loudon, Samford University. Names, selected data, and corporate identities have been disguised.

Case 17   Europska Databanka

Pavel Jisa, co-owner of Europska Databanka, shifted his weight and leaned forward in his chair as he contemplated the question that his friend Richard, the 84th Duke of Siebenlugner, had just asked him and his partner, Dalibor Dusek. "Are there any ways that you two might use marketing research to improve the operations of your company?" had been Richard's query. The Europska Databanka office in Prague, Czech Republic, had been launched in 1991. It was now May of 1997. The company had been so successful that the question of marketing research had never been raised. But perhaps now was the time to determine whether engaging in some research on the effectiveness of their organization might allow the partners to be even more efficient in their operations.

Background on Europska Databanka

Pavel let his mind race back to the launching of the company. The Velvet Revolution which had occurred in Czechoslovakia in November 1989 had presented unique opportunities to latent entrepreneurs in the country. Not in 50 years had the possibility of beginning their own businesses existed for citizens of Czechoslovakia. The Revolution was ushered in by hundreds of thousands of citizens jingling their keys in the streets of Prague around the popular Wenceslas Square and shouting, "Closing time," or "We shall overcome." The mood at that time in history was that of an endless carnival.

Before the Revolution, Pavel and Dalibor had worked for a transit company that shipped goods transported in containers on the company's trucks and scheduled the containers for shipment on railway cars when needed. Pavel was a computer technician and had the responsibility of working with the logistics of using the company's trucks in the most efficient manner. Dalibor was the supervisor of the computer department on one of the three shifts of the day and was Pavel's supervisor. After the Velvet Revolution, Pavel and Dalibor began thinking about their business options. Dalibor had suggested: "It seems to me that there will be a great need for information about new companies that are producing specific goods and services that customers may need. The Yellow Page Directory published by the telephone company is only distributed once a year, and new businesses are starting every day." Pavel had responded, "Since we've both been involved in getting goods on containers to the right place at the right time and keeping accurate records about the transportation of these goods, we should be able to use those skills to start a company that delivers information to people in a timely manner about companies that provide the goods and services that they desire."

Someone had told Pavel and Dalibor about a man named Schwanzen who had started a business in Brno, Czechoslovakia, similar to the one they were thinking about launching. They contacted him, talked about their desire to start a similar company, and discovered that he was franchising his business throughout the Czech Republic and Slovakia.

They learned from Schwanzen that the company operated in the following manner:

1   Salespeople from Europska Databanka contacted businesses that offered goods or services to the public and agreed to represent them and refer callers inquiring about such products or services to their offerings. They charged the companies that they represented a fee which could range from 5,000 korunas to 30,000 korunas per year based on the size of the company and the number of their products. Not only did they handle goods and services of companies but also offers of travel services and accommodations for travelers. Some of the companies that had signed contracts with them were Skoda, VW Group, IBM, Hewlett Packard, Credit Management, British Petrol Oil, Nissan, Citibank, and Dun and Bradstreet. Detailed information about the client firms was stored in the company's databank in Germany and made available to all of their foreign clients.

2   The company publicized its services to consumers through ads in various Yellow Pages, billboard posters along the highways, sponsoring a television show on aerobics, and advertising on the sides of buses and trams.

3   The company distributed information to consumers regarding the availability of products and services they were interested in through the use of the following means of communication: a bank of telephone receptionists who were available from 7:00 a.m. until 7:00 p.m. to take calls for information; a web site on the internet to offer the same information; and compact disks also bearing information about the companies and their products. Unlike the 1-900 numbers in the United States that received revenues by charging the caller a fee, this company secured their revenues from the companies they represented. The contracts from the companies were renegotiated each year.

Pavel and Dalibor were even more interested in the business after their conversation with Schwanzen. They knew that beginning a new business could be risky, so they decided to put together a business plan to test the feasibility of such a franchise in Prague. After working on the business plan for three months, they decided that there was a market for such a company in Prague; and they entered into an agreement with Schwanzen for exclusive franchise rights in the city.

The first step Pavel and Dalibor took was to raise the needed 100,000 Czech korunas that it would take to launch the business. Since the newly-formed private banks were not lending money to anyone, they raised their start-up capital from friends and relatives. They decided to borrow the money rather than bringing in additional owners of the company.

After the money had been raised, Pavel and Dalibor applied for a concession (certificate or business license) with the Concession Office in Prague. They had to pay 1,000 Czech korunas to pay for the concession. In addition to filling out the form for the concession and paying the 1,000 koruna fee, they also had to bring with them a certificate from the court stating that neither of the partners had ever been convicted of a criminal offense. In one week, they received their certificate from the Concession Office. The next step they had to take was to present the business certificate to the Taxation Department and receive a tax number. Finally, they located a site for the business at # 15 Husitska in the heart of the Prague business district.

Pavel had read in a publication for entrepreneurs that in the first six years since the Velvet Revolution, 1.5 million certificates to begin a business had been issued by the government. It had been estimated by the government that for only 150,000 of these business certificate recipients would the business be their primary jobs. For the rest, the ventures would merely be a way to supplement their full-time jobs.

Most businesses that were begun in 1990 had been launched by former Communist leaders because they had the right contacts and sufficient money to begin a business. A popular saying in the United States, "It's not what you know, but who you know," applied also to the burgeoning new Czech economy. However, by 1991 other people were finding ways to raise money to begin their own businesses.

Privatization in Czechoslovakia

Before the revolutions that shook the countries of Eastern Europe in 1989, there were basically two kinds of firms in operation: state-owned and cooperatives. Whereas Poland had a rather strong private sector with many cooperatives, Czechoslovakia did not. In fact, in 1986, 96.7 percent of Czechoslavokia's net national product was produced by the state-owned firms. East Germany, the Soviet Union and Czechoslovakia had the highest percentage of state production of all of the Communist countries.

Czechoslovakia had several advantages as it moved toward a free market economy. The country's annual inflation rate never exceeded 5 percent throughout the decade of the 1980s; the external debt of Czechoslovakia was low by international standards; and the country had a well-educated and skilled labor force. However, the country also had some major disadvantages. It had no private sector and all prices had been centrally controlled. Also, Czech exports had been aimed at the countries of the Soviet Union and Eastern Europe. In fact, 40 percent of their exports had been to the Soviet Union. Most of their products were not saleable in Western markets because of their poor quality.

By the Spring of 1997, there was another problem that bothered economists, economic journalists and politicians: the fraudulent activities which had recently surfaced in the economy. It was apparent that shady speculators were destroying small investment funds by selling off their assets and "tunneling" the money out of the country. Thomas Jezek, a godfather of speedy privatization, used to cry that, "We must be faster than the lawyers" to keep the process (of privatization) from bogging down in needless controls. By 1997, the same Mr. Jezek, as Chairman of the Prague Stock Exchange, spoke in horror of the lack of controls on business in the new Czech Republic.

Emergence of the Czech Republic Economy

After the 1993 split between the northwestern, primarily Bohemian, section of Czechoslovakia into the Czech Republic and the southeastern, mostly Moravian, section of the country into Slovakia, the economy of the Czech Republic initially held up quite well. Although the Czech gross domestic product (GDP) fell precipitously in 1991–92 because of economic problems in the eastern markets that were formerly their primary customers and a fall in domestic demand as a result of rising prices, there were still many bright spots in the economy. Most encouraging was the very low unemployment rate and the growth of the private sector. A Czech economist named Kamil Janacek speculated:

> One can infer that faster progress of the private sector in the Czech Republic is one of the reasons for the less adverse impact of transformation there. In the Czech Republic, private sector's share of the GDP was almost 10% in 1991 compared to 4% in Slovakia.

However, as the months turned into years since the Revolution, the Czech Republic found itself in the Spring of 1997 facing serious economic problems. To begin with, there had been very little restructuring in the older, recently privatized Czech companies. This situation was responsible for the low unemployment rate in the country. The country's trade deficit had also grown. This was coupled with a concern about some underhanded dealings in the Czech capital markets and a compromised position at some of the big banks. In January and February of 1997, industrial production slumped 4 percent, wages soared 16 percent, and the budget deficit hit 8.5 billion korunas.

In response to the shocking financial news, an emergency economic package was unveiled by Prime Minister Vaclav Klaus in late Spring of 1997. The most striking provisions were for large budget cuts through cuts in investment and welfare spending, a public sector wage growth limited to 7.3 percent with pressure on the private sector to follow suit, the immediate introduction of 20 percent import deposits on foodstuffs and consumer goods (to stop the hemorrhage in the balance of payments), and the completion of privatization of government-owned businesses and sales to foreign strategic partners or managerial groups.

One resource that had not been sufficiently utilized in solving many of the economic problems of the new economy was the brain power of the local schools of higher learning. Within Prague, there was the prestigious Charles University which was well known for its programs in medicine, law, computer animation and economics. Another school that drew many foreign students to study was the University of Economics in Prague. There were also technical schools which had business programs.

The Challenges for Europska Databanka

The early months of Europska Databanka had been more successful than Pavel and Dalibor could have imagined. They had paid off all of their loans to friends and family within the first six months of operation. The company continued to grow, but they wondered if there were ways of making it grow faster.

Pavel and Dalibor had not been able to open a bank account initially because the banks told them they would have to have 50,000 korunas before they could open an account. And even if they had that much cash, the bank suggested they did not have an account number to give them. They were instructed to come back in a year and a half and perhaps then they would allow the company to open a checking account. Most people in the Czech Republic paid cash in all of their transactions, so a bank account was not a necessity. However, there were those who realized that a cash economy has very few controls for violating the tax laws.

There were other challenges for entrepreneurs in the new Czech Republic. Although in the early years of the Czech free market economy sole proprietorships and partnerships had limited liability, in 1996 the law had changed and proprietorships and partnerships now had unlimited liability. Pavel and Dalibor realized they could lose all of the money they had invested in the company plus anything else of value that they owned if the business went under and they were sued by their creditors. The partners knew unlimited liability made sense for an economy that was attempting to establish sufficient ground rules to keep the possibility of fraud out, but it did make their position much riskier.

By May of 1997, the company had 10 women working on the telephones supplying information on goods and services to callers and 10 people working in the field as salespeople. The sales force called on prospective companies and attempted to get them to agree to sign a contract with Europska Databanka. One of the primary problems of the business was the difficulty of hiring good employees. Because the unemployment rate in the Czech Republic was so low, it was almost impossible to find qualified employees. In fact, the company had recently run an advertisement in the newspaper for new salespeople and had received 50 inquiries about the position. However, only four people showed up for an interview, and only one of the four people was qualified for the job. The low unemployment rate also meant that workers were not afraid to lose their jobs because of low productivity; they knew they could always get another job.

There were a few employment search agencies in Prague; however, they were not utilized by the companies because the idea of search agencies was completely new. The primary customers of these agencies were foreigners seeking jobs in the Czech Republic.

As to competition, Pavel and Dalibor believed at the present time the only competition was from the Yellow Pages printed by the telephone company. However, they also knew there were few barriers to entry into the industry. Another entrepreneur could simply observe what they were doing and copy their operations. The primary barrier to entry was the massive task of organizing all of the information about the companies that they represented. They wondered if there were other barriers to entry that they could construct. Richard had suggested to them that if they could offer superior customer service, this might prove to be a barrier to entry. Pavel liked the idea of customer service but had to laugh when he thought of the lack of customer service that existed under the former command economy. He remembered that customers were treated as slaves who had to beg for products from the government-owned businesses. He wondered how they could implement customer service in their operations.

Pavel reflected on a question that a young American named Suzanna Pierce had asked him yesterday. Susanna was a student at the University of Economics in Prague and was keenly interested in the economic changes that were taking place in the economy. Her question had been, "What do you consider to be the greatest challenges for new businesses in a country that has recently moved from a command economy to a free market economy?" He thought about the state of the former and present Czech economy and began in his mind to formulate a response to that intriguing question.

Pavel's thoughts came back to the present when Richard rose from the desk on the mezzanine at #15 Husitska where the two of them and Dalibor had been sitting. As Richard put his wide-brimmed black hat on his head and moved toward the door, he suggested again that they consider utilizing market research to improve the performance of the company. There must be some way, he urged, to find out if consumers are actually taking the firm's advice and buying the products that it had recommended to them. Also, there must be a way of determining how the callers found out about the company so that the company could be assured that it had used the most effective method of advertising. Pavel wondered how they would accomplish these things.

This case was prepared by Dr. Marlene Reed, Visiting Professor of Entrepreneurship at Baylor University, and Dr. Edward Felton, William and Mary University.

Case 18   Northside Chiropractic Services

Jill Anderson, administrator of Northside Chiropractic Services, was becoming increasingly concerned about the lack of response to the clinic's promotional expenditures. Significant increases in expenditures over the last two years had resulted in very few new patients. She felt that there may other factors involved in the patient decision-making process that she had not evaluated. She was interested in determining if there were negative attitudes among the general public toward chiropractors and the services they provide.

Northside Chiropractic Services is located in a southern city with a population base of about 150,000. The city is considered by many to be a regional medical center based on the large number of medical services available. The clinic was established by a husband/wife chiropractic team about 25 years ago and is located along a major street in the city. Expansion of the clinic has included remodeling of the present location and adding two new chiropractors and a massage therapist. About 90 percent of the current clients came to the clinic on the basis of referrals from other clients while the remainder came as walk-ins based on a yellow page ad or other advertising media.

A variety of promotional tools have been utilized over the past two years including team/event sponsorships, television and radio spots, a yellow page ad, and a billboard ad. Each new client is asked how he or she found out about Northside and most of them report that they were referred to the clinic by a relative or friend who is a current or past client of Northside.

To help evaluate the lack of response to the promotional campaign, a local consulting firm was asked to submit a research proposal to Northside and that proposal was accepted. Excerpts from the proposal and the questionnaire used in the study are shown in the following.

Research Proposal

Consumers will be surveyed to determine the following: 1) prior knowledge of chiropractors and their services, 2) whether the consumer has ever visited a chiropractor or used chiropractic services, 3) attitudes toward chiropractors and their services, and 4) the demographic profile of respondents.

The main purpose of this study will be to determine the market acceptability of chiropractors and their services. The study will also evaluate price perceptions, chiropractic use, and reasons for patient visits. Finally, this research project will develop and evaluate demographic profiles of consumers. Strategic implications of the results will be presented to guide Northside in promotional planning.

Research Objectives

To guide the research, the following objectives were developed:

1   To determine perceptions of chiropractors relative to other health care providers.
2   To evaluate the use of chiropractic services.
3   To evaluate satisfaction with chiropractic services including fees charged.
4   To evaluate differences in perceptions based on socio-economic characteristics of respondents.

Methodology

To accomplish these objectives, a probability sample of 120 will be drawn from the local telephone directory using a cluster sample design. The directory is only three months old and should include most of the area residents who have listed numbers.

A structured questionnaire will be designed and administered by telephone. The questionnaire will be pre-tested and administered by our staff of trained interviewers.

The resulting data will be processed using the SPSS statistical analysis software. The analyses will include percentages, mean scores, and chi-square analysis. Other statistical techniques will be used as deemed necessary to accomplish the project objectives.

Report

The final bound report along with an oral presentation of findings will be ready by September 1. Three copies of the bound report will be furnished to Northside. Additional copies will be available upon request.

The report will include a detailed executive summary, findings, tables, and charts. The findings section of the report will use a question-by-question format to provide a more thorough analysis of the data.

Survey Questionnaire

Interviewer
Person interviewed
Telephone number
Date

Northside Chiropractic Survey

Hi! My name is…… I work for ABC Consulting and we are doing a survey of area residents. Would you take a few moments and answer some questions for me? Your answers will be held in strict confidence and combined with the answers of other respondents. (If the answer is yes, begin the survey with question 1.)

1.   Are you or anyone else living in your home presently employed by a health care provider such as a hospital, doctor, or a chiropractor?
   Yes[1] no[2] (if yes, thank and terminate)
2.   How long have you lived in this area?
   Less than a year[1]
   1–5 years[2]
   6–10 years[3]
   11–15 years[4]
   16–20 years[5]
   more than 20 years[6]

3. Do you have a family doctor?
    Yes[1] no[2]

4. How often do you go to the doctor's office?
    Once a month[1]
    Once every 3 months[2]
    Once every 6 months[3]
    Once a year[4]
    Other[5]

5. Have any of your family members been to a chiropractor?
    Yes[1] no[2] don't know[3]

6. Do you think your doctor would ever refer you to a chiropractor for care?
    Yes[1] no[2] don't know[3] (if no, why)

7. Do you consider chiropractors to be a part of the medical profession?
    Yes[1] no[2]

8. Do you have health insurance?
    Yes[1] no[2]

9. Does your insurance cover chiropractic care?
    Yes[1] no[2] don't know[3]

10. Would you expect chiropractic services to cost:
    About the same as a doctor[1] (read choices)
    Less than a doctor[2]
    More than a doctor[3]

11. Have you ever been to a chiropractor?
    Yes[1] no[2] (If the answer is no, skip to question 19)

12. What was your reason for going to a chiropractor? (mark all that apply)
    back pain
    headaches
    leg pain
    arm pain
    other

13. What type of treatment did or do you receive? (mark all that apply)
    Adjustment   (read choices)
    Therapy
    Massage

14. How often did you or do you use chiropractic services?
    once a month[1]   (read choices)
    twice a month[2]
    once every 3 months[3]
    once every 6 months[4]
    once a year[5]
    other[6]

15. On a scale of 1 to 5 with 1 being extremely dissatisfied and 5 being extremely satisfied,
    how would you rate the following:

Friendliness of the staff	1	2	3	4	5
Cleanliness of the office	1	2	3	4	5
Atmosphere of the office	1	2	3	4	5
Promptness of service	1	2	3	4	5
Quality of care	1	2	3	4	5
Professionalism of the doctor	1	2	3	4	5
Reasonableness of fees charged	1	2	3	4	5

16. Would you recommend chiropractic care to your friend and family?
    Yes[1] no[2]   (if no, why) .
17. How did you find out about the chiropractor you used?
    referral by a friend[1] (read)
    referral by a doctor[2]
    advertisements[3]
    word of mouth[4]
    other[5] .

    Now we would like to have some information about you.
19. Which of the following categories contains your age? (read)
    18–25[1]
    26–34[2]
    35–44[3]
    45–54[4]
    55–64[5]
    65 and over[6]
20. What is you current family status? (read)
    single[1]
    married[2] (with no children at home)
    divorced[3] (with no children at home)
    widowed[4] (with no children at home)
    married with children at home[5]
    divorced with children at home[6]
    widowed with children at home[7]
21. Sex: (Don't ask unless absolutely necessary)
     male[1]
    female[2]
22. What is the highest level of education you have completed?   (read)
    completed middle school[1]
    completed high school[2]
    completed college[3]
    completed advanced degree[5]
23. What is your occupation? (read)
    homemaker[1]
    student[2]
    laborer[3]
    skilled[4]
    professional[5]
    retired[6]
24. Which of the following categories contains your family's annual income? (read)
    less than $10,000[1]
    $10,001–$30,000[2]
    $30,001–$50,000[3]
    $50,001–$70,000[4]
    $70,001–$90,000[5]
    $90,001–$100,000[6]
    over $100,000[7]

Thank you very much for your time and cooperation

Discussion Questions

1 Are the study objectives and methodology appropriate for management's information needs given in the case? Discuss.
2 Evaluate the questionnaire in relation to the research objectives. Are the appropriate topics covered? Is the sequence of questions logical? Is the structure of the individual questions appropriate for the needed data?

SPSS Applications

Use the SPSS file to analyze the data and answer the following questions:

1 What is the demographic profile of respondents surveyed?
2 Are respondents who have used chiropractic services satisfied with these services?
3 Are chiropractors considered to be part of the medical community?
4 Are there significant differences among respondents on the ratings of the seven factors listed in Question 15?

This case was prepared by Dr. Robert Stevens, Southeastern Oklahoma State University, Dr. David Loudon, Stamford University, and Dr. Phylis Mansfield, Pennsylvania State University. Names, selected data, and corporate identities have been disguised.

Case 19   Internet Versus Mail Surveys

Two university professors who are involved in doing both mail and Internet surveys were challenged by an intriguing question: "Do the results of internet surveys differ from results of other data collection techniques?" Due to limited budgets, much of their research involved mail surveys. However, the advent of Internet service companies providing the ability to do as many surveys as desired with only a nominal fee ($10 a month) and other companies providing bulk email addresses, the feasibility of using Internet surveys was greatly improved. To determine if Internet results were as valid as mail survey results, they decided to set up an experiment to test for differences in responses to the same questionnaire delivered using two media—a mail survey and an Internet survey. The cost of this research project would be low since one of them had already subscribed to an Internet survey service.

Research Objectives

To guide the research the following objectives were developed:

1   Determine differences in response rates between mail surveys and Internet surveys.
2   Determine differences in responses to individual questions between mail surveys and Internet surveys.

Research Methodology

To accomplish these objectives, an experimental design was used. The design is represented as follows:

$$R_1 T_1 O_1$$
$$R_2 T_2 O_2$$

where R=random group assignment (mail or Internet), T=Treatment (mail or survey), and O=Observation.

The questionnaire contained 15 Likert-type scales with four possible responses ranging from strongly agree to strongly disagree. No neutral response option was offered so that the respondent would be forced into either a positive or negative response. In addition, five classification questions concerning the institution and experience of the respondent were asked to determine differences in responses based on institution size, years of experience of the respondent, etc. The questionnaire was pre-tested and revised prior to actual use.

One of the keys to the research was to have a relative large group of potential respondents with both their mailing address and their email address. Using a recent directory of accounting faculty in the U.S., respondents were randomly assigned to the mail group or the Internet group.

If no email address was given for an individual, their name was dropped from the Internet survey list of potential respondents. The mail survey was sent to 410 professors and the Internet survey participation request was emailed to 412 professors. The surveys were emailed using an independent email account and a link was provided to the survey's web page in each email message. The potential respondent would simply need to click on the link to go to the Web page and begin responding to the questionnaire. After completing the questions, clicking on the submit option completed their participation in the survey and their data was added to the database for the survey. This data could then be downloaded into a spreadsheet format for statistical analysis.

After both groups of surveys were sent, a one-month cut-off period was used to allow enough time for the responses to be returned. A Z-test for sample proportions was used to test for significant differences in response rate and t-tests were used on the scaled statements to identify significant differences in responses to individual questions between the two media. Cross-tabulations were used to identify differences in responses using the classification questions.

Findings

Of the 410 questionnaires mailed out, 408 were actually delivered. Of the 408 delivered 71 usable responses were received yielding a 17.4% response rate. Of the 412 email requests to potential survey participants, only 212 were opened and 48 responded giving us a response rate of 22.6% response to the Internet survey. Five subjects deleted the email without opening. Ninety-three emails were returned to sender because of faulty addresses. One hundred and eighty-eight emails were unaccounted for. While the response rate to the Internet survey was higher than the mail survey, the difference was not significant at the .05 level of significance.

Survey Questionnaire

University of Louisiana at Monroe
Accounting Opinion Survey

Research Purpose:

The uncovering of unethical accounting practices involving companies like Arthur Andersen, Enron, and WorldCom has been highly publicized over the past months. This questionnaire is designed by marketing research students at the University of Louisiana at Monroe to assess the impact of these events on the accounting profession with an emphasis on the educational field. Faculty members from 519 accounting departments are being surveyed in order to collect this data. Results will be tabulated and available to survey participants. Thanks for your participation in this study.

Instructions:

The statements listed below relate to the impact of the recent accounting scandals on the accounting profession. Please circle the number corresponding to your level of agreement with each statement using the following scale:

1=Strongly Agree, 2=Agree, 3=Disagree, 4=Strongly Disagree

		Strongly Agree	Agree	Disagree	Strongly Disagree
1.	The recent accounting scandals have impacted the accounting profession.	1	2	3	4
2.	My institution has felt the impact of the scandals.	1	2	3	4
3.	Accounting students at my institution have more negative attitudes toward accounting since the scandals were discovered.	1	2	3	4
4.	As a result of the unethical practices, the number of accounting majors at my institution will probably decrease.	1	2	3	4
5.	Students at my university believe there will be fewer employment opportunities in the accounting profession as a result of the scandals.	1	2	3	4
6.	Job placement of accounting students will be affected by the scandals.	1	2	3	4
7.	Private financial support of my institution's accounting department will be affected by the scandals.	1	2	3	4
8.	My institution's accounting curriculum adequately covers ethics.	1	2	3	4
9.	Universities in general should reformat their degree programs and curricula to include a greater emphasis on ethics.	1	2	3	4
10.	In the future, there will be increased government regulations of the accounting profession.	1	2	3	4
11.	Accounting curricula will have to change to reflect increased government regulations.	1	2	3	4
12.	The overall image and prestige of the accounting profession has been tarnished by the scandals.	1	2	3	4
13.	The number of companies developing in-house accounting departments, instead of outsourcing the services, will increase.	1	2	3	4
14.	There is nothing wrong with public accounting firms offering both accounting and financial consulting services.	1	2	3	4
15.	I feel the impact of the accounting scandals on the profession will be long-term.	1	2	3	4

Classification Information:

16. At what educational institution are you currently employed?
    _____ What is your position? _____
    Years experience? _____
17. What is your institution's current student enrollment?
    ___Less than 1,000
    ___1,001–5,000
    ___5,001–10,000
    ___10,001–15,000
    ___More than 15,001
18. What accounting degree programs are offered at your institution? (check all that apply)
    ___Associate's Degree
    ___Bachelor's Degree
    ___Master's Degree
    ___Doctor's Degree
19. Outside of education, do you have any other accounting experience?
    Yes ____No____ If so, in what field? _____
    How many years? _____
20. Are you a CPA? Yes ____No____

Discussion Questions

1   Are the study objectives and methodology appropriate for the information needs given in the case? Discuss.
2   Evaluate the questionnaire in relation to the research objectives. Are the appropriate topics covered? Is the sequence of questions logical? Is the structure of the individual questions appropriate for the needed data? Is the use of a 4 point scale with no neutral point appropriate? Discuss.

SPSS Applications

Use the SPSS file to analyze the data and answer the following questions:

1   Are there significant differences in the responses to individual statements between the two groups-mail and Internet?
2   Are there significant differences among respondents on the 15 statements?
3   On the basis of the analysis, what conclusions can be drawn on the basis of this research?

This case was prepared by Dr. Robert Stevens, Southeastern Oklahoma State University and Dr. C. William McConkey, University of Louisiana at Monroe, retired. Names, selected data, and corporate identities have been disguised.

Case 20 Louisiana Purchase Gardens and Zoo

Louisiana Purchase Gardens and Zoo's Director had just taken over management of the property after a successful turnaround of another zoo located in an adjacent state. One of the first things he noticed was a lack of any meaningful data from the target market served by the property. While fairly accurate attendance records were maintained from ticket sales, there was very little other data to use to develop a marketing plan to increase awareness and attendance.

The Louisiana Purchase Gardens and Zoo opened to the public in 1923. It was remodeled in 1967 with a $2.5 million dollar rebuilding phase, opening to the public once again in 1971. The property consists of 83 acres with another 80 acres available for future development. Louisiana Purchase Gardens and Zoo is subsidized each year by a $500,000 grant from the city park commission.

The Director sought help from the local university to develop a research project to collect the data he felt he needed as input to the marketing plan he wanted to put together and present to the park commission board. The project was taken on by a group of students in a marketing research class as their semester project. Excerpts from their proposal along with a questionnaire are shown below.

Detailed Study Objectives

The market research study objectives were as follows:

1 Determine the features that consumers desire in a zoo.
   - Size
   - Location
   - Cost
   - Local businesses
   - Others
2 Evaluate the importance of these features to consumers.
3 Evaluate the community's perception of the zoo.
   - Positive
   - Negative
   - Indifferent
4 Evaluate the community's knowledge of the zoo.
   - Ability to locate the zoo
   - Types of exhibits
   - Promotional events
5 Determine consumer awareness.

6   Determine the present consumer's usage of the zoo.
- Within the last month
- One to six months ago
- Seven to twelve months ago
- Over one year ago
- Over two years ago
- Do not know

7   Develop and evaluate the profile of consumers according to:
- Consumer Classifications
  - Age
  - Marital Status
  - Children
  - Income
  - Education
  - Sex
  - Geographic Areas
- Relationship with Zoo
  - Attended
  - Not Attended

Methodology

We propose collecting data from a random sample of 100 area residents using a telephone survey. The new telephone directory, which includes most of the listing for the parish, will be used as a sampling frame. A questionnaire will be developed to help estimate awareness, usage patterns, and concerns respondents have about the Louisiana Purchase Gardens and Zoo.

The frequency of responses to each question will be measured along with cross tabulations by demographics such as sex, age, marital status, and income. Tests of statistical significance will be used where appropriate.

The respondents will be surveyed using a structured questionnaire designed to respond to the project's specific study objectives. The information gathered from the structured telephone survey will be edited, tabulated, and processed by computer to provide a comprehensive set of tables and cross tabulations. These tables include percentages, mean scores, and cross tabulations that are required to answer the research questions.

Proposed Questionnaire

Interviewer: _____
Telephone number: _____
Person interviewed: _____
Date of interview: _____

Louisiana Purchase Gardens & Zoo

"Hi, my name is _____, and I'm a student at the University. As part of a class project we are conducting a marketing research project among local residents. Am I speaking with the man/lady of the household? Would you mind taking a few moments to answer a few questions? Your answers will remain confidential and will be combined with the answers of other respondents. We are not trying to sell anything, and it will only take a few minutes."

1. How long have you resided in this parish?
   ___less than a year[1]
   ___1–5 years[2]
   ___6–10 years[3]
   ___11–15 years[4]
   ___16–20 years[5]
   ___more than 20 years[6]

2. Have you ever heard of the Louisiana Purchase Gardens & Zoo? (if 'no', skip to #8)
   ___yes[1]
   ___no[2]
   If 'yes', how did you hear about it?
   ___saw sign[1]
   ___newspaper ad[2]
   ___television ad[3]
   ___radio[4]
   ___word of mouth[5]
   ___don't know[6]
   ___other[7] _____
   If 'no', do you know where it is located? (yes[1]) or (no[2]) ____

3. Have you ever visited the Louisiana Purchase Gardens & Zoo? (if 'no', skip to #7)
   ___yes[1] (if 'yes', answer 12a)
   ___no[2] (if 'no', answer 12b)
   If 'yes', when was the last time you went?
   ___within the last month[1]
   ___1–6 months ago[2]
   ___7–12 months ago[3]
   ___over one year ago[4]
   ___over two years ago[5]
   ___don't know[6]

4. Have you ever attended: (check all that apply)
   ___Zoobilation?
   ___Boo at the Zoo?

5. While at the zoo, did you feel safe?
   ___yes[1]
   ___no[2]
   If 'no', why? _____

6. Did you notice security on the grounds of the zoo at all times?
   ___yes[1]
   ___no[2]

7. While on vacation, have you ever been to: (check all that apply)
   ___the Jackson Zoo?
   ___the Alexandria Zoo?
   ___the Audubon Zoo in New Orleans?
   ___other
   If 'yes' to any of the above, when was the last time you went?
   ___within the last month[1]
   ___1–6 months ago[2]
   ___7–12 months ago[3]
   ___over one year ago[4]
   ___over two years ago[5]
   ___don't know[6]

8. Have you ever been to: (check all that apply)
   ___the Biedenharn Museum & Gardens?
   ___the Northeast Louisiana Children's Museum?
   ___the Masur Museum of Art?
   ___Kiroli Park & Gardens?
   ___Antique Alley?
   ___the Aviation Historical Museum of Louisiana Inc.?

9. If the Louisiana Purchase Gardens & Zoo formed 'partnerships' with other organizations in order to offer discounts, would you be more likely to attend?
   ___yes[1]
   ___no[2]

10. If the company you worked for sponsored a 'family day' at the zoo, would you be likely to attend?
   ___yes[1]
   ___no[2]
   ___not applicable[3]

11. Specifically, what would attract you to the Louisiana Purchase Gardens & Zoo on a more frequent basis? _____

12a. (if 'yes' to #3) Please rate the following items pertaining to the Louisiana Purchase Gardens & Zoo on how important each of them is to you personally on a scale of 1 to 5 with 1 being the least important and 5 being the most important: least important most important

admission price	1	2	3	4	5
number of animals	1	2	3	4	5
condition of the animals	1	2	3	4	5
zoo personnel	1	2	3	4	5
quality of the facilities	1	2	3	4	5
rides	1	2	3	4	5
food/snack bar	1	2	3	4	5
gift shop	1	2	3	4	5
location	1	2	3	4	5
hours of operation	1	2	3	4	5

12b. (if 'no' to #3) Please rate the following items pertaining to any zoo on how important each of them is to you personally on a scale of 1 to 5 with 1 being the least important and 5 being the most important: least important most important

admission price	1	2	3	4	5
number of animals	1	2	3	4	5
condition of the animals	1	2	3	4	5
zoo personnel	1	2	3	4	5
quality of the facilities	1	2	3	4	5
ides	1	2	3	4	5
food/snack bar	1	2	3	4	5
gift shop	1	2	3	4	5
location	1	2	3	4	5
hours of operation	1	2	3	4	5

13. Are you:
   ___male[1]
   ___female[2]

14. Are you:
    ___single/divorced/widowed with no children[1]
    ___single/divorced/widowed with no children at home[2]
    ___single/divorced/widowed with children at home[3]
    ___married with no children[4]
    ___married with no children at home[5]
    ___married with children at home[6]
    if 'yes' to children: how many _____
    what are their ages _____

15. Which age category do you fit into:
    ___18–25 years old[1]
    ___26–34 years old[2]
    ___35–44 years old[3]
    ___45–54 years old[4]
    ___55–64 years old[5]
    ___65 and older[6]

16. What category best describes your family's total income:
    ___less than $10,000[1]
    ___$10,001–$20,000[2]
    ___$20,001–$40,000[3]
    ___$40,001–$60,000[4]
    ___$60,001–$80,000[5]
    ___$80,001–$100,000[6]
    ___over $100,000[7]

17. What is the highest level of education you have completed:
    ___did not complete high school[1]
    ___high school graduate[2]
    ___high school with some college[3]
    ___college graduate[4]
    ___college graduate with some graduate work[5]
    ___graduate degree holder[6]

18. What is your race:
    ___Caucasian[1]
    ___African-American[2]
    ___Hispanic[3]
    ___Asian[4]
    ___other[5]

19. What is your occupation:
    ___homemaker[1]
    ___student[2]
    ___laborer[3]
    ___skilled worker[4]
    ___professional[5]
    ___retired[6]
    ___other[7]

Discussion Questions

1   Are the study objectives and methodology appropriate for management's information needs given in the case? Discuss.
2   Evaluate the questionnaire in relation to the research objectives. Are the appropriate topics covered? Is the sequence of questions logical? Is the structure of the individual questions appropriate for the needed data?
3   Evaluate the sampling process and sample size. Is a sample of 100 adequate to represent the population? Is the telephone book a good sampling frame? What problems could the sampling frame and sample cause in this situation?

SPSS Applications

Use the SPSS file to analyze the data and answer the following questions:

1   What is the demographic profile of respondents surveyed?
2   What is the overall awareness of Louisiana Purchase Gardens and Zoo?
3   How did respondents hear about Louisiana Gardens and Zoo and what does this tell you about the effectiveness of their advertising?
4   How did respondents rate Louisiana Purchase Gardens and Zoo on the 10 items included in the questionnaire?
5   Are there significant differences among respondents on the ratings of the 10 factors listed in Question 12a?

This case was prepared by Dr. Robert Stevens Southeastern Oklahoma State University and Dr. David Loudon, Samford University . Names, selected data, and corporate identities have been disguised.

Case 21 Mac's Sausage Company

Mac's Sausage Company is a custom slaughter and processing plant, which was established in 1988. Mac's Sausage Company currently distributes smoked sausage to a few select grocers in a local metropolitan area. Mac's prepares three different flavors of smoked sausage: regular, jalapeno, and jalapeno and cheese.

Jim MacDonald contracted with a consultant to perform a study in the local area. The study was to be conducted to assess the consumption patterns and awareness levels of area consumers regarding Mac's Sausage Company products. The main objective of the study was to determine the feasibility, from a consumer perspective, of increasing sales volume from 500–700 pounds per week to 3000–5000 pounds per week, while gaining two new accounts per month over the next few years. The resulting survey was to (1) identify levels of sausage consumption, (2) identify levels of awareness, (3) identify demographic characteristics, (4) evaluate results based on factors important to sausage users, and (5) develop strategic implications of results.

Excerpts from the consultant's proposal and the questionnaire to be used in the study are shown below.

Study Objectives

The market research study objectives are as follows:

1 Identify the levels of sausage consumption in the area.
   - Frequency of consumption
   - Price sensitivity
   - Quality preferences
   - Serving size preferences
   - Brand preference
   - Flavor preference
2 Identify levels of brand awareness in the area.
   - Unaided awareness
   - Aided awareness
3 Identify demographics
   - Age
   - Sex
   - Occupation
   - Income
   - Education
   - Marital Status
   - Ethnic Group
4 Evaluate results based on factors important to sausage users.

Research Methodology

A cluster probability sample approach will be used in the study. To insure a quality sample, a total of 115 respondents will be randomly selected from the area telephone book.

The respondents will be surveyed using a structured questionnaire designed to answer the research objectives. Before the questionnaire is administered, it will be pre-tested to insure clarity and accuracy. Information gathered from the questionnaire will be edited, tabulated, and processed by the SPSS software program to provide a comprehensive set of tables, frequencies, cross tabulations, and statistical tests. The tables include data of frequencies and percentages. Frequencies were run to determine awareness levels, important purchase factors, brand and flavor preferences.

Proposed Questionnaire

Telephone Number_____
Person Interviewed_____
Interviewer_____

McCain Farms, Inc Study

"Is the man or woman of the house in?"

"Hi! My name is _____. I'm with Triad Consulting and we are conducting a survey among local residents. Would you mind taking a few moments and answer some questions for me? Your answers will remain confidential and will be combined with the answer of other respondents. (If yes, go to question 1)

1. How long have you been a resident of the area?
   ___Less than 5 years[1] ___11–20 years[3]
   ___6–10 years[2] ___More than 20 years[4]
2. How many people live at your home?
   ___One[1] ___Three[3]
   ___Two[2] ___Four or more[4]
3. How many times a month do you shop for groceries?
   ___ 1–3[1] ___11–12[4]
   ___ 4–6[2] ___Over 12[5]
   ___ 7–10[3]
4. Do you ever prepare meals that include smoked sausage?
   ___Yes[1] ___No[2] [skip to #12]
5. How many times per year do you prepare meals that include smoked sausage?
   ___1–2[1] ___5–6[3] ___8–9[5] ___12 or more[7]
   ___3–4[2] ___ 6–7[4] ___10–11[6]
6. Please rate how the following factors affect your purchase of smoked sausage with 1 being very unimportant to 4 being very important.

Price	1	2	3	4
Quality	1	2	3	4
Brand Name	1	2	3	4
Size of Servings	1	2	3	4

7. Do you have a brand preference for smoked sausage?
   ___Yes[1] (if yes, what brand_____) ___No[2]

8. Do you have flavor preference in smoked sausage?
   ___Yes[1] (If yes, what flavor _____) ___No[2]
9. Have you ever heard of Mac's Sausage Company smoked sausage?
   ___Yes[1] ___No[2] [Skip to #12]
10. Have you purchased Mac's Sausage Company smoked sausage?
    ___Yes[1] ___No[2] [Skip to #12]
11. Please rate McCain Farms smoked sausage with 1 being very satisfied to 4 being very dissatisfied.

Price	1	2	3	4
Quality	1	2	3	4
Taste	1	2	3	4
Size of Servings	1	2	3	4

12. Which age category do you fit into?
    ___18–24[1] ___45–54[4]
    ___25–34[2] ___55–64[5]
    ___35–44[3] ___65 and older[6]
13. Sex: (Don't ask!)
    ___Male[1] ___Female[2]
14. Which of the following categories contains your family's annual income?
    ___Less than $10,000[1]
    ___$10,001–$30,000[2]
    ___$30,001–$50,000[3]
    ___$50,001–$70,000[4]
    ___$70,001–$90,000[5]
    ___$90,001 –$100,000[6]
    ___Over $100,000[7]
15. What is the occupation of the chief income earner in your household?
    ___Clerical[1]
    ___Student[2]
    ___Laborer[3]
    ___Skilled craftsman[4]
    ___Business owner/manager[5]
    ___Retired[6]
    ___Other, please specify[7]_____
16. What is the highest level of education you have obtained? (Don't read choices)
    ___Did not complete high school[1]
    ___High school graduate[2]
    ___High School graduate with some college[3]
    ___College graduate[4]
    ___College graduate with some graduate work[5]
    ___Graduate degree[6]
17. What is you current family status?
    ___Single[1] (with no children)
    ___Single[2] (with children)
    ___Married[3] (with no children)
    ___Divorced[4] (with no children)
    ___Widowed[5] (with no children)
    ___Married with children at home[6]
    ___Divorced with children at home[7]

___Widowed with children at home[8]
18. What is your race?
    ___Caucasian[1]
    ___Oriental[2]
    ___Hispanic[3]
    ___African-American[4]
    ___Other[5]

Thank you for your time and cooperation

Discussion Questions

1   Are the study objectives and methodology appropriate for management's information needs given in the case? Discuss.
2   Evaluate the questionnaire in relation to the research objectives. Are the appropriate topics covered? Is the sequence of questions logical? Is the structure of the individual questions appropriate for the needed data?
3   Evaluate the sampling process and sample size. Is a sample of 115 adequate to represent the population? Is the telephone book a good sampling frame? What problems could the sampling frame and sample cause in this situation?

SPSS Applications

Use the SPSS file to analyze the data and answer the following questions:

1   What is the demographic profile of respondents surveyed?
2   What is the overall awareness of Mac's Sausage Company?
3   How did respondents rate the four items on sausage consumption included in the questionnaire?
4   Are there significant differences among respondents on the ratings of these factors?

This case was prepared by Dr. Robert Stevens, Southeastern Oklahoma State University and Dr. David Loudon, Samford University . Names, selected data, and corporate identities have been disguised.

Case 22   The Online Marketplace

Late one night while Jack Reynolds was looking through items for sale on eBay, he had what he thought was a fabulous idea. He figured there must be a lot of people in the surrounding area that would be interested in buying and selling things online, but just didn't know how to go about doing it – or didn't have the time. His idea, The Online Marketplace, would be a local company who would assist people in buying and selling things they had online. He had seen garage sales all spring and summer this year as he drove to work each day, so he knew that people had things they wanted to sell. His company would help facilitate the sale by offering several different services.

The Online Marketplace would set up an eBay site for the seller, provide a post office box for receiving payment via check and money order, provide fax and copying services, and would take care of all the logistics in mailing sold items. Jack had a hunch that this idea would be profitable, but he didn't want to make any financial investments until he had some additional information. He contacted a local marketing research firm to see if they could provide some information about consumers in the local area and their likelihood to use an online marketplace. The research firm submitted a proposal that included the following.

Detailed Study Objectives

The market research study objectives were as follows:

1   Determine the frequency of the residents' buying and selling activity
2   Determine the residents' current methods of buying and selling items.
   - Through garage sales
   - Through the newspaper
   - On the internet
   - At pawnshops
   - At estate sales
3   Evaluate the level of interest in the type of services the online marketplace would offer, including the willingness to pay for the service.
   - Their level of interest in an online service
   - If not interested, the reasons for disinterest
   - What price they would be willing to pay for the service
4   Evaluate differences in the activity levels by demographic profile.
   - By age
   - By gender
   - By occupation
   - By race

- By level of household income
- By zip code
- By time living in the area

5   Evaluate differences in the interest in an on-line marketplace by demographic profile.

- By age
- By gender
- By occupation
- By race
- By level of household income
- By zip code
- By time living in the area

Methodology

Consumers in six small towns in the surrounding area will be contacted through a telephone survey to determine the following: 1) length of time they had been in the area, 2) their experience with buying and selling items through several types of venues, including the internet, 3) the number of times they bought or sold items through these venues, 4) their interest in an on-line marketplace, and 5) the demographic profile of respondents.

To accomplish the research objectives, a random sample of 113 respondents from the six towns will be selected, including both sellers and non-sellers of personal items. The sample will be selected from the local towns' telephone directories. A structured questionnaire will be developed specifically for this project and will be pre-tested with a group of volunteers prior to conducting the telephone survey. The data will be analyzed through various types of statistical techniques, including t-tests, ANOVA, frequency tables, and chi-square analysis. Information will be provided in the form of percentages, mean scores, and recommendations.

Proposed Questionnaire

Interviewer_____

Telephone number_____

Date_____

"Hello my name is_____ and I am with Services Research Association and we are conducting a study in the local area. We are asking local residents about how they buy and sell personal items. This interview takes a few minutes of your time and we'd appreciate your cooperation. Your responses will be confidential and used in combination with the responses of other people.

1.   How long have you lived in this area?
   ___Less than a year[1]
   ___1–5 years[2]
   ___6–10 years[3]
   ___11–15 years[4]
   ___16–20 years[5]
   ___more than 20 years[6]

2.   Have you ever bought or sold anything from the following? (mark all that apply)
   ___garage sales
   ___newspaper
   ___pawnshops

___estate sale
___internet
If internet: which websites?

_____

3. How often do you use these services?
   ___Once a month[1] (read choices)
   ___twice a month[2]
   ___once every 3 months[3]
   ___once every 6 months[4]
   ___once a year[5]
   ___other[6] _____
4. Do you use any outside sources to assist in your buying or selling?
   Used items? ___Yes[1] ___No[2]
   If yes: What sources? _____
   If internet was not chosen on question 3, ask questions 5 and 6
5. Do you have access to a computer? ___Yes[1] ___No[2]
   If yes: Do you have access to the internet? ___Yes[1] ___No[2]
6. Have you considered using the internet to buy or sell items?
   Yes[1] ___   No[2]___
7. Would you be interested in a service that would package, store, and sell your items for you on the internet?
   Yes[1]___   No[2]___
   If yes what percentage of the selling price would you be willing to pay for such a service?
   ___5% or less   ___21–25%
   ___6–10%   ___26–30%
   ___11–15%   ___31–35%
   ___16–20%   ___over 35%
   If No, what are your main reasons for not being interested in such a service? (Mark all that apply)
   ___can do it myself
   ___don't trust others to sell
   ___may not get my price
   ___don't want to pay for such a service
   ___other
8. Sex: (Don't ask unless absolutely necessary)
   ___Male[1]
   ___Female[2]
9. Which of the following categories contains your age? (read)
   ___18–25[1]   ___45–54[4]
   ___26–34[2]   ___55–64[5]
   ___35–44[3]   ___65 and over[6]
10. What is your race? (read)
   _____Caucasian[1] _____Asian[4]
   _____African American[2]   _____Other[5]
   _____Hispanic[3]
11. What is your occupation? (read)
   ___homemaker[1]   ___skilled[4]
   ___student[2]   ___professional[5]
   ___laborer[3]   ___retired[6]

12. Which of the following categories contains your family's annual income? (read)
    ___less than $ 10,000[1]   ___$70,001–$90,000[5]
    ___$10,001–$30, 000[2]   ___$90,001–$100,000[6]
    ___$30,001–$50,000[3]   ___over $100,000[7]
    ___$50, 001–$70,000[4]

13 What is your Zip code____

Thank you very much for your time and cooperation

Discussion Questions

1 Are the study objectives and methodology appropriate for management's information needs given in the case? Discuss.
2 Evaluate the questionnaire in relation to the research objectives. Are the appropriate topics covered? Is the sequence of questions logical? Is the structure of the individual questions appropriate for the needed data?
3 Evaluate the sampling process and sample size. Is a sample of 113 respondents from six small towns adequate to represent the population? Are the local telephone books a good sampling frame? Why or why not? What problems could the sampling frame and sample cause in this situation?

SPSS Application

Use the SPSS file to analyze the data and answer the following questions:

1 Prepare a demographic profile of the respondents surveyed.
2 What types of selling techniques (garage sales, internet, etc.) do the respondents use? What is their frequency of use for these types of sales techniques?
3 How many of the respondents have considered using the internet to buy or sell items? What number of them would be interested in using an internet sales service to help them in their on-line activity? If respondents are not interested in this type of service, what are their reasons?
4 For those respondents who are interested in the internet service, what percentage of the sales price would the majority of them be willing to pay?
5 Are there significant differences among respondents based on demographics for the following:
   a. Have they ever considered the internet to buy or sell items?
   b. How often do they use buying/selling services (garage sales, etc.)?
   c. Are they interested in an internet support service?
   d. If interested, what percentage would they be willing to pay?

This case was prepared by Dr. Robert Stevens, Southeastern Oklahoma State University and Dr. Phylis Mansfield, Pennsylvania State University Erie, Names, selected data, and corporate identities have been disguised.

Case 23   Victorian Rose Gift and Flower Shop

Rose Jackson, owner of Victorian Rose Gift and Flower Shop, is considering expanding into other segments of the market, specifically, the small business segment. She has been quite successful for the past twenty years as a florist selling primarily to individual customers however she knows that the business market may be different from the consumer market. She is interested in finding out what factors small businesses use in the selection of a florist, as well as their awareness of and attitude toward Victorian Rose. She would also like to know what their usage patterns are when it comes to buying floral gifts.

While Ms. Jackson has accumulated data for the past several years on her customers' buying habits, she doesn't have a clue as to what the small businesses think. She has decided to contact a local marketing research firm to see if they can help her find this information. Excerpts from the proposal they have developed are shown in the following paragraphs.

Detailed Study Objectives

To guide the research project, the following objectives were developed:

1 Determine the factors that influence the choice of a florist by small businesses
   - Quality
   - Promptness
   - Friendly service
   - Delivery
   - Reasonable prices
   - Variety
   - Cleanliness of shop
   - Atmosphere
2 Evaluate the satisfaction levels with current florists.
   - Atmosphere
   - Cleanliness
   - Delivery
   - Promptness
   - Quality
   - Friendly service
   - Reasonable prices
   - Variety

3   Determine small businesses' floral purchase patterns for certain holidays and/or special situations.
  - Birthdays
  - Boss' day
  - Christmas
  - Funerals
  - Secretary's day
  - Thanksgiving
  - Valentine's day

4   Determine the demographic profile of the small business customer.

Methodology

To accomplish the research objectives, data will be gathered through a telephone survey, which will be developed specifically for this project and pre-tested for clarity. The survey will be administered to a random sample, which will be drawn from the local Yellow Pages phone directory of 100 small businesses in the area. The sample may include both current and prospective business customers. The survey will be administered by a trained staff of interviewers. The data collected will be analyzed using SPSS software and various statistical techniques. The analyses will provide information in the form of percentages and mean scores.

The main purpose of this study will be to determine the potential market demand for the services of Victorian Rose Gift and Flower Shop. The study will also evaluate perceptions of Victorian Rose, the businesses' satisfaction with current florist services, and a profile of the business customer. Information and implications for market expansion will be presented to guide Ms. Jackson in her business decision.

Proposed Questionnaire

Telephone Number: _____
Person Interviewed: _____
Interviewer: _____

Telephone Survey for Victorian Rose

Hello. Am I currently speaking to the owner or manager of _____? (If not, ask to speak to the owner/manager).
Hello. My name is _____. I am with Services Research Association and I am conducting a marketing research survey on the awareness and attitude of people toward local flower and gift shops. Would you please help me by answering a few questions? Your responses will be confidential and used in combination with the responses of other people.

1. Do you ever purchase flowers and gifts?
    _____ Yes   _____No (if no terminate)
2. How often do you purchase flowers or related items?
    ___0–5 months __6–12months __1–2years __Never __Weekly __Other
    (Specify)_____

3. On what occasions would you most likely purchase flowers? (Mark all that apply.)
    ___Birthdays
    ___Boss' Day
    ___Christmas
    ___Funerals
    ___Secretary's Day
    ___Thanksgiving
    ___Valentine's Day
    ___Other (Specify)_____

4. Please rate each of the following factors in terms of their importance in selecting a florist
    with
    1 being very important, 2 being important, 3 being somewhat important, and 4 being not
    important.

Atmosphere	1	2	3	4
Cleanliness	1	2	3	4
Friendly services	1	2	3	4
Prompt service	1	2	3	4
Quality of flowers	1	2	3	4
Variety of flowers and gifts	1	2	3	4
Reasonable prices	1	2	3	4
Delivery services	1	2	3	4

5. Which florist do you most frequently buy floral arrangements from?
    ___Brook's Florists
    ___College Town Florists
    ___The Flower Basket
    ___Grand Floral
    ___Green Earth
    ___Henderson's Flower Shop
    ___LaPetite Fleur
    ___Maxwell's Florist
    ___McMullen Flower Shop
    ___Monroe City Florist Inc.
    ___Mulhearn Flowers Inc.
    ___Patti's Flower & Wholesale
    ___Rhapsody in Bloom
    ___Roark's North Monroe Flower & Gifts
    ___Tisket-A-Tasket
    ___Victorian Rose Flower & Gifts
    ___Vee's Flowers
    ___Westside Flower & Gift Shop
    ___Other _____

6. Have you ever heard of Victorian Rose Flower and Gifts?
    ____ Yes   ____No (If no go to number 11)

7. How did you hear about Victorian Rose?
    _____ Billboards
    _____ Newspaper
    _____ Word of mouth
    _____ Television
    _____ Radio
    _____ Other _____

8. Have you ever purchased anything from Victorian Rose?
    _____ Yes   _____No (If no go to number11)
9. How often do you make purchases from Victorian Rose?
    ___1–3 times a week
    ___4–6 times a week
    ___6 or more times a week
    ___Once a month
    ___Once a year
    ___Other _____
10. Please rate your satisfaction with Victorian Rose on the following factors with 1 being
    very satisfied, 2 being somewhat satisfied, 3 being somewhat dissatisfied, and 4 being very
    dissatisfied.

Atmosphere	1	2	3	4
Cleanliness	1	2	3	4
Friendly services	1	2	3	4
Prompt service	1	2	3	4
Quality of flowers	1	2	3	4
Variety of flowers and gifts	1	2	3	4
Reasonable prices	1	2	3	4
Delivery services	1	2	3	4

11. How likely are you to switch florists?
    ___Extremely
    ___Fairly
    ___Maybe
    ___Never

Now, I have a few questions about your company.

12. Which category best describes your business?
    ___Retailer
    ___Wholesaler
    ___Manufacturer
    ___Service
13. How many employees do you currently have?
    ___Less than 15 employees
    ___16 to 25 employees
    ___26 to 35 employees
    ___36 to 45 employees
    ___46 to 55 employees
    ___56 to 65 employees
    ___66 to 75 employees
    ___over 75 employees
14. How long have you been in this area?
    ___Less than 5 years   ___5 to 10 years
    ___11 to 15 years   ___16 to 20 years
    ___21 to 25 years   ___26 to 30 years
    ___31 to 35 years   ___36 to 40 years
    ___41 to 45 years   ___46 to 50 years
    ___over 50 years

This concludes our survey. Thank you for your time and cooperation.

Discussion Questions

1 Are the study objectives and methodology appropriate for management's information needs given in the case? Discuss.
2 Evaluate the questionnaire in relation to the research objectives. Are the appropriate topics covered? Is the sequence of the questions logical? Is the structure of the individual questions appropriate for the needed data? Are they appropriate for the method of survey collection?
3 Evaluate the sampling process and sample size. Is a sample of 100 small businesses adequate to represent the total population in the area? Is the use of the telephone directory a good sampling frame for the population being studied? What problems could the sampling frame and sample cause in this situation?

SPSS Applications

Use the SPSS file to analyze the data and answer the following questions:

1 What is the demographic profile of the respondents surveyed?
2 What is the importance level of various factors when small businesses are selecting a florist?
3 How aware are the respondents of the floral shop, Victorian Rose? Where did they receive their information about Victorian Rose? Have they ever purchased flowers from Victorian Rose?
4 How satisfied are the small business respondents with their current florist? Provide specific satisfaction levels for the different elements (atmosphere, cleanliness, etc.).
5 What is the likelihood of the respondents' purchasing flowers on holidays and special situations?

This case was prepared by Dr. Robert Stevens, Southeastern Oklahoma State University and Dr. Phylis Mansfield, Pennsylvania State University Erie. Names, selected data, and corporate identities have been disguised.

Case 24 MCS Publishing Company

In 1992, MCS Publishing launched its first academic business journal because of the demand for more outlets for college professors to publish their research. Because the primary accreditation agency for colleges of business required professors to demonstrate currency in their discipline through research and publishing of their findings, the demand for appropriate journal outlets grew. Within the next five years, 23 more journal titles were added. MCS's success in this arena was due primarily to its printing technology and ability to print small volumes of a publication at a profit.

The success of these journals spurred the management at MCS to consider the college textbook market. A sale of textbooks and related materials is estimated at $6.9 billon dollars (National Association of College Stores, www.nacs.org/public/research/higher_ed_retail.asp, March 16, 2006). While MCS recognized it did not have the resources to compete with the large publishers such as McGraw-Hill, Thomson, and Prentice-Hall, they believed the market was large enough for them to capture a small portion and make a profit doing it. Thus, the decision was made to enter this market by focusing on a subset of the market – colleges of business.

MCS had already developed relationships with business professors through its academic journals since many served as editors, co-editors, and on editorial review boards. Business publications accounted for over half of their academic journals. The company already had the technology to print textbooks, they owned their own printing presses, and they already had a highly-developed database of business professors throughout the United States. The only thing MCS did not have was an understanding of the process business professors used in deciding on a particular textbook.

To gather this critical information, MCS contracted with a marketing research firm in Louisiana. The firm prepared a research proposal and used MCS's current list of business professors as their sampling frame. Excerpts of their research proposal as well as the questionnaire follow.

Detailed Study Objectives

The market research study objectives were as follows:

1   Identify the relative importance of various criteria used in the adoption of a textbook.
    - Content
    - Edition of text
    - Author(s) of text
    - Advertising
    - Cost
    - Length
    - Online material

2 Identify the relative importance of various ancillary materials.
- Test bank (electronic and paper)
- PowerPoint slides (basic and video-enhanced)
- Online materials (testing, quizzes, class material)
- Instructor's manual (CD and paper)
- Cases
- Videos

3 Explore reasons a professor switches textbooks.

4 Determine desirability of various methods of promoting a textbook.
- Direct contact (email, telephone, direct mail)
- Publisher's website
- Examination copy
- Advertisements
- Booth displays at conferences
- Contact by book reps

5 Determine desirability and frequency of contact methods.
- Method (personal visit, telephone, e-mail)
- Frequency of current contact
- Frequency of desired contact

6 Explore the helpfulness of direct mail promotions.
- Specific book promotion
- Multiple book promotion

7 Evaluate various book promotion options in terms of encouraging a professor to take a closer look at a new book.
- Email
- Direct mail
- Magazine
- Website
- Telephone
- Contact by book rep
- Examination copy

8 Evaluate impact of demographic information on textbook adoption.
- Years of teaching experience
- Rank
- School size

Methodology

MCS's business professor database contained 13,041 names and corresponding email addresses. Since the professors represented a good cross-section of universities throughout all of the United States, the marketing research firm believed the database was a good representation of the business professor population.

An email was sent to each of the 13,041 names in the database asking the individual if they would be willing to participate in the research. Embedded in the email was a link to the actual survey. Once the survey was completed, it was submitted by the respondent to the marketing research firm.

For various reasons, such as wrong email address, insufficient email address, or the email was viewed as spam by the university's email filter system, 1,274 emails were returned. This resulted in 11,767 emails being delivered. From this sample, 1,192 responded to the questionnaire, yielding a response rate of 10.13 percent.

Individuals were surveyed using a structured-undisguised questionnaire approach. Responses were automatically tabulated by the computerized system and placed in an Excel spreadsheet. This process greatly reduced data entry errors by clerks. The data were then analyzed by using frequency counts and means of each item. Significance tests were conducted based on the respondent's rank, years of teaching experience, and the size of the institution.

Questionnaire

MCS Publishing

The Textbook Adoption Process Used by College of Business Professors

"For each of the statements listed below, please indicate your answer by clicking in the circle or box. If you teach more than one course, answer the questions for the course or courses you teach most frequently."

1) Please identify the relative importance of the following criteria in your decision to adopt a textbook.

	Very unimportant			Very important	
Content	1	2	3	4	5
Edition of text	1	2	3	4	5
Ancillary materials	1	2	3	4	5
Author(s) of text	1	2	3	4	5
Advertising of text	1	2	3	4	5
Cost of text	1	2	3	4	5
Length of text	1	2	3	4	5
Online textbook only	1	2	3	4	5
Online and hard copy	1	2	3	4	5

2) Please identify the relative importance of the following ancillary materials in your decision to adopt a textbook.

	Very unimportant			Very important	
Electronic test bank	1	2	3	4	5
Online testing	1	2	3	4	5
Hard copy of test bank	1	2	3	4	5
Video-enhanced PowerPoint slides	1	2	3	4	5
Basic PowerPoint slides	1	2	3	4	5
Hard copy of instructor's manual	1	2	3	4	5
Instructor's manual on CD	1	2	3	4	5
Cases	1	2	3	4	5
Online student quizzes	1	2	3	4	5
Online class material	1	2	3	4	5
CD for students	1	2	3	4	5
Videos	1	2	3	4	5

3. Why do you switch textbooks from the edition you are currently using? (Please mark all that apply.)
   ___Unhappy with the current textbook
   ___Unhappy with the publisher of the current textbook
   ___Dissatisfied with the ancillary materials of the current textbook
   ___New edition of my current text is coming out and I want to change
   ___Content of a new textbook
   ___New textbook is better suited to my teaching style
   ___Better ancillaries in the new textbook

4. In terms of learning about new textbooks, evaluate each of the following methods on a scale of 1 to 5 with 1 being very undesirable to 5 being very desirable.

	Very undesirable			Very desirable	
Email	1	2	3	4	5
Direct mail	1	2	3	4	5
Publisher's website	1	2	3	4	5
Telephone	1	2	3	4	5
Examination copy	1	2	3	4	5
Advertisements in media	1	2	3	4	5
Booth displays at conferences	1	2	3	4	5
Contact by book representative	1	2	3	4	5

5. In terms of communication from your book reps, how desirable are each of the following methods?

	Very undesirable			Very desirable	
Personal visit	1	2	3	4	5
Telephone contact	1	2	3	4	5
Email contact	1	2	3	4	5

6. How often, if at all, do book reps contact you?
   ___Four or more times a semester
   ___Two to three times a semester
   ___Once a semester
   ___Once a year
   ___Less than once a year
   ___Never

7. How often would you like to be contacted by your book rep?
   ___Four or more times a semester
   ___Two to three times a semester
   ___Once a semester
   ___Once a year
   ___Less than once a year

8. How helpful are the following types of direct mail promotions from a publisher?

	Not helpful			Very helpful	
Specific book promotions	1	2	3	4	5
Multiple book promotions in one piece	1	2	3	4	5

9. What, if any, types of book promotions encourage you to take a closer look at a textbook? Please rate each methodology below on a scale of 1 to 5 with 1 being most ineffective to 5 being most effective.

	Most ineffective				Most effective
Email	1	2	3	4	5
Direct mail	1	2	3	4	5
Magazine	1	2	3	4	5
Website	1	2	3	4	5
Telephone	1	2	3	4	5
Contact with book representative	1	2	3	4	5
Examination copy	1	2	3	4	5

10. How long have you been teaching?
    ___5 years or less
    ___6–10 years
    ___11–15 years
    ___16–20 years
    ___More than 20 years

11. What is your current rank?
    ___Adjunct
    ___Instructor
    ___Assistant professor
    ___Associate professor
    ___Full professor

12. What is your institution's current student enrollment?
    ___Less than 1,000
    ___1,000–4,999
    ___5,000–9,999
    ___10,000–14,999
    ___15,000–19,999
    ___20,000–24,999
    ___25,000 or more

Discussion Questions

1 Are the study objectives and methodology appropriate for management's information needs given in the case? Discuss.
2 Evaluate the questionnaire in relation to the research objectives. Are the appropriate topics covered? Is the sequence of questions logical? Is the structure of the individual questions appropriate for the needed data?
3 Evaluate the sampling process and sample size. What type of sampling methodology is being used? Is the publishing company's professor database a good sampling frame since it does not contain the e-mails of every business professor within the United States? What problems could the sampling frame and sample cause in this situation?

Basic SPSS Applications

Use the SPSS file to analyze the data and answer the following questions:

1 What is the demographic profile of the respondents in this survey?
2 What criteria do professors use in selecting a textbook?
3 How important are the various ancillary materials provided by publishing companies?
4 Why do professors switch textbooks?
5 In terms of learning about new books, what methods are the most desirable?
6 How are professors being contacted by book reps? How often are professors being contacted and how does that compare to what they prefer?
7 What types of book promotions encourage a professor to take a closer look at a textbook?

Advanced SPSS Applications

1 Are there any significant differences in responses based on the number of years an individual has been teaching? (For this analysis, it is recommended that you collapse the number of years the respondent has been teaching into three categories: 10 years or less, 11–20 years, and more than 20 years.)
2 Are there any significant differences in responses based on the respondent's rank? (For this analysis, it is recommended that you collapse the respondent's rank into three categories: Assistant and below, Associate, and Full.)
3 Does school size have any significant impact on the respondent's answers to the survey questions? (For this analysis, it is recommended that you collapse the student enrollment of the institution into four categories: Less than 5,000, 5,000–9,999, 10,000–19,999, and 20,000 or more.)

This case was prepared by Dr. Robert Stevens, Southeastern Oklahoma State University, Dr. David Loudon, Samford University and Dr. C. William McConkey, University of Louisiana at Monroe, retired. Names, selected data, and corporate identities have been disguised.

Notes

1 Introduction to Marketing Research

1. For a discussion of studies conducted on the value of being market oriented see Bruce Wrenn, "The Marketing Orientation Construct: Measurement and Scaling Issues," *Journal of Marketing Theory and Practice*, 5(3), (1997), 31–54.
2. "The Perils of Typecasting," *American Demographics*, (February 1997), p. 60; Karen Benezra, "Fritos Around the World," *Brandweek*, (March 27, 1995), p. 32; "Chinese Chee-tos," *The New York Times*, (November 27, 1994), p. 31; "Chee-tos Make Debut in China but Lose Cheese in Translation," *USA Today*, (September 2, 1994), B-1.
3. See John Yokum, "Invest for Success: It's Research That Makes Winning Programs," *Marketing News*, (June 6, 1994), 22.
4. Peter D. Bennett (ed.), *Dictionary of Marketing Terms* (Chicago: American Marketing Association, 1988), 117.
5. See William D. Neal, " 'Marketing' or 'Market' Research?" *The Research Report*, (Summer 1989), 1.
6. See William D. Perreault, Jr., "The Shifting Paradigm in Marketing Research," *Journal of the Academy of Marketing Science*, 20(4), (1992), 369–381.
7. See N. B. Zabriskie and A. B. Hurellmantel, "Marketing Research As a Strategic Tool," *Long-Range Planning*, 27, (1994), 107–118.
8. Christine Moorman, Gerald Yaltman, and Rohit Desponde, "Relationships Between Providers and Users of Marketing Research: The Dynamics of Trust Within and Between Organizations," *Journal of Marketing Research*, 24(3), (1992), 314–328.
9. Adapted from Irving D. Canton, "Do You Know Who Your Customer Is?" *Journal of Marketing*, (April 1976), 83.
10. Discussion of research purpose and research objective is adapted from David Aaker, V. Kumar, and George Day, *Marketing Research* (New York: John Wiley and Sons, 1998).

2 Ethics in Marketing Research

1. S. Alsmadi, "Marketing Research and Social Responsibility: Ethical Obligation Toward the Society," *Journal of Accounting, Business & Management*, 17(1), (2010) 42–47.
2. M. Constantineseu, "The Relationship Between Quality of Life and Marketing Ethics," *Romanian Journal of Marketing*, 6(3), (2011) 41–44.
3. http://www.casro.org/iso_faq.cfm Accessed 04/11/2012
4. Robert V. Kozinets, "The Field Behind the Screen: Using Netnography for Marketing Research in Online Communities," *Journal of Marketing Research*, 39(1), (2002) 68.
5. E. Head, "The Ethics and Implications of Paying Participants in Qualitative Research," *International Journal of Social Research Methodology*, 12 (4), (October 2009), 335–344.
6. Alsmadi,op. cit.
7. Chase E. Thiel, Zhanna Bagdasarov, Lauren Harkrider, James F. Johnson, and Michael D. Mumford "Leader Ethical Decision-Making in Organizations: Strategies for Sensemaking," *Journal of Business Ethics*, 107, (2012).49–64.

3 Secondary Data

1. See Marcia Stepanek, "Weblining," *Business Week E-Biz Supplement,* (April 3, 2000), pp. EB26–EB34.
2. See Heather Green, "The Information Gold Mine," *Business Week E-Biz Supplement,* (July 26, 1999), EB17–EB30.

4 Research Designs: Exploratory and Qualitative Research

1. G. Zaltman, "Rethinking Market Research: Putting People Back In," *Journal of Marketing Research,* 34(4), (1997) 454–437.
2. N. Denzin, and Y.S. Lincoln, "Introduction: Entering the Field of Qualitative Research," in N. K. Dentin and Y. S. Lincoln (eds), *Handbook of Qualitative Research:* 1–32. (Thousand Oaks, CA: Sage, 1994).
3. Pamela Mayut, *Beginning Qualitative Research: A Philosophical and Practical Guide.* (Brighton, Falmer Press, 1994).
4. N. Denzin, and Y.S. Lincoln, "Introduction: Entering the Field of Qualitative Research," in N. K. Dentin and Y. S. Lincoln (eds), *Handbook of Qualitative Research:* 1–32. (Thousand Oaks, CA: Sage, 1994).
5. See David Kiley, "Shoot the Focus Group," *Business Week*, (November 14, 2005), 120–121.
6. Gina Chon, "VW's American Road Trip," *Wall Street Journal,* (January 4, 2006), B1ff.
7. Emily Nelson "P&G Checks Out Real Life," *Wall Street Journal,* (May 17, 2001), B1ff.
8. Robert V. Kozinets, "The Field Behind the Screen: Using Ethnography for Marketing Research in Online Communities," *Journal of Marketing Research*, 39(1), (February 2002) 61–72.

5 Research Designs: Descriptive and Casual Research

1. Donald R. Cooper and Pamela S. Schindler, *Business Research Methods*, 10th edn, (New York: McGraw-Hill Irwin, 2008), 151.
2. Adapted from Gilbert A. Churchill, *Basic Marketing Research,* 2nd edn (Fort Worth, TX: Dryden Press, 1992), 130–131.
3. Robert Ferber, Donald F. Blankertz, and Stanley Hollander, *Marketing Research* (New York: The Ronald Press, 1964), 153.
4. Ibid., 171.
5. For a discussion of the ethics of marketing research see N. Craig Smith and John A. Quelch, "Ethical Issues in Researching and Targeting Consumers," in N. Craig Smith and John A. Quelch (eds.), *Ethics in Marketing*: 145–195 (Homewood, IL: Irwin, 1993).
6. Thomas C. Kinnear and James R. Taylor, *Marketing Research* (New York: McGraw-Hill, 1991), 285.
7. William R. Dillon, Thomas J. Madden, and Heil H. Firtle, *Marketing Research in a Marketing Environment*, 3rd edn (Burr Ridge, IL: Irwin, 1994), 180.
8. These points were taken from N. D. Cadbury, "When, Where, and How to Test Market," *Harvard Business Review,* (May–June 1985), 97–98.
9. "Test Marketing: What's in Store?" *Sales and Marketing Management,* 128 (March 15, 1982), 57–58.
10. Donald S. Tull and Del L. Hawkins, *Marketing Research,* 6th edn (New York: Macmillan, 1993), 252–258.
11. Material provided by the Burke Institute on their BASES simulated test-marketing program.

6 Measurement

1. Jim C. Nunnally, *Psychometric Theory,* 2nd edn (New York: McGraw-Hill, 1978), 3.
2. Shelby D. Hunt and Robert N. Morgan, "The Comparative Advantage Theory of Competition," *Journal of Marketing,* 59 (April 1995), 1–15.
3. Bruce Wrenn, "What Really Counts When Hospitals Adopt a Marketing Orientation: The Contribution of the Components of Marketing Orientation to Hospital Performance," *Journal of NonProfit and Public Sector Marketing,* 7(1/2), (1996), 111–133.
4. Bernard J. Jaworski and Ajay K. Kohl, "Marketing Orientation: Antecedents and Consequences," *Journal of Marketing,* 57 (July 1993), 53–70.
5. Gilbert Churchill, "A Paradigm for Developing Better Measures of Marketing Constructs," *Journal of Marketing Research,* 16 (February 1979), 64–73.

6. Robert D. Buzzell, Donald F. Cox, and Rex V. Brown, *Marketing Research and Information Systems: Text and Cases* (New York: McGraw-Hill, 1969), 133.
7. Joan Raymond, "For Richer and for Poorer," *American Demographics,* (July 2000), 58–64.
8. John B. Ford, Michael S. LaTour, and Tony L. Henthorne, "Perceptions of Marital Roles in Purchase Decision Processes: A Cross-Cultural Study," *Journal of the Academy of Marketing Science,* 23(2), (1995). 120–131.
9. J. Labrecque and L. Ricard, "Children's Influence on Family Decision-Making: A Restaurant Study," *Journal of Business Research* (November 2001), 173–176.
10. Michael D. Hutt and Thomas W. Spegh, *Industrial Marketing Management* (Hinsdale, IL: The Dryden Press, 1985), 65–69.
11. Thomas C. Kinnear and James R. Taylor, *Marketing Research* (New York: McGraw-Hill, 1996), 231.
12. For an in-depth discussion of the measure process see Jim C. Nunnally, *Psychometric Theory,* 2nd edn (New York: McGraw-Hill, 1978); Claire Selltiz, Lawrence S. Wrightsman, and Stuart W. Cook, *Research Methods in Social Relations,* 3rd edn (New York: Holt, Rinehart and Winston, 1976); Fred N. Kerlinger, *Foundations of Behavioral Research,* 3rd edn (New York: Holt, Rinehart and Winston, 1986).
13. For a discussion of some of the associations between attitudes and behavior see Richard Lutz, "The Role of Attitude Theory in Marketing," in Harold Kassarjian and Thomas Robertson (Eds.), *Perspectives in Consumer Behavior,*4th edn: 317–339 (Upper Saddle River, NJ: Prentice-Hall, 1991); John Mowen and Michael Minor, *Consumer Behavior.* 263 (Upper Saddle River, NJ: Prentice-Hall, 1998).
14. Gilbert A. Churchill, Jr. and J. Paul Peter, "Research Design Effects on the Reliability of Rating Scales: A Meta-Analysis," *Journal of Marketing Research,* 21 (November 1984), 360–375.
15. Rensis Likert, "A Technique for the Measurement of Attitudes," *Archives of Psychology,* 140, (1932).

7 Primary Data Collection

1. Joe L. Welch, "Research Marketing Problems and Opportunities with Focus Groups," *Industrial Marketing Management,* 14, (1985), 248.
2. Thomas L. Greenbaum, "Do You Have the Right Moderator for Your Focus Groups? Here Are 10 Questions to Ask Yourself," *Bank Marketing,* 23(1), (1991), 43.
3. *The Group Depth Interview,* 170–182.
4. The following sources were referred to in writing this section on Internet research: James Watt, "Using the Internet for Quantitative Survey Research," *Quirk's Marketing Research Review,* (June/July 1997), 18–19, 67–71; "Pro and Con: Internet Interviewing," *Marketing Research,* 11(2), (1999), 33–37; Diane K. Bowers, "FAQs on Online Research," *Marketing Research,* 10(4),(Winter 1998/Spring 1999), 45–49; Don Dillman, *Mail and Internet Surveys* (New York: John Wiley and Sons, 2000), 352–361.
5. See, for example, Don Dillman's *Internet, Mail, and Mixed-Mode Surveys: The Tailored Design Method,* New York: John Wiley and Sons, 2009
6. *Mail and Internet Surveys,* 356.

8 Designing the Data-gathering Instrument

1. Patricia Labaw, *Advanced Questionnaire Design* (Cambridge, MA: Abt Books, 1980), 12.
2. Ibid., 61.
3. See Stanley L. Payne, *The Art of Asking Questions* (Princeton, NJ: Princeton University Press, 1951); Seymour Sudman and Norman M. Bradburn, *Asking Questions: A Practical Guide to Questionnaire Design* (San Francisco, CA: Jossey-Bass, 1982); Jean M. Converse and Stanley Presser, *Survey Questions: Handcrafting the Standardized Questionnaire* (Beverly Hills, CA: Sage Publications, 1986). Another good source on designing and implementing a mail or Internet questionnaire is Don Dillman, *Mail and Internet Surveys* (New York: John Wiley and Sons, 2000).

9 Sampling Methods and Sample Size

1. This section is based upon a discussion in Seymour Sudman and Edward Blair, *Marketing Research* (New York: McGraw-Hill, 1998), 375–378. This book is an excellent reference for marketing research sampling issues.

10 Fielding the Data-gathering Instrument

1. Don A. Dillman, *Mail and Internet Surveys* (New York: John Wiley and Sons, 2000).
2. Technically, sampling frame error could be thought of as one subcategory of sampling error. However, we will follow convention and describe it here as a nonsampling error, and leave sample error to be that random error described in Chapter 7.

11 Analyzing and Interpreting Data for Decisions

1. Adapted from Philip Kotler, *Marketing Management* 8th edn (Englewood Cliffs, NJ: Prentice-Hall, 1994), 24
2. Some reference works for those readers interested in a more in-depth discussion of analysis include: For analysis of qualitative research see Matthew B. Miles and A. Michael Huberman, *Qualitative Data Analysis,* (Thousand Oaks, CA: Sage, 1994); Norman K. Denzin and Yvonna S. Lincoln (eds), *Handbook of Qualitative Research*, (Thousand Oaks, CA: Sage, 1994); Harry F. Wolcott, *Writing Up Qualitative Research,* (Thousand Oaks, CA: Sage, 1990). For statistical analysis, including multivariate statistical techniques see Sam Kash Kachigan, *Statistical Analysis* (New York: Radius Press, 1986); Joseph F. Hair, Ralph E. Anderson, Ronald L. Tatham, and William C. Black, *Multivariate Data Analysis*, 4th edn (Englewood Cliffs, NJ: Prentice-Hall, 1995). Harvey J. Brightman, *Statistics in Plain English* (Cincinnati: South-Western Publishing Co. 1986).
3. It should be noted, however, that there is definitely a place for research findings which may not lead to an immediate decision, but which educate decision makers in a more general way. Well-informed, knowledgeable decision makers are valuable by-products of the analysis of decision-oriented research information. Therefore, researchers would not fail to report findings which may not in themselves suggest a decision, but which serve to edify management in important ways about the company's markets, customers, or significant trends in the environment.
4. We will assume that the researcher/analyst has a computer printout which shows both the mean and standard deviation (and standard error of the mean) for the intervally scaled questions in the survey. Readers who desire more information on how to compute and interpret standard deviations and other descriptive or inferential statistics are referred to any of the standard statistical texts such as the Kachigan or Brightman books listed in note 2.
5. See for example, pp. 342–356 of the Kachigan book listed in note 2.

12 Advanced Data Analysis

1. Much of this discussion of hypothesis testing is adapted from Harvey J. Brightman's *Statistics in Plain English* (Cincinnati, OH: South-Western Publishing Co., 1986), 160–173.
2. See Paul Newbold, *Statistics for Business and Economics* (Englewood Cliffs, NJ: Prentice-Hall, 1991).
3. Fred N. Kerlinger, *Foundations of Behavioral Research*, 3rd edn (New York: Holt, Rinehart and Winston, 1986).
4. Joseph F. Hair, Rolph E. Anderson, Ronald L. Tatham, and William C. Black, *Multivariate Data Analysis,* 4th edn (Englewood Cliffs, NJ: Prentice-Hall, 1995).
5. Fred N. Kerlinger, (1980). Analysis of Covariance Structure Tests of a Criterial Referents Theory of Attitudes. *Multivariate Behavioral Research*, 15, 403–422.
6. *Foundations of Behavioral Research*
7. R. L. Dipboye, H. D. D. Zultowski, and R. D. Arvey, Self-Esteem as a Moderator of the Relationship Between Scientific Interests and the Job Satisfaction of Physicists and Engineers, *Journal of Applied Psychology,* (1978)63, 289–294.
8. David A. Aaker and George S. Day, *Marketing Research: Private and Public Sector Dimensions* (New York: John Wiley and Sons, Inc., 1980).
9. *Multivariate Data Analysis*.

13 The Research Report

1. Kenneth Roman and Joel Raphaelson, *Writing That Works* (New York: Harper and Row, 1981); William Strunk, Jr. and E. B.White, *The Elements of Style*, 3rd edn (New York: Macmillan, 1979); William Zinsser, *On Writing Well*, 3rd edn (New York: Harper and Row, 1985); Tim J. Saben, *Practical Business Communications* (Burr Ridge, IL: Irwin/Mirror Press, 1994); David Morris and Satish Chandra, *Guidelines for Writing a Research Report* (Chicago: American Marketing Association, 1993).

Index